ISBN 978-1-332-34748-3
PIBN 10317080

1 MONTH OF
FREE
READING

at

www.ForgottenBooks.com

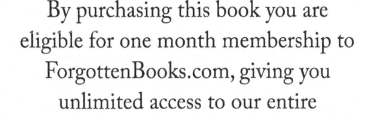

By purchasing this book you are eligible for one month membership to ForgottenBooks.com, giving you unlimited access to our entire collection of over 700,000 titles via our web site and mobile apps.

To claim your free month visit:

www.forgottenbooks.com/free317080

English
Français
Deutsche
Italiano
Español
Português

www.forgottenbooks.com

Mythology Photography **Fiction**
Fishing Christianity **Art** Cooking
Essays Buddhism Freemasonry
Medicine **Biology** Music **Ancient**
Egypt Evolution Carpentry Physics
Dance Geology **Mathematics** Fitness
Shakespeare **Folklore** Yoga Marketing
Confidence Immortality Biographies
Poetry **Psychology** Witchcraft
Electronics Chemistry History **Law**
Accounting **Philosophy** Anthropology
Alchemy Drama Quantum Mechanics
Atheism Sexual Health **Ancient History**
Entrepreneurship Languages Sport
Paleontology Needlework Islam
Metaphysics Investment Archaeology
Parenting Statistics Criminology
Motivational

THE PRIVATE JOURNAL

OF

AARON BURR

Eng by E G Williams & Bro NY

Painted by J Vandyke

PRIVATE JOURNAL

OF

AARON BURR

*REPRINTED IN FULL FROM THE ORIGINAL
MANUSCRIPT IN THE LIBRARY OF
MR. WILLIAM K. BIXBY,
OF ST. LOUIS, MO.*

WITH

AN INTRODUCTION, EXPLANATORY NOTES,
AND A GLOSSARY

IN TWO VOLUMES

VOL. I

ROCHESTER, N. Y.
1903

THE GENESEE PRESS
THE POST EXPRESS PRINTING CO.
ROCHESTER, N. Y.

INTRODUCTION

FOR a century Aaron Burr has been so persistently and vindictively misrepresented and villified that he is now commonly regarded as one of the blackest characters in American history. He had, indeed, some conspicuous faults, which can neither be concealed nor condoned. He made promises easily, and often broke them without regret; he was extremely careless, though not intentionally dishonest, in his financial transactions; he was a scoffer at religion, though his father and grandfather had been clergymen; his political principles sat lightly upon him, and after the death of his wife he was notorious for the immorality of his private life. This notoriety, however, was due in some degree to the entire absence of hypocrisy in his character; it was a more immoral age than this, many of the prominent men of his time were as fond of gallantries, intrigues, and amours as Burr himself, but he was less disposed than they to resort to duplicity and concealment. His public career, on the other hand, was such as to win for a time the applause of his fellow-citizens. He was a gallant soldier in the Revolutionary war, famous alike for personal bravery and the skill to plan and execute the boldest movements; he was a politician of extraordinary skill, one of the most brilliant lawyers of his time, and a statesman of high ideals and lofty purposes. In his domestic relations and among his friends he was the most charming of men. One of his biographers speaks of Burr's courage and fortitude, his generosity, his magnanimity, and his capacity for family affection, and adds: "No heartless villain, such as Burr has been represented, could have won and retained the love of such a wife and of such a daughter as Burr had. When all the other witnesses have been heard, let the two Theodosias be summoned, and especially that daughter who showed toward him an affectionate veneration unsurpassed by any recorded in history or romance. Such an advocate as Theodosia the younger must avail in some degree, even though the culprit were brought before the bar of Heaven itself."

Aaron Burr was born in Newark, N. J., February 6, 1756, of the purest and best New England stock. His father, the Rev. Aaron Burr, a scholarly and eloquent man, was the first president of Princeton College and his mother was a daughter of Jonathan Edwards, the famous Colonial divine. The boy was left an orphan at an early age, but was carefully educated under the direction of his relatives and was graduated from Princeton at the age of 16 with the highest honours of his class. When the news of the battle of Lexington reached him, he was studying law at Litchfield, Conn. His soul glowed with patriotic ardor and he soon joined Washington's army, to do his share toward winning the independence of his country. He accompanied Arnold's expedition through the wilds of Maine, participated in the assault on Quebec, was at Montgomery's side when the American general fell, and endeavored to bear his body from the field of battle when the attack failed and the army began the retreat. At the battle of Monmouth he commanded a brigade and again greatly distinguished himself. In 1779 he was in command of the debatable ground in Westchester county that lay between the lines of the British and American armies, and was again proving his worth as a soldier when a long illness terminated his military career.

In January, 1782, he was admitted to the bar at Albany,

N. Y., and began the practice of law in that city. On July 2d of the same year he was married to Theodosia Prevost, the widow of an officer in the British army who had died several years before in the West Indies. She was a native of Switzerland, was well educated, was literary in her tastes, and had a most pleasing manner. Years after her death, Burr spoke of her as "the best woman and the most charming lady" he had ever met. Their correspondence both before and after marriage was most affectionate and their married life was one of unalloyed happiness. Their daughter Theodosia was born in 1783. Mrs. Burr died in the spring of 1794, and thereafter the affections of the father concentrated upon the daughter. He took all possible pains with her education and the development of her character, and she became not only one of the most beautiful but one of the most brilliant of American women. The affection of the father was returned with passionate ardour, and throughout all the vicissitudes of his career she was his enthusiastic champion. In one of her letters written when he was in sore straits in Paris and she had failed to procure a supply of funds for his support, she wrote: "I witness your extraordinary fortitude with new wonder at every new misfortune. Often, after reflecting on this subject, you appear to me so superior, so elevated above all other men, I contemplate you with such a strange mixture of humility, admiration, reverence, love, and pride, that very little superstition would be necessary to make me worship you as a superior being, such enthusiasm does your character excite in me. When I afterward revert to myself, how insignificant do my best qualities appear! My vanity would be greater if I had not been placed so near you; and yet my pride is our relationship. I had rather not live than not be the daughter of such a man." In 1801 Theodosia was married to Joseph Alston, of South Carolina, a young man of fine family and high character, who became governor of his native state.

In 1783 Colonel Burr removed to New York city and soon shared with Alexander Hamilton the most important law business of the metropolis. One of their contemporaries thus compared them: " As a lawyer and a scholar, Burr was not inferior to Hamilton. His reasoning powers were at least equal. Their modes of argument were very different. Hamilton was very diffuse and wordy. His words were well chosen, and his sentences so finely formed into a swelling current, that the hearer would be captivated. The listener would admire if he was not convinced. Burr's arguments were generally methodized and compact. I used to say of them when they were rivals at the bar, that Burr would say as much in half an hour as Hamilton in two hours. Burr was terse and convincing, while Hamilton was flowing and rapturous. They were much the greatest men in this state, and perhaps the greatest men in the United States."

Colonel Burr was nominally an anti-Federalist in politics, though his political convictions were never strong. In 1791 he was elected to the Senate of the United States, defeating General Schuyler, Hamilton's father-in-law, though the Federalists had a majority in the legislature. Burr was approachable, able, adroit, firm in the confidence of the people, intensely loyal to his friends, and had a fine record as a soldier, while Schuyler, though an honourable man, was aristocratic and unpopular. Hamilton took an active part in this contest, bore his defeat ungracefully, and for thirteen years thereafter was Burr's bitterest and most implacable political and personal enemy.

In 1792 Colonel Burr was suggested for Governor of New York, but Hamilton's interference was successful and Clinton was nominated. In the same year his friends brought him forward for the office of Vice-President, but again Hamilton thwarted his ambition. In 1794 Burr's appointment as Minister to France was urged upon President Washington by Madison and Monroe, and he was the unanimous choice of his associates in congress, but for a third time Hamilton prevailed over him. In 1797 Burr was defeated for re-election to the Senate and Hamilton triumphed again. In 1800 Burr rallied his party in New York and by infinite tact and skill carried the State for the anti-Federalists, and in the Electoral College received as many votes as Thomas Jefferson for President of the United States. On account of the tie the election of the President was devolved on congress. Once more Hamilton brought his marvelous power of detraction into play, and Jefferson was elected, Burr being chosen for Vice-President. During this contest Burr's friends complained bitterly because he would do nothing in his own behalf. One of his opponents declared, while the contest was going on, " Had Burr done anything for himself he would long ere this have been President." Colonel Burr was often accused of discreditable methods in politics, but here, when the highest of all offices was at stake, the true character of the man was revealed; he would promise no patronage and pledge himself to no policy, and deaf to the impassioned importunities of his friends, refused absolutely to influence a single vote in his own behalf. And yet it was asserted subsequently that he was actively engaged in the very intrigue to which, through a sense of the highest honour and the greatest delicacy, he would not stoop, even to gain the Presidency; but the jealousy of the rival leaders of his party had been aroused, and when Burr, as usual, condescended to no explanations, made no excuses, and attempted no justification of his conduct, they resolved upon his overthrow.

Colonel Burr presided over the deliberations of the Senate

with great dignity and impartiality, but his re-election seemed unlikely and he accordingly resolved to appeal to the people of New York; in 1804, therefore, he announced himself as an independent candidate for Governor. Again Hamilton sprang forward to thwart him, and, emboldened by former immunity, increased the bitterness of the attack. Burr was beaten in the election, and considering himself the victim of innumerable wrongs inflicted through a long series of years, sought an explanation from Hamilton. Nothing but evasions were forthcoming and finally a challenge was sent and accepted. The two men, long rivals in politics and at the bar, met under the heights of Weehawken on the morning of July 11, 1804; both fired when the word was given, and Hamilton fell mortally wounded. His death resulted in a tremendous popular upheaval. Burr was denounced as a murderer, was indicted for murder in both New York and New Jersey, and was compelled to flee to the Southern States. But both before and after the duel there was nothing censurable in Burr's conduct, when measured by the standards of the times in which he lived. It was an age of duelling; both Burr and Hamilton were military men; both were strenuous on points of honour, and at that time there was no man in public life who would have hesitated to send a challenge when honour was wounded or who would have refused to accept a challenge if one was received. Hamilton himself bore testimony to this effect. He declared that his "religious and moral principles were strongly opposed to the practice of duelling," and yet he did not have the moral courage to decline a challenge, saying that "the ability to be in future useful, whether in resisting mischief or effecting good, in these crises of our public affairs, would probably be inseparable from a conformity with public prejudice in this particular." The duel was conducted with the utmost propriety, the participants took equal chances of life or death, and, according to the ethics of that age, though not of this, neither was in the slightest degree censurable.

After a short tour through the South, where he was received by the best society, Colonel Burr returned to Washington to resume his duties as Vice-President of the United States. He presided over the Senate during the trial of Judge Chase of Maryland " with the dignity and impartiality of an angel and the rigor of a demon," and the day after the trial closed, his term being about to expire, delivered a farewell address to the Senate, which was so full of eloquence and pathos that most of the Senators were in tears when he concluded.

Ruined politically and financially, with his beautiful home at Richmond Hill sold for debt, ostracised by society and shunned by men of all parties, Burr now resolved upon a journey to the West. Floating down the Ohio, he stopped at Blennerhasset's island, a few miles below Marietta, where he fascinated Blennerhasset and his wife with the brilliancy of his conversation and the charm and polish of his manner. At Nashville he was entertained by General Jackson. At Fort Massac he met General Wilkinson, commander of the Western armies, an old friend and army commander, who received him graciously. At New Orleans he was entertained like a prince. After his return to Philadelphia he applied to Jefferson for a foreign appointment, which was refused on the ground that he had forfeited the confidence of the country. His thoughts then turned to the Southwest. He resolved upon the establishment of a colony, and purchased 400,000 acres of land on the banks of the Washita, a tributary of the Red river. At that time there were many prominent Americans who expected and, indeed, advocated war with Spain. Burr was one of these, and he determined to be on the frontier when hostilities broke out, and be ready to take part in them. But when his expedition reached Frankfort he was arrested, charged with conspiring to injure a foreign power with which the United States was at peace. Henry Clay defended him, Burr himself made an eloquent speech, and he was triumphantly acquitted, a result that was celebrated with a grand ball and great popular rejoicings. Burr went on to Bayou Pierre, near Natchez. Here he was arrested again, and again released. But further legal proceedings were set on foot and Burr, despairing of success in his expedition, abandoned it, crossed the Mississippi, and disappeared in the wilderness. A few weeks later he was arrested near Fort Stoddart on the Alabama river, and taken under guard to Richmond, Va. Here he was indicted for treason and misdemeanor. The trial that followed was one of the most remarkable in the history of the United States. The presiding judge was John Marshall, Chief Justice of the Supreme Court, and one of the greatest and purest judges that ever lived. Several of the ablest lawyers in the country appeared for Burr and for the government, and the whole power of President Jefferson's administration was exerted to bring about a conviction. Colonel Burr took an active part in his own defense, conducting himself with great dignity and constantly manifesting his remarkable ability as a lawyer. The result of the trial was a triumphant acquittal. Burr had, indeed, discussed warlike enterprises, but, as the prosecution's own witnesses admitted, his plans were not to be put into execution till the United States itself had taken the initiative and had declared war against Spain. He may have had some visionary schemes; he may have dwelt upon the project of driving the Spaniards out of Mexico and founding an empire; but there is no reason to suppose that he intended to attack New Orleans, that he intrigued to bring about the secession of the West, that he intended at any time to defy the military power or violate the laws of his country, or that his projects were in any respect treasonable.

Partly to escape the importunities of creditors whom he could not satisfy, partly to allow the popular resentment to cool, and partly with the hope of inducing some European government to interfere in Mexico, and give him employment suitable to his abilities, Colonel Burr sailed for Europe on June 1, 1808, and remained abroad for four years.

During his absence he visited England, Scotland, Sweden, Germany, France, and Holland in turn and sailed for home· from England. Though American diplomatic representatives at all foreign capitals looked upon him with suspicion and endeavoured in every possible way to embarrass him, he was everywhere received with the greatest cordiality, and moved always in the highest society. His political projects, however, were a failure, the European governments not being willing to countenance interference with the trans-Atlantic possessions of Spain. When he realized this, Burr was desirous of returning to the United States. But the power of his personal and political enemies was so great that for many weary months he could not obtain the necessary passport from the French authorities, and was virtually a prisoner in Paris. His supply of money was soon exhausted; he either could not or would not do anything to earn a living; remittances from home were interrupted or had become impossible, and he finally became absolutely dependent upon his new friends in Paris. For weeks at a time he suffered severely for lack of fire, clothing, and food. When, however, he succeeded in borrowing money he became utterly reckless in his expenditure, buying costly presents, useless books, unnecessary wearing apparel, and expensive wines, and making liberal payments to women whose acquaintance he formed on the street.

When his funds ran low, he would again feel the pinch of poverty, and after exhausting his credit at the pawnshops would sink once more into abject misery. Through it all he preserved wonderful good humour, displayed a most astonishing faith in himself, and never doubted that fortune's wheel would turn. In these trials he exhibited one of his remarkable characteristics. No matter how poverty stricken, how cold, or how hungry, he never complained, never denounced his enemies, never entered upon a justification, or even an explanation, of his own conduct, and never lost his serenity of mind.

Upon his return to the United States Colonel Burr settled in New York and resumed the practice of law. There was still a strong popular prejudice against him and progress was slow and difficult. When, however, some degree of success seemed certain, he suffered two crushing blows, the death of his grandson, followed within six months by the tragic death of his dearly beloved daughter, Theodosia. The boy, the " little Gampy " so often mentioned in Burr's letters, died on June 30, 1812, and the poor mother was heartbroken. She became listless, apathetic and morose; happiness had fled, hope was gone, and life itself became a dreary burden. Her father, deeply distressed as he learned of her pitiable condition, sent a physician to South Carolina to bring her to New York; for in change of scene and the loving care of the father lay the only possibilities of saving her life. She accordingly embarked at Charleston on the schooner Patriot on December 30, 1812, but within a few days all on board were lost in a gale off Cape Hatteras. The father watched with constantly growing anxiety for the arrival of the vessel, and haunted the docks in search of news as the weary days dragged on. When the terrible truth was borne in upon him by lapse of time and the entire absence of news,

Colonel Burr, who had withstood a succession of calamities, nearly succumbed to this the most awful blow of his tragic career. Thereafter life had no allurements for him; 'there were no incentives to effort, and the broken-hearted man sank slowly into poverty and obscurity. In 1830, at the age of 78, he married Eliza Bowen Jumel, the widow of a rich wine merchant. The union soon proved unhappy, owing to the husband's management of the wife's property, and they finally separated, though they were not divorced. In 1833 Colonel Burr suffered two strokes of apoplexy, which rendered him nearly helpless. He lingered for three years, a constant burden on charitable friends, and died at Port Richmond, Staten Island, New York, on the afternoon of September 14, 1836, in his eighty-first year. By his own request he was buried at Princeton near the graves of his father and grandfather.

During his tour of Europe, Colonel Burr kept a Journal, intended for his own information and the amusement of his daughter. Apparently he made a copy of what he had written and mailed it to her from time to time. Her copy, however, must have varied in many respects from the original, for it is simply inconceivable that a father who loved and respected a daughter as Burr loved and respected Theodosia could have written for her perusal many of the things contained in his Journal. Shortly before his death, Colonel Burr put all his papers into the hands of his personal friend and chosen biographer, Matthew L. Davis, of New York. In 1837, Mr. Davis published the "Memoirs of Aaron Burr," in two volumes. This was well received and in the following year he published, also in two volumes, "The Private Journal of Aaron Burr During his Residence of Four Years in Europe, with Selections from His Correspondence." Though Mr. Davis had Colonel Burr's own copy of the Journal, he did not publish it in full. On the contrary, he took the most astonishing liberties with it, leaving out hundreds of pages, omitting nearly all the passages in French, which were very numerous, and occasionally inserting words that Burr never used. His reason may have been that Colonel Burr's reputation was in his keeping and that personal loyalty to him required that nothing should be printed that might tend to lower it in the opinion of the people. But certainly this reason has no force now, and in the following pages the Journal appears as nearly as possible as Burr wrote it, and is reprinted from the original MS. The work is prepared for private and gratuitous distribution; the edition is limited to 250 copies, the type has been distributed, and no copies will ever be offered for sale. The Journal will be of very great interest and value to those who would understand the remarkable man whose inmost secrets are here revealed. He wrote with the freedom of a Rousseau, and attempted no concealment except such as might be effected by the use of the French language, the persistent abbreviation of important words, and careless and often scarcely legible handwriting.

The liberties which Davis took with the Journal were amazing and some of his changes were ridiculous. For example, Burr wrote, " I saw her home "; Davis prints it, " I waited upon her home." Again, Burr wrote : " This cursed platina pen is too stiff; see what devilish scrawls it makes." Davis printed it, " This platina pen is too stiff; see what scrawls it makes." A third example : Burr wrote, referring to a servant named Juliet, " I opened my eyes and lo ! Ju. with a bowl of *bouillon gras* in her hand." Davis prints this, " I opened my eyes, and lo ! there she was with my breakfast." Hundreds of changes of this kind might be cited. Some changes were made in the hope of saving the feelings or the reputation of particular individuals. Here is an example: At Paris on June 28, 1811, Burr wrote, "Vanderlyn came in. If he does not go to United States he will be in jail here within a year." Davis gives it, "I anticipate much trouble for him in another year." A thousand changes were made by Davis because he could not read or understand the MS. On one occasion when he was not feeling well, Burr wrote that he had been " taking *rhad. rhei*," meaning *radix Rhei*. Rhubarb was a favourite remedy with him, but in Davis's reprint the words *rhad. rhei.* are printed "good wine." In the notes to the present edition attention is called to many other examples of this kind. Colonel Burr made very frequent references to his amorous escapades. His biographer usually omitted them entirely. Occasionally they were admitted after free revision. For example, under date of Paris, October 1, 1810, Burr wrote: "Had an hour to spare and I maliciously set out on mischief. Called on Edwards; out. On Prevost; out, and meeting no obstacles in the way, got safe to Vanderlyn's at ½ p. 3. Dined there and at 6 came off together. Parted at the Pont des Arts, he to go on some errand, I to come home; but went round by Viol.; out. On the way, however, a *renc.*; 6 francs for pros. only; home at 8. Read two hours in my Sp. grammar. Made *caf. blanc*. Having no sug., took of that infernal *sirop de raisin*, which with sour milk made a mess fit for the devil's feast, but swallowed it and am still alive as you see at ½ p. 12." This is the way Davis printed the passage: " Had an hour to spare. Called on Prevost and Edwards; both out; and, meeting no obstacle in the way, got safe to Vanderlyn's at half past three. Dined, and at six came off together. Parted at the Pont Desarts. He to go on some errand, and I to come home. Read two hours in my Spanish grammar. Made coffee *blanc*; having no sugar, took of that horrid *sirop de raisin*, which, with sour milk, made a mess unfit for man or beast; but swallowed it, and am still alive, as you see."

It seems improbable that Davis understood French, for nearly all of Burr's French is omitted in the Davis reprint. Burr used French when referring to his discreditable adventures, ("accidents," he called them), but he used it very frequently for other purposes. He shows, indeed, throughout the entire Journal a singular fondness for using words from languages other than his own. This is childish at times. In Sweden he learned the words *bröd* and *mjolk*, and then used them almost exclusively for three years thereafter, instead of the English words, bread and milk. He seemed immensely pleased when he could draw upon several languages to form a single sentence. For example, he wrote · " *Bro.* and *cas.* for *din.*" Here we have four languages represented in a sentence of five words! *Bro.* is an abbreviation of the Swedish word *bröd*, bread; *cas.* is probably Burr's attempt to write the German word *Käse*, cheese, and *din.* is his abbreviation of the French word *diner*, dinner.

In the notes an attempt is made to give a correct rendering of all phrases in foreign languages which Burr used, and to accompany these with translations. Necessarily many words are translated that are familiar to those who read these pages, and to such, unfortunately, the notes may seem burdensome. But to those entirely unfamiliar with foreign languages and particularly with French, the translations will be necessary to an understanding of the text. In the Glossary at the end of the second volume all the phrases used by Burr will be found alphabetically arranged and convenient for reference.

PRIVATE JOURNAL
OF AARON BURR

UNE 1, 1808. Having paid $60 for the cabin of the Clarissa Ann, and also for a pilot-boat to put me on board, I was to meet the pilot-boat near the Narrows. At 10 A. M., T. arrived at———, where I lodged. At 4 P. M., left in a skiff, with a man and a boy. Heavy wind. We went on Long Island at the place agreed on, and there passed the night.

2. At 9 A. M. crossed to Staten Island, having seen neither S. nor pilot-boat. Returned. At 11 A. M. took boat and landed at Communipas. The boy and I went to the Vineyard, and reached there 1 P. M.

3. Remained till 8 A. M. Left for the Narrows with——— Reached the house of G. Kemble.

4. G. Kemble arrived. Very politely received by Mr. K———

5. Remained here.

6. R. Swartwout. At 9 P. M. went with him to New York. Lodged with J. S.

7. H. introduced W. E. Hosack. 10 P. M., met T. At 11 A. M. went on board pilot-boat with F. B. O. Set sail.

8. No wind. At 3 P. M. anchored between Narrows and Sandy Hook.

9. At 7 P. M. set sail. At 6 P. M. see the packet Queen Charlotte. Fair wind. Passengers, Edwards[1], Luscomb, Clough, Hosack[2], Mackay, Harrison, wife of Judge Thorpe and six children, Henley, and Charles Alexander Williamson.

July 13, 1808[3]. Arrived at Falmouth at 8 P. M. Custom house, &c.

14. At 9 P. M. took mail, with Captain Gerrard of the Marines and Mr. Luscomb. Breakfast at Tinro. Insolence of landlord. Arrived at Exeter at 9 P. M.

15. Leave Exeter at 4 A. M. Breakfast at————. Very bad and very disobliging. Luscomb leaves us.

16. Arrived at ½ p. 6 at London. Set down at Gloster Coffee-house, Piccadilly, with Gerrard. Garret rooms. No breakfast till 9. Breakfast in coffee-room. Call at John Lewis Mallet[4]—*bien recu*[5]. On Reeves[6] with letter of Willot; his surprise—joy. On Castlereagh and Cooke; out of town. *Soir*[7]—*opera*—*galere*[8].

26. Rode in stage to Weybridge to see Madame Prevost[9], about nineteen miles. Arrive at 1 P. M. Dine at Robson's with Hosack *et ux*[10]. Ma-

1 H. E. Edwards—Aaron Burr's assumed name.
2 "W. E. Hosack, a Scotch merchant of very respectable standing and character, who is established at New York, and is now on his way to Scotland."—Burr, in a private letter, July 19, 1808.
3 In the Journal the memoranda of the voyage are merely brief notices of the wind and weather.
4 Mallet was a second cousin of Frederic Prevost, son of Mrs. Aaron Burr by her first husband.
5 Well received.
6 John Reeves, an official of the British Alien Office.
7 Evening
8 For *galerie*. Gallery.
9 A relative of the Mrs. Prevost whom Burr had married, now dead.
10 For *et uxor*. And wife.

dame Prevost, Constant *et ux.* Dinner very simple.
After dinner, cards. Retire with Madame Prevost
and Madame C. at 11. Lodge at inn called The
Ship. (Mem : Picture of Sir George Prevost, painted
by Miss de Tott, daughter of Baron de Tott, who
now resides with the Margravine of Anspach.)

August 10, 1808. Declaration of Aaron Burr,
an alien, taken before John Reeves, Esq., the 10th
day of August, 1808 :

Declare, 1st, your name, age place of birth, rank, occupation
or profession [the same in French]. *Aaron Burr, United States,
rank of citizen, forty and upward.*

2d. Your residence, when last in your own country. *New
York.*

3d. Your last and principal residence before your arrival in
this kingdom. *New York.*

4th. To whom known in this kingdom and the place of his or
her residence.

5th. For what reason or purpose are you come ? *I am known
personally to Lord Mulgrave and Mr. Canning, to whom the motives to
my visit have been declared. These reasons have long been known to
Lord Melville.*

6th. When and where did you land in this kingdom ? *July.
Falmouth.*

7th. Where you now reside, and have resided since your last
arrival ? *London, Craven street, No. 30.*

Sign your name.

*The undersigned was born within the King's allegiance and his
parents British subjects.*

A. BURR.

21. Received invitation from Jeremy Bentham[1]
inviting me to pass some days, *chez lui.*[2]

---

1 Jeremy Bentham was born in London in 1748, and died there in 1832. He was graduated
from Queen's College, Oxford, in 1763, was admitted to the bar, but gave up the practice of the
law to devote himself to literary pursuits. On the death of his father, in 1792, he inherited a
fortune which enabled him fully to indulge his literary tastes. His chief works are : "Introduction to the Principles of Morals and Legislation" (1789), "Fragment on Government" (1776),
"The Constitutional Code" (1830), and "Rationale of Judicial Evidence" (1827).

2 At his home.

13. Dr. Joseph Moore introduced me to Fuseli, to view Royal Academy.

18. At 9 this morning found my trunk. At 10 got into the stage for Gadstone. To Croydon 10 miles, where waited two hours, and then hired post-chaise to take me to Barrow Green, near Gadstone, 13 miles; in fact 12. Arrived there at 4 P. M. Found Jeremy Bentham, and his secretary J. Herbert Koe, waiting for me at the gate. Affectionate reception. Introduced to his "workshop." License over his papers[1].

19 and 20. With Bentham at Barrow Green.

21. Sunday. Returned to town. Took bed at 30 Craven street.

22. Lodged at Bentham's house at Queen's Square Place. Very kind reception by Madame Stoker[2]. Wrote Bentham by mail this afternoon, and by baggage wagon this evening. Letter from Beckett, first under secretary to Lord Hawkesbury, asking me to call on Friday last.

24. Letter to D. M. Randolph to consult Marquis Iruko about J. Bentham's "Tactics." At 10 got into stage-coach for Croydon. Stopped to see the railway. *Four* horses were drawing *sixteen* wagons, containing two tons fifteen hundred, equal to *forty-four* tons; being *eleven* tons to each horse.

26, 27, 28 and 29. At Barrow Green. Amiable simplicity of J. Bentham. He was interested by the

---

1 Meaning that license to examine Bentham's papers was given. In a letter to an American correspondent, Burr said that Bentham gave him " an unqualified privilege to read anything and at any time."
2 Bentham's housekeeper.

picture of Theo[1]. "Dear little creature. Let her take care." Gave me a letter to General Bentham.

London, September 24, 1808. Received Guillemard's note, and cards of Gov. Franklin and Mr. Luscomb.

26. Took post-chaise for Little Gaddesden, and arrived at Major Gamble's at 7 P. M. Kind and hospitable reception.

27. Visited Bartlett. *Les dames*[2] Bartlett ordered horses, and rode with me eight or ten miles.

28. Visited Lord Bridgwater (Egerton, Earl of Bridgwater), not *chez lui*[3]; left cards. His building, three hundred feet front; wall, three hundred feet deep. Went with Mrs. Bartlett and Mrs. Span, her daughter, in their carriage, to dine at 6 P. M. at Asp Ridge House. Handed in Madame Bartlett. Lord Bridgwater hands Miss Bartlett to dinner. Lady Bridgwater and Madame Span get on as they can at dinner. Came off at 10. Lord Bridgwater going to-morrow to London. Apologizes for postponing his visit. Offer of service; *politesse*[4] On returning *chez*[5] Gamble, debate on handing in a lady— on English ease and politeness. Proposed to call next day on Lord Bridgwater—"very correct." That Lord Bridgwater might hand in, but nobody else— "no ceremony." Debate about etiquette at the Court of France. "But the Court of France is here."

---

1 Meaning Theodosia, his daughter. Usually referred to as T. hereafter.
2 The ladies.
3 At home.
4 Politeness, i. e., for politeness' sake.
5 *Chez* means at or to the house of; hence here, to Gamble's house.

29. Mr. Gilbert, the rector, and Bartlett call. Visit *les dames* Bartlett, &c. Walked to see the garden of Asp Ridge. Dine at Gamble's at 5. Bartlett *ux.* and Span. Renew debate on etiquette, handing in, &c. McCarthy and *les dames* sustain Gamp[1]. Cards. Visited Gilbert, who walked with us to see the church, supposed to be built when the Monastery *des Bonhommes*[2] was Asp Ridge in 1200. Lord Bridgwater calls, and with him Mr.————. Lord Bridgwater invites me to dine, take bed, &c., &c.

30. Left Little Gaddesden at 6 A. M., having engaged to return on Tuesday. Arrive in London, 27 miles, at 11. At 30 Craven street, found note and card from Captain Sinclair. Called on him at the Virginia Coffee-house, and being abroad, left note inviting him to dine with me.

October 1, 1808. S. Swartwout called with his letter from Lees. Called on Dr. Lettsome, who was not at home. Being engaged to the play with S. and M., was obliged to send excuse, feeling the approaches of a headache.

2. Kept bed till 4 P. M., fasting; hard headache. At 9 took tea.

3. Rose at ½ p. 8, quite well. At Ridgway's; left with madame, an obliging woman, a mem. of books for A. B. A[3]. At Gilbert's, bootmaker—a great liar; boots not done. At Madame Mallet,

---

1 Meaning himself. Gamp was a family nickname, applied by Burr to himself and by Burr and others to Theodosia's son, Aaron Burr Alston. It is conjectured that " Gamp " might have been the result of the child's early attempt to say " grandpa."
2 For *des Bonhommes.*
3 Aaron Burr Alston, Theodosia Burr Alston's son.

veuve[1]. Catherine went yesterday to Weybridge, having left a civil message for A. B.[2] at Madame Achaud's[3]. All the family, except Mr. Achaud, gone to Tunbridge, whither Constant *et ux.* had gone some days before. Madame Wilken, Craven street; in the evening, at the trunkmaker's. Coach hire, 9 shillings. But first in the morning on Reeves. Prayed to dine, which accepted. Υ[4]: George Chalmers[5], author of certain compilations; Brown, who had been in Russia; Madame B. *sa mere*[6]. Stayed till 9 o'clock.

4. Rose at 6. Sent porter for trunk and boots. Neither done. Clothes not come from wash. Stage for Gaddesden to start at 12, and nothing ready; bought two shirts. Clothes and trunk came at ½ p. 11. Packed up *tout suite*[7] and drove *comme diable*[8] to stage-house, Oxford street. Discovered that the hour of departure was *one*, and not *twelve* o'clock. Start at ½ p. 1 o'clock. Arrive at 7. Servant of Major Gamble waiting at the inn to receive and conduct me. Took tea at Bartlett's. History of ball at —— *Nonchalance de Madame*[9]. Mode of leading out *dames*.

5. Rose at 7. Called on Mr. Gilbert, the rector, to return his visit. He got up horses to ride with me. Called on Lord Bridgwater. Υ: Lord

---

1 Widow.
2 Aaron Burr.
3 Madame Achaud was first cousin to Frederick Prevost, son of Mrs. Aaron Burr by her first husband. Mrs. Constant was Mrs. Achaud's eldest daughter. The houses of Achaud and Mallet (previously mentioned) were frequented by famous literary personages.
4 Υ. French word meaning there. It is used throughout the Journal for there were present.
5 Born at Fochabers, Scotland, 1759; died at London, 1825. Historian and antiquary. Author of "Caledonia" (1807-24), "Life of Mary, Queen of Scots" (1818), and numerous other works.
6 His mother.
7 For *tout de suite*. At once.
8 For *comme le diable*. Like the devil.
9 The nonchalance or unconcern of Madame.

Grimstone and two daughters. Went on to Berk-hamstead, into the church ———— to Queen Elizabeth. Left horses at the Swan. Called at Ford's, Berkham-stead Place, half a mile from town, to see the ruins of the castle. Returned at 4; dinner at 5. *Υ*: Rev. Mr. Gilbert and Bartlett. *Cards. Won two shillings and sixpence of the rector.*

6. Rose at 8. Bartlett and the rector rode to show me the remains of a Roman camp, eight miles off. Magnificent and extensive view. Returned by Dunstable, famous for straw-hat making. Strange dialect of the peasants. At 6 to dine at Asp Ridge. *Υ*: Rev. Nor *et ux.* Mr. Nor is one of the King's chaplains. At ½ p. 8 start in four carriages for the ball at Berkhamstead. Dancing had commenced when we arrived. Supper at 1. Got home at 3.

7. Called at Asp Ridge; *personne*[1], all airing. During my absence to-day, Lady Bridgwater called in her gig, driving herself, and left for me C.'s " History of Hertfordshire."

8. Dined at Bartlett's. Barker *et ux.* He is uncle of Lord Lake, Rector of ————, and Chaplain to the Prince of Wales. Music and dancing. Barker invites me to dine on Monday, which I accept. Break up before 12.

9. Breakfast at M'Carthy's at 10, having agreed to ride with him to see the place of the Earl of Bute, said to have the best collection of pictures in England. M'Carthy has eight children, all handsome and most

---

1 For *Personne n'y était.* Nobody was there.

of them beautiful. Having staid longer than was intended, thought it was too late to visit the Earl of Bute's, so rode over to Hamel Hemstead. Called on Meade, brother-in-law of M'Carthy. Returned by Berkhamstead, and reached home at 4.

10. Called by appointment on Lord Bridgwater. Left for his perusal, letter of J. Bentham. M'Carthy called at 11. Rode with him and Bartlett. Called on ———, amiable, frank old man, very deaf; uncle of Mrs. Gordon, also of Whitbread. Polite and hospitable overtures. Tea with the Bartletts. Came home at 9. Retire to write and pack up. Wrote Lord Bridgwater, returning the book and paper, and asking for Bentham's letter.

12. Rose at 5. Got in stage at 6, intending to take post-chaise from Hamel Hemstead to St. Albans to visit Lord Grimstone; but no chaise was to be had, so came into town, where arrived at 10 o'clock. To Faleur; not content with his work. Impertinence of his goldsmith, whom I ordered out of the room for obtruding his opinions. F. is to mend his work, and I am to call to-morrow—thence to S. Swartwout. It was fortunate that I came to town, for yesterday he received orders to go on to Liverpool forthwith. Received letter from D. M. Randolph; very melancholy. Speaks of the death of a most valued friend in America, which must be particularly afflicting to me. Who can he mean? I have heard of no death of the least consequence to anybody. To Beck, tailor, about *culots*[1]; badly made. Bentham has writ-

---

1 For *culottes.* Breeches.

ten that he will be in town on Friday. Mrs. S. says I may lodge————. Received a very civil letter from Sir Andrew Grant, enclosing the letter of his correspondent near Carlisle, about Mrs. Miller's legacy, which turns out to be just nothing. Also a very pretty letter from Miss C. Mallet, as well in her own as on Madame Prevost's behalf, inviting me to Weybridge. At 4, walked to Ridgeway's; Madame had procured the books for which I had left a memorandum.

14. Called at Queen's Square Place; Mrs. Stoker has received a letter from Bentham delaying his return until Monday 16th, unless I shall be in town and wish him to come sooner. It is now 12, and, having suffered my fire to go out two hours ago, I am going to bed[1].

15. Rose at 8. After saying at 12 last night that I was going to bed, I made a good fire, got wine, water, and sugar, and sat up till ½ p. 2. I went on Thursday to Robert Shedden, Gower street, on the business of the lovely Anabella, now, I hope, Mrs. A. B. R. Mr. Shedden was not at home, so I left a note, written at his house, of which, see the copy made from memory[2].

London, November 13, 1808. Sir Mark A. Gerrard and Captain Percival of the Marines came to breakfast. The former was fellow-passenger with me

---

1 Under this date Burr wrote to Bentham: "I have no longer the slightest hope of the countenance of the ministry for anything which might be proposed. I am an object of suspicion and alarm." He was anxious that the British government should assist him in his plan to drive the Spaniards from Mexico.

2 From this time until November 13th, there are no entries in the Journal.

from Halifax. The latter was introduced to me by him yesterday. We took dinner together at Story's Gate Coffee-house. After breakfast Sir Mark walked with me to Miss Beetham's to pay for a picture—*profile en noir*[1]. Miss B. not at home. Paid her sister, Mrs. ———, 21 shillings. *Belle femme et d'esprit*[2] Called on Dumont at 5, and went together to dine at Achaud's. *Y:* Sir Samuel Romilly *et ux.,* formerly Miss ———, of K., where now lives her brother, *belle et bien elevee*[3]; the young Baron D'Albert and his sister, wards of Constant. Sir Samuel has an amiable and intelligent countenance. Came off at 10 o'clock.

14. Don Castella called on me at 10. He had yesterday seen 89[4]. Three letters on X[5] affairs. Went to Falieri's; got home, *sans accident*[6]. William Graves called at 5. The Hopewell does not sail till the 16th. No vessel yet provided to take the mail to New York.

15. Wrote Sir Mark to call on me. Note from Captain Percival that Lady Hamilton was not in town. G. called with Captain Stewart, an amiable young Scotchman. Sir Mark has discovered *les personages*[7], and will present A. B.[8] on Friday. Passed the day in writing to the United States; at home, except calling on Reeves at 4 about passports. Did not see him.

---

1 Profile in black, i. e., a silhouette.
2 A fine-looking, intellectual woman.
3 Fine looking and well-bred.
4 Some individual who is referred to by number rather than by name. Burr left with his daughter a long list of names to which numbers were attached. He was obliged to be very guarded in his communications.
5 Used several times in the Journal. X signifies Burr's secret projects with regard to Mexico.
6 Without accident.
7 The persons.
8 Aaron Burr.

K. abroad. Evening with Bentham; conversed of tattooing, and how to be made useful; of infanticide; of crimes against Nature, &c., &c.

16. Castella called at 11 and sat an hour. Called at 4 on Dawe, painter; *pas talents*[1]. At 5 home, safe. Dinner with B. and K. Tea ditto. Passed evening with ———

17. Did nothing till 2, then called on Reeves about passports. He had done nothing, would do nothing, and was just going out of town for four days! *Me voila prisonier d'etat*[2]! At J. Wedgwood's, 328 Oxford—*elle ne veut plus me parler*[3]. Strolled and *pensant a T. et tous mes petits plans*[4]. Called on Madame Beetham; *dehors*[5]. Sat half an hour *av la mere*[6], who did not know me, but received me with politeness. On Madame Langworthy, *la mere de la belle* Catherine[7].

18. Castella called before I was up. Breakfasted with me, and gave me many interesting details respecting South America and of persons there. Called on General Picton, Dr. Blackburn, and on Mr. Duval; waited till he came in to dinner, and dined with him. To Madame H. Surry, who confessed that there was no such person as the Hon. Madame Bruce, but that the whole was a fable imposed on her by Madame G., sister of Madame C., and so on me. Madame G. lives in handsome style, handsome carriages, and many

1 For *Il n'a pas de talents.* He has no talents.
2 Here I am a state prisoner.
3 She won't speak to me any more.
4 Thinking of Theodosia and all my little plans.
5 Out.
6 For *avec la mère.* With the mother.
7 The mother of the beautiful Catherine.

servants l Called on Madame W., found there a card from General Picton and a note from Mr. Duval, with whom I am to dine on Sunday. Tea with Bentham, Wrote to Hosack in reply to his of the 17th, and a long letter to Mrs. Prevost. Confab an hour with K. Read Thierry[1] an hour with B.

20. To Madame W.; abroad. To Madame H. Surrey, to see further about the Hon. Madame Bruce. To the Salopian Coffee-house, to meet Sir Mark by appointment. He came not, but met there Captain Percival. *Chez nous*[2] to dress. To Duval's to dine at 5. A family party. Only the two sons, who are amiable and pleasant. The counsellor, Lewis, very intelligent. I had lent for a few days the picture of Theodosia, which was hung up there, and employed more of my thoughts than the dinner and company. We drank her health, &c. It is very remarkable that one of the sons looks like Phil, and the other speaks like him. You will be struck with it at your first interview. Read an hour more of Thierry, and laughed a great deal. Made out a law opinion requested by Hosack, which took me two hours, being obliged to hunt up the treaty of 1794[3], and certain laws of the State of New York. General Picton called on me yesterday at the hour I was *chez lui.*

21. At War Office to confer with General Hope about license, &c. Note: I had met General Hope

---

1 There were several French authors of this name.
2 At our house, at home.
3 This was probably the treaty with regard to Indian lands in Western New York, signed at Canandaigua, N.Y., by representatives of the United States and the principal chiefs of the Seneca Nation of Indians.

at dinner at Mr. Cooke's. He declared himself to have been an intimate friend of the late Colonel Williamson[1]; to have heard him speak much and affectionately of me; to have greatly desired my acquaintance. Gave me his address, &c. To Madame Onslow's, about two and a half miles, New road. *Au retour pres 5*[2], called again at the War Office to see General H., having been told by the porter that he would certainly be in at that hour. His carriage waiting at the door. *Denied!* Dinner *chez nous* with B. *seul*[3]. Koe came in and we read Thierry. B. always goes to bed at 11, at which hour, of course, I come down to my room. Wrote to you, and for you, and about you, till 2.

22. Sir Mark came in at 12 to apologize for his default on Sunday. Walked with him to be introduced to Signora ———; truly a very lovely woman; native of Corsica; widow of a British officer; *peut-etre* 32; *parl.* Italian, French, and English; *une physionomie tres interressante*[4]; *nous y rencontrames* four *autres dames etrangeres*[5]. Walked with the General to Tottenham Court Road, having twice *egarêd*[6] on the way. We parted. To Madame Onslow's—*je la trouvee superbement mise et av. beaucoup de gout. Jouames Echec—je gagnai. Elle me joua quelques airs assez joliment sur la Harpe*[7]. Left at ½ p. 4. *En ret.*[8]

1 Charles Williamson, who managed the lands in Western New York owned by Sir William Pulteney.
2 On my return at nearly 5.
3 Alone.
4 Perhaps 32; speaks Italian, French, and English; a very interesting face.
5 We met there four other strange ladies.
6 Lost the way, strayed. Burr here makes an English verb from a French perfect participle.
7 I found her dressed superbly and with much taste. We played chess. I won. She played me some airs quite prettily on the harp.
8 On returning.

stopped moment *chez* Ridgeway. She dare not undertake the ———— of Jovellianoz. *Chez nous* at 5¼. *Din. seul av.* B. K. *ent. a* 6, read Thierry a little[1]. Part at 11. Wrote till 2 to United States.

23. Castella came in at 10 and took breakfast. Stayed two hours. Had received a very interesting letter from his friend C. in Spain. Had seen M. de G. He is to call again on Friday. Many things proposed for consideration. Baron N. left word that he had called at the particular request of the sister of Sir W. Pulteney. This another inquiry about American laws. Left card at Baron Norton's. To Falieri's. After essaying an hour, he determined to abandon this, his second work, and try again. Note: I have already paid him £30!! Returning, at Madame Duval's, to thank her for the pretty manner in which the picture was sent home. She said rolling injured it, and she had procured a very handsome portfolio, made just to receive it; an attention which very much pleased me. To Achaud's; saw Madame only; gave instructions about the letters they are to write to Portsmouth, Falmouth, and Liverpool, to secure the reception of T[2]. To Reeves's, who prayed me to dine; engaged to return after dinner. Dinner *chez nous* B. *seul.* Koe enters at 6. At 7 went to Reeves's. Gave him up his license. Claimed the privilege of a British subject as a birthright, which I had a right to resume, and gave him notice that I should go where I pleased. This violent measure, however, grew out of his sug-

---

1 Dinner alone with B., K. entering at 6, read Thierry a little.
2 Theodosia, his daughter. He hoped she would join him in Europe.

gestions. He promised to report the case to Lord Hawkesbury, who would probably refer it to the Attorney-General. R. is to communicate to me the result. Returned to tea. Read Thierry an hour with B. and K. Part at 11. Wrote till 3. On returning home, called at Turnevelli's, the statuary, and engaged to give him a sitting to-morrow at 11.

24. Rose at 9. Wrote to Sir Mark not to call till 1. Went to Turnevelli's. He would have a mask. I consented, because Bentham, *et al*[1]. had. A very unpleasant ceremony. To Sir Mark's; he was sitting down to breakfast. Walked together. Called at Herries and Farquar's, St. James's street, agents of the late Colonel Charles Williamson, to see for letters from T————. None! none 11 Returning with G., *chez moi*[2] found a note from Baron Norton, requesting an interview. No doubt some law business. Wrote him to call at 12 to morrow. Sir Mark had engaged me to call on Signora B. Just as we were going out, casting my eyes in the mirror I observed a great purple mark on my nose. Went up and washed it and rubbed it—all to no purpose. It was indelible. That cursed mask business has occasioned it. I believe the fellow used quicklime instead of plaister[3] of Paris, for I felt a very unpleasant degree of heat during the operation. I sent Sir Mark off, resolved to see no Signora till the proboscis be in order. Wrote Ons.[4], with whom I had engaged to pass the evening, apolo-

---

1 Latin for *et alii*. And others.
2 At home.
3 So in the MS.
4 Madame Onslow.

gizing. Sent Tom with the packet for T., to be put into the mail for Falmouth. Also a letter for E. in French. Dinner *chez nous* with B. *seul*, Koe being gone to Hamstead. I have been applying a dozen different applications to the nose, which have only inflamed it. How many curses have I heaped on that Italian! Read to B. review of Leckie's work, which took till 9. K. came in, and we finished Thierry. I shall go early to bed (say 12), in hopes to sleep off my nasology.

25. Did not get to bed till 1. Rose at 9. Nose the same. At 11, went to Turnevelli's to sit. Relieved myself by cursing him for the nose disaster. He bore it like one conscious, and endeavored to console me by stating that the same thing happened to Lord Melville and to several others, and that the appearance passed off in a few days. Took a hack, not liking to walk and exhibit my nose. Stayed two hours with Turnevelli. He will make a most hideous, frightful thing, but much like the original. After leaving Tur., being unfit for any reasonable thing, rode to Madame O.'s to apprise her that if she were disengaged I would call after dinner and *play chess*. It was agreed. Rode to F's to give him a written mem. pointing out the defects and containing precise directions. Paid off the coach, 3 shillings, and walked to O.'s. On the way eat cakes and custard, 1 shilling, by way of dinner. Got to O.'s at ½ p. 5. Staid till ¼ p. 9. Play two games—each won alternately and paid. *Chez nous a dix*[1]. B. was writing. *Chez moi*, where

---

1 At home at 10.

I do nothing but muse for two hours. *Couché*[1] at 1.

26. Rose at ½ p. 9. Went to Turnevelli's at 11; nose a little improved. Sat one hour. The thing grows more hideous at every touch. Called at the house which C. gave me as his residence. The lady said he did not lodge there, she not being able to accommodate his family—that is, his *niece*. . . . . "Old enough to be my grand-father!" *Helas! quand reviendrai*[2]? Roved about two or three hours hunting a chess table, or stand with chess board inlaid; did not find one to please me. Home at ½ p. 3 to dress for dinner, being engaged to General Picton at the Tower Coffee-house. Went there, the nose notwithstanding, at ½ p. 5. *Y:* Captain Charles Smith; Baron Montalbert, who had served in St. Domingo, and said De Pestre was one of his officers, i. e., under his command. Spoke of De Pestre handsomely, but not in the warm terms which his virtues, his courage, and his talents merit. Also Dr. ———, an Irish gentleman who was in the medical department of Trinidad with Picton, and his particular friend, a frank, intelligent man. General Picton was governor of Trinidad, and had here a very unpleasant lawsuit, on a charge of applying torture to a mulatto girl to extort a confession of a theft to which there was a reason to believe she was a party. The ministry did not support him.

Friday (25th) again. I come back to Friday to say that Baron Norton, agreeably to my appointment,

---

1 Go to bed. One of the French words often employed in the Journal.
2 Alas! when shall I return.

called promptly at 12. His errand was to inquire about the estate of the late Lady Buth', the daughter of Sir W. Pulteney, and particularly as to the laws of descent in New York. He is a judicial baron of Scotland, whither he is going in a few days. Gave me his address, and offered me all sorts of civilities. Madame Norton, his wife, is a niece of the late Sir W. P. Perhaps a sister. No, it is a niece, and sister of the late Lady Buth.

Saturday (26th) again. Our dinner was a very good one, of three courses and four kinds of wine. Being in very bad order for society, I left them before coffee and got home at ½ p. 10. Just spoke to B. and came to my room. After ruminating and doing nothing for two hours, to bed about 1. In the course of the day called on Madame W. and found her in tears, with a gentleman by her side, consoling her in his manner, and from which I supposed something very melancholy had happened. He went off, and on inquiring the cause, which was—too long to be written—I found it so ridiculous that I scolded and laughed at her until she also laughed.

27. Sent Tom to Walbrooke to Madame W., which is his daily tour. At 12 called at Reeves's. He showed me a letter from Colonel Jenkinson about my pretensions as a British subject. Dampier has given opinion that I may resume at pleasure, the Lord Chancellor, Eldon, that I cannot, and am forever an alien. The Attorney-General is doubt-

---

1 For Lady Bath, for whom the village of Bath in New York state was named.

ing. Lord Hawkesbury thinks the claim monstrous. I begin to think the policy of this brusque move-- ment very doubtful. I am out of all patience at being detained in town, and am in danger of weary- ing out my great and good friend Bentham. From Reeves's walked on to visit the Donna; but, recollecting my nose, walked home. Tom had brought a letter from Graves, who is a most indefatigable and good creature. At 2 went over Westminster Bridge, and through Southwark to the London Bridge. Then round by the Tower, which I had never before seen. It is surrounded by a ditch, through which the Thames water flows; but it would not resist an enemy provided with heavy cannon for twenty-four hours. It may do very well to keep the lions and state prisoners. Called on Crockatt, 22 Throgmorton street; not at home. Gamp was tired and stopped a quarter of an hour to eat a jelly and cake, 8 pence. Came back by Blackfriars' and Westminster Bridges, and got home *safe* at ½ p. 4, having walked, as your map will show you, at least eight miles. Dinner below. B. and K. went up, and, against my advice, began the reading of the Preface and Eloge[1] of Thierry. B. got asleep, and I, approaching to it, came down to bring up my journal for the last three days, lest my little Min.[2] scold.

28. Rose at ½ p. 9. Nose a little improved. Sent Tom to Graves for the laws of New York, and to Miller, bootmaker. It is now five weeks since I

---

1 Eulogy.
2 Does he mean Minerva?

put into Miller's hands some of Bellamy's leather for a pair of boots. One pair which I could not get on, were sent and were returned. Since that I have had daily promises, but no boots. The shoes, which cost 17 shillings, I could not wear, and have given them away. Thus it is with every mechanic I have employed in London except my tailor, Beck, who lies a little, but far less than any other. Waited till 1 for Tom's return, and then went to Turnevelli's. Sat one hour. Worse and worse! This was meant to please you ; but if I had suspected that I had become so infernally ugly, I would sooner have ————. Roved about for two hours, ruminating on this sort of non-existence and on you. E. A., too, often accompanies me. Got home safe at ½ p. 4. Mr. Elkton Hammond, merchant, to dine with us. A very intelligent young man ; admiring the works of B. Has two sisters ; one studies legislation, the other chymistry[1]. The chymist said to be pretty. I am to dine there with B. on Thursday, when you shall hear more of them. This is the first time of Bentham's dining out. Mr. Slade sent me this morning a dozen Boston newspapers down to 14th October. What a nation of scoundrels you are, if one is to believe the gazettes !

29. *Couche* at 3. Rose at 9. I don't recollect to have told you that on my return from Weybridge, I had determined to set off immediately for Scotland. Six weeks have elapsed, and I am apparently (what

---

1 So in the MS. An old form of spelling.

hellish scrawls'; I must try to do better, or this
precious mem. will be lost to you and to the world),
apparently no nearer departure than on the day of my
return. Castella called with his friend P. at 11. P.
is a pleasant, amiable young man. Each a niece!
*Pauv. dia.*² P. has offered me some interesting maps
and papers. Had determined to go to-day to Weybridge; but having neglected to secure a passage, the
stage was full, &c. Went out at 1 to hunt a chess-
table; bought one, which, after buying, I found was
not the thing. Gave it up on paying 2 shillings.
Home at 2. A letter from Graves by Tom. American news to November 8th, by a schooner which ran
out of New York, the embargo notwithstanding.
You go on exactly as I expected, and as I declared
four months ago. At 3 to Donna. A very interesting woman; a tall, graceful figure, and the eyes and
hair of Italian beauty. No rouge, but interesting
physiognomy. If I were to stay in town should
pass many hours with Donna. To Falieri's at 5.
Thence to Madame O.'s, having taken, by way of
dinner, a jelly and biscuit on the way, 7 pence.
Played two games of chess, and won both. Prompt
payment—alarm—all ends well. Got home at ½ p.
8. Read with Bentham an hour in Semple's "Travels in Spain."

30. It is in the evening only that I write to you
in this manner. After writing what you see of yesterday, Koe came into my room about 12, and

---

1 The description is perfect '—Editor.
2 For *pauvre diable.* Poor devil.

challenged me at chess. We played till 4 this morning. I had ordered Anna to wake me at 7. She called at the hour. I answered and slept on till 10. Went out at 12. To Vickery, the celebrated *perrukier*[1], Covent Garden, to get a peruke for my country tour. Dressing my head in any fashion takes some time, and cannot be done on a journey; so I have taken again to the wig. Called at Madame W.'s on my return. She says several have called without leaving their names, perhaps some one with letters from you! The sight of your handwriting would make a jubilee in my heart. Found there a letter from Madame Prevost, and a very pretty one from Madame Godwin. Came home, answered Mrs. G.'s. Wrote also to Guillemard, from whom a second note came to-day. Found waiting for me in my room Captain C. Smith, whose civilities are unremitted, and of the most friendly kind. Went out again at 3. To a dozen cabinet-makers for a chess *table*. In vain; there is no such thing. Got her, however, a Dupre seal, 7 shillings 6 pence. To Falieri's. He has tried again, and I think has now succeeded. He had adopted an improvement on my suggestion, which he now values very much; but I had great trouble to make him do so. To Madame O.'s at ½ p. 5, having on the way taken a custard, a tart, and a cake for dinner, 1 and 2 pence. Pence are of some value here, but guineas of none. Took tea and played chess with O. and settled the winnings. Each score a

---

1 For *perruquier*. Peruke-maker.

game. Got home at 9. Found that D. M.[1] had called. What can have brought him? I am, however, most heartily glad he has come. I was just going to write him to come. He has been for some time at Bath. Read with B. and K. an hour in Semple. Wrote Madame Prevost and am now going to bed, ½ p. 1. The nose improves apace; hope it will be exhibitable to-morrow, and be fit for inspection of the legislatrix and the chymistress. *Bon soir[2]!*

London, December 1, 1808. Up at 7. Breakfast at 8. Some hopes of reform. Wrote several notes. At 11 came in D. M. R. Poetry! A little cracked, I fear. Perhaps the champignons he ate at Cheltenham of which *il manquoit de mourir[3]*—no doubt a little cracked. *Soir[4]* at 2 to Turnevelli's; abroad. Glad of it, for I would give 5 guineas that the thing were demolished! To twenty cabinet-makers for chess table. None. To ———— for seal for O. To Madame W————. *Chez moi* at 3. B., K., and self began our march at 4. The distance 3 miles. Arrive at 5. *Y:* Elton H.; two *souers, assez bien. Mais ne disent mot. Le jeune frere* ———— *bon franc physion. Un* ————, *pas homme. Un tres jeun hom.* Clark *probablement un* clerk. *Din. simpl. assez bon. A 8 sor. pour rendezvous de Madame G. La vû seule. Un develupment tres franc. Elle a un excellent esprit. Ses projects sur U. S. Promis de don. un rendez. chez moi a mon retour a* Weybridge. *Retour a H. a 9.*

---

1 D. M. Randolph.
2 Good evening.
3 He almost died.
4 Evening, or afternoon.

Music ——— *par* Gam. La, la. *Chez nous* at 11[1].
Chess with K. till 2.

    2. Rose at 9. Breakfast at 10. D. M. R. at 11.
Not quite so mad as yesterday, yet a little out. Consents to lay by the poem for some months. A very
civil note from Guillemard, to which replied. Wrote
several other notes. Sent trunks to get better locks.
So much plague as I had to get trunks, and the locks
are naught. *Sor.*[2] at ½ p. 2. To Turnevelli's, who had
been to hunt me. Sat only twenty minutes. He is
determined to go through with it; tries to encourage
me; finds it wonderfully like Voltaire; but all won't
do. It is a horrid piece of deformity. To Falieri;
not ready. To Miss Mallet. The most rational
being I have seen. Staid a whole hour, and greatly
pleased with her. Good breeding and social talents in
a degree very rare. Why don't I go there oftener?
Because I do nothing that I wish or intend. At ½
p. 5 to Colonel Charles Smith, 14 Beaumont street.
Y: Colonel Kearney; Von Sent, a respectable, quiet
subject, living thirty miles from London; Dr. Flanagan, who was in Trinidad with Picton, whom he
represents to be a man of rigid integrity and great
disinterestedness. Took no fees or perquisites while
governor. Such a man will not suit, and hence out of
favour. Dr. F. is a sprightly, sensible, frank, well-

---

1 Two sisters, pretty good. But they don't say a word. The young brother——a good,
open countenance. A ———, not a man. A very young man Clark, probably a clerk. Dinner
simple, pretty good. At 8 go out to Madame G.'s rendezvous. Saw her alone. A very frank
explanation. She has an excellent mind. Her schemes as to U. S. Her promise to give a rendezvous at my house on my return to Weybridge. Return to H. at 9. Music——by Gamp.
La, la. At home at 11. [In this case La, la, might be French, *Là, là*. There now!]
2 For *sors*. I go out. Used all through the Journal.

informed man. Tendered many civilities. An abominable tale was told of the P. of W———— of the annuity of £200 to ————, the famous groom and jockey; General ————, who has gone to command at Lisbon. His eulogy—Shaving the Seapoys—when secretary in Ireland. General Picton has two brothers in Wales. One a private gentleman, the other a clergyman. Three brothers, Pictons. *Chez nous* at ½ p. 10. Passed one-half hour with B. and K. Prepare for journey. *Couche* at ½ p. 2.

3. Had very carefully put Mr. Achaud's letter, my handkerchiefs, and other small articles in the pockets of the coat I intended to wear. Anna had *put my room in order* before I got down. After being two hours on the way, missed my handkerchiefs, and, upon quiet examination, discovered that I had taken the wrong coat. What a curse to have two coats at a time! But the letter; the letter of Madame A. to Madame P.! Met at Brentford the coach going to town. Engaged the driver for half a crown to go to Bentham's for the letter. Wrote K. to give him it. Breakfast at Brentford, 1 shilling 6 pence. A sensible elderly lady in the coach, going to Madame Merry's, Chelsea. This cannot be our Madame Merry. Arrived at Weybridge at ½ p. 1, having been five and a quarter hours on the road. Distance twenty-one miles. This is the usual rate of stage-coaching in this country, except the mail. At Madame Prevost's, her son, Lieutenant-Colonel William Prevost, and wife; an Irish lady, Miss Hamilton. Her father now at ————,

in Somerset, one brother, merchant in Liverpool, one, very young, merchant at Quebec, making a fortune out of the embargo. She offered a letter for you to her brother in Liverpool, in case you should land there. Dinner at 5 *en famille*[1] Cards *au soir*[2]—*perd.*[3] 3 shilling 6 pence. In the forenoon walked with Madame Prevost. Met several Gunns, but not Eliza. After returning, called at Gunn's. He abroad. Madame and the five daughters *chez elle*[4]. All very accomplished. All talents. The mother and Eliza superior. Came home (to the tavern) at ½ p. 10. I refused a bed at Madame's, being more at my ease to smoke my segar and tell little T. what I have been about. But I don't tell ½ nor ¼. These are only notes to write from. Afraid to write *out*.

4. Rose at 8. Breakfast at Madame P.'s. Walked through Oatland's Park to Walton, to see Mr. O'Callahan. Stopped at the outer Park gate, and got a passage after much difficulty. Mr. and M'lle O'C. abroad. M'lle *chez elle et comme me paroit un peu s.*[5] Urged to dine. Mr. Gunn came in; going out, met Mr. O'C., who, with Gunn, walked with me over the commons, not choosing to try the Park on my return. Pointed out to me on an eminence, about one mile distant, a place formerly the residence of Edward III., and afterward of Cardinal Wolsey, now the property of a broker, who has taken down the ancient struc-

---

1 In or with the family ; informally, as one of them.
2 In the evening.
3 For *perdis*, or *perdu*. Lost.
4 At her house.
5 At her house, and as it seems to me, a little s———.

tures, and put up a modern house in very bad taste. Near Weybridge met Madame Gunn and five daughters, with whom walked in the Park, and went to see the congaroos[1] and other beasts. Called on Mr. Bissett, once a very respectable clergyman at New York, now corrector of the press to a printing-office in Weybridge. He went home with me and staid till 5. *Din. chez*[2] Madame Prevost. *Y:* Colonel P. *et ux.;* Captain ———— *et ux.* Came home at 9. Mr. Gunn sent me a letter for his steward in Ireland. Madame Colonel P. gave letter to her brother at Liverpool, to whom she also wrote about T. The lost letter from Madame Achaud to Madame P. came by this day's mail, but charged with 8 pence postage.

5. Got in stage at ½ p. 7. Breakfast at Brentford. Arrived at ½ p. 11. Thus you see the rate of traveling. Stage fare going and coming, 14 shillings. To the coachman 2 shillings; bill at Weybridge 11 shillings 6 pence; maid 2 shillings 6 pence; two breakfasts 3 shillings; an extra 2 shillings and 6 pence to the driver, who took my letter to Bentham. Total, 35 shillings and 6 pence, though I lived at Madame P.'s. Took coach at Charing Cross, and went to Madame W.'s. My little villain, Tom, had been without orders and taken up my letters. Home at 1. Found letter from Guillemard, transmitting the laws of N. Y., and an invitation to dine to-morrow, which was obliged to refuse. *Sors* at 2. To the Tower

---

1 So in the MS.
2 For *diner chez.* Dinner at the house of.

Coffee-house, Bond street, to see Dr. Flanagan. Denied that he lived there, though he gave it to me as his address. To Miss Mallet, with Madame Prevost's letter; abroad. To Major-General Picton's, Edwards street; abroad. To Falieri's, where staid an hour. Still not done. Returning, called at Madame Achaud's; nobody at home. *Quod mirum*[1] *!* By way of dinner, three oysters, jelly, and cake, 10 pence. Called at Godwin's at ½ p. 5, knowing that he dines at 4. Found them at tea, and joined—the three daughters and little son. Agreed with Madame for rendezvous to-morrow at 11 at Mr. Lamb's[2] rooms. He is a writer, and lives with a maiden sister, also *literaire*[3], in a fourth story. Forgot—on my way from Achaud's, called on D. M. R., and walked half an hour with him. Mad again on poetry and politics. *Chez nous* ½ p. 8. Read an hour in the " Edinburgh Review " of the " Life of Washington." Descend at ½ p. 10. Spent two hours in hunting for some bank bills, my whole stock, and finally gave them up as lost. Found them when and where least expected. *Couch*[4] at 1.

6. Rose at ½ p. 9. *Sor.* at ¼ before 11 to meet Madame G. Met at the door of the place. Walked about the Temple, which comprises a large, irregular square; several small courts and alleys; many handsome buildings; two gardens on the banks of the Thames, very pretty. Madame had found a

---

1 Latin. How remarkable ı
2 Charles Lamb.
3 Literary.
4 For *couche.*

more convenient place at the house of Mr. Norris, treasurer of something. A handsome parlour. Passed an hour and a half talking over the affairs of G., &c. Walked with her to Holborn, and then went to Turnevelli's, where sat an hour. Home at 4. Caught in the rain, having yesterday left my umbrella at Brentford—no doubt lost. Dinner, B. and K. Read out the review of the " Life of Washington" by Marshall and Ramsay. The review is full as stupid, and as illy¹ written, as either of the books. Came down to bring up your journal since Saturday, the 7th, lest such important incidents should not be recorded. I know you will rave like a little Juno if you are not told what I do, and where I go every day. I could write six or eight very amusing pages of the incidents of the last three days, but they must be said and not written. Sir M. G. called on me just as I got home to-day, and gave me his address at his new lodgings. Omitted: Yesterday called at O.'s; she was engaged. Have not seen Donna, but hear that she is very ill. (My journal is four days in arrear. Half will be forgotten. This is Saturday evening. I will try to recollect.)

7. Rose *at ten*. Such is the mode in London. *Sor.* at 1. Going up Haymarket, met Madame O., and walked with her half an hour. Went to the stage-house in Piccadilly to inquire for my umbrella, but with little hope. It was there, brought by the coachman; 1 shilling 6 pence. How very honest

---

¹ So in the MS.

people are here, and yet I am cheated most impudently every hour! Met Sir Mark, and walked an hour with him. To Madame Duval. To Falieri's. To Turnevelli's; not at home; shall never be done with that fellow, and yet he tries his best; but the strange irregularities and deformities of the face defy all art. To O.'s for ten minutes, to say I would come to-morrow. To Sir M. Gerrard's to dine at———— Plagued to find the house. Like a true Irishman, he had mistaken his address. The same happened with Dr. Flanagan on Monday. Monsieur ————, the host of Sir Mark, has seen better days. He is now one of the pensioners of this government. *Sa femme,* a pretty, amiable *Angloise*[1], who speaks French perfectly. Captain ———— came in. Left Sir G. at 8, and went by way of Gray's Inn Lane to Godwin's, where stayed till ½ p. 10, and then at a very rapid rate home—26 minutes by the watch, being about three miles. Two shillings to beggar girls—pure benevolence. Just said *bon soir* to B., and came to my room. Chess with K. till 1. Sat up two hours after, packing up. Shall I ever get out of town to make this long-projected tour? Yes, on Saturday evening, pos.[2]

8. Rose at 10. Wrote to Reeves; to General Hope; to Crockatt; to Dr. Flanagan. *Sor.* at 1. Left Reeves's letter at his house, he not being at home. Left Dr. F.'s at the Tower Coffee-house. But before going out, Graves came in to tell me that the mail for

---

1 His wife, a pretty, amiable English lady.
2 For positively or possibly.

the packet would close at 5 P. M. this day; yet instead of sitting down to write to you, you see what I did. From the Tower Coffee-house to Madame Duval's. Called at Beetham's and got my picture of Catherine L. To Reeves's; he was reading my letter, and begged me to dine, being then ½ p. 4. I told him my distress about the packet. He sent a messenger to inquire. The mail would close at 5, but sailing orders would not go till to-morrow's mail, and he is to get your letter along with those of government. So staid to dine. Left them at 7, under pretence of my great impatience to write, and went off three miles to O.'s, where I staid till 10. Two games of chess, and was beaten both games, though I tried my best. Got home at ¼ after 11. Note: O. has found me out. Just spoke to B. and immediately came down to write. *Couche* at 3.

9. Rose at 8; breakfast at 9. Castella came and took breakfast with me. Sent him off, being busy, and engaged to walk with him at 8. To Putney 5 miles to see Judge ———— *et ux.* Had omitted to send yesterday to Mrs. W. Tom brought me the note of General Hope. Enclosed your letter and E. A.'s to Reeves—tried to write M. L. D. for G———— *Sor.* at 2. To Turnevelli's. To Horse Guards to meet General Hope by appointment. Had an hour's confab and received an explanation. To testify his intimacy with Colonel Williamson, he showed me the very *chiffre*[1] which I had given Williamson. Many

---

1 Cipher, figure.

courtesies and two letters for Scotland. *Chez nous* ½ p. 4. Dinner—Bentham and Koe. *Post prandium*[1], went to see Godwin. Staid till 9. Took tea. The children all very glad to see Gamp. Home at 10. Talked an hour with B. and K. To bed at 12.

10. Rose at 8. Breakfast at 9. Just as I had done, Castella came in. Gave him breakfast, and at ½ p. 10 began our march. Walked to Putney in 1 h. 10 m. Saw Madame Th. only. He sick and child at school. Came off in wherry at 12, and got to Weybridge in 50 minutes; 2 shillings 6 pence. The distance by water at least six miles. But Gamp has walked a great deal and is tired—now 2 o'clock. He will finish in the morning. When shall I begin my journey? Alas! alas!

Saturday, 10th, continued. On the way to Putney, we pass through the small towns of Chelsea, Battersea, and Fulham. At the last, cross a bridge over the Thames. The return by water is very beautiful. To Turnevelli's at 2. I wish I had never begun with him. To Falieri's. He has succeeded very well, except the colour. Home at 5. *Din.* B. *seul.* K dines abroad. The whole evening with K., *seul.* At 11 came down to my room. Read newspaper one hour. The poor Dons come out as I told you. Whether the British will get safe off is now the question. Just discovered that the under sheet of the last page is bottom upwards, which would have puzzled your luminous head for an hour if I

---

1 Latin. After breakfast.

had not told you. Journalized for an hour and went
to bed at 2.

11, Sunday. Slept like a log till 10, and then
was called. The atmosphere is certainly narcotic.
You see all along how enormously I have slept.
Wrote Meeker to call. He came at 12. Captain
Percival also an hour. Went to see the Donna; she
had gone to mass. Called at Bridgwater's and
Grimstone's, Grosvenor square. Neither of them in
town, but Grimstone expected. Nevertheless I will
go to St. Albans to-morrow to see him. His daughters, two, are very sensible, amiable women. Went
by Oxford street to Holborn, and took coach to
Smithfield to see for a passage to St. Albans.
Engaged a seat, and also a bed at the Angel Inn; to
go at 4 to-morrow morning. Paid 1 shilling earnest.
To Godwin's, where discharged coach; 2 shillings.
Half an hour with M. J. G.; then walked home by
way of Covent Garden to avoid the Strand, which is
forever so crowded and so dirty that there's no getting
on with comfort. Home at 5. Dinner—B. and K.
Immediately after dinner to work packing up. Wrote
long letter to M. L. D. about Madame G.'s business.
At ½ p. 10 all ready. Took leave of B., and sent
for hack to transport me and my trunk, being, as you
will see by your map, three good miles. No coach
was to be had. Went myself—no coach; so here is
Gamp, at 2 in the morning, at Queen's Square Place,
writing nonsense to T. B. A.', having let all his fire

---

1 His daughter.

go out and the last candle just gone. Played chess an hour with K. I have ordered Ann to wake me at 7. For what? When shall I get off?

12. Ann did call me at 7, but I slept, nevertheless, *a l'Anglois*[1], till ½ p. 9. Sent off Tom with notes written last night, but dated this morning, to M. J. G. and Mr. Graves, enclosing to him my letter to Davis. Tom is to bring word of the hour of the stage going to Gaddesden, being determined to go somewhere to-day. Tom did not return till 1, and brought word that the stage would go at ½ p. 1; so got coach and went off at a great rate. The stage had been gone 10 m. before I got there. *Quoi faire*[2]? Resolved not to go back to Q. S. P[3]. I thought I would go and hunt for some coach going any hour to-day or night; but having no place to put my trunk, was obliged to keep the coach. After running about for two hours and spending 9 shillings in coach hire, I discovered, what at any stage-house they might have told me, that no coach would go to Gaddesden till 1 P. M. to-morrow. Persisting in not going to Q. S. P., I e'en sat down with my trunk at the stage tavern in Oxford street, corner of Swallow. After depositing my trunk and ordering a fire in my room, sallied forth once more to Faleur's—then to see Graves, 10 Walgrove. Took coffee with Graves, a very respectable and intelligent young man, and extremely obliging. He makes inquiries, and does

---

1 For *à l' anglaise.* After the English manner.
2 What was to be done?
3 Queen's Square Place, where Bentham resided.

me many kind offices, which save me a deal of trouble. He is, I believe, a broker. The mother was there; a very comely, decent Quakeress. The mother of eight or ten grown children. It is wonderful how the women wear in this country. In all my stage rambling to-day, I could not discover how to get to York. Graves has undertaken for me. Thursday is the day fixed for my grand tour to Scotland, Ireland, Wales, &c. On my way home took musk of a very indifferent quality, 10 shillings 1 pence. Got home to the tavern at 8, and ordered coffee again, having only dined on a jelly, cake and tart, 10 pence. Great debate whether I would have it in my room or must descend to the coffee room. Note: I am in the third story, what is here called second floor. Finally the lady relaxed, and I had my coffee *chez moi.* Tobacco interdicted; but I ventured to smoke my pipe up chimney, with a window open. No segar to be had. Tobacco very bad, 3½ p. an ounce. Something more than a dollar a pound. The Virginians would, at this time, be glad to get 10 cents per pound for tobacco of much better quality. A bed with very dirty sheets, to which I objected; but the maid assured me, upon her honour, that they were very clean, and that she put them on herself. So I am bound to think them clean; but shall, nevertheless, not undress. It is quite impracticable to get a good fire in any tavern. At 10 took bread and cheese and cider, by way of supper. Wrote all this, and after writing two letters to my Gaddesden friends, having a

presentiment that I shall not get there, shall *coucher*[1]
Since beginning the preceding page, the servants have
been three different times in my room to inquire
whether they should put out my candles. To the
first message I replied very distinctly that I always
put out my own candles, and desired that I might not
be again interrupted. This did not defend me against
the two subsequent intrusions. The object of this
affected civility is to save one inch of tallow. This
very rigid calculation is *universal.*

13. Rose at 9. At the tavern. No soap.
Asked for a piece to wash hands. The maid said
soap was so dear that she could not give it without
leave, but she would go and ask her mistress, which I
forbid, but gave her 2 shillings to go and buy me a
piece. She " would tell the footman "—every one in
their department ! A cake of soap was brought for
15 pence, which will probably last me three months,
which is at the rate of 1 penny ¼ a week, and at
this rate, if there should be twelve lodgers in the house,
the value of the soap used by the whole would be 1
shilling 3 pence per week and about 3 guineas per
annum ! Had my breakfast in my room and at 11
sor. To Vickery's to get the wig made more scratch-
like and less dressy. To cabinet-maker's about that
same chess-board. Returned to the tavern at 1, and
found stage at the door. One shilling to the waiter,
and bid him bring down my trunk and put it in the
stage. He brought it down, but at the door handed

---

1 Shall go to bed. Here *coucher* is an infinitive.

it to the porter, who handed it to the coachman, this
being the porter's department. Two pence to the
porter. At Hemel Hempstead (look at your map)
found a beer club of about a dozen, smoking and
drinking ale. Joined them. Took my pipe and
called for my pint of beer. They bring a pipe, with
a small bowl with tobacco. The tobacco is never put
on the table. The maid fills it and hands it to you ;
for each pipeful a ½ penny ; pint of beer 3 pence.
Arrived at Little Gaddesden ½ p. 8. A note to
Bartlett, inquiring, &c., and that I should call in half
an hour. He being abroad, it was opened by Madame
Bartlett, who immediately sent a servant to conduct
me. But to be in order with my precise friend, Major
G., I went first to his house ; there found a party of
ten gentlemen over their wine, of which it appeared
they had then drank *quan. suf.*[1] Bartlett and M'Carthy were there ; also Halsey, M. P., lately married
(two years ago) to a wealthy and pretty heiress, whose
name he assumed ; Dr. ——— and his son (a lieutenant of navy) ; Mr. ———, a handsome young
man. After twenty minutes went to Bartlett's, where
found Madame B., Madame Span, Mrs. and Miss
———. Took tea and passed the evening. At 10,
Bartlett, M'Carthy, &c. came in. Urged to take bed
both here and at Major G.'s ; but intending to set off
at ½ p. 6 in the morning, preferred the tavern, where,
after great efforts, I got a very small fire. Asked for
more coal. The mistress brought up in her hand two

---

1 Latin for *quantum sufficit.* As much as suffices.

pieces, each about the size of a biscuit. Got a bottle of very good cider, and sat down to write. Note to Major Gamble ; to McCarthy ; to Dr. Bartlett desiring him to apologize for me to Lord Bridgwater. To bed at ½ p. 2.

14. Rose at 6. Set off at 7. I sleep very soundly in these stage coaches. By sleeping, however, forgot to ask for my umbrella, which I had left at Stanmore. Took breakfast at Edgware, 1 shilling 3 pence. Coffee, bread, and butter. If you have an egg or any other article, it is charged in addition. Arrived at 12 at the Bell and Crown, Holborn, where left my trunk till I should see about getting off to-morrow. Went on to the Berwick wharf in Burr street. The packet course ; passage 2 guineas for *half a birth*[1], 3 guineas for a whole one. You are found in provisions. Stage-coaches go every morning at 7 for York, &c. Doubting which mode to adopt, walked back to the Bell and Crown. Paid 2 pence for leaving my trunk. Took hack and drove to Queen's Square Place at 4. Received in the most affectionate manner. How inexhaustible is the goodness of Bentham ! Hurried to dress, being engaged to dine with Judge Thorpe at Putney. Walked there and arrived just before 6, being five miles. They had despaired of me, and just sat down to dinner. The family and Castella. Affection of the children. Very pleasant. At ½ p. 8 returned by the Richmond coach, which goes every hour from 8 A. M. to 8 P. M. Thorpe

---

1 So in the MS.

and Castella along. Set down in Pecad. and got to Q. S. P. at ½ p. 9. An hour with Bentham to give an account of myself.

THE ADVENTURES OF GIL BLAS MOHEAGUNGK DE MANHATTAN.

London, December 21, 1808. In a garret at the Black Lion, Water Lane, London. Having made half a dinner at Queen's Square Place, drove off furiously to the White Horse, Piccadilly, to be in time for the Oxford stage. Having waited half an hour and the coach not come, the weather cool, went in to warm. Having warmed half an hour, and wondering at the delay, went out to see. The coach had been gone twenty minutes. My honest coachman, as well to be sheltered from the storm as for repose, had got inside and was sound asleep. Drove to Gloucester Coffeehouse to take the mail. Was advised to go to the Golden something, Charing Cross. Thither went. The mail was full, inside and out. Thence to the Saracen's Head. Thence to Fister Lane. Coach full. To the Black Lion, Water Lane, Fleet — full, inside and out. To the Old Crown, Holborn—no coach hence till Friday. To the Bolt Inn, where found a seat in a coach to go at 7 to-morrow, but no bed to be had. Went to the nearest inn, being the same Black Lion, where I am occupant of a garret room, up four flights of stairs, and a very dirty bed. In the public room, however, I have been amused for an hour with a very handsome young Dane. Don't smile. It is a male ! A merchant. I would have slept on the porch or walked the street all night sooner than have returned to Q. S. P. Coach hire 9 shillings.

Oxford, December 22. Was called at 6, to be ready for the coach at 7. Gave my baggage to a porter, but, being stopped a minute to make change, he got out of my sight. I missed the way, and when I got to the Bolt Inn the coach had gone. My passage having been paid in the evening, there was no inducement to wait for me. Pursued and had the good fortune to overtake the coach. Found in it one man. Having preserved perfect silence for a few minutes by way of experiment, I remarked that the day was very mild, which he flatly denied, and in a tone and manner as if he would have bit me. I laughed out heartily, and very kindly inquired into his morning's adventures. He was old, gouty and very fat. No hack to be had at that early hour, or, what is more probable, choosing to save the shilling he had walked from his house to the inn. Had fallen twice ; got wet and bruised, and was very sure that he should be laid up with the gout for six months. I sympathized with his misfortunes. Wondered at the complacency with which he bore them, and joined him in cursing the weather, the streets, and the hackney coachmen. He became complacent and talkative. Such is John Bull. We took in another fat man, a woman still fatter, and a boy. Afterwards, a very pretty, graceful, arch-looking girl, about 18, going on a visit to her aunt, Lady W. But M'lle was reserved and distant. At the first change of horses she agreed to take breakfast, which we did, *tete-a-tete*[1]. I was charmed to find her all animation, gayety, ease, badinage. By the aid of drink to the coachman, our companions were kept three-quarters of an hour cooling in the coach. They had breakfasted. When we joined them the reserve of my little siren returned. After various fruitless essays, and at first without suspecting the cause, finding it impossible to provoke anything beyond a cold monosyllable, I composed myself to sleep, and slept soundly about eight hours, between London and this place, where we arrived at 8 this evening. (There must be something narcotic in the air of this island. I have slept more during my six months' residence in Great Britain than in any preceding three years of my life since the age of 14.) Took leave of my little Spartan. Mem: To write an essay, historical and critical, on the education and treatment of women in England. Its influence on morals and happiness. Thinking it too late to call on the provost (your instructions are not lost on me), I wrote him a "*polite*" note, enclosing the letter, and proposing to see him in the morning, to which a *polite* answer was received.

23. I was received with the distinction due to such a letter. His manner is mild, cheerful and courteous. He engaged me to dine, and sent for a young "fellow," who went with me through all the great buildings, and showed me all the strange things. Many of those for which I inquired he had never

---

1 For *tête-à-tête.* Together.

before heard of. Everything here is for ostentation, and nothing for use. A manuscript of Horne's "Mirror" was shown me, but evidently modern. A handwriting much like our Mr. Koe's. The librarian acknowledged that it was but a copy, and professed no knowledge of the original. The bust of Aristotle has a forehead very like yours. We were more than three hours traversing the various buildings. I was much gratified. My poor conductor nearly frozen. Two plump, hale "fellows" joined us at dinner. Study and abstinence had not yet impaired their rosy complexions. All is canonicals. The dinner was excellent and well served. The details of the conversation shall amuse you at another time; but they cannot be written. A few hints may serve as memoranda. "I would rather our friend Bentham should write on legislation than on morals!" Holy Father, if ever one of thy creatures was endued with benevolence without alloy —— All this was admitted, and the expression was qualified and qualified, till finally it settled on the single point of *divorce*, and Hume was quoted. By mutual consent divine authority was laid aside, and I made a speech, which was very silly, for I ought to have turned it off with levity. The *innate* sense of religion. "The most barbarous nations have some religion. Has it not a great influence on the morals of your Indians?" We then got on American politics, statistics, geography, laws, &c., &c., on all which a most profound and learned ignorance was displayed. The evening wound up pleasantly, and we parted with many expressions of courtesy. He appears to be of cheerful temper and amiable disposition. Yet, though he speaks of Bentham with reverence, and, probably, prays for him, I presume he thinks that he will be eternally damned, and I have no doubt he expects to be lolling in Abraham's bosom with great complacency, hearing Bentham sing out for a drop of water. Such is the mild genius of our holy religion.

Brummigem, December 24, (though, indeed, I have heard it several times called *Birmingham*.) Left Oxford at 7 this morning. We were four inside. The only article of any interest was a pretty little comely brunette, who had been through Blenheim Castle, and all the other places of note within twenty miles. Could describe all the pictures and statues; had read all the fashionable novels and poetry, and seemed to know everybody and everything. I was never more at a loss in what rank of beings to class her; but was very much amused. At twenty miles we put her down at a very respectable farmhouse. I handed her in; was introduced to her aunt: " My dear aunt, this gentleman has been extremely polite to me on the road." I received from aunt and niece a very warm invitation to call on my return, which I very faithfully promised to do, " whensoever," &c. " If," &c., &c. At Stratford, where lie the bones of Shakespeare, the barmaid gave me a very detailed account of the jubilee in honour of his memory. At about twenty miles farther was pointed out a very handsome establishment of Sir ———— Smith, *dit frère de* Madame[1] Fitzherbert. For the last forty or fifty miles we had on board a strange, vulgar-looking fellow, who had been all over the world; spoke Latin, French, and Spanish; and in the course of three hours told me more than a hundred lies; probably some itinerant Irish schoolmaster. The market place and the principal street, adjacent to which I am set down, is full of people. Tents, booths, lamps, candles, fiddlers, pipers, horns. Seeing nothing to amuse me within, I shall sally forth to see what's going forward without. But, first, I have taken passage for Liverpool, to set off at ½ p. 11, being advised that there is no other way to get on. Against my will, therefore, I go to Liverpool. We shall, from appearances, make a lively party. At this hour to-morrow I may have something more amusing to say. Now I go.

12 o'clock. Still at Birmingham. Full of contrition and remorse. Lost my passage. Lost or spent 28 shillings and a pair of gloves. Every bed in the house engaged. No hope of getting on but by the mail at 7 to-morrow morning. The office shut, and no passage to be taken to-night. What business had I to go sauntering about the streets of a strange place, alone and unarmed, on a Christmas eve? Truly, I want a guardian more than at 15. It was K.'s fault that I left my dirk, and I could choke him for it. I have often heard that great sinners have relieved their consciences by full confession. Let us try. I sallied forth. There were hundreds of pretty

---

1 Said to be the brother of Madame F.

45

dressed folks of all sexes and ages, in little groups and very gay. I joined one party, and then another, and another. At length I got so well suited with a couple that we agreed to walk and see the town. I have always had a passion for certain branches of natural history. These, I thought, afforded me an opportunity of acquiring information ; and even now, amid all my regrets, I must acknowledge that it was a most instructive and, abating one rencounter, which had very nearly ended in a riot, a most amusing lesson. Hence it would seem that all this penitence is for the money and not for the folly, on which a very good theological dis course might be written. The subject shall be recommended to our friend the provost. Indeed, I was very much amused. I heard many amusing anecdotes of the grandees of the town, and some strange and pretty things. At this moment it comes into my head how to redeem this 28 shillings. It shall be done and then peace of conscience will be restored. I will take passage outside. Half price only. I am resolved, and you shall see how I execute.

Edinburgh, January 1, 1809. Got my best parlour in order, expecting Lord Justice Clerk[1]. At 12

---

1 Charles Hope, Lord Granton (1763–1851), was educated at Edinburgh, admitted an advocate in 1784, and in 1801 was appointed Lord Advocate. In 1804 he was appointed an ordinary Lord of Session and Lord Justice Clerk in the place of Sir David Rae, and assuming the title of Lord Granton, took his seat on the bench on December 6, 1804. On November 12, 1811, he succeeded Robert Blair of Avontoun as Lord President of the Court of Sessions. In December, 1836, he became Lord Justice General. In 1793 Hope married his cousin, Lady Charlotte Hope, second daughter of John, second Earl of Hopetoun, by his third wife, Lady Elizabeth Leslie. Burr's letter of introduction to Lord Justice Clerk was written by A. Cochrane Johnstone, of London, who said : " Permit me to introduce to your Lordship the bearer of this, the celebrated Colonel Burr, with whom our worthy friend, Charles Williamson, was very intimate. His talents, abilities, and amiable qualities will, I am confident, ensure him a place in your esteem. He proposes making a stay of only a few days in Scotland, during which time I have to request that you will render him any attention in your power. He is anxious to have an opportunity of making the acquaintance of the most learned of our profession, and to whom can I apply so well as to you to bring this about ? "

Arbuthnot came in, and afterward Colonel Smith. At 2 went out. Met in the street and was introduced to Alexander M'Kenzie[1], author of " Man of Feeling," being on the way to his house. Called on Jeffrey[2] and handed him a letter. Called on Walter Scott; on Lord Provost (Mayor). While Arbuthnot and Smith were sitting with me this morning, Lord Justice Clerk called, and was refused by the stupidity of a servant. Wrote Lord Justice Clerk, apologizing, accepting his invitation and enclosing Colonel J.'s letter. At 5 went to dine with Mr. Jardine, an advocate. Delayed a whole hour, not being able to find the house. The coachman more ignorant than myself. Met there Erskine, brother of the Lord Chancellor and of the Earl of Buchan, and heir apparent to the title; Colonel Alexander Munro; Madame Munro; the Colonel has been fifteen years in India, and very lately returned; the Rev. Mr. Morehead; Mr. Forbes, son of Sir ——— Forbes; Madame Bruce, *femme de* ——— Bruce, son of the traveler. He was confined with the rheumatism, and did not appear. Henry M'Kenzie, advocate, son of the author of the " Man of Feeling."

2. Note from Lord Justice Clerk. Message that the Lord Provost would call. Waited at home

---

1 But it was Henry M' Kenzie, not Alexander, who wrote the novel of this name. He was also the author of " The Man of the World " (1773), " Julia de Roubigné " (1777), etc. Under date of February 12, 1809, Burr wrote to his daughter : " Among the literary men of England I have met M'Kenzie, author of the ' Man of Feeling,' and Scott, author of the ' Minstrel.' I met both frequently, and from both received civilities and hospitality. M'Kenzie has twelve children—six daughters, all very interesting and handsome. He is remarkably sprightly in company, amiable, witty—might pass for 42, though certainly much older. Scott, with less softness than M'Kenzie, has still more animation; talks much, and very agreeably." At this time M'Kenzie was 64 and Scott 38.

2 Lord Francis Jeffrey (1773–1850), founder, and for twenty-six years editor of *The Edinburgh Review*.

till 2, he not coming, *sorti*[1]. Called on Bishop Cameron; thence to Arbuthnot's. Snowstorm; returned home. Robert Dundas, during my absence, left a card. While dressing, Mr. and Mrs. Erskine called—denied. Madame left an invitation for the evening of the 6th. While dressing, also, Mr. Jeffrey and brother, nephew of Jeffrey of Boston. The brother had known A. B.[2] in Philadelphia; also, Sir H. Camp bell, for twenty-five years Lord President of the Court of Sessions; also, Lord Frederic Campbell, uncle of Duke of Argyle, Lord Register.

4. *Lev.* at ½ p. 8. Mr. Gordon, by appointment, called; sat half an hour, and tendered all sort of civilities. *Sor.* at 12. To Mrs. Lockhart, 3 Heriot Row. She was a Crawford, born in Holland of Scotch parents; Madame Court-Lockhart; has now charge of M'lle D. V.; not at home. To Mr. Jardine's, where saw Mr. and Mrs. ———; urge me to pass a day at ———, the residence of the late traveler Bruce, and now of his son and heir. To Mr. Arbuthnot's, 47 Queen Street. Madame and M'lle. Home at 2. Mr. Hume came in and claimed acquaintance, having dined at my house with Madame and his two nieces, Houstons, about 1803; is passing some weeks in town at Mr. Walker's, who has made a fortune in the East Indies. *Sor.* at ½ p. 2. To Walker's, 21 Queen's Place, to see Mr. and Madame Hume. *Υ:* also Mr. and Madame Walker and three daughters. Invited to dine, which accepted, hoping to hear fine music.

---

1 For *je suis sorti*, or *je sortis*. I went out.
2 Meaning himself.

The daughters very fine; the two elder, *jolie, belle—la jeune, genie*[1]. To D. Williamson's[2], from whom had just received a very friendly note. He showed me many letters addressed to Charles Williamson. Saw there little Charles Alexander. Took coach to come home for dispatch; 2 shillings. Dress and out at 5; coach 1 shilling 6 pence. While I was out the Mr. M'Kenzies, father and son, called and left cards. Found, also, an invitation from George Dundas and wife, for Wednesday, to which wrote yes. At dinner at Walker's. The family, Mr. and Mrs. Hume, Mr. Ogilvie, who had made a fortune in the East Indies, and wife, very sprightly; Sir William Fettus, Madame Wauchope, sister of Sir ———— Baird; her daughter, a most lovely and fascinating girl. In face and person something like Miss M'Kevers (Van Ness)[3], but all animation, sensibility, and intelligence; a son of Madame Wauchope, a very handsome and intelligent lad, 18, in the navy; a son of Mr. Ogilvie, 22, also supposed navy; *les trois* M'lles Walker[4] played and sang Scotch songs for me. Took one rubber at whist; won 1 shilling. Off at 10. *Trop bu*[5], drank lemonade and smoked black tobacco till 1. Amused by the singing of a jovial party in an adjoining room.

5. Rose at 8. Took chaise and drove out to Lord Justice Clerk's to breakfast. He had breakfasted, but got [breakfast] for me. A pair of Shetland

---

1 The two older ones pretty, beautiful—the young one a genius.
2 David Williamson, Lord Balgray, was a brother of the late Colonel Charles Williamson.
3 Mrs. William P. Van Ness, whose husband, an eminent New York lawyer, was Burr's second in the duel with Hamilton.
4 The three Misses Walker.
5 Having drunk too much.

Island knit gloves. Lady Charlotte Hope. Very interesting confab. Lord Hope walked two miles with me. Got home at ½ p. 3. Found card from Colonel Smith, and notice to dine at 4. Note from Mrs. Gordon with the letters of "Amicus" in answer to Lord Selkirk. *Din. chez moi.* At 8 to Mrs. Erskine. Duchess Gordon, Lord Tweedale, Miss Dallas, Mrs. Munro, from Jamaica by way of New York, Lady ———, who introduced me to her husband, Mrs. ———, who came with a gentleman in black scratch, Mrs. Erskine, Lady Jane, Miss Dalzelle and brother with crutch.

6. Rose at 8. *Sor.* at 11 to M'Kenzie's, No. 6 Heriot Row; out. To Walker's. Mr. W. and Mr. Hume were just going out to see me. Mrs. W. prayed us to dine. To Jeffrey's; the two brothers. *Chez moi*, where found Mr. Hope's card. He had called to remind me of Saturday evening; music. To Mrs. Erskine's; not at home. *Chez moi.* Mr. Jardine called while I was dressing. To Colonel Smith's to dine at ½ p. 4. Fourth story. Colonel S. and his sister, Mrs. Dundas; Captain Duncan, an old sea captain who has been much in North America; Mr. M'Cormick, cousin of David, lived ante-war in Virginia; was at New York during the war; Dr.———; Captain McDowell, four years in the army; very impressive young man; married to ———, a correspondent of Madame Sp.

7. Rose at 11. *Sor.* at 1. To D. Williamson's who had received a letter from Lord Hopetoun,

inviting me to visit Hopetoun House, with any friends I pleased. To dine. Walked with D. W. to the ————, where are warm baths. To Jardine's; all out. *Chez moi.* Found note from Mrs. Gordon inviting me at request of Mrs. Johnstone to pass some days at her place near Sterling. To dinner at Jeffrey's. *Y.:* Scott, minstrel; Johnstone; two Jeffreys, &c. At 9 took chair and went to J. Hope's, 54 Prince street. *Y.:* The three Misses Hope, daughters of ———— Hope; Miss H., sister of ditto; M'lle Houston, *bien jolie*[1]; two Misses Walker, sisters of Mrs. Hope; Miss ————, *anglois*[2]; Mrs. Clarke, elderly; Mr. and Madame (or Miss) Duff. The second Miss Hope plays *superieurement*[3] on piano. Jane Walker sang in a style quite new to me and very delightful, several Scotch songs. *Chez moi* at 12.

8. Rose at 11. *Sor.* at 1. *Chez* James H.; *pas*[4]. *Chez* Arbuthnot; *sor. av.*[5] to Magdalene Asylum; *pas admis*[6]. To Colonel Smith's. *Y.:* Captain Duncan who engaged me to dine on Saturday. *Chez moi* at 3. Found cards of Hume and Walker. At 4½ to dine. *Y.:* M'Kenzie, Clerk, Vic. Ker[7], *b. d'esprit*[8], Mr. Arbuthnot, and *sa mere*. *Ancien. connaissance de* Madame Bartlett[9] who was Mrs. Munro. Left at about 10. Received a letter.

9. Vigils till 6. Rose at 11. Mr. Clune, the

---

1 Very pretty.
2 For *anglaise*. English.
3 In a superior manner.
4 For *pas chez lui*. Not at home.
5 For *sors avec*. Go with him.
6 Not admitted.
  Vicompte Ker. Viscount Ker.
7 For *beaucoup d'esprit*. Lots of wit, or intelligence.
8 For *ancienne connaissance de*. Old acquaintance of Madame Bartlett.

Sheriff, called before I was up. Left card and invited to sup the 10th. Before I had breakfast, Colonel Smith and Captain M'Dowell, whose wife is niece of Bartlett, sat ½ hour, and engaged me to dine Friday. Breakfast at 1. *Sor.* to Jeffrey's. Left with him Bayard's speech and " Agrestis'". Interrupted by a lady To D. Williamson's ; not at home ; left note for him about dining at Lord Justice Clerk's, and the medi tated visit to Hopetoun House. Met him as I went out. Sat ½ hour. *Chez moi* to dress at ½ p. 3. While dressing, Hume called, and left card and mem. reminding of engagement to dine Saturday. At 4 took post-chaise and went to Lord J. Clerk's. *Y*: Mrs. Hope, wife of General Hope, now in Spain, *belle, interess., chev. jaune*[2]; Wedderburne ; Lord Ch. Baron Dundas, nephew and son-in-law of Lord Melville ; Lord J. Clerk *toujour pol.*[3]; his arrangements for Hopetoun House. Return at ½ p. 9. Paid postchaise and coachman 16 shillings 6 pence. Wrote note to Arbuthnot asking interview this night (about Walsh) ; to Mr. Clerk, accepting his invitation ; to Williamson about the visit to Hopetoun House. *Renc. en ret.*[4] Mary McKay at Madame's. Dr. Hume, son-in-law of Captain Duncan, called and left card and invited to dine on Saturday.

    10. *Couche* ½ p. 2. Rose at 11. Raining. Still warm. *Sor.* at 1. Mr. Williamson *chez* Madame

---

1 A pamphlet detailing General Wilkinson's intrigues at New Orleans. Alston, Burr's son-in-law, was suspected of the authorship. Blennerhasset said that that was " preposterous ", but that Alston's wife, Theodosia Burr Alston, might have written it.
2 For *belle, intéressante, cheveux jaunes.* Fine-looking, interesting, yellow hair.
3 For *toujours poli.* Always polite.
4 For *Rencontrai en retournant.* On returning met.

Major Robertson. *Belle taille*[1] *Tres poliment recu.*[2] To Duchess of Gordon at Dornbeck's hotel. *Elle seul*[3]. The medal, &c. Half an hour. To the Bridewell. Panopticon. *Vid.* notes *inde*[4]. *Chez moi. Din. seule en chamb*[5]. *Rien fa. jusq. a 9*[6]. To Mr. Clerk's. *Υ:* Admiral ———, who lost an arm at Dogger Banks; Mr. Duff; M'lle Duff; Mr. and Mrs. Clerk; son of ditto, aged 15; Mr. and Mrs. James Hope; Dr. Hope, professor of chemistry; Judge Hume. Staid till 12. Invitation from Mr. Walker for Wednesday the 18th. Question about accepting. Before going out this evening wrote to D. Williamson proposing Thursday for the Hopetoun House party. *Chez* Duchess Gordon. Lady Jane Montague, 18, and her little sister.

11. Having eat and drunk too much yesterday, was obliged to sit up till 5. Rose at 12. Note from D. Williamson before I was up, proposing Thursday for Hopetoun House, to which assented. *Sor.* ½ p. 2. To Dr. Hume's, 34 Yorke Place; not at home, but saw Captain Duncan. To Mr. Arbuthnot's, ½ hour. To Jeffrey's; not at home. *Chez moi* at 4. Williamson called for me to go with him to our dining room before I was dressed; kept him waiting ½ hour and went to Mr. John Dundas. *Υ:* Mr. J. D; Robert D., wife, and her sister, the same I met at

---

1 Fine figure.
2 Very politely received.
3 She alone.
4 Latin and English. See notes thence i. e., taken from that. " Panopticon " was the title of one of Bentham's works.
5 Dinner alone in my room.
6 For *rien fait jusqu à 9.* Nothing done till 9.

Charles Smith's in London; D. Williamson; Mr. and Madame Irvine; Mrs. Ferguson; her son and daughter, he an average American young man; Mrs. Wallace; two Misses Rollo, sisters of Lord Rollo; and Major William Drummond, who had served in the West Indies and is now going to Spain, a fine, sensible, soldierly, well-bred man. We came off together and he urged me to go and take supper and pass an hour with him at his hotel. Went, supposing he was a bachelor; came in Madame D., a most lovely woman, his wife, who had been three years with him in the West Indies; Lord and Lady Rollo and another Miss Rollo. Passed an hour pleasantly. *Chez moi* at ½ p. 11. Wrote to Madame Gordon.

12. Rose at ½ p. 7. Mr. Williamson called in a post-chaise. At ½ p. 9 we drove off; a fine, clear day. Stopped for an hour at ———— Ferry; a compact village. Great number of fishing boats. Views. Cromwell's mother. Miss Stewart of the blood royal. Dinner; two wines; four fries. Pictures. Herculaneum. Home at ½ p. 8. *Sor.;* 37 shillings.

13. Rose at ½ p. 10 in very bad order, having been up three or four hours with the *bu*[1] Took *de* cre. tar. punch[2]. At 12 Mr. Walker and Dr. Hume called and were denied. American newspaper. Packet arrived in twenty-three days. Colonel Smith called and denied. Dr. Hume called again at 3 and sat ½ hour. Colonel G. at 4. Walked to dinner at Captain

---

[1] Drinking. Literally, with (having) drunk. On this day Burr wrote a letter to Jeremy Bentham in London in which he said: "I lead a life of the utmost dissipation. Driving out every day and at some party almost every night. Wasting time and doing many silly things."

[2] Took cream tartar punch—a favorite cure of Burr's when he was "in bad order" in the morning.

M'Dowell's in snow storm. *Y.:* Captain M'Dowell's two mothers and Miss Donald; Colonel Patterson; Major Cameron; Dr. Spence. Rode home in Colonel P.'s carriage with him and Miss Donald—which was *tres mal fai*[1]. Captain M'Dowell urged us to sup. *Chez moi* ½ p. 9. *Sor.* 10. Major Cameron's. *Y.:* Johnston, *la chanteuse*[2]; two Madame Camerons. *Chez moi* at ½ p. 11, *tres mecon. de moi*[3]. Finished letter to Koe. Began one of apology to J. B. All flat and bad. *Couche* at 2. Invaded by *tous les Diab. de reprou*[4]. Vigils till 5. Omitted: Mr. Arbuthnot called this forenoon to let me know that Mrs. A. had brought him a daughter.

14. Rose ½ p. 10. *Mieux qu' on doit attendre*[5]. Before I had done breakfast Lord Justice Clerk called and sat ½ hour. He has written to Lord Melville. The Lord Justice is colonel of a regiment of volunteers and had been out exercising them three hours this morning. *Moi dor!*[6] At 12 Robert Dundas and Dr. Coventry called and were received. The Dr. a pleasant, sprightly, sensible man; *par. aimable*[7]; asked me to dine, but I declined to fix a day. R. Dundas said he was writing to Captain Smith, and asked my commands. Desired him to order on my letters and did not send the letter written for that purpose to Captain S. Finished my letter to J. B., a mere note

---

1 Very badly arranged (*fai* for *fait.* Done.)
2 The vocalist.
3 For *très mécontent de moi.* Greatly displeased with myself.
4 *Reprou.* for *reprouvé.* Reprobate. Hence, invaded by all the demons of the lost, the reprobate.
5 Better than one ought to expect.
6 For *moi dormeur!* Sluggard that I am!
7 For *particulièrement aimable.* Especially amiable.

on the same sheet with that of K.; also one to
Meeker; sent both to post-office. *Sor.* at 3 to
Arbuthnot's; out; compliments and enquiries to
Madame, who had yesterday a daughter. Home at
4. Dress and at ¼ before 5 called on Colonel Smith
to go with him to Dr. Horne's, 34 Yorke Place, to
dine. He was not going; arrived at Horne's too
soon. Mr. Horne abroad; nevertheless Madame H.
received me very politely. At dinner, Mr. Horne
and wife and Captain ———, her father, an old sea
captain, Madame H. the only child; Mr. Ferguson,
barrister, *et ux.*, a pretty, pale, delicate blonde, *tres
jeune*[1]; Mr. Thompson, author of a collection of
Scotch songs in four volumes and himself *bien fer. en
Mus*[2].—advocate, *je croi*[3]; Mr. Gillespie, a very handsome, gentlemanly young man; Mr. Huyck or Hyck
et ux.—un fem. aimable and comely[4]; a lovely little
daughter of 9, *qui danse comme une ange*[5]; Mrs. Gil-
more, *jeu. veu. 22 tres ri*[6]. and very beautiful; Miss
Brown, daughter of Captain Brown, handsome *et
aimable et* well bred; two M'lles ———; the elder
sings divinely, the *cadette*[7] pretty, *manque tournure*[8];
Judge Hume and wife. Much good music and sev-
eral Scotch songs in a very superior style. Madame
H. plays and sings extremely well. Miss Brown was
intimate with Miss M'Pherson, now Mrs. Pringle,

---

1 Very young.
2 For *bien fervent* (fervent in) or *fertile* (fruitful, abounding in) the Muses, i. e., poetry.
Mus. may refer to *musique.* Music.
3 A lawyer, I believe (*je crois*).
4 For *une femme*, etc. A comely and amiable woman.
5 Who dances like an angel.
6 For *jeune veuve*, 22, *très riche* or *riante.* A young widow of 22, very rich (or smiling, cheerful).
7 The younger.
8 Lacks figure.

and asked her address. Met her at Bath. Mr. Thompson begged I would accept from him a letter to Mrs. Grant (Sterling), author of ———. Dr. H. begged me to fix a day to meet a literary party at his house and to name any whom I particularly wished to see.

16. Rose at 11. To Arbuthnot's; out. To D. Williamson's to confer about conflicting dinners. To James Gordon's, 8 South Castle street. *Tres bi. recu par* Mr. *et* Madame[1]. Author of "Amicus." Bought Brown's reply to Selkirk.

17. Rose at 1. Captain M'Dowell called before I had breakfasted. Walked with him to Leith. The docks. Engaged to dine with him on Friday. On return, found cards of Baron Norton and Colonel Smith. Note to Dr. Horne to inform M'lle Brown of the address of Miss M'Pherson, and asking for Ashe's "Travels." Read two hours in Ashe[2] Full of lies. Believe he has never been over the country he describes. His letter of introduction from Burr to Colonel Bruin! At ½ p. 9 went to the Duchess of Gordon's. *Υ:* Lady Montfort; Charlotte Hope; Duchess of Manchester; M'lle M'Kenzie. Mr. Walsh causes himself to be introduced to me by Jeffrey. Duchess of Manchester opened ball with reel, and then at head of common dance; Lady Jane Montague; her daughter next. Supper very handsome. All very gay. Left them dancing at 5. Mrs. Dundas *ux. du*

---

1 For *très bien reçu par.* Very well received by.
2 "Travels in America, performed in 1806, for the purpose of exploring the rivers Allegany, Monongahela, Ohio, and Mississippi, and ascrtaining the Produce and Condition of the Banks and Vicinity." By T. Ashe. London: 1808; three volumes.

chef baron[1] engages to receive me at Sir H. Campbell's.
Mrs. Lockhart ———; D. V. not there. The reels
after supper—pure Scotch reels—catches, glees, all
very social. Mem : While walking this morning with
Mr. D., met Lord Justice Clerk, who said that he had
just received a letter from Lord Melville about Gamp,
which will require him at London. Arbuthnot called
this morning to introduce Governor Houston, a
sprightly, well-bred man, *c. d.*[2] governor of Grenada.
Married, but *pas enf. Ric.*[3] M'lle Erskine, daughter
of the late Chancellor—the form, the eyes, the hair,
and manner of Theodosia.

18. Queen's birthday. Rose at 11. *Sor.* ½ p.
12. Mr. Moir; out. Dr. Horne ; found Madame at
home with a lame eye. Lady Charlotte Hope ; out.
Madame Erskine ; out. Madame Clerk ; out. Governor Houston ; out. Baron Norton ; out. D. Williamson ; out. Left note for him asking to write that
I must come to Sir H. Campbell's. Arbuthnot ; sat
with him 5 minutes. *Chez moi* at ½ p. 3. At 5 went
to dine at Walker's. *Y :* General Maxwell ; Mr.
Baron Hepburn and wife, a very lively old lady ; Miss
Trotter, *bien grand. fait mal.*[4] 32 ; Miss ——— and
Miss ———, a relation of the family ; Dr. Horne ;
two M'lles Walker ; Mr. and Mrs. Walker ; Judge
Hume *et ux.* After dinner sat ½ hour *av. les dames*[5].
Took hack and went to Sir H. Campbell's. Madame
chef baron has agreed to patronize me. *Tres bien recu*

---

1 Wife of the head baron.
2 For *ci-devant*. Hitherto or formerly.
3 For *pas d'enfants. Riche.* No children. Rich.
4 For *bien grande, malfaite.* Very tall, ill-shaped.
5 With the ladies.

par Sir J. C. *Y:* Lord Campbell; Margaret Truesdale; Mr. Chief Baron *et ux.;* Mr. Dundas *et ux., son frere*[1]; Madame *interressante*[2], 32; *un fis*[3], ill; Miss Campbell; Madame Colquhoun, her younger sister, a widow of two years *sans enf.*[4]; Justice Clerke *et ux*; Colonel ———— and ————, an old advocate, once a man of wit; a young gentleman not named, but *apparement*[5] related to the family. Staid till 10. Then walked to the assembly room, 1 mile, very cold. *Sans surtout ou gans*[6]; continued badly. At the assembly rooms, which are very handsome, Duchess Gordon, Duchess B., Lady Montfort, Lady Primrose, Lady Duncan, Lady Sinclair, and her daughters, M'lle Walker, and others. Home at 1.

19. Rose at 11. Duchess of Gordon, who said many civil things; Madame Ferguson; Mr. and Madame F., Mrs. F., his brother's wife, *belle femme;* two loving children; a pretty child of Madame F. To Mr. Moir's, 20 Queen; out. To Mr. Gordon's, 8 South Castle street, to dine. *Y:* Baron Norton and wife; Mr. Young, advocate; Mr. Moir, of Aberdeen, cousin of Madame Gordon, *un excellent homme*[7]; Mr. Story; Mr. and Mrs. Boyle, (soldier gent.).

20. Rose at 11. Answered M'lle Williamson's note. Arbuthnot called and brought me letters from Koe, T. B. A.[8], Bollman, and Madame d'Auvergne.

---

1 His or her brother.
2 An interesting woman.
3 For *un fils.* A son.
4 For *sans enfants.* Without children.
5 Apparently.
6 For *gants.* Without overcoat or gloves.
7 An excellent man.
8 Theodosia Alston Burr, his daughter.

The Hopewell taken, with all my letters, the bust, &c. My presence in London demanded. Message from Castella. *Sor.* at 1. To Mr. Williamson's; Mr. Horne. *Y:* Captain Duncan and M'lle ————, the *chanteuse;* ridiculous blunder not recollecting M'lle. To Walker's. *Y:* Madame ———— and the two Mademoiselles. To Arbuthnot's; Lord Justice Clerk urges my going to London. Lord Melville's letter to him. Returning home found cards from Mr. Young, Mr. Hope, and Colonel Smith. At 5 walked with Colonel Smith to Captain M'Dowell's. *Y:* Captain Kemp, a young Englishman who was in the army and three years in the East Indies; Mr. Kennedy of Ayrshire, a sprightly gentlemen of 50; Madame Knight and son; two daughters Madame K., relation of David M'Cormick. Off at 9. Colonel Smith, Captain K., and Captain M'D. walked with me to my lodgings.

21. Rose at 12. Up all night with crem. ta. pun.[1] *Sor.* at 2. To Dr. Horne's; Mr. H. and Captain Duncan. To Alexander Young, 48 Queen; out. To M'lle M'Kenzie's; out. To Gordon's; ½ hour with Mr. and Madame. To Jardine's; out. To Vic. Clerk's; out. To Sir H. Campbell's; all out, but when I had got a few paces, sent for by Sir H.; passed ½ hour in his library; of trial by jury, &c.; elegant house. To D. Williamson's. He has written to General A. Hope about Gamp and expects answer on Tuesday. *Chez moi* at ½ p. 4. Found letter from Meeker assenting to my draft, and note from Mr.

---

1 Cream of tartar punch.

Gordon inviting me to go to the theatre with Mr. Irvine. *Sor.* at 5 to dine with Ferguson, 41 George street. *Y:* Mr. and Mrs. F.; *blonde, mince, delicat, aimable*[1]*, ci dev.*[2] Horne; her uncle the author of "Douglass." Mr. and Madame Boyle, advocate-general; Mr. and Mrs. Fletcher. *Mad. est d'un esprit forte*[3]; principal directress of the House of Industry. Mr. ———— who was in U. S. before *guerre*[4]; *de bon sens*[5]. Mr. and Mrs. ————; Mr. and M'llse ————; Madame F. *ux. de* Dr. F. who is in Portugal, *belle fem.*[6] with three lovely children. After dinner, American affairs. *Sor.* at 9. To theatre. *Y:* Madame Gordon; Mr. and Mrs. Irvine and her sister; both handsome. Cinderella. The little Miss Rock or Rocque; lovely child.

22. *Couche* at 2. Rose at 8. Read an hour in Ashe's "Travels," and did nothing till 12, when Captain M'Dowell came in and we walked to Holyrood Palace; a grand structure far above St. James's. To the Horse Guard's barracks, a very handsome establishment. To Porto Bello, a place for sea-bathing, hot or cold, in doors or out. A very pretty village, greatly resorted to by the Edinburghers and Leithites in summer, two and a half miles from Edinburgh and on the sea. Walked along the shore (a fine beach), to Leith. The glassworks; about the docks, which cannot be too much admired. Leith supposed to contain

---

1 Blond, thin, delicate, amiable.
2 For *ci-devant.* Formerly, heretofore; probably here meaning " whose name was formerly Horne."
3 Madame has a strong mind.
4 The war.
5 Of good *sense*, or has good *sense*.
6 For *belle femme.*

20,000 inhabitants. Home at 3. Ferguson had called and left his pamphlets. An invitation from Mr. and Mrs. Young for the 31st inst., to which wrote negative, intending to leave town on Thursday. N. B.—This is the coldest day this year, and many say within memory. Walked an hour *seul* in quest of adventure; got home without any, but with mischievous intentions. Dinner *seul.* Sent out porter to notify Ma dame that I would take tea there; went. E. G. Staid till 11. Ten shillings 6 pence to Madame; 14 shillings to E. G.; 2 shillings to *dom's.*¹; 26 shillings 6 pence. Tea at home. *Couche* 2.

23. Rose at 8. Mr. Hume (Judge Hume) called. The Lord Advocate left card and invitation to dine on Friday. Went to consult Williamson whether I ought to stay. He said I must; that the Lord Advocate is the intimate friend of Lord Melville, &c., so sent acceptance. On the way home, met Judge Hume, and walked with him. Governor Tonyn's ideas about the west country. Various good suggestions and a most friendly interest. To Gordon's, 8 Castle street. Saw Mr. and Madame. Home at 3. Took coach at 5 to dine with Baron Norton. *Y:* Mr. Young, advocate; Mr. Ferguson, M. P. for ———; Mr. Gordon, son of Sir A. Gordon, near Dumfries; Mr. Storey, whom I met at J. Gordon's; Mr. and Mrs. James Gordon; Baron Norton *et ux.*, cousin of Madame Gordon. Baron Norton has seven children, very beautiful. M'lle Hastie. Excellent

---

¹ For *domestiques.* Servants.

dinner, and excellent wines. The hermitage[1] and claret the best. Staid till 10 and came home with Mr. Gordon of D. and Mr. Ferguson. The Baron repeats his invitation to take a bed, &c. Invitation to dine on Wednesday with all the Barons, which accepted. At ½ p. 10 to E. G.; out and shut. To theatre to hunt for; not found. To Madame D., who sent for G. Sat an hour; 7 shillings to D.; 21 shillings to G. Agreed to Wednesday. *Chez l.*[2] at 1. Went, staid 1 hour, but came not. *Couche* ½ p. 2. Note: Judge Hume thinks Mr. Jackson would be a valuable acquaintance, and proposes to introduce him.

24. Rose at 10. Judge Hume called at 11 with Mr. James Hume or Horne, writer to the Signet. Go to view the register's office: a noble building and perfectly adapted to its purposes; half the original plan only is executed. A statue of George III. by Mrs. Darner; an act of Parliament of 1300. To M'lle Williamson's; ½ hour. Home. Mr. Gordon of Kurkuthbright[3] came in; sat ½ hour and offered all sorts of civility and friendship. Three brothers; a counsellor of the Court for Divorces; major of militia. Spoke much of Mrs. Lenox and M'lle Keene; of the latter with admiration; that they had told him much of Gamp as the greatest and most am.[4] in America.

---

1 Hermitage wine, that of the Côtes du Rhône in Southern France. Of this there are three kinds: The red with its peculiar purple colour; the white, which is really yellow in tone, and the very unctuous, luscious, sweet *liqueur*-like *vin de paille*, somewhat like a tawney port in colour, and reminding one somewhat of a sweet old Madeira or port. It is called *vin de paille* because the bunches of grapes were dried in the sun on straw. Now they are dried in glass houses until the grapes become almost raisins. But very little of this is made now and it commands high prices because it takes seven or eight times the quantity of these dried grapes to make a cask of wine, and longer time is required for maturing the wine.
2 Perhaps for *chez elle.* At her house.
3 Meaning Kirkcudbright, probably.
4 Amiable?

To Madame Gordon's, 8 Castle street, by appointment to walk. Found her waiting impatiently. Walked to Baron Norton's. Took with us Miss Norton, Mrs. N., M'lle Hastie. Walked on to Hawke Hill, the residence of Mrs. or Miss Johnston, 80, sister of Sir William Pulteney. Passed the Loch. At Hawke Hill, Miss Laurie, daughter of clergyman. *jo. vif. sp.*[1] Asked into Mrs. J.'s room. Pretty place; view of the Forth; island and ocean in the rear; from the Hill in front, of Edinburgh and its beautiful environs. Repast; *delic. vin Mad.*[2] Mr. Laurie walked with us on return to Baron Norton's. Continued on with Madame G. to 8 Castle street. Her zeal about lunatics. Put into my hands report of House of Commons and a pamphlet by her young friend, Andrew Duncan, Jr., M. D. Mrs. Norton's passion for the chase; of the cries of the hare; dialect; Diana. At 4, *chez moi.* Found note from Mr. Young with the Etym. Dic.[3] and invitation to family dinner on Thursday, which accepted. Judge Hume, who is indefatigable to serve me, called while I was out and left note that he would call at $\frac{1}{4}$ p. 12 on Thursday to view Hariots[4] Hospital. Note: Madame G.'s affecting stories of the treatment of lunatics. Her zeal and perseverance in reforming the madhouse in Edinburgh; of Miss ———, who is leading manager of the House of Industry in Edinburgh; burning at

---

1 For *jolie, vive, spirituelle.* Pretty, vivacious, refined.
2 For *délicieux vin de Madère.* Delicious Madeira wine.
3 Etymological Dictionary of the Scottish language.
4 Heriot's Hospital, founded for the education and maintenance of poor boys.

Alsa; of the benevolent Captain Lowes, 28 George's square.

25. Writing to Bentham till 3. Went to bed, but my head had got so awake and so full of B. that sleep fled. Poor little dear T., you are rivalled but not superseded nor even diminished in my affections, but another is associated with our joint existence; another who will love you as I do. At 8 I got asleep and slept till 11. Whilst at breakfast, Colonel Smith came in. Then Judge Hume, who comes always to discover how he can serve me and always succeeds. At 2 came in Mr. Walker to ask me to breakfast to-morrow, seeing that all my dinner hours were pre-occupied; assented. *Sor.* at 3. To Mr. Gordon's of Kircudbright; out. To Ferguson's; out. To Colquhoun, the Lord Advocate; out. To Madame Gordon's of Craig, 8 Castle; out. Home at 4. Found a note and large package from Mrs. Gordon, of Craig, containing publications and plans about lunatic asylums. To Baron Norton's, Abbey Hill, to dine. Had, by appointment, ½ hour with him before dinner. The company were Mrs. Dundas, the mother of the *chef* baron; the *chef* baron; Mr. Boyle, the Solicitor General; Mr. and Mrs. Jardine; Miss Skeene, sister of Mrs. Jardine; Mr. Stewart; Mr. William Dundas; Baron Hepburn; Lady Jane; Baron Norton *ux.* and M'lle Norton. Miss Hastie, reported to be sick abed, did not appear. Baron N. has seven children: Grace, 13; ———, 11; a boy, 10; ———, 9; George, 7; Helen, 5½; Augusta, 4. Extraordi-

nary attachment of Augusta; all love Gamp. After dinner taken up stairs by Augusta; sent for soon by Baron Norton. Dinner and wines excellent. Madeira, champagne, hermitage, Frontignan, malmsey, claret, port, sherry. Baron Hepburn's very warm invitation to come and pass days or weeks with him in E. Lothian, twenty-two miles from Edinburgh. Came home with him at 10. Conversation at table general, and current trifles, and wit. A general wish that England would go to war with the United States. Home at 10. *Sor.* Madame D. *Υ*: E. G.; ½ hour; 10 shillings 6 pence; *dom.*, 1 shilling; engagement for 8 to-morrow. Two hours reading Mrs. Gordon's pamphlets, &c.

26. Went to bed last night at 2; lay sleepless till 5; rose at 7. Dressed by candlelight. At 8 *sor.* to E. G. as per engagement. After much difficulty to gain admission, G. was *sub. vi*[1]*!* Home; breakfasted. The knitting woman. At ½ p. 9 walked to Walker's, 23 Queen street, to breakfast again, as per engagement. *Υ:* The family, Judge Hume *et ux.* Sat till 12. Amusing and amd.[2] Home to give orders (a most furious snow-storm). *Sor.* immediately in hack to Walker's. Took up Judge Hume and went to Jackson's, who with Mr. Gray escorted us to Heriot's Hospital; 140 boys at dinner; keeperess and ten *fem.*[3] servants. Three sick, of whom one lame, one feeble constitution. Boys under 10 and above 7 are admitted. Sent out to trades, &c., at 14; ——— pounds

---

1 Probably for *subter vi* or *vim.* Under constraint.
2 Amusing and amused (?)
3 For *femmes.* Women.

to each on going out. More to those exhibiting literary talents. Income £5,000, and will in six years be £10,000. Food; clothing. Good faith to prevent detection of one who had plundered potatoes; all cut piece from their coats. During Jackson's administration, 5½ years, not a death. Thence to Bank. Plan by Read, a young Scotchman. Twenty clerks; about twenty offices or branches in the different towns of Scotland; capital, $1,500,000. Home at ½ p. 3. Sent reply to Baron Norton's note to dine on Saturday, accepting. Chair to dine at Alexander Young's, 48 Queen street. *Y:* Mr. Stewart, very handsome, intelligent young man, £5,000 per annum; residence nearly opposite Isle of Man; near relation of Lord ———; Mr. ———, an intelligent young man; been some years in East Indies; prisoner at Mauritius; his plan for taking Isle of France; knew mad[1] Hulot. *Tres gal.*[2] Bathing room. His son, *un matelot en marine*[3]. Hon. M'lle Crofton, Ireland. *Mere* Baroness Crofton. *Belle.* Social. Mr. and Mrs. Y. Miss Y., *jo. interes. esprit*[4]. Music. Miss ———, whose name was not heard. [Conversation] of the education and talents of women; great debate; of J. B.; of Dug. Stewart. Mr. Y. is agent of Lord ———. Home at 11. At the instance of M'lle Crofton, took home and read review of "Cavallos" and of Hon. Parnell on penal laws against Irish Papists. On our return

---

1 The writing is not clear. The word may be "mad," as given, or intended for an abbreviation of Madame.
2 For *très galant.* Very courteous, genteel.
3 A sailor in the navy.
4 For *jolie, intéressante, esprit.* Pretty, interesting, and endowed with wit, intellect.

from Heriot's Hospital to-day we heard the news of the battle of Corunna, and of the death of Moore[1].

27. To bed at 2. Slept till 5. Rose at 7. Sent note to D. W. that I would breakfast with him. Waited an hour in vain for return of messenger; went and found breakfast over; he had written that being occupied, he would prefer another hour; staid 2 hours; much talk of X affairs, modes of access; proposed introduction to Melville and Moira. Home at 12; very stupid; want of sleep and intemperance. *Couche* and slept 2 hours. Dr. Horne and J. Hope called while asleep. Much refreshed, however. Took coach to dine. Dined with Lord Advocate. *Sa fem. encore (mere de 7 enf.) tres jol.*[2] and of most fascinating sweetness and loveliness. *Y:* Sir A. M. M'Kenzie; Madame ———; Miss Crofton; the Rev. Mr. ———, 70 and appearing 45. At ½ p. 9 being about to go, the Lord Advocate and Madame urged so much that I would stay to sup, and Sir A. and others joining, that I assented and staid till 12. The Lord Advocate spoke properly of J. B.; that he had endeavored but in vain to get access to him. Madame C. took a lively interest in all that was said of him; took list of his works. Sir A. M'K. loaded me with all sorts of civilities, urged to visit, &c. Home at 12. Sir A. M'K. walked with me.

28. *Couche* at 2. Rose at 10, having slept. *Sor.* at 1. To Dr. Horne; Madame H. and Captain; sat

---

1 Corunna is in northwestern Spain. The battle (between 15,000 British and 20,000 French) was fought January 16, 1809. Sir John Moore was killed by a cannon ball and was buried at Corunna by his soldiers.

2 His wife still very pretty, although mother of seven children.

½ hour. To Lord Justice Clerk's, where left note requesting interview and announcing my departure for Tuesday morning; out. To Lord Advocate's; out. To Arbuthnot's; sat ¼ hour. Home. Took coach to dine at Baron Norton's at 5. *Y:* Sir Campbell and daughters, *bizarre*[1]; Colonel or General Trotter and sister, the older sister of her I met at Walker's; Madame ———; Miss Hastie. Children all gathered around me and became familiar. Grace, 13; Fletcher, 12; Caroline, 11; George, 9; Helen, 6; *William Augusta Ann*, 4½. W. A. A. would not leave table after dinner without me; finally she permitted to stay with me. At 9 joined the ladies. Miss Campbell played on the organ, and Miss Norton. The Baron and his other male guests came up at 10. Stole off and brought back by Caroline. Passed all my time with the children; their frankness and gaiety. Came off at 11. Talked of judiciary; jury trial; not one had read Bentham. Home at 11. *Sor.* to E. G.; full and noisy[2]; ½ hour; 7 shillings. A little sore throat which I hope to sleep off.

29. Went to bed at 2 in bad order. Was waked at 8; a most infernal sore throat and too drowsy to rise; lay till ½ p. 11. John M'Donald came in at least twenty times. At 1 came in Lord Justice Clerk in consequence of my note. Sat ¾ hour, when J. Hope came in. Lord Justice Clerk zealous in X affairs, but does not go to work right. *Sor.* ½ p. 2. To Captain M'Dowell's, whom I found alone. Sat ½ hour and

---

1 Odd.
2 Burr or the room ?

parted *com. fau.*[1] Called on M'lle Williamson, who was at dinner. At 5 went to dine at J. Gordon's of Craig. *Y:* Mr. and Madame Gordon; Dr. ———, *hom. disp.*[2]; Mr. Gordon of Kirkb't; Mrs. Hill, born in Halifax, and M'lle Hill. Madame H. is one of the committee of the House of Industry; M'lle much interested. After dinner talked very freely of judiciary, of jury, of lunatics and paupers. No one knew anything of J. B. except Madame G., to whom I had talked before. Mr. Gordon, son of Sir Alexander, walked home with me. Found invitation from the Lord Advocate and cards of Sir A. H. M'Kenzie and Mr. Vic. Clerk.

30. Had been intemperate. By way of cure drank *excessively* of cr. tar. punch; kept going till 5; very little sleep; rose at 9. Bad order; very bad, but sore throat gone. Sent John M'D. about stockings; wrote to Mr. Young with his books; to Lord Advocate in answer to his invitation; to David Williamson about arrangements for departure. Received a very friendly note from Lord Justice Clerk, enclosing letter for General A. Hope. At ½ p. 10 Judge Hume called to notify the appointment made by Mr. Jackson to go with me to Read's, the architect, at 12. Mr. Gordon of Kirk. called. Received note from Madame Gordon of Craig that Captain ——— would be at her house at 1 to meet me. *Sor.* at 12. To Jackson's; with him and Hume to Read's, where was greatly amused with his plans for improvement of the city.

---

1 For *comme il faut.* As was fitting, i. e., as men should part.
2 Probably for *homme disputeur.* A disputatious man.

He gave me his plans of lunatic asylum and the address, bound. To Mr. Gordon's, where met Captain ———; sat ½ hour. To the Lord Advocate's; all out. To Ferguson's; all out. To Mr. Young's; sat ½ hour with Madame and M'lle, the two Hunters (John Hunter consul in Spain), Jane and Margaret; *bien jol.*[1], 11 and 12. To Mr. Walker's; *M'lle la cadette*; sat ½ hour; met Horne at the door. Home at 3. To Baron Norton's, Abbey Hill, one mile. *Y:* The family, except two children; Mr. and M'lle H., whom I met on my return; also Mr. Gordon of Kirk., who walked with me to Holyrood House; saw only the gallery of pictures. Home at ½ p. 4. Took bowl soup. *Sor.* at ½ p. 5 to E. G., whom saw and * * * *[2]; 1 hour. Ten shillings 6 pence. P.[3] handkerchief and gloves. To D. Williamson's. He gave me two letters which I wrote last summer to Charles; a third, more material, had not been found. Note: He has many of the letters of John and S. Swartwout. Talked an hour on X affairs during which I twice got asleep, and came off. Home at 9. Omitted: Yesterday as I was going out to dine, a servant of the Duchess of Gordon gave me a verbal message, with compliments, asking me to sup with her that evening! Did not go nor send any answer. Called this morning and saw her. Some civil reproaches. Invited to the like this evening. Just before I went to Williamson's, her servant called to say that, being suddenly much indisposed, she could

---

1 For *bien jolie.* Very pretty.
2 An undecipherable word.
3 Probably for presented.

not see company this evening. Doubtless the decease of her nephew, Colonel Maxwell, who died of a wound received at Corunna.

31. Went to bed at 12, being excessively tired and sleepy. Nevertheless, could not sleep. Took ten dr. of laud. Still no sleep; took sixteen more, and about 4 got dozing and lay till 10. Rose very stupid. Arbuthnot called and sat half an hour. *Sor.* at 12 to Manners & Miller's bookstore, to meet James Gordon of K., as per appointment, to go to court. Gordon had waited ½ hour and had gone. Mr. Miller's politeness. Went with me to court. Lord Justice Clerk sends a clerk to provide me a proper seat, &c. F. Jeffrey speaking. Stayed one hour. "My lud and my luds." In very bad order. Home at 2, intending to go and discharge all my visits; but too stupid with the laudanum. At 3 to the Duchess of Gordon's. [Conversation]: Duke of York and the attack on him. Very angry about the report of the death of Colonel Maxwell. Of the Duke of York's mistresses. Of Moss; of the Shaws, father and son. To Miller & Manner's store; bought two maps. Returning, M'Kenzie overtook me; invited to his house to-morrow evening. Home at 4. Ordered a bowl of soup, but when it came could not touch it. Went to bed and slept two hours. Something refreshed. Mr. Walker called while I was asleep to ask me to go to the concert with his family this evening. Instead of soup, took tea. D. Williamson called and gave me two letters, one for General

Hope and one for Dr. Braid. Sat an hour. Of Braid; of Moira; of Cochrane Johnstone; of Picton; D. of Y. A note and a long letter from Madame Gordon. Note from James Gordon of K., which answered.

February 1, 1809. Wrote to J. B. an hour. *Couche* at 2. *Lev.*[1] at 10. Slept a little and still in bad order. Note from Madame G. with plans, &c., which I had left at her house; answered her note. Wrote to Lord Advocate for franks, &c. To Meeker; to Koe; further to J. B. Mr. Gordon of K. came in and sat ½ hour. Received answer from Lord Advocate with the franks and notice that he was ready for M'lle H. Note from David Williamson with two great letters. Wrote him to remind him of Sir J. Sinclair and Lord Moira. Wrote Colonel Smith, asking his commands, &c. Sent my letters to the post office, having enclosed to J. B., T.'s letter of December 5th and Clara's[2]. Received note from Baron Norton requesting me to dine with him to-day *en. fam.*[3], which answered by his servant, negative. *Sor.* ¾ p. 2. To Duchess of Gordon's; sat ½ hour; of politics; D. of Y.; revolution; asked to see her in London. To Lord Advocate's; met and went together to M'lle Hamilton's. *Υ:* Miss Hamilton; *pas mal*[4]; Mr. Edgeworth, brother of Miss E., the author, and two ladies. Sat ½ hour. Many civilities from the Lord Advocate. To A. Young's. Madame and M'lle.

---

1 For *live* in expression *je me live*. I get up. Burr often uses this word for I get up, as he does *sor.* for I go out, and *couche* for I go to bed.
2 Madame d'Auvergne, better known as Leonora Sansay, author of the "Horrors of St. Domingo," etc.
3 For *en famille*.
4 Not bad.

Madame is a native of the island of Guernsey, *a d'esprit. M'lle tres interessante* and *plein d'esp.*[1] To Walker's; regret of Emily that Gamp failed at the concert; most affectionate adieu. To Mr. R. Dunbar's; after waiting ten minutes in carriage at the door for answer, left card of *conge.*[2] To Mrs. Erskine's. To Hope's. To Vic. Clerk's. Hope chased and overtook me to bring me back to dine with him, which declined. To Governor Houston's; out. To M'lle Williamson's; out. Home. Ordered beefsteak and *sor.* at ½ p. 5 to Arbuthnot's. Saw Mr. and Madame, and her *mere* and four children. " I ken'd ye." He offers to take my bill for £50. Home at ½ p. 6. Dined and dressed for the evening at M'Kenzie's. Note received from Lord Justice Clerk's inviting me to sup there, which answered, declining. At ¼ before 8 *sor.* to M'Kenzie's. *Y:* Mr. and Madame M'Kenzie; his elder and second sons; Madame and M'lle M'K.; Miss Hope; M'K. *jol.*[3] Lord Webb Seymour came in. *A del esprit* and *connaisences*[4]. Tea and supper. Conversation general; wit and anecdote; of Judge Cullen, a mimic; of banks; paupers; of J. B. (ignorant); of juries, codes of laws. Tea and supper; oysters, &c. The two older women were engaged to a ball, but Hope sat till 11 and M'lle M'K. till 12. Home at ½ p. 12. Found note from Colonel Smith

---

1 Has intelligence. Mademoiselle very interesting and abounding in intellect or wit (*pleine d'esprit*).
2 For *congé.* Leave-taking.
3 For *jolie.*
4 For *a de l'esprit et des connaissances.* Has intellect (wit) and attainments.

inclosing letter from Sir J. Sinclair. Drank hot whisky toddy to balance the oysters.

2. Sleepless night. Rose at 10. Judge Hume called. Colonel Smith. Wrote to Captain M'Dowell. *Sor.* 12. To Arbuthnot's about money; out. To Holyrood Palace; see Mary's rooms. To Arbuthnot's again; he took my bill on Graves for £50. Home at ½ p. 1. Went to take passage in mail. It is full; so kept till to-morrow; very lucky, for it was impossible to clear out reputably. Took passage in Union coach for to-morrow, 5 A. M., 7 guineas. Tavern bill £20. The burnt carpet. *Sor.* at 3. Dr. Horne's. *Y:* Madame and Miss Brown; Captain Duncan and Mrs. ————. To Jeffrey's; sat ½ hour. Home at ½ p. 4. Wrote long letter to Madame Gordon; to J. B. Sorting papers, 3 hours. Note to General A. Hope. At 2 began to pack up. Three guineas to servants. In the evening a note to Arbuthnot, and his reply. Mr. and Mrs. M'Dowell's note enclosing letter for Span, which I did not answer!

London, February 7, 1809. Arrived at 11 this evening at the Saracen's Head, Snowhill. The usual time of arrival is 1 P. M., but the coachman and the guard both got a little boozy, and each had a girl. Stopped every few minutes to drink. The coachman extremely insolent. With great difficulty got a very dirty bed, in a room with another, and, after an hour's perseverance, got a little fire and a glass of hot lemonade. Went below in the public room to smoke a pipe. No segars. Two very intelligent young men there. One a foreigner, looking very like Gallatin[1]. They both made approaches for acquaintance, which, *pour des raisons*[2], I received distantly.

8. Breakfasted in coffee-room. To hotel, Convent Garden, to see Randolph[3] and Meeker. Both gone. Took their address from the barkeeper. To the Horse Guards, where saw General A. Hope; *bien recu*. To Queen's Square Place. *Υ:* J. B. and J. H. K., and a young deputy secretary; *bien recu*. Stayed to dinner. Out at 10; raining, took K.'s umbrella, having lost my own. Koe overtook me, having run all that way in the rain; sent by Bentham to bring me back to sleep, he not suspecting that I was going off. Apologized. At Bentham's found Theodosia's letter of the 3d of January, and one of September.

9. Breakfasted at 11 at Saracen's Head. Domestic demanded my name. To Graves's; he had been a fortnight out of town. Returned home; paid my bill, 10 shillings and 6 pence. Domestic, 4 shillings and 6 pence. Took my baggage and went to call on W. P. M.; out. Left for his perusal the letter I had written to Graves. To Horse Guards to deliver General Hope another letter, which I had overlooked. He being engaged, left the letter. To Q. S. P.[4] at 3. Note from General Hope, proposing an interview to-

---

1 Albert Gallatin, who was Secretary of the Treasury of the United States from 1801 to 1813.
2 For reasons.
3 D. M. Randolph, who was an associate of Burr's on the latter's first visit to London. Writing to Mrs. M. J. Goodwin, and referring to Randolph, Burr said : " If it should happen that you should meet, be not discouraged by the unpromising appearance of a tall, meagre, pale, white-headed man. There is truth, and honour, and goodness within."
4 Queen's Square Place, where Bentham resided.

morrow. W. P. Meeker came in at 7. The bill from Edinburgh paid.

10. Castella came in, and we walked out together. It was with regret that I left Bentham, having intended to join in his morning walk; K. not having returned from Hempstead, where he went yesterday to dine at General Bentham's with Miranda, who had known the General in Russia. To D. M. R.'s; he has abandoned poetry and taken to the manufacture of shoes, which I think will turn out something. To Mrs. Duval's, who gave me the new address of Lewis. Madame Duval knew Miss Emily Devisme, daughter of Gerrard; says she is 25, and has 200 pounds per annum. To Lewis Duval's, to whom told the story of White, bookseller. He advised me to employ an attorney[1], and sent for Humphrey, to whom I gave the papers. Resolved to change my residence. Bentham's house is too full with this new secretary; but for a more cogent reason, arising out of the difficulty with White respecting the books sent to Alston. The benevolent heart of J. B. shall never be saddened by the spectacle of Gamp's arrest! So I have said that I should dine abroad to-day. At 2 to Horse Guards. Interview and free conversation with General Hope. He says Lord M. will write to me, inviting an interview at his first moment of leisure. To Q. S. P. at 3.

---

1 Burr was afraid of being arrested for debt. It was an old transaction. In a letter to Alston, he wrote: " White, the bookseller, has made a peremptory demand against me of the amount of his account against us both. It is impossible that I should enter into a lawsuit on this trifling affair, and, trifling as it is, by no means convenient to pay it out of my slender resources. The sum is 117 pounds, and he demands four years' interest, but would probably take up with the principal. I wrote to E. W. Laight in September, requesting him to send his papers, showing how the seizure of the books was made by the government. I have no doubt it was the fault of White."

Remain an hour. Out to look for obscure lodgings. Got suited at a huckster's (Dunn), 35 James street. Roved about for two hours without any object. At 7 to D. M. R.'s; he gave me a letter which he got from General Lyman, United States consul general. It is from E. Bollman, dated *August*, and brought by Prime, an Englishmnn. Took coffee with D. M. Randolph. Mr. Skipworth, late United States consul to Paris, came in; cold and formal. Sat ½ hour and came home, Q. S. P., at ½ p. 8, *sans accident.* Three hours spent with K. in deciphering. *Couche* at 2. Note: Humphrey did not send any letter to D. M. R. for me as was directed and promised.

11. *Lev. 9 pa tran'.* Castella came in at 10. *Sor.* at 11 to Duval's, whence wrote a note to Humphrey asking what he had to communicate. Received reply, requesting an interview. To his house, Harper street. He had written to Tal.[2], who agreed to suspend prosecution till Tal. should have seen the papers; but Tal. says it is probable he will do something on Monday, being the last return day this term. He will see T. to-day. To Vickery's about peruke. To Gilbert's about shoes. Mem: On the way to Duval's bought a settee, 12 shillings, *pourquoi*[3]? for the chess player, to whom I am in debt. Called on —— to apologize and atone for the failure on Wednesday evening; out. To Q. S. P. at ½ p. 4. Dine *seul av.* J. B. [Conversation] of Mendoza; Colquhoun; Chancellor Erskine; superstitions; thirteen at table.

---

1 Probably for *pas tranquille.* Not calm, not easy in mind.
2 The attorney for White.
3 Why?

Sor. at 7 P. M. to 35 James street to engage the rooms, order fires for to-morrow evening ; gave 7 shillings to buy coals, &c. On my return to Q. S. P. told J. B. what I had been doing and of my resolution to go ; said nothing of Tal. After a free, candid, and friendly explanation, he consented to my departure, my address to be still at Q. S. P. From 9 to 1 with K., deciphering ; got through both letters. Began letter to D. M'K., but determined to wait to learn whether he be not in town, and if not, doubting whether I would not go to Hastings to see him ; 65 miles.

12. *Lev.* at 10. *Sor.* at ½ p. 11. To D. M. R. ; had just gone out to call on me ; got lost an hour. To Vickery's, where got peruke. To Duval's ; out and all locked up. To W. R. M. ; out ; wrote in his room a note requesting to appoint a place and time of interview and to enquire about Grandpré mentioned in previous letter as having come out in November with letter for me from Min. and E. A. To Mr. Duval's, 44 Great Russell street, where wrote note to Lewis D. desiring him to get M'K.'s address from Mr. England, his attorney. To Castella's, Fitzroy square ; saw him and his *two* nieces. He walked with me to Charles Smith's, 14 Beaumont Place. Charged Castella to inquire for Grandpré. Smith out ; left his brother's letter and card. To Cochrane Johnstone's, 13 Alsop's buildings, New Road ; out. Returning, took coach and drove to Surrey street, Mrs. Hick's. Gamp tired. Message from Galley. Marriage of Miss Chase. Home at ½ p. 4 in coach ; 4 shillings 6 pence. Din-

ner with J. B. and K. At 6 began to pack up for removal. To Anna; 7 shillings. Porter to take my things to Charing Cross; there took coach. To D. M. R.; out. To 35 James street. Porter, 3 shillings; coach, 3 shillings. Madame ———, *d'ou diab. vient elle*[1]? Sent by the Devil to scd.[2] Gamp. Set to unpacking and stowing away, which with smoking and idling and thinking about writing, kept me up till 2. How many beautiful letters I should write were it not for the mechanical labour of writing, which I hate!

13. *Couche* 2. *Lev.* 7. A strange figure in the drama. Madame P. Breakfast at 9. Till 2 bringing up Journal for T. K. came in; apologized for the mistake and was going off, not suspecting it to be ab. a *cause de Peru*.[3] Brought me one pound coffee, and 3¼ pounds tea. A letter from L. Duval saying that he had sent to Mr. England for M'K.'s address and it was denied. Kept K. waiting while I wrote note to England, to Humphrey, and to Duval, the two former enclosed in the latter. Cochrane Johnstone going to Vera Cruz. The Berlin decree withdrawn! *Dub.*[4] Assorting, filing, burning papers all day. Read again J. B.'s "Emancipation." *Couche* 12. Mem.: K. also wrote to General Hope inquiring about the sailing of the packet.

14. Slept *one* sound nap from 12 to 9! What has happened to make me such a sluggard? It must be the air of this country. They all sleep. My

---

1 For *d'où diable vient-elle?* Where in the devil does she come from?
2 For seduce.
3 About a *cause de Perou*, i. e., about a matter of great importance (?).
4 Probably for *dubito*, Latin for I doubt; or else for dubious.

habits are as temperate as you have heretofore known and yet I absolutely require seven hours sleep. Whence this strange revolution? Madame Prevost is extremely attentive—*Un air d'elegance et d'abbatement*[1]. *Peutetre* 28[2]. While I was at breakfast, J. B. and K. came in; a quiet laugh; brought me letter from Meeker proposing an interview and advising that he will leave town this evening for eight days. Cannot find Grandpré. Note from General Hope about packets. Message from Castella that Grandpré is here but his address denied at the Alien Office. Message from Colonel A. C. J. requesting an interview at 12 this day at Q. S. P. *Sor.* at 12. To Q. S. P.; waited till ½ p. 1. A. C. J. came not. To D. M. R.'s; out; left there my great coat, being too warm. To Green street cabinet-maker for chess-table. To L. Duval's, 4 New Square, Lincoln Inn; there received answer from Mr. England giving address of M'K.—Binfield, Berks; his father lying dead there. Answer from Humphrey; he had had no further communication with T. or W., and asks my "determination." Wrote him reminding him of the determination already made known to him. To Meeker's, 14 King street, Holborn; gone. To D. M. R.'s, whom found waiting for me; sent out for mutton and potatoes, and staid till 7. Returning home, *corsettiere. Bru. che. noi. bo. su.*[3]; 7 shillings. Drink, 1 shilling 6 pence. Fruit and chestnuts for Madame

---

1 An air of elegance and dejection.
2 For *peut-être* 28. Perhaps 28.
3 For *corsetière. Brunette. Cheveux* noirs. *Bon sujet.* Corset-maker. Brunette; black hair; good subject.

P., 2 shillings. Carpet for the foot-board of O.'s chess-table, 2 shillings. To Q. S. P. at ½ p. 8. Sat ½ hour; refused tea. Home at 9. Madame P. not yet come in. *Mais bientot venoit*[1]. Foreseeing that we might go the round of sentiment, though I think we shall go rapidly through it, thought it necessary to *coo dow. Ce pung. l corsettiere*[2]. An hour with Madame P. *La 2 lecon car. et souprs*[3]. *Des progres; ça je finira en deux jours*[4]. Two hours arranging papers, noting down and arranging names. Took tea *seul* at 10. *Couche* at ½ p. 10, having lost 2½ hours with P. *Des progr. rapides*[5].

16. Rose at 9, having slept sound just 6½ hours. *P. rougisse. Proteste. Jamais revenir*, &c. *Au milieu de tou. Ça pleurs. Jo. melange*[6].

17. *Couche* 3. *Lev.* 10. J. H. K. came in just after I got up and brought note from Lord M. inviting an interview at 11 to-morrow morning. *Sor.* 11 to Gilbert's, shoemaker, Bond street. To cabinet-maker's, Green street, Leicester square, about chess-table. Bought chess-men and boards, 15 shillings.

18. Rose ½ p. 9. *Pas tro. bi. Hate m'habiller. Conge peruke*[7]. *Sor.* ¼ before p. 11. To 6 Arlington street. Lord M. not up. Desired to call at 12.

---

1 But she came soon.
2 This is a great riddle. Possibly meant for: Thought it necessary to *kotow* (formerly spelled *kootoo* and various other ways); *cependant la corsetière.* It would then mean : Thought it necessary to bow, i. e., say good-by, in the meantime, to the corset-maker. (The word *kotow*, introduced into English from China, was used in England even before Burr's visit there.)
3 For *la deuxième leçon [des] caresses et [des] soupirs.* The second lesson consists of caresses and sighs.
4 Progress. I'll finish that in two days. (*Finirai.*)
5 For *Des progrès rapides.* Rapid progress.
6 Madame P. blushes (*rougit.*) Vows she'll never come back, &c. In the midst of all that [*tout cela*] tears. Pretty mess !
7 Not very well. Hasten to dress myself. (*Je me hâte de m'habiller.*) Take leave of my wig.

Walked home in the rain. At 12 took coach, 2 shillings 6 pence; found him; received in the most kind and frank manner. After sitting ½ hour, he was called down, a gentleman desiring to say one word to him. It was to inquire if C. B.[1] were not there, which being answered in the affirmative, he apologized and went of!! Not known to Lord M. Sat an hour. Of his advising the ministry of being taken into the administration; of the war in Spain. To cabinet-maker's, Green street. To Mr. Duval's; out. To Mr. Achaud's. M'lle A. began to ask of M'lle Duval. *Tres hon't rec. par*[2] Madame A. and M'lle. Stopped to take jelly and cake. *Faib. et fat.*[3] *Voila* Madame P.[4] To 14 Harper street, Mr. Humphreys; he has seen T. and arranged a suspension of hostilities for eight days. *Fatig*[5]. Took coach to Horse Guards; General Hope out; got the daily table of packets, &c. The packet Express, with my interesting letters of October and December, still in port at Falmouth. What fatality! Home at 5. Coach-hire, 3 shillings. Mem.: *Renc.* Madame Harris; *pri. ad.*[6] Dinner, ham and potatoes. At 7 *sor.* to Gilbert's, shoe-maker. *Renc. pet.*; 3 shillings 6 pence. *Mal.*[7] To Q. S. P. at 8. *Recontra* J. B. *Son avis*[8], &c. Home ½ p. 9. *Mal tête*[9]. Cre. tar. punch, which

---

1 Meaning himself—Colonel Burr.
2 For *très honnêtement reçu par.* Very genteelly received by.
3 For *faible et fatigué.* Weak and tired.
4 There is Madame P.
5 For *fatigué.* Tired.
6 For *Rencontrai* Madame Harris; [*je la*] *priai* [*de me donner son*] *adresse.* Met Madame Harris and asked her for her address.
7 For *Rencontrai* [*une*] *petite* [*demoiselle* or *femme.*] 3 shillings 6 pence. *Mal.* Fell in with a little woman. 3 shillings 6 pence. Bad!
8 Met J. B. His opinion, &c. (*rencontrai.*)
9 For *mal à la tête.* Headache.

kept me up till 5. Madame P. sat with me till 3 and nursed me with great tenderness.

19. K. called at 10. I was still abed. Rose at ½ p. 11. K. called again at 1. Says the orders in council are to be repealed. Hard cred[1]. Took a note from me to A. G. Milne enquiring about vessels for New York and Spain. *Pas bien. Faib[2].* P. sat by me on the *canape ou je reposoit*[3] the whole day and evening. At 7 P. M. made me coffee and *causait de ses af.*[4] Did nothing all day; at 10 to Q. S. P. to get change of linen. J. B. gone out to dine; 'K. gone to Hempstead.

23. Madame P. rose at 6, made my fire and called me; then made my breakfast; boiled and brought up the kettle; washed and put strings to my night-cap; hemmed my handkerchief. At ½ p. 7 left my quarters with a shirt in post-chaise. To Gilbert's, who had found my shoe, but had done nothing for me. To the W. Horse Cellar, Piccadilly. Sat waiting in the coach from ½ p. 8 till 9. An elderly, plain man and a very pretty girl of 15, sad, silent, and apparently *enfantic*[5]. At B———, twenty-eight miles from London, being the nearest point to Binfield, the elderly man and I got out. An elegant equipage and two servants in livery were waiting for him. He begged me so kindly to take a seat with him that I did so. Arrived at his gate, he got out and ordered the

---

1 Probably for hardly credible.
2 Not well, weak.
3 On the couche (*canapé*) where I lay (*reposais*).
4 For *causait de ses affaires.* Chatted about her affairs.
5 Evidently a manufactured word from the French word *enfant*, child. Hence for infantile.

coachman to take me to the tavern at which I had said I should stop, which I declined. He asked me to his house; declined also; walked not 300 yards to the inn. A better bed than at any inn in Edinburgh. Wrote to D. M'K. asking him to call on me at the inn. Received answer from Madame De Powe that D. M'K. was gone to Bath, and that the family could not receive me. So wrote note of thanks to Claude Russell, Esq., paid my bill, 5 shillings 3 pence; *dom.*, 1 shilling 9 pence, and walked off. At ¼ p. 5, sunset. Missed the road, and walked 4 miles to get to Bridewell. Continued on, rather dark and a little rain; arrived at the Sunny Hill Tavern and Spring, *dit medical*[1], at ¼ before 8, having walked 8 miles. Well received for the second time in England. The more surprising as I was afoot, but this is off the general road! Tea, *sangree*[2], pipe and tobacco; jollity.

27. *Couche* 2. Rose at ½ p. 7, intending to have breakfast with Colonel A. C. J. Thinking I was too late for that, took breakfast *chez moi* and *sor.* at 10 to his house. Found him alone, but in 20 minutes we were interrupted and he proposed to call on me at Q. S. P. at 4, to which I agreed.

28. *Couche* 2. Rose 9. *Sor.* at 11 to see the Hon. *Madame Bruce* by appointment. Called at Q. S. P. on the way. K. had forgot to send my note to Graves. To Surrey street, where saw Madame, the best looking woman of 63 I ever saw; she avowed 61;

---

1 Said to be medicinal.
2 For *sangaree*. A drink of red wine and water.

½ hour. Took coach at Charing Cross and drove on to Walbrooke; Graves not at home. Left the note for him. Discharged coachman; 2 shillings 6 pence. To Dr. Lettsome's. Owing to stupid directions, walked a mile out of the way. But wrote him note about Gardiner for Mexico. To 90 Gray's Inn Lane; paid Bellamy 30 shillings 6 pence. Through Convent Garden to Q. S. P. K. out. Home at 4. K. called. Wrote Bartlett, enclosing Mrs. S.'s letter. Went to Q. S. P. at 6 to get it franked, but Mr. H. had not come, so the letter will lie over a day. Dined at home at 4; ham, potatoes, and eggs, cheese and butter; *vin et* delicacies[1]. Lounged and smoked an hour and then finished my letter to T. Made my coffee at 9. *Rencont. av.* Mr. Dunn *qui a ete 3 jou. ici incog. Pourquoi*[2]? A subject of the mysterious regions. Madame P. came up at 11 and sat till 1, when separated. Directed a letter to Lord Justice Clerk.

March 1, 1809. *Couche* at 3. Rose ½ p. 8. *Sor.* at 12. To Q. S. P. My letter to Bartlett did not go till to-day. Saw K. only. To Gilbert, shoemaker; effect of offer of ½ crown. To D. M. R; out. To corner Swallow and Oxford to enquire for stage to Little Gaddesden. To D. M. R., where dined; 2 shillings 6 pence each. Bought razor strop which I did not want, 2 shillings 6 pence; 1 pound honey, 2 shillings 6 pence. To Q. S. P.; saw K; no letter from Lettsome or Graves! Home at 7.

---

1 Wine and delicacies.
2 For *Rencontre avec* Mr. Dunn *qui a été trois jours ici* incognito. *Pourqoui?* Rencounter with Mr. Dunn, who has been here 3 days incog. Why?

Madame P. out   Wrote to Lord Justice Clerk.
Madame P. came in at 12. *Mauv. hum.*, supposing I
had seen *en Rue sans parl. Entete. Pas* in *hum'*.

4. *Couche* at 2.   Rose at 8. *Bruillè hier au soir
av.* Madame P² Madame had been out and met
some one who talked of Gamp! That she should
have met any one who spoke of Gamp was a little
surprising and not pleasant. *Inde³* many conjectures,
under what name. Of R. was impossible ; of B. not
probable, yet possible! The first suggestion was that
he must instantly remove. Went to bed thinking
much and concluding nothing. Madame would not
explain. Parted *boudeuse⁴*. Madame made the fire
and got breakfast as usual. *Regard triste, sombre. Pas
maligne⁵*. A sort of explanation ensued. Madame
said that one of her acquaintances had met us walking
the evening of the second, and knowing *lui⁶*, had followed and on meeting *lui* on Friday had made the
remarks by description and not by name. Consoled
but not satisfied, parted *amis⁷*. Packed up some, and
transported to Q. S. P. other of my things. Mem.:
Wrote last evening to Mr. Gordon of Craig. To Q.
S. P. ¼ before 1. To Gilbert's bootmaker's ; boots
not done! To corner of Swallow and Oxford streets ;
stage not arrived. Bought paper of Wedgewood, 4
shillings ; two pamphlets, 2 shillings ; coach hire 3

---

1 A strange mixture of English and bad French. For *Mauvaise humeur.* Supposing I had
seen (her) *en rue sans parler. Entêté. Pas* in *humeur :* In bad humor, supposing I had seen
her in the street without speaking to her. Obstinate. Not in [good] humor.
2 Had a fuss last evening with Madame P. (*Brouillé.*)
3 Latin. Hence.
4 Sulky.
5 Her look sad, melancholy. Not malicious.
6 Him.
7 Friends.

shillings 6 pence. Set out at ½ p. 1. A decent young man and the French paper-maker. The *jeu. hom.*[1] complimented me on my speaking English so well that he did not know I was a foreigner till he heard me speak French! Arrived at Little Gaddesden at 7. Bartlett's servant waiting to receive me. Engaged bed at tavern and went up to B.'s. *Y:* The family and M'lle Baillie. *Grand, blanche, chev. noi. bel. tranq*[2]. *Bien rec.*[3] After tea called on Major Gamble, who offered me a room, but Madame Bartlett had provided a room, fire, &c.; would take no refusal. So went for my trunk and took my quarters at B.'s. (Mem.: Passing through Nettleden this evening, saw McCarthy and family.) *Couche* 12.

Little Gaddesden, March 5, 1809. *Lev.* at 8. Breakfast at 10. *Sor.* at 11 to Lord Bridgwater's; Madame dressing; Lord B. engaged. To Major Gamble's. Dinner at 5. Major G.; M'Carthy; M'lle Bingham, daughter of Rev. Dr. Bingham, has three brothers, one major in army, another lieutenant in navy, and the third studying theology. *M. a bon. taille, bon. phys., gai., fran., ma. quelq. malad au fig.*[4] The Major B. and the youngest brother came in at 10, having dined with the second brother. Music. Span *touche qu.lq. airs ecossais sur la harpe superieurement*[5]. Lord Crew of Cheshire; created baron under

---

1 For *jeune homme.* Young man.
2 For *grande, blanche, cheveux noirs, belle, tranquille.* Tall, white, black hair, good-looking, calm.
3 For *bien reçu.*
4 For M'lle *a bonne taille, bon physique; gai, franche, mais quelque malade à la figure.* M'lle has a good figure, good physique; is gay and frank, but rather sickly in the face.
5 Span plays a few (*quelques*) Scotch airs on the harp in a superior manner.

the Fox administration, has an only child, Will Crew. *Dit aimab. Am. de* Spa.[1]

6. *Couche* at 1. *Lev.* at ½ p. 9. Family at breakfast before I got down. Walked with Mr. Bartlett through the park to Nettleden. Met M'Carthy, who engaged to dine with us. Wrote to W. Graves to hunt for Bartlett's letter and forward all letters to me at this place. Dinner at ½ p. 5. The family and M'Carthy. *Mus. et dans. le soir*[2]. Story of Princess Amelia and an Irish gent., her partner at cards. " Five love." " So we are, my dear." *La belle sauvage*[3]; Ludgate Hill; a savage and a church bell. While walking in the park, Bridgwater, at a distance on a horse, saw and galloped up to us.

7. *Couche* at 2. *Lev.* at 9. *Promen. av.*[4] Span, Bart. and Baillie. J. B.'s amusing letter. Dined at Nettleden with M'Carthy. Walked there with Bartlett. Met Bridgwater, who talked of a dinner. In the evening came Span, Madame Bridgwater and Baillie. Music, dancing, &c. Note : In letter of J. B. came one from Hosack (supposed William E.), saying that Mr. Edwards (you [know] what Edwards) had written to me and wished to see me.

8. *Couche* at 2. *Lev.* at 9. Walk in the Park with the whole family to see the building. Met ———, who is on a visit to Mr. Heaton. (Note: Mr. H. is uncle of Whitbread and of his sister, Mrs. Gordon *dit d'esprit*[5].) Walked two hours. Return-

---

1 For *Dit aimable. Ami de* Span. Said to be amiable; a friend of Span.
2 For [*La*] *musique et* [*la*] *danse le soir*. Music and dancing in the evening.
3 The fair barbarian.
4 *Promenade avec*, etc. Took a walk with, etc.
5 Said to be intellectual.

ing, Betty Bustle, 5. Dinner *en fam.* Music, &c.
Wrote J. B. that I would be in town on Friday;
a line to K. desiring him to tell Madame P.
Wrote Graves also to stop my letters.

9. *Couche* 2. *Lev.* at 9. Dinner *en fam. au
soir*[1] as usual. In the morning walked *seul* to Nettleden to take leave of M'Carthy. Two families.
Called on Major Gamble. Betty Bustle—*charmante
enf.*[2]

London, March 19, 1809. Arrived in Madame
A.'s chariot with M'lle E. M. at ½ p. 4. Very ill
with a headache. I could not sit up in the carriage.
Kind solicitude *des dames*[3]. Got to my den at 5.
Madame P. and Mr. Hosack abroad; no fire; lay on
sofa till 8. From anxiety about some letters expected,
made great effort and went to Q. S. P. *Y:* A letter
from D. M'K., barely civil and a flat refusal; note
from Mr. Forbes; ditto from Guillemard, containing
a most curious sort of apology, *q. v.*[4] Returned *chez
moi*, and again took to sofa. Drank cr. tar. punch.
No effect. Mr. H. came in at 10, and amused me
with the news of the day and his little incidents.
Says Captain S. of the Herkimer is a great friend of
Gamp and offers his service. Also Captain ———,
of the Jupiter, who lately sailed. Madame P. came
in at ½ p. 10; did not see; at 12, went to her chamber; in violent hysterics. Would not see Gamp.
Went to bed at 12. Slept, or rather dozed till ½ p.

---

1 With the family in the evening.
2 *Charmante enfant.* Charming child.
3 Of the ladies.
4 For Latin *quod vide.* Which see. Burr kept letters received and copies of those sent.

9. No better. Drank cr. tar. punch; no effect; could not borrow or hire a *machine a lave't*[1] in all the town. At 2 P. M., however, was relieved and took a slight breakfast, the first morsel since Friday dinner. Dressed and went to Q. S. P. to meet Captain Skinner; waited till ½ p. 4; came not. Wrote note to M'lle C. M. Home at 5. H. came in; he had not found Captain Skinner; made another appointment to meet him at D. M. R.'s rooms at 11 to-morrow. Took a very little boiled rice for dinner; coffee with Madame P. Read over my letters of November and December to T. and by examining the sailing of the packets am in hopes that she got my duplicate by the Princess Amelia, which is said to have sailed December 8th and arrived January 27th; quite renovated by this discovery.

25. *Couche* 2. Rose 9. Sent H. to Somerset House to hunt for letters by the Princess Amelia, of whose arrival heard last night. *Sor.* at 11 to Q. S. P. No letters yet come. Note from D. M. R. At ½ p. 11 Hosack returned *sans*[2] letters. Went with him in hack to Somerset House, where Captain Skinner; not ready; agreed to wait till 2. To William Graves's, whence sent express to Q. S. P. for my letters. He returned just as we were seated in the post-chaise, with a letter from T. Paid hack, 5 shillings 6 pence; express, 3 shillings 6 pence; 9 shillings. At ¼ p. 2 drove off with Captain Skinner and Mr. Brigham, a handsome young Englishman who is going out to the

---

1 For *machine à lavement*. Enema-syringe.
2 Without.

United States. Arrived at Gravesend ½ p. 6. At White Hart. Mr. Lane of Boston, a young man educated at Montreal, and who has been in East Indies on miscellaneous affairs, joined our mess. He is going in the Herkimer. Dinner and tea. Captain Steel of New York, now a merchant, and Captain Thomas, who lately sailed in his employ and was seized and condemned at Copenhagen. Steel had a copy of the United States non-intercourse and non-embargo bill. Called at Steel's quarters in the evening and there saw W. P. Meeker and Mr. Boggs of New Jersey, brother of the lawyer. Mr. Mullett of London, merchant, arrived about 11, having come on business to Captain Skinner. Wrote to T. and A. B. A.

30. *Couche* 1. *Lev.* 6. *Sor.* at ½ p. 8. To toyman, 209 Piccadilly, about chess-men. To Gilbert, shoemaker; boots not done; promised every day for five weeks. To D. M. R.'s, where left note and also one for Meeker. To J. L. Mallett's, to get him to speak to Sir F. Romilly about alien or not. To Faleur's. Returned to D. M. R.'s at ½ p. 11 to meet Hosack by appointment. He came not, but W. P. M. came; ½ hour about finances. He sais' there is advertised at the Exchange a vessel to take passengers for Holland, and the Atlantis will sail for New York on Monday. While at D. M. R.'s, Mr. Crew, Quaker, American merchant, came; doubtless he is acquainted with Sansom. Left D. M. R.'s at 2. Stopped at a small shop of old books and bought 4

---

1 So in the MS.

shillings 6 pence; a comb, 6 shillings; two oranges, 6 pence. To Wedgewood's, to give order about October tablet and paper of a size to suit the tablet. To Bradbury's; paid for nose specs., 10 shillings 6 pence. Over to Tottenham Court road, intending to see Madame O., but changed my mind. Roving back without noticing what course, found myself again at D. M. R.'s, so stepped in to order a joint dinner; mutton chops and potatoes.

4. 35 James street. The evening passed with Madame P., who assured me that she has ascertained that Mr. Dunn's negotiation had no reference to me. *Couche* at 2. *Lev.* at 8. Having a confused presenti ment that something was wrong, packed up my papers and clothes with intent to go out and seek other lodg ings. At 1 o'clock came in, without knocking, four coarse-looking men, who said they had a state warrant for seizing me and my papers; but refused to show the warrant. I was peremptory, and the warrant was pro duced, signed Liverpool[1]; but I was not permitted to read the whole. They took possession of my trunks, searched every part of the room for papers, threw all the loose articles into a sack, called a coach, and away we went to the Alien Office. Before going I wrote a note to Reeves, *q. v.*, and on our arrival sent it in. Waited one hour in the coach, very cold, but I refused to go in. Wrote in pencil to Reeves another note. He came out. We had a little conversation. He could not then explain, but said I must have patience.

---

1 Lord Liverpool, British minister. Burr was under grave suspicion, and the ministry were determined that he should leave the country.

After half an hour more orders came that I must go with one of the messengers (Hughes) to his house. On this order I first went into the office to see Brooks, the under secretary, whom I knew. You may recollect the transaction in July, which must have fixed me in his memory. He did not know me except that I was Mr. K. None of them knew me, though every devil of them knew me as well as I know you. Seeing the measure was resolved on, and having inquired of the sort of restraint to which I was doomed, I wrote a note to Koe, which Brooks took to show to Lord Liverpool for his approbation to forward it. Arrived at my prison, 31 Stafford Place, at 4. The wife, a very pretty young Welsh girl with a young child. Both very civil. Here we are, husband, wife and child. After dinner looked out for amusement. His books were all German except " The Secret," a play, and Tacitus's " Life of Agricola," translated by Aiken, both of which I read ; but happening to discover that Hughes played chess, we took to that, and, having played till the poor fellow is almost crazed, I wrote this, and am now going to bed in a small room on the same floor, where is a neat, comfortable bed.

5. Slept very sound till 8, and was then wakened by Hughes, as I had ordered. Breakfast at 9. The only thing that disturbed me was some apprehension about my papers. They have got everything. No plots or treasons, to be sure, but, what is worse, all my ridiculous Journal, and all my letters and copies. Wrote Reeves, *q. v.* Hughes sent the letter. No

person is permitted to see me. There being no other books in any language intelligible to me, went to chess, our only resource. Played till 5, dinner-time. A very good dinner, and then Hughes, his wife, and I make a party of whist. I took the dead hand, the child fortunately asleep. This child annoys us a great deal, having the hooping[1] cough. At ½ p. 11 Hughes and I engaged in another game of chess, which lasted till 1. I give him a castle to make us equal. The following are the notes referred to in my Journal of yesterday:

> My person, under the name of Kirby, papers, and effects are seized by warrant from Lord Liverpool. I wait in a coach at the door. Explain who Mr. K. is, and step to the door to save me the vexation of going in.　　　　A. BURR.

> 3 P. M. I sent in a note to you; has it been received? I am still waiting in the carriage at your door.　　A. BURR.

6. Cards last evening till 12. Chess till 1. *Couche* ½ p. 1. Rose ½ p. 8. Reeves, *q. v.* Just as the letter was going a message came requiring our attendance at the Alien Office at 10; so we did not send the letter. Went at the hour in a hack. *Y.* Brooks and Beckett; both very civil. Apology and message from Lord Liverpool. Discharged, and papers and effects restored. The papers had not been opened. Beckett and Brooks went with a message from me to Lord Liverpool. In the interim came in Reeves. His advice about alienism. Brooks returned. £50! Heligoland! He ordered Hughes to take my baggage where I might direct, which was

---

1 So in the MS.

to Q. S. P. At 3 called at 35 James street. Madame P. out. To 16 Palace street; gloomy faces. W. A. Hosack, his papers and effects seized on Tuesday night. Zeal and firmness of Madame P. Fearing that Gamp's interference might do harm, wrote to Captain Newton, *q. v.* To Q. S. P., where dined. Received a letter from Captain Edwards, advising that he would be here on Friday noon. Note from A. O., postponing the proposed interview till Saturday. Wrote Graves. Note to Mr. Achaud that I would call at 9 to see him and take leave. Received note and book from William Godwin. At 8 walked to William Godwin's. *Υ:* The family and Madame Cooper, mother of the actor. At 9 to Achaud's. Morose. Saw him and Madame. At 10, 35 James street; Madame P. *de ret. Bien aim.*[1] The story of the last two days and her dreams.

7. *Couche* 2. Rose 9. To J. Reeves's of whom learned the place of W. A. Hosack's confinement. Went there, but could not get admittance (10 Charles street). To Alien Office to ask of Brooks permission to see him. Refused. Wrote him a note, which Brooks promised to send. Passed the door several times, and at length Hosack raised the window, and I spoke to him. To Q. S. P., where dressed. To Reeves at 2, by appointment, to meet Brooks, who came. Confab one hour. Departure postponed till this day week. Appointed another meeting at 2 P. M., *Lundi*[2]. To Grace Church street to take passage

---

1 Madame P. back (*de retour*). Very amiable.
2 Monday.

to Camberville. Coach being full took seat on the top; 8 shillings. Arrived at Camberville at 5. Dr. Lettsome and family in town, where the dinner is to which I am invited. Set out to walk back, but overtaken by stage and got in; 1 shilling 3 pence. Arrived at Dr. Lettsome's at 6. They had but that moment sat down to dinner. Colonel Elliott; Smith, *avoc.*[1], solicitor to Board of Ordnance; Norris, surgeon; Cooke, physician; Temple, physician. Very gay and social. Dinner and wines excellent. Norris engages me to dine on Monday. To William Godwin's at ½ p. 9. At 35 James street, [Burr's residence] ½ p. 11. *Y.:* Madame P ; *bruill.*[2] "There is another source of danger." " I know it." *Sed faisait.* 2 *h. Bruit. J'obstinoit*[3]. [*Pas couchè.* Bkt. at 6. *Sor.* 7.][4] (Mem.: Get from Lettsome letter in favor W. A. Hosack.)

The following is a copy of the memorandum left with Reeves to be shown to Lord Liverpool:

Whether I may take one or two companions. There are now here a number of young Americans who would be glad to accompany me.

An assurance that there will be no restraint on my movements from Heligoland. I would willingly stay there till it might be proper to go to the United States, if this government would give me proper patronage and introduction.

Something to show that I have not imposed on the government by assuming the name of G. H. Edwards.

Having in my late letters engaged to my friends in America to wait here till June, I ought to have something to testify why I now leave the country.

---

1 For *avocat*. Advocate.
2 For *brouille*, quarrel, or *brouillé*, at variance with.
3 For *Sed* [*je le*] *faisais*. [*cela dura*] *deux heures* [*Du*] *bruit.* *J* [*e m*] *'obstinais.* But I did it. It took two hours. Racket. I insisted.
4 That which is put in brackets in the text was written and crossed out by Burr. It reads: Didn't go to bed. Breakfast at 6. Go out at 7.

8. *Pas couche*[1]   Breakfast at ½ p. 5. *Sor.* at 7.
To Q. S. P.   To Reeves's at 8 to aid Hosack;
Reeves not up.   To Gilbert's, shoemaker.   To 209
Piccadilly; small chessmen and table, 13 shillings 6
pence.   To Reeves's ¼ p. 9; not up.   Waited till
he got up and gave him Dr. L.'s letter, first taking a
copy.   Left with J. R. also a mem. *q. v.*, about my own
concerns.   He promised to attend to both.   Walked
past W. A. H.'s *prison* for ½ hour but could not get
sight of him; called and left message with his keeper.
To D. M. R.   Slept 2 hours on his sofa.   To Wedgewood's; paid 25 shillings for sundries.   To Flax-
man's.   The Italian wife!   To Achaud's to inform
them of the postponement of my journey.   (Mem.:
At 3 got mutton chop and potatoes at D. M. R.'s.)
Mem.: On leaving 35 James street bid *dom.* to get
something for my dinner at 6, and to buy coal, &c.
At 6 at Madame Onslow's.   *Υ:* Tea and two games
chess, &c.   *Par. a* 10[2].   At 11 *chez* D. M. R.; alone.
Couche on his sofa.

9. *Couche* at 1.   *Lev.* at 8.   After breakfast went
to Q. S. P.

10.   Dined with Norris, surgeon Old Jewry.
The guests were all *athletæ*[3] and the same as at
Lettsome's on Friday, with the addition of Dr. Vaux
and Dr. Babington; a very social day.   Dr. Bab. and
Dr. Temple particularly civil to me.   At 9 went up
to take tea with the ladies, but the stile[4] seemed to be

---

1 For *Je ne me suis pas couché.* I did not retire.
2 For *Partis à* 10. I departed at 10.
3 Latin. Athletes.
4 So in the MS.

for each sex to keep separate. Two of the ladies had intelligent and social faces, but I was obliged to conform. Staid till 10. Told Norris of my ostracism. Returning, stopped at Godwin's.

13. Still at D. M. R.'s. Lay down at 2. Slept not a wink. At ½ p. 5 got up and dressed; no fire till 7.

14. *Couche* at 12. *Lev.* at ½ p. 6. Breakfast at 8. At 9 came in a note from Reeves (which had been sent last evening to Q. S. P.) requesting my attendance at his home at 10 to meet Brooks and settle the treaty[1]. To Mallett's at 9 in consequence of his message of last evening. He was not up, but came down presently. His zeal and interest; he had been both to Reeves and Beckett to remonstrate, &c. Took coach to D. M. R. to meet Hosack, but he had not come. *Y.:* Brooks; offers £100, which refused. " Lord Liverpool expects that you will leave town this day and the kingdom to-morrow." Refused to go till arrival of the Pacific. Sent message to Lord Liverpool. Further meeting agreed on at 3 this day.

24. *Couche* at 12. Rose at 6. William Graves, who effected settlement with White. William P. M ; Achaud; Dumont; Lieutenant-Colonel Mosheim. Went to Godwin's. To Baron Bunkman, the Swedish minister, where dined. *Y.:* Captain Nordenskold of the Swedish navy; Mr. ——— and *le secretaire*[2]. Off at ½ p. 8. At 9 to W. Godwin's. Returned at 10. D. M. Randolph. (Mem.: Hosack all day sick abed.)

---

1 His agreement with the British government whereby he was to leave the country.
2 The secretary. (*Secrétaire.*)

At 11 went in earnest to work writing letters; wrote all night.

25. At 6 waked Hosack and set him to work. To Achaud's both Monday and Tuesday about change of money. Interview with Beckett on Monday. Tuesday evening to Reeves for passports. To Q. S. P. at 9. There found the passport from Reeves. One hour with J. B. Home. T. T. E. and Hosack assisting in packing. Everything to do at the last moment. Left my quarters at ½ p. 1 to take stage at Grace Church street. Stopped at W. G.'s to get the Coestus¹, which was beautifully executed. Family up to *congé;* affectionate *congè de tous²*. Arrive at stage-house just in time. Hosack with me. He returns, not being ready. Six inside. Arrive at Harwich at 2 P. M.; seventy-two miles. At 4 had passed through the forms at the Alien Office and custom-house. Wrote Hosack, Bunkman, Lettsome, and Eliza P. On board at 8, and made sail immediately. His Britannic Majesty's packet, the Diana, Captain ———, a sloop of sixty tons. Fourteen passengers, of whom two *dames* and one little girl. Mrs. Barnes and Mrs. Daily, going to join their husbands in Sweden. Great confusion settling berths, &c. Fair wind, yet at 10 cast anchor! At 11 turned in, being the first moment I had lain down since rising at 6 yesterday morning.

27. On board the Diana in Harwich Bay. Under weigh at 8. The wind fair, but light. Dull sailor.

---

1 The Journal contains several references to the Coestus. The reference is obscure and uncertain.

2 An affectionate farewell from all.

28. Wind N. E. and rose to a gale. Beating all Friday and Saturday. On Friday no one at dinner but captain, mate, and myself. Friday evening (28th) I was taken seasick. Kept bed all Saturday and Sunday, eating nothing.

30. Wind N., light and veering. Heavy rolling sea. Caught two fine codfish. At 4 P. M., wind came round to S. W. Ran all night before the wind, about 6 knots.

May 1, 1809. Rose at 4. Well and hungry. Shaved, changed, &c., and got breakfast at 6. At noon supposed we had made 250 miles from Harwich; about half our passage. Wind fair all day; average about five knots. At night, though clear and a steady light breeze from S. W. took in all sail except mainsail, *a l'Angloise*[1].

2. Wind all night good, and still on. Two sprightly, sensible women on board, Mrs. Daily and Mrs. Barnes, going to join their husbands, who are in Sweden. Mrs. B. has a very fine little girl about 4 years. I took possession of the long boat. Made a sort of lounging place, where, with an umbrella, I read much at my ease; taking no notice of any one, not even *les dames*. My territories were invaded yesterday by Madame D. Reads remarkably well, and is indefatigable. Read to me all M'lle Wollstonecraft's " Tour through Sweden," and the greater part of Sheridan's " Revolution of 1772." Madame B. has been some years in Russia. Shipwrecked on the

---

1 For *à l'anglaise.* After the English fashion.

Russian coast lately on her way to England. Passed through a variety of adventures. Played much at chess with Captain Nordenskold, of the Swedish navy, who is rather my superior at chess. Wind still good. At 5 we saw the church and lighthouse of Gottenburg[1], on the shore. Entered the harbour at 12. Anchored at the lower town. Sent up our passports by the captain. At 2 came on board the two husbands of the ladies. Both prepossessing appearance and manners. Permission came by a custom-house officer to land; our baggage to be taken to the custom-house. Went in custom-house boat with several of the passengers, being nearly two miles to the city. Enter the canal of the main street. Our baggage all passed without any troublesome search. Trunks merely opened for form. My sack, the article about which I was most apprehensive of trouble, on account of the books it contained, passed without opening. But my large trunk, containing all my clothes, is missing. I sent by the captain M'Donnaugh's letter to Malm *et fils*[2], with a note requesting them to provide me a lodging. While at the custom-house, a brother-in-law of Malm came from him to show me my lodgings. Smith, the British consul, hearing that I had a letter for him from Colonel Mosheim, came also to tender his services. Mr. Oppenheim, of Memel, merchant, fellow passenger, very civil. Offered me a room at his quarters, which, fool-like, I did not accept. Alas! my trunk, my trunk! My

---

1 For Gothenburg. In Swedish, *Göteborg*, Goth-city.
2 And son.

lodgings very commodious. Three large rooms well furnished, but not a creature in the house speaks one word of any language of which I have the slightest knowledge. Made my landlord understand that I wished to go to the theatre. He went with me. Paid for two seats in the pit, the boxes being all full. All pantomime to me. Much amused with two young girls in boys' clothes, tight pantaloons and short waistcoats, one of whom played admirably. The ballet and pantomime amusing enough by force of novelty. Two good dancers. One of each sex. Malm's young man, seeing me in the pit, got me a place in the box. Out at 10. Got home, but could not make my host understand that I wanted a dish of tea. After labouring in vain for a quarter of an hour, was obliged to take him out to the house of a Frenchman, who spoke Swedish, and who explained for us. Tea was got very cheerfully. A long pipe and tobacco. My bed had a single light coverlet, not heavier than a sheet. No other covering. But, being quilted down, found it very warm. Mem.: While at the custom-house, Captain Nordenskold brought and introduced to me his brother, a lieutenant of artillery, and desired him to devote himself to me. The Lieutenant speaks a few words of French, but no English.

4. The tea kept me awake till 4, and I had ordered the host to wake me at 7, which he did most punctually, and I got up. Dressed as well as could be without my trunk, and breakfasted. Not in good order. Lieutenant N. came in to tender himself.

We walked to Malm's; to Consul Smith's; to book-seller's; to the custom-house. No news from the trunk. At 2 the Lieutenant took me to a coffee-house to dine. A public table. A bill of fare produced, and each guest orders what he likes, which is brought him on a plate, with bread and napkin. We drank porter. Paid and Lieutenant *remercied*[1]. Met here the captain and mate of the Diana. Both swear the trunk is not on board! The mate agreed to meet me at 7 at Todd's, at the landing. Walked there with the Lieutenant, one and a half miles. The mate not there. Took punch and pipe, and walked on a mile and a half further. Met the captain on return. Still insists that the trunk was put into the custom-house boat. The steward says the same. Engaged Smith and Malm to aid in search. Home at 9. Tea. *Couche* 10.

5. Yesterday the Lieutenant took my passport to show to the Commandant, Col. ———, and to the police. It was returned, the production being endorsed by both. At the instance of the Lieutenant, also, I went yesterday with him to pay my respects to the Commandant. A very awkward visit. He did not ask me to sit down. A stout, square man of 55, speaking tolerable French. As the packet will sail to-morrow for Harwich, and the mail closes this evening at 5, wrote a postscript to my letters to T. B. A. and a letter to W. Graves about my trunk, enclosing to him the two letters for T. B. A. and a letter to

---

1 A French verb, *remercier*, to thank, anglicized by Burr. Thanked.

Bellington, the agent of aliens at Harwich—a civil-looking animal—also about the trunk. Not only all my clothes, but my four letter-books, gone, gone! Went to Smith and Malm to urge them to search; but it is probable that my trunk never left Harwich. At 5 went to Smith's to give my letters, and lo, his young Swede had found my trunk on board the Diana! Huzza! Went to the same coffee-house to dine. Salmon, potatoes, wine and water, cheese and butter, ½ rix dollar[1] Went with my Lieutenant to hunt a carriage (a sort of cabriole), of which, it is said, one must be bought. To bookseller's; bought a map, 2 rix dollars. Mr. Hedboom and the Russian mineralogist called, and proposed to journey to Stockholm. Hedboom has a carriage which will hold three. As he is a Swede, and speaks tolerable English, this is a most acceptable overture. Neither Malm nor Smith has called on me, or offered any hospitality!!

6. At Gotheborg yet, which we write Gothenburg. Breakfast at 8. *Sor.* to Malm's, where learn that an English packet from Harwich arrived last evening. Walked to the landing, 2 miles, with Hedboom. On board the packet found Hosack. Took my trunk from on board the Diana, and came up in a boat, rowed by two boys, with Hosack. Paid ½ rix dollar. My trunk passed and taken home. Noth-

---

1 From Swedish *riksdaler* or Danish *rigsdaler*, imperial dollar—a silver coin varying in value in different European countries from about 36 cents to a dollar or more. There was a considerable difference between a rix dollar *banco* and a rix dollar *rikigåld*, or, as Burr spells it, *rixelt* or *rexelt*, the former being undepreciated currency and worth a half more than the latter. According to a statement of Burr to be found further on, a " rix dollar rixelt " was worth " nominally 3 shillings sterling, but in fact only 2 shillings and 6 pence."

ing demanded at the custom-house. I was permitted
to give a few copper pieces to the under officers. The
principal expressed great indignation at learning that I
had, on the former occasion, paid a guinea to a person
whom I supposed to be the custom-house officer, but
who, it is found, is a broker. On my return home,
sent for that broker and got back my guinea, paying
him 2 rix dollars for his trouble, viz., coming on
board the packet, getting a boat for us, and attending
us to the custom-house. Showed Hosack to the
quarters of Hedboom, where he got a room, and is to
go with us to-morrow. We are to set off at 7 to-
morrow morning.

11. Stockholm at 10. Were detained at the
gate about an hour by the custom-house officers, but
they were not unreasonable or troublesome. The
trunks not unpacked. All the taverns and hotels full.
Through the good offices of our good-natured fellow-
traveler, Mr. Hedboom, we got beds at the house of
an obscure mechanic in an alley near the Exchange.
The approach to Stockholm was nothing striking;
nothing to indicate an approach to the capital. No
view of the town, but it was dusk.

12. Rose at 6. At 10 to Professor Gahn's, who
was out. Saw his wife, who speaks French. Left
with her the letter from the consul, H. Gahn. Returning, called on the Count or Baron Munck, Governor of the Palace, and having apartments therein.
Was in his court dress, with the Spanish cloak. A
handsome man, and has the air of a man of the

world. Left the letter of Colonel Mosheim. At 1 called on Baron Armfelt with the letter of Baron Bunkman. The Baron a good, firm, soldierly appearance; might pass for 50, but must be older. Took dinner at an ordinary. Fish, potatoes, pudding, bread, butter, cheese, and brandy and wine, 3 shillings sterling. In the evening Hedboom came in, and asked us to dine to-morrow. Professor Gahn called on me in the forenoon, and engaged me to dine on Sunday. The hour, in both cases, ½ p. 2.

13. *Couche* at 1. Rose at 6. To a bookseller's; bought map of Stockholm. At 11 called on ———— with the letter of Achaud. Mr. C., a good, respectable-looking merchant. Appeared much indisposed. His head bound up. On Mr. Wennerquiest, with the letter of Colonel Mosheim. A house very handsomely furnished. Many fine paintings. Is a wealthy broker. Proposed to walk with me to several places. At 12 we went to the ————, where is the Society of Nobles. He inscribed my name, which gives me the freedom of the house. Very magnificent apartments. A hotel; a public table, where, at a moderate price, the members, or one introduced, may dine; see all the newspapers, &c. Thence to the gardens, where walked an hour. *Pas beaucoup de monde*[1]. It is yet cold. At ½ p. 2 to Hedboom's to dine. *T:* His wife and her sister, M'lle Poussett; two very pretty women, but, *malheureusement*[2], speaking nothing but Swedish; Mr. Heuland; two clerks of Mr. H., and

---

1 Not many people.
2 Unfortunately.

Hosack. Before dinner, brandy, bread and cheese, salt herring, cut into small pieces and handed round. Fish, then soup, then *bouilli and roti*[1]*;* good claret, of which the ladies partook. *Trinquè*[2]. All rose at once from table. Bows and salutations. Coffee served immediately. Then open rooms, third story. At 7 came off with Heuland and Hosack. *Chez nous.* The adventure. Frederica. The bath in the forenoon. *Couche* 12.

14. Wennerquiest said I must positively change my lodgings ; that they are not reputable. Went to look at chambers. Ten rix dollars asked for such as could be had for a guinea in London. To the post-office, which is open on Sunday. Letters are called for, and not sent out. At ½ p. 2 to Gahn's to dine. Wife, daughter, and niece, two brothers ; the member from Fahlun[3] and the Colonel ; a cousin, Diedron, very handsome young man ; Mr. Foster, the British *charge d'affaires.* At 7 to the ball with Colonel Gahn. Country dances ; how managed ; *valse*[4]; cotillions. Met Armfelt ; his apologies. Captain Baker or Becker of the British navy. *Couche* 12.

15. Rose at 8. *Un peu stupide*[5] with Gahn's good wine. Breakfast at 9. At 11 *sor.* to Gahn's ; saw the family. He also came in. To Colonel Gahn's. Walked with him and Hosack to the Observatory. The views, the pictures. Dinner at the French Hotel with Colonel Gahn, Hosack being

---

1 Boiled meat and roast meat. (*Rôts.*)
2 Glasses were touched in drinking. (*Trinqué.*)
3 Now Falun.
4 Waltz.
5 Rather stupid.

engaged to dine at the Merchants Society with Hedboom. After dinner walked to see the College. The
gardens and park extensive, and the trees fine. Met
the Countess C. and her niece. Took tea with her.
Madame often *folle*[1]. *Tous deux*[2] speak in French and
M'lle some English. The Baron W Music.
Politesse de Madame[3]

16. Having very *mal apropos*[4] taken a little
physic last evening, it kept me up till 5; took cold,
lay till 9, and rose quite ill. While I was in bed
Baron Munck's servant called and left the Baron's
card (*peut etre* a visit *a la Suedoise*[5]), and inquired
whether I was engaged for Friday. An hour after he
returned with an invitation from the Baron and Baroness to dine on Friday, which accepted. At 10
Baron Armfelt's servant called to ascertain where I
lodged. No message. Colonel Gahn came in at 11;
sat half an hour. *Sor.* at 12. To Wennerquiest's,
whom I met at his door. Strolled about for an hour.
Then to Colonel Gahn's, and took him to introduce
me to Catteau[6], whom we found at home. A sprightly,
well-bred man, apparently not more than 48. His
congregation being principally dispersed, he proposes
to return to Paris. Is now engaged in writing a View
Physique et Commercial[7] of the Baltic, which will,

---

1 Frolicsome.
2 For *toutes les deux.* Both of them.
3 Madame's politeness.
4 Inappropriately.
5 Possibly (*peut-être*) a visit after the Swedish fashion. (*À la suédoise.*)
6 Jean Pierre Guillaume Catteau-Calleville (1759-1819) was a historian and geographer of
some repute whose life was spent partly in Stockholm and partly in Paris. For some years he
was minister of the French Reformed Church of Stockholm. He also became a member of the
Royal Academy and of the Academy of Sciences of that city. His written works referred
mainly to Scandinavian countries.
7 A physical and commercial view.

undoubtedly, be very interesting. He will not publish it until he reaches Paris. He had not a copy of
his View of Sweden, nor have I been able to find one.
An imperfect English translation I brought with me.
Took a bowl of soup at home. At 6, went with
Hosack to introduce him to Professor Gahn's family,
and to take tea. *Y:* The family (except the Doctor),
two elderly ladies; a daughter of Gahn of Falun.
Left Hosack there and came off at 8. Supped on
bread, butter, and cheese, with porter, hot water, and
sugar. M'lle Gahn was engaged in making shoes
a la[1] Melville. Eva Munck, granddaughter of Dr.
Gahn. Beautiful child of 5. Writes a handsome
hand. *Couche* at 11, intending to rise at 5.

17. Rose at 9. A charming spring day. At
11 came in Wennerquiest, with Slade and Hartshorne.
The latter left New York on March 24th. They had
just arrived from London, by the route of Harwich
and Gothenburg. To Colonel Gahn's, who was in his
nightgown, and writing. Took his servant to pilot me
to the *Marechal du Royaume*[2], Count Klingstrop (or
near that), and Count Brae, governor of Gothenburg.
By mistake the rascal took me to a Count ———,
where I left a card, supposing it to be the *marechal.*
Left cards, also, with the real *marechal*—up two flights
of stairs. Spent half an hour hunting lodgings.
Home at 1. Heuland came in, and we had three
games of chess. At ½ p. 2, to the Society of Nobles,
to dine; an elegant, magnificent hotel, where none but

---

1 After the manner of.
2 Field-Marshal of the Kingdom (*maréchal*).

the society, and those introduced by a member, are admitted. You meet persons of the first distinction; the first officers of state, foreign ministers, &c. A variety of dishes, and dessert; and coffee served after dinner. A billiard room, card tables, a news-room, all the domestic and foreign gazettes, new publications, &c., a library beautifully situated. Four of us had two bottles of French wine, and our bill was 2 rix dollars each. Home at 5. Heuland came in and we had three games of chess. At ½ p. 6 to the quarters of Slade and Hartshorne. To the theatre. A comedy and farce in Swedish. Silence; order; not one laugh, except Hosack's. Less buffoonery than in England or the United States. The acting natural and sprightly. Curtain continues up till the end of the play, and again from beginning to the end of the farce. No change of siene[1]. The same through the whole performance. The orchestra good, and one of the women a very fine voice. Not a light except on the stage; but between the pieces a large *lustre*[2], with about twenty Argand lamps, let down from the ceiling, so that we could then see each other. No noise, even between the pieces, except cheerful talk, in the tone of common conversation. The dresses very good. No handsome or elegant women, but it is said that there is one who did not appear. A box ticket is a rix dollar; but the highest places (they were all taken) a dollar *banco*[3]. At home a little past 10. Still daylight.

---

1 So in the MS.
2 A fine chandelier.
3 A dollar in undepreciated bank currency. See Glossary.

Read an hour in Acerbi[1]. Smoked and journalized. *Couche* at 1.

18. Mr. Gahn, nephew of the Professor, and a member of the Diet, called before I was up. Just looked into my room and went off. He called again at 11. Sent by Professor Gahn to show us lodgings. Hosack went out with him and got suited. Two rooms at 7 rix dollars (one guinea) per week, firewood (which is nothing at this season) included. Colonel Gahn having informed me that I was this day to be presented to the Regent, dressed for the purpose, and sat in state waiting for him till 2. Sent Hosack to see what was the matter. The Colonel had gone out early and left no message. *Quod mirum[2]!* Went with Hosack to see our new quarters, which are commodious and decent. H. went to dine at the hotel. I took three eggs at home. At 4 Heuland called by appointment to go to see the *manufacture de fayance[3]*, about 1½ miles. The principal was out and we saw nothing. Being near to the Comtesse C., went on to see her. They were dressing to go out. Returned alone. On the way the Comtesse overtook me, and stopped the carriage to parley. Reminded me of the ball to-morrow. *M'lle la niece bien belle et bien mise.[4]* Home at 6, a little weary. These stones fatigue. *Point de trotoir[5]* and all the pavements pebbles. Before the arrival of Heuland this afternoon came in to see

---

1 Giuseppe Acerbi (1773-1846), an Italian traveler and naturalist, author of "Travels Through Sweden, Finland, and Lapland" (1802.)
2 Latin. How strange!
3 For *fayence* or *faience.* The *faience* manufactory.
4 The niece very good-looking and well dressed.
5 For *point de trottoirs.* No sidewalks at all.

Hosack, by appointment, Potter, an old negroe[1], who has married in this place a young lady of decent family. Appears a shrewd old dog. About 60. As ugly as possible. Gentlemen and ladies talk and walk with him in the street. On coming in he laid aside his Spanish cloak, which is the fashionable costume, took a chair, and sat near an hour. Heuland called at 7, and we chessed till ½ p. 9. Sent for Hedboom to aid us to settle with our landlord. He would have 12 rix dollars per week for rooms not worth 4, and which he offered for 6. Compounded for 10. Our week's living in this den is 3 guineas, though we had to go abroad for our dinners.

19. We were up at 1 last night gathering and packing for removal this morning. Rose at 6 and to work at packing. Sent for Mr. Gahn, the *apothek*[2], the son of the member from Falun, to interpret and assist in settling. At 9 he came. Our host, determined to make the most of us, charged 12 rix dollars per week for the two rooms which he would gladly have let for 5; 12 sch[3]. per day for the servants' attendance. We finally settled at 21 rix dollars, 10.24 each. We had breakfast and tea with them. Paid 1 rix dollar to the boy. Our new quarters, two handsomely furnished and pleasant rooms, with the use of a third in common with one other person, at 7 rix dollars per week. The rooms are worth double those we left, yet the price is double what it would be if the

---

[1] So in the MS.

[2] This word means in Swedish apothecary's shop, not the apothecary himself, which should be *apotekare*.

[3] Evidently Burr's abbreviation for the Swedish *skilling*, a copper coin now worth about a cent in American money.

Diet¹ were off. No person in our new quarters speaks a word of French or English; hence much vexation. Unpacked and settled ourselves. At ½ p. 2 to dine with Baron Munck. *Y:* The Baron *et ux.* and a little niece (12), Professor Arnt, and Dr. Domcier, the German physician to the Duke of Sussex, who is here a missionary for benevolent purposes from the Philanthropic Society, invited, but did not come. The sideboard and brandy before dinner. At dinner, eggs, and slices of salt salmon; roast beef; fish, then soup, veal, and spinach; wild fowl. At table about two hours, then all rose together. Our bows, &c. Adjourned to the saloon. *Y:* coffee. At ½ p. 5 came off with Professor Arnt. On our way he took me to the German doctor's (Sussex) to introduce me; out; left card. Arnt came home with me and sat a while. At 6 Mr. Gahn (*nev.*²) came to take us to the ball. Hosack, not being able to make his toilet, was left. On our way met Mr. ——— of the City College, who went with us. Took boat (to save about five hundred going by the bridge); all these boats rowed by women. Paid ½ sch. At the ball about sixty ladies, (not so splendid as that at the Exchange); Countess of ——— and her niece; Baron Wrangle; Baron Armfelt, who introduced me to his daughter, the Baroness of ———, a very fine woman; a physiognomy of great intelligence; *tres belle.* *La* Baroness de B. *cru la plus belle. Pas par moi.*³ M'lle Sergel *fl.*

---

1 The national parliament, then in session.
2 For *neveu.* Nephew.
3 Believed to be the most beautiful. Not by me.

nat. du statuaire[1]. Left the ball at 10; *mal. a. t. ayant tro. bu.*[2] Hosack came in at 9; left him there. Home at ½ p. 10. *Rhea.*[3] *Couche* at 11 on the *can-opie*[4]; can't endure the down bed.

20. Rose at 5. *Gueri de mal a T. mais pas bien.*[5] A servant recommended by Gahn as speaking English. He asked a dollar *banco* per day. Sent off. I could not understand a sentence he said in any language. Mr. Bergström of the City College came in. Walked with him ½ hour. Went to Professor Arnt's, whom saw. He proposes to walk with me on Sunday to see some objects of curiosity. A note from Professor (Dr.) Gahn asking H. and me to dine on Monday; agreed. Home at 1. H. out. Slept on the *can.*[4] two hours. Read one hour in Acerbi. Tea at 6 *pour dine*[6]. Great vexation to make myself understood *par Madame ou la jolie jungfru*[7]. Professor Arnt came in from Baron Munck to ask me to dine at Haga (*sa campagne*[8]) on Monday, but was engaged to Gahn. *Amus. av. jungf. deux heur. Tres b.*[9] H. came in at 11, having dined at the country house of Wennerquiest, where met Slade. Invitation to me was sent but not received in season. Captain ———, adjutant, called in the fore-noon and amused me with details of the disposition of the Swedish forces and those of Russia which are on the frontier. Great vexation about the key. *A trav-*

---

1 Miss Sergel, natural daughter [*fille naturelle*] of the statuary.
2 For *mal à la tête, ayant trop bu.* Headache from having drunk too much.
3 Probably meant for Latin of rhubarb. See Glossary.
4 For *canapé.* Sofa.
5 Cured of headache, but not well.
6 *Pour dinè* or *diner.* For dinner.
7 By madame or the pretty maid. From now on Burr talks much of the *jungfrus.*
8 His country-house.
9 For *m'amusai avec la jungfru deux heures. Très bien.* Had fun with the *jungfru* (maid) for two hours. Fine!

erse l'antichambre. U. muse venoit. Ne saur. renvoir[1].

21. *Couche* at 12. Rose at 5. Breakfast at 7. Mr. ———, a military officer and very gentlemanlike ; speaks French and English; has been at Paris, &c., came in at 11. We walked together to hear Catteau preach. The service was nearly concluded before we got there. The congregation consisted of nine women and thirteen men. Walked with ——— to the King's Garden (or Vauxhall); full of *monde*[2]. Home at 1. Catteau came in and sat half an hour. Pleasant, cheerful, and instructive. Tea at 6 *pour dinè*. H. went out at 1 and returned at 10. Passed the evening *seul* reading Acerbi.

22. *Couche* at 12. Rose ½ p. 6. Breakfast at 8. Always sweet rye bread and very bad butter, of which the pound will last us a month. Have eaten nothing, nothing but this bread, since Friday. At 11 called on Hartshorne and Slade ; then home. Dr. Domcier, physician to Duke of Sussex and physician to his B. M.[2] for Hanover, called during my absence. This is the missionary of the Philosophic Society of London. Heuland, and soon after, Charles Forsfell, lieutenant *topographe*[3], called ; though we were dressing, both sat, and we continued our toilet. Agreed to meet the Lieutenant at 6 in the King's Garden. At ¾ p. 2 to Dr. Gahn's to dine. We were late. Dinner was on the table. *Y:* J. G. Gahn ; Madame ———,

---

1 Probably for *à travers l'antichambre. U muse Venait. Ne saurais [la] renvoyer.* Across the hall, maid *muse* came. I couldn't send her back. (The word *muse* is used throughout the Journal by Burr in describing his amorous adventures. The literal meaning in French is "the beginning of rutting time." He evidently uses a very unusual word for the purpose of veiling his meaning.)
2 People.
3 Britannic Majesty ?
4 Topographer.

jol.[1] *blonde,* married fifteen days ago ; *sa soeur* M'lle
————, *aussi belle et interessante ; chev. brun enfoncè ;
touche la harpe superieurement*[2] ; their brother, a very
handsome and genteel young man. At 6, to the Garden to meet the Lieutenant. He was not there.
Madame ———— and M'lle Gahn *de* Falun came in
with the son and daughter of Dr. Gahn ; walked with
them ½ hour and met the Lieutenant. Went with
him to the puppet show ; very well for such a throng,
but very silly for Gamp. *Auprè a tres jo. U. Un
arran. ft. mais manq ; ne scais par quoi*[3]. Home at 9.
Tea. Mem.: Wrote to Mr. Achaud and sent the
letter to Hedboom to be forwarded. On coming to
Dr. Gahn's to-day, the little Eva, who speaks not one
word of French or English, ran and seized me around
the neck in the most affectionate manner. She talks
to me a great deal, and imagines that I understand
every word. She is one of the most beautiful and
interesting children I ever saw. The dinner was sumptuous, and would, in any part of the world, have been
thought *tres bien.* The forms, as before, except that
soup followed immediately the salt herring. Three of
the ladies very sprightly and animated in conversation.
An officer of the rank of————remarked to me that I
spoke French much better than English, and inquired
which of the European languages the native language
of the Americans most resembled !

---

1 For *jolie blonde.*
2 Her sister, M'lle ————, also fine looking and interesting; dark ,brown hair (*foncé*),
plays the harp in a superior manner.
3 For *Auprès une très jolie U.* [*jungfru ?*]. *Un arrangement fait, mais manqua ; ne sais
pourquoi.* With a very pretty maid; an arrangement made, but failed ; I know not why.

23. *Couche* at 12, but *insomnie*[1]; got asleep at 5
and slept till past 9. When I rose, H. had just got
up. Professor Arnt being expected at 10, we had
enough to do to get dressed and breakfast. He came
in just after 10. Our miserable breakfast just ready.
Went with him at 11 to the Palace to see the pictures,
the statues, and library. Passed there an hour. Home
at 1. Slade and Hartshorne came in and sat a few
minutes. Seven American vessels taken by the Danes.
At two went to Hedboom's; out. Thence to the
Bad Huset[2]; ordered water to be heated and walked
out. Bought small piece of soap; 1 rix dollar; they
have none but soft soap at the bath. With some difficulty got it ready by 4. Two *U's*[3] to assist, rub, &c.
Paid 3 rix dollars; 2 ff[4]. Home at ½ p. 5. Bought
bread, 3 sch.; cheese, 14 sch. Tea *pour dine*. *Sor.*
at 8. To Dr. Gahn's. *Y:* The family and Don
Morinos, the Spanish Junta minister. Supped there,
and home at 10. Mem.: Baron Munck invites us for
Wednesday to Haga. Message by Professer Arnt.
Agreed to go.

24. *Couche* at 12. Rose at 6. The supper at
Dr. G.'s disagreed with me. Not well sleep. Breakfast at 8. At 9 *sor*. to Hedboom's. Left him with
10 guineas to be changed into Swedish paper. *Pours'i
un U. ba. eng. 9 c. soi*[5]. *Chez moi* at 10. Gahn came in

---

1 Wakefulness.
2 For *badhuset*. Swedish. The bath-house.
3 For *jungfrus?*
4 A riddle.
5 This is a fair sample of the sort of riddles frequently introduced by Burr in the Journal.
They are generally in French, in part, at least, and consist largely of abbreviations. This probably stands for *Poursuivis une jungfru* (or *fille*) *badine* (or *banale*). *Engagement pour 9 ce soir*.
Pursued a sportive (or common-place) lass. Made an engagement with her for 9 o'clock
to-night. *Ba.* may stand for *basse*, inferior, vile.

and staid an hour. Went with him to Heuland's to introduce him, they being both mineralogists. Found Heuland *y*[1] and left them together. *Sortant*[2] met M'lle Posse *belle souer*[3] *de* Hedboom. Entered and talked a few moments by signs. *Qu'ell. es jo*[4]. *Chez moi* at 12. At 1 *barouche fiakre*[5] to take us to Haga. Mr. Potter *noir de Boston* m'd *ici un blanche d'un famille*[6]. Very civil and useful. To *Vieux*[7] Haga. *Y:* The Baron, *ux. et* niece; *le* General Baron C. de Morner, *ch. d'un reg. de Hussards*[8]. Dined in the room in which the revolution of 1772 was projected and matured by Gustavus III. The pavilion; three cabinets and six stoves; six *canop.*[9] *de* crimson velvet. *Le General si bieu bu. qu'il se couche ivr. sur can. en bot.*[10] At dinner Gamp gave "*Les Prisoniers Royaux,*"[11] which was received by Baron Munck with inexpressible sensibility, tears, &c. *Apres din. un promenade.*[12] Called back to meet the Countess of ———— and ————, the former being her we saw at Desbero's; *belle femme;* all speak French fluently. The Prince and his elder sister walk with the two ladies of the Queen's suite to New Haga. Beautiful promenade along the lake. The temple; the pavilion; echo. Went through the lower story of

---

1 There.
2 For *en sortant*. On going forth.
3 For *belle-soeur*. Sister-in-law.
4 For *Qu'elle est jolie !* How pretty she is !
5 Note the spelling and also the queer tautology! One might as well say in English, coach-coupé !
6 Mr. Potter, a negro from Boston, married here a well-to-do white woman. (*Une blanche de famille.*)
7 Old. He speaks of both a New Haga and a *Vieux* Haga.
8 General Baron C. de Morner, chief of a regiment of Hussars. (*Chef.*)
9 For *canapés*. Couches.
10 For *le Général est si bien buveur qu'il se couche ivre sur le canapé en bottes.* The General so much of a drinker that he goes to bed drunk on the sofa with his boots on.
11 "The Royal Prisoners." This probably referred to Ferdinand VII., Baron Muuck's father, then recently detained by Napoleon in France.
12 A promenade after dinner.

the Palace. Four beautiful rooms. Picture of Gustavus III. To the new Palace. Magnificent plan.
The model. The place for the guard. Singular effect
produced by copper pavilions and tents painted *a la
Chinois*[1]. Back to Old Haga at 9. Supper. The
Baron walks with us to town. *Υ arr.*[2] at ½ p. 10;
very light; daylight. Locked out and great plague;
a la fin[3], got in but spoiled lock. Paid for hack 2½
rix dollars, the distance being about two and a half
English miles. The *Hermaph. stat.*[4] at Baron Munck's.
Professor Arnt *restoit a Vieux* Haga[5]. *Tro. bu et tro.
mang. Fum.* till 1[6]. Mem.: On returning home
found Baron Armfelt's card. The Prince is a fine boy
of 9; eyes and forehead very good; the lower part
not corresponding. The Princess, 7, not handsome.
Neither of them looking very healthy. They were in
a little barouche, drawn by four little horses. Near
the Palace saw the youngest Princess, about 1 year
old; pretty. The second daughter, about 5, is a
cripple.

    25. *Lev.* at 6. *Chauffé*[7]. *Sor.* at 8 *av. dejeun.
cherch. bague. Pas trouv*[8]. *Ret. 9*[9]. Heuland came in;
took breakfast with us and we played two games chess;
won both. *La. be. Mar. Sentm. su. le bag*[10] Paid 7

---

1 For *à la chinoise.* After the Chinese fashion.
2 For *y arrivons.* We arrive there.
3 Finally.
4 The statue of Hermaproditus, the fabled son of Hermes and Aphrodite, combining both
sexes in one body, and regarded as the emblem of indissoluble marriage. There are numerous
statues of this mythological personage, *e. g.* in Florence, Rome, Naples, and Paris.
5 Professor Arnt remained at Old Haga.
6 For [*J'avais*] *trop bu et trop mangé. Fumai* till 1. I had eaten and drunk too much.
Smoked till 1.
7 Probably for *Je me suis chauffé.* I warmed myself.
8 Went out at 8 before breakfast looking for ring. Didn't find it. (*Sors avant déjeuner
cherchant* [*une*] *bague.* [*Je ne la*]*trouve pas.*)
9 For *retournai à 9.* Returned at 9.
10 *La belle Marie; ses sentiments sur la bague.* Pretty Marie; her feelings about the ring.

rix dollars for one that pleased. Potter came in at 8 and staid till 1. A good fellow. After he and Hosack went out settled for *le bag; tres cont. tou. du*[1]. He returned at ½ p. 2. Got from Hedboom 78.10 rix dollars for 10 guineas, that is, 7.40 each. Paid Hosack 16.36, balance of his account for sundries. Hosack *sort'd*[2] and I got bottle of beer, of which with bread and butter and three eggs made a good dinner. At 6 to Dr. Gahn's, where met the family; *la belle* ———; Madame Wedenberg and her beautiful daughter. Pretty manner of saluting. The young ladies went to walk *au jardin du roi*.[3] Came home at 9.

26. *Couche* at ½ p. 11. Rose at 6. Mr. Gahn the younger of Falun came to breakfast with us. Heuland also came in. At 9 to Baron Armfelt's. *Reçu tres grac.*[4] Proposes to arrange for my presentation to the Regent. Will make a visit for me to Prime Minister by *sending his servant with my card!* Home at 10. *Sor.* at 11 to the Palace to see Baron Munck; out, at Haga. In Palace yard met *la U* noted *le* 22d, 2d pag. *Don. addr.*[5] *Chez nous* at 12. Settled for our rooms, 7 rix dollars 32 sch.; ½ equals 3.40. To the lodgings of Slade & company, where met Slade. To dine at the Nobles Society. This place is well described by Acerbi. Mr. Andrè there and civil. Hartshorne and Slade. Hosack came in

---

1 Settled for the ring. Very much pleased. The rest is a riddle. Possibly for *toute douce.* Very sweet, gentle.

2 Here Burr again turns a French verb into an English verb. This means Hosack went out.

3 To or in the King's garden.

4 For *Reçu très gracieusement.* Very graciously received.

5 For met *la jungfru* noted *le* 22d, 2d page. *Me donna son adresse* Met the maid noted on the 22d, 2d page. She gave me her address.

whilst here. Dinner: Ice cream, bottle of wine for three; bill 1 rix dollar 24 sch. each. To Mr. Heu land's. He came home with me and we played chess an hour. Took boat to go to the theatre at Uregong. Towed by two old women about 1½ miles. Paid 12 shillings rix. All the water*men* are *women*. What a little barn! Thirty-two persons in the boxes. Amused with the pantomime and ballet. The site of the theatre romantic and beautiful. Returned at ½ p. 9; broad daylight. To read or what you please. Returned across the island. The King's ferries; pay nothing; gave 2 sch. at each. 2 *U's. 15. Rendev.*; 1 *banco*[1]. Potter went as our pilot. Hosack returned at 10. *Com. pr. 3 jou. pas. silen. com. ang. et* uncommun[2]. Women are fisher*men* as well as water*men*. Two in a small boat, each a line attached to a small stick in each hand; these they keep moving gently up and down.

27. *Couche* at ½ p. 11. Rose at 6. Hosack *tre grav.*[3] *Dejeu. 8*[4]. Heuland came in; chess for two hours. Walked an hour before breakfast; to the markets, &c. At 11 called on Baron Munck; made arrangements to meet him on Tuesday to see the Museum and the Palace. Gahn *nev.*[5] came in. We walked to see the *attelier de*[6] Sergel. The Pshyche[7]

---

1 For two *jungfrus*, 15, *rendex-vous ;* 1 [dollar] *banco.*
2 Another riddle. May it not stand for : *Compagnon pour trois jours passés silencieux comme un Anglais et* uncommunicative. For the past three days my chum has been silent as an Englishman and uncommunicative.
3 For Hosack *très grave.* Hosack very solemn.
4 For *déjeuner à 8.* Breakfast at 8.
5 For *neveu.* Nephew.
6 The studio (*atelier*) of Sergel. Jean Tobie Sergel was a very celebrated Swedish sculptor. He lived in Stockholm until his death in 1814.
7 So in the MS. The Psyche and Cupid was one of Sergel's best known works.

and Cupid; the minister; Muse of history; the Mars carrying off Venus, wounded and fainting; the boy picking a thorn out of his foot, and the statue of Gustavus III. are works of great merit. Some of his copies, too, are fine, but the preceding are said to be original. In the bust of Gustavus III. a great likeness to Baron Munck. The Queen who was Princess of Baden, said to be handsome, but in the bust very defective in the nose and mouth. Sergel hypocond.[1] and confined to his room, seeing no company. Home at 2. Found waiting, Bergström. He offers to give me a lesson in Swedish every day, to which I agree. A raw egg, bread and butter and water *pour boisson, pour dine*[2]. At 6 to Dr. Gahn's; out, all out. Roved about ½ hour. Home and took tea. At 8 to Dr. Gahn's again; all out. Hosack quite ill with a pain in the ear. In the morning called on Slade and Hartshorne. While I was out, Arvfedson called and left card. This morning an invitation from Wennerquiest to dine on Tuesday, which accepted. Home at 9. Mem.: Returning from Sergel's parted with Gahn on the bridge. *Sedu. par* a *laid vir.* Ent'd. X'd 2. *Mauv.* 1 R. D.[3]

28. *Couche* at 12. Rose at ½ p. 6. Hosack says he has slept none; but the swelling in his ear has discharged and he is better. Our valet did not come till ½ p. 8. Got our breakfast at 8. No butter, and being Sunday, none to be had. At 10 came in Dr.

---

1 For hypochondriac.
2 And water for a beverage for dinner.
3 Probably *seduit par une laide virago.* Entered, etc. *Mauvais.* Led astray by an ugly virago. Entered. ——ed twice. Bad. 1 rix dollar.

Gahn, sent for medically; thinks the cure is already performed. Sat an hour. Says the President Enger-ström, Minister of Foreign Affairs, expects me to-day. Gave me his address; so dressed; took Potter and sallied forth ; arrived at the Palace we found that the President did not live there, though he had hired the house and was expected there in a few days. He lives now on the Stade Holmen[1]; thought this very odd ; did not go to see him lest the whole affair should be a mistake as well as what regarded the residence. Home at 12. Wrote to Dr. G. the failure. Read an hour. At ½ p. 2 walked, alone, on the Soder Malm, the island south of this. (Note: I live on the Stade Holmen, 119½ Lilla Nygatan[2].) Sought the high ground, but could get no distant view, not above two or three miles. This part of the city very clean and neat; most of the houses are white. Roved about for two hours without seeing or meeting anything remarkable or amusing. *Chez nous* at ½ p. 4. At 7 *sor.* again *seul.* Across the Palace bridge, across the Kung's Holmen[3], to the Transberg's Bron ; being from my lodgings about three miles. In the midst of rocky eminences, most beautiful verdure and bloom. Many pretty farms and country seats. This is the road to Drottningholm where I was to have passed the the day ; but the distance, being about eight English miles, I thought too great to walk and return. The wind strong ahead prevented a water passage and 5 rix dollars was asked for a horse and chair, which I did

---

1 For Stadsholmen. Swedish. City island.
2 Swedish. Little New street.
3 For Kungsholmen. King's island.

not choose to give. Nothing but a *tres bel. bra.*[1] at a window, both going and returning. Home at ½ p. 8. Not a soul has been near our quarters since Dr. G. this morning. At 2 before going out took bread, one raw egg, and water. At 6, tea, bread, butter, and three eggs boiled.

29. *Couche* at 12. *Lev.* at 6. Before I was out of bed a servant of Armfelt came in with a note from him informing me that there would be a levee at the Regent's at 9 when I would be presented. Dressed and went to General A.'s a little before 9, but it seems that I must have a sword, *chapeau bra.*[2], and buckles; so put off the presentation till Thursday. At 11 to manufacturer of hosiery. To d'Aries', French *emig. libraire*[3], to see about lodgings. He offers rooms which we shall take principally for the convenience of his library, of which he offers the use, and for that of being in a family whose language we can understand. Agreed to call at 4. Dinner *chez moi. Skropel et eau.*[4] At 4 to d'Aries's; raining hard; agreed to send final answer by H. this evening. On the way to D.'s *Vis. inv. pr. fois U. pa. bi. jo. ma. bi. fa. Bo. suj. 1 r. d.*[5] *Chez moi.* at 6. Coffee, and three eggs for supper. *Mar. ne. vin. pa.*[6] Hosack dines at the Society of the Nobles. Note from Baron Munck that at 12 to-mor-

---

1 For *très beau bras.* Very pretty arm; or possibly the last word is *bru.* for *brunette,* in which case it should read *une très belle brunette.*

2 *Chapeau.* Hat. The reference of *bra.* is doubtful. It might mean *brave,* spruce or smart, or *brodé,* embroidered.

3 French emigrant [*émigré*], bookseller.

4 Probably for *skorpa et eau.* Biscuit and water. The Swedish food *skorpa* was much like the German *zwieback* or the English rusk, a light, sweetened bread or biscuit, browned.

5 Another mystery. May be: *Visitai invité plusieurs fois une jungfru pas bien jolie mais bien faite. Bon sujet.* 1 rix dollar. I visited after repeated invitations a maid not very handsome, but well put together. A good subject. 1 rix dollar.

6 For *Marie ne vint pas.* Marie didn't come.

row he would show the Palace. Dr. Gahn called this morning, professing to see H. Bergström this P. M.

30. *Couche* at 1. Having drank strong coffee, kept awake till 4. Rose at ½ p. 7. At 10 walked an hour. At 12 to the Palace. Baron Munck went through the whole with me. The magnificence, extent, and elegance of the apartments. Manner of seizing the King *y* explained. At 2 *chez nous*. Slade and Hartshorne came in just before 3 to walk with me to dinner. Dinner *chez* Wennerquiest. *Υ:* Hartshorne, Slade, Hosack, ———, a sensible Swede speaking English; ———, a German speaking French and English, and a brother of Wennerquiest's. Dinner passed gaily; served *al' Anglois*[1]. All drank much and some too much. Stole off at 6. Home. Gahn *neveu* came in; we walked to d'Aries's. All out to Drottningholm, leaving a note for me saying that they expected me and *l'aimable sec.*[2] to dine there at 2. To the King's garden. *Vin de*———[3] To Dr. Gahn's. *Υ:* The family; the president of the committee for preparing the plan of a constitution. Colonel G. came in, but scarcely spoke to me. For the first two days he devoted himself to me with great assiduity, and since that time *tout d'un coup*[4] perfectly cold. Came off at 8. Home. Mem.: This morning called on Mrs. Daily with whom I was fellow passanger from Harwich. Saw her and Mr. D. Engaged me to dine on Thursday next. Mem.: Baron Munck gave me

1 Notice his incorrect way of writing the expression *à l'anglaise.*
2 For *l'aimable secrétaire.* The amiable secretary.
3 Wine of ———, or rather ——— wine.
4 All of a sudden.

the names of five gentlemen (holding office about the person of the Regent) whom I ought to visit previous to being presented. Offered to make the visits for me if I would give him five cards, which I did. The visits will be made by sending those cards by a servant. Baron M. also offered to introduce me to-morrow morning at 9, to which agreed.

31. *Couche* ½ p. 11. Rose at 6. *Un peu lourd. Trop bû hier*[1]. At 10 *sor.* to buy chapeau, &c. Was asked 25 rix dollars for a very indifferent castor hat and 15 rix dollars for one much worse; the best of them not worth ½ guinea. For a pair of common plated buckles, 3 rix dollars, not worth 2 shillings 6 pence. These are rather too heavy taxes to pay for the honor of visiting the Regent. Baron Armfelt's servant was here at 7 this morning with a message from the Baron that he would meet me at the Palace at ½ p. 9 to-morrow morning to introduce me. Note from Baron Munck inviting us to dine at Haga on Friday. Replied *oui*[2]. Tried to borrow hat, but in vain. *Quoi faire?* Am committed to the two barons and to the five gentlemen in waiting.

Stockholm, June 1, 1809. The Journal has been neglected since Wednesday last, and now, on Tuesday evening, at 10 at night, writing by daylight, I sit down to recollect the trifling incidents of the last six days. Trifling, indeed! but if the operations of my head and heart could be delineated, each day would fill a volume. *Couche* at 12. Rose at 6. Full of

---

[1] Rather heavy (thick-headed). Drank too much yesterday (*Trop bu.*).
[2] Yes.

business for the levee, and am at length accoutred with the three deficient articles of buckles, sword, and hat. The buckles were bought for 1 rix dollar, being worth about 9 pence. Sword borrowed from Dr. Gahn, and hat, which was the greatest trouble, borrowed by H. from a good-natured French *marchand*[1]. Baron M. sent his servant last evening to say that I must be at his chambers in the Palace at ¼ before 9. Went punctually and found him ready. The levee commenced exactly at 9. We were on the spot at the moment. You would have laughed to see Gamp with his sword and immense three-cornered hat. We waited one hour exactly before the Regent made his appearance. He is 61 years of age, but appears much older, and an air *use*[2]; something like Mr. Samuel Hatchin's, only not so tall by about three inches, and has a flat nose. Mr. H., too, has rather the advantage in point of dignity and grace. His Royal Highness exchanged a few words with me in French. He was in the room about twenty minutes. Spoke to about fifteen or twenty persons. A few kissed his hand. There were present sixty-three persons. I counted them. Vice-Admiral Stedingk was particularly attentive to me. Got home at 11, excessively fatigued. Lay an hour on the sofa reading Catteau. Made agreement to-day with Mons. d'Aries for one room on a first floor (which is what we call second story), and the occasional use of a parlour to receive visitors, and two rooms for Hosack in the *fifth* story at 7 rix dollars per week. Took tea at 6 *pour din.*

---

1 Merchant.
2 Worn out (*usé*).

2. *Couche* at 12. Rose at 6. Set to work to packing, &c., as we are to move this morning. Made several attempts to wake H., but in vain. At 8 he got up and said he would pack his things in 5 minutes and would then help me. By 11 I had done and went out, leaving him at work. Went to d'Aries's, where H. came with the things at 1. On my way to D.'s called on *U.* and agreed to call again at 10 to-night. At 2 walked to Haga, about two and a half miles, to dine with Baron Munck. *Y:* His *beaufrer*[1], a handsome young man who lives in Westmania[2]; his name is ————, being the brother of Madame Munck; Dr. Domcier; Mr. Laing or some such name, a Russian merchant; Professor Arnt; Baron Armfelt; Munck's wife and niece, and Hosack. The dinner good and cheerful. After dinner we walked two hours and returned to tea. Armfelt, Domcier, and Laing had gone. After tea walked with Baron M. and the rest two hours again. Then came in to supper. The supper is a very substantial meal; fish, roast, *fricasses*[3], &c. Two cards were received by the Muncks whilst I was there announcing the death, one of a husband, the other of a father, both concluding with this caution, " Condolences are not received." Came off at ½ p. 10 with Professor Arnt and Hosack. Home at ½ p. 11. *Sor.* at 12 to *U.* Fredrick[4], *suiv arrgt.*[5]; heard several voices; *frappe*[6] and off. Professor Arnt's

---

1 For *beau-frère*. Brother-in-law.
2 For Westmannia or Westmanland, an old province of Sweden.
3 For *fricassées*. Fricassees.
4 Elsewhere Burr refers to this personage as Frederica.
5 For *suivant l'arrangement*. According to arrangement.
6 Knock.

opinion that all women ought to be shut up as in Persia.

3. *Couche* at 12. Rose at 7. *Tro. bu. Pas bien*[1]. *Sor.* before breakfast to *U.* Fredrick; 1 rix dollar. *Tro. usé*[2]. Breakfast at 9. Read a romance, "*Les Amour de Daphnis et Cloe*[3]," *traduit du Grec de* Longus *par* Arryot[4]. This romance is supposed to have been written after that of Heliodorus ("Theagenes and Chariclea"). Dined on sugar, water, and bread. A promenade *seul* to Kongl. Djur Garden[5], about two miles. Returned *sans aventure*[6]. Tea at 9.

4. *Couche* at 11. Rose at ½ p. 5. *Dejeun.*[7] at 7. Read variously and desultorily. *Eau suc. et pain pr. din.*[8] At 6 set out for Lisbon Hill, where we are invited by Wennerquiest to a musical party. Very much amused on the way to see the mode of passing Sunday. Vast numbers of both sexes engaged in various sports. Fiddles and other musical instruments. Dancing parties in many houses. Always a *comedie*[9] on Sunday. Went half a mile beyond the house of W. before I could ascertain where it was. At length found it. He was in town. One Swedish servant only at home. No preparation for any party. Returned home at 9 and took coffee, wondering at this disappointment. Note: In the forenoon called on Madame Daily.

---

1 Had drunk too much and did not feel well.
2 Too much used up.
3 So in the MS.
4 " The Amours of Daphnis and Chloe," translated from the Greek of Longus by Arryot.
5 See Glossary.
6 Without adventure.
7 For *déjeuner*. Breakfast.
8 For *Eau sucrée et pain pour dîner*. Sugar-water and bread by way of dinner.
9 For *comédie*. Comedy.

5. The coffee kept me awake all night. At 3 or a little before, walked out to see the sun rise at 3. A beautiful horizon from the Observatory hill. Got my breakfast at 6. During the night formed a plan for return to the United States. Full of it all day. New Jersey was to be my location. This forenoon saw Hosack for the first time since living at this house. He had been charged by Wennerquiest to tell me that the party intended for Sunday was postponed, but omitted to do it. Breakfast as usual, with the addition of a salt herring. *Din. eau et pain.*[1] *Sor.* at 3. *Une blan. jeun. jo. embon.*[2]; 1 rix dollar. Read desultorily and *sans objet que distraire.*[3] Hartshorne came in P. M. and a game of chess.

6. *Couche* at 11. *Lev.* at 6. At 7 came in Mari *de* Lil. Ny. gat.[4] about some demands of the lady. A very seasonable visit; 1 rix dollar. The demands left unsettled; will call on Thursday. The proclamation of the new King; great show; heralds; trumpets; music; military, &c. *Moi*[5] in the midst enticed off by a lit. *brun.*[6]; 2 rix dollars. This day we receive news of the new arrangement between the United States and Great Britain; the proclamation of the President opening intercourse with Great Britain.

7. Note from Laing, the Russian merchant, to remind me of the dinner to-day at Albino—*Cravi Tiske* or *royaume des ecrivisses*[7] Walked, being about

---

1 Bread and water for dinner.
2 For *une blanche jeune jolie* [*femme*]. *Embonpoint.* A pale, pretty, young woman. Plump.
3 And without other object than amusement.
4 Swedish for Little New Street. (*Lilla Nygatan.*)
5 I.
6 A little brunette ?
7 Kingdom of the crabs. Burr's words *Cravi Tiske* may represent the Swedish word *Krabbtaska,* Crabs. The restaurant may have received that nickname from the fact that a specialty was made of crawfish.

two miles; a most beautiful and picturesque promenade. *Υ.:* About twenty, *i. e.,* ten of each sex. A
very expensive and splendid dinner. Baron Stedingk,
late minister to Russia, *fem.* and two children. *U's*[1] 10
and 13 and *leur gouvernante*[2]; the elder *fille*[3] intelligent
and well educated. *La gouvernante* M'lle ———— *jol.
et* interesting. Madame ————, two daughters and a
son; the daughters both handsome; *belle embonp*[4]
Mr. Phillipson *et ux.;* a very amiable woman, 30; the
secretary of Stedingk, a well-informed young man;
Dr. Domcier; his singular position that in England
there were 3,000 to a square mile; Mr. Foster, the
British *charge d'affaires. Tro. bu* and stole off alone
at 9. Note: The wife of the vice-admiral, Stedingk,
has several sisters of much renown.

    8. *Couche* at 12. *Lev.* at 6 *un peu lourd*[5].
Mari came in at 7 to settle accounts; 2 rix dollars.
Sor. at 11 with Dr. Gahn, who called to invite me to
go and see the show. All the troops, as well militia
as regulars, under arms, to be sworn to the new King
and constitution. Sworn by regiments and by word
of command. Immense concourse of people of all
sexes and ages. The King rode about on horseback,
saluting and saluted. At 2 *chez moi. Eau et pain.*
Finished reading Eustace's "Letter to Cleomenes,"
430 octavo pages. A strange medley of things personal, of Grecian and Roman history and maxims, of
anecdotes, &c., but not badly put together, and amus-

---

1 *Jungfrus.*
2 Their governess.
3 Daughter, girl.
4 Fine looking, plump.
5 Rather dull.

ing. Written in 1730. Says he is the nearest male relation of the late Mr. Addison. At 6 to tea at Gahn's by invitation. *Y* Colonel Gahn to attend me to the levee, which is announced for this evening at 7. Put on my sword and tripod, and went. A very splendid display of beauty. There were many hundreds. Those who pretended to be able to form a judgment said 1,600. The King looked much better than when I last saw him; went very well through the forms. The Queen still better. The Princess Louisa appeared to labour, and to be fatigued with it. Met there all my acquaintances of both sexes. Came off at 9 and supped at Gahn's. Hosack there. The family and M'lle————. *La belle boit. qui touche si bien la harpe. Et sa soeur ainèe*[1]————. Gahn the nephew left town for Falun this day to my great regret for he was my most useful and willing guide. He called to take leave. Home at ½ p. 10.

9. *Couche* at ½ p. 12. *Lev.* at 6. How very regular we are grown! Breakfast at 9. Read the life of Captain John Smith, who went with the first colony to Virginia and afterward to New England. It is extracted from Belknap into an English compilation entitled " Polyanthea, or Collection of Interesting Fragments." *Sor.* at ½ p. 1. *Un* strolle[2]. Met Wennerquiest, who asked me to a musical party on Sunday at Djurgarden. Home at ½ p. 2. *Eau et pain. Sor.* at 5. *Rencont. U. que vis hier. Mar.*

---

1 The pretty lame girl (*boiteuse*) who plays the harp so well, and her elder sister (*soeur ainée*).

2 Notice the puerile mixture of French and misspelled English.

Carol. blo. jeu. 1½ r. d. *Rendev. pr. Lund.* 3 P. M.[1]
D'Aries brought in to see me the Baron————, who
is a member of the Diet and a lodger in this house ;
a frank, sensible man, speaking French fluently. He
is on a committee to reform judicial proceedings. Not
heard of our J. B.[2] Supped with Mons. d'A. Took
neither tea nor coffee this P. M.

10. *Couche* at ½ p. 12. Slept till waked by my
noir[3] at ½ p. 7. I am better without the afternoon
tea and coffee and resolve to discontinue it. Raining
hard, which prevents my intended walk to Drottningholm, about eight miles. Read two or three hours
this morning in a French work printed in 1804,
entitled, " *De la Philosophie de la Nature ou Traite de
Morale pour le Genre Humain tirè de la Philosophie et
fondè sur la Nature.*" *7me edit.*[4] The style very fine.
Great advocate for *natural law,* as the foundation of all
law and morals. "*Cette loi naturelle gravèe sur le
coeur.*"[5] A great deal of pretty and ingenious nonsense
of the like kind. Pretending to quote and confute all
writers, ancient and modern, who hold a contrary doc-
trine ; but not naming Bentham, though published at
Paris. The book is anonymous, but said to be the
————[6]. Dinner by invitation with d'Aries. *Lui,
Madame, et Madame*————*veuve du consul Portugais*

---

1 For *Rencontrai la jungfru que vis hier. Marie Caroline ; blonde, jeune.* 1½ rix dollars.
Rendez-vous pour Lundi, 3 P. M. Met the maid whom I saw yesterday. By name Marie Caroline ; blonde, young. 1½ rix-dollars. Appointment for 3 P. M. Monday.
2 Jeremy Bentham.
3 Negro.
4 " Of the Philosophy of Nature ; or Treatise on Ethics for the Human Race, drawn from
Philosophy, and Founded on Nature." Seventh edition.
5 This natural law graven on the heart.
6 Sentence unfinished.

mais nee italienne.[1] This morning while I was shaving, came into my room a tall, graceful, pretty woman, plainly but neatly dressed. Asked if I could speak Swedish. No. German. No. Italian. No. I then asked her if she could speak English. No. French? No. So that it seemed that communication by words was out of question. I made her, however, understand that I was going to the country, and would be glad to see her again on Tuesday morning at the same hour, viz., 7 o'clock. Who she is, or what the *pretence* of the visit, I can form no conjecture.

11. Mr. d'Aries waked me at 5. At ½ p. 7 went with him and his son in their one-horse phaeton, to Drottningholm. A very beautiful ride; cross four large bridges. Madame D. went last evening with Mr. de Castre. At 11 went to witness the service at a country church, about 1½ miles from the Palace. A neat, pretty, ancient building; low, arched; several pictures; a narrow alley through the middle, and seats (pews) on each side. The women on the left and men on the right; about an equal number on each side; perhaps 150 of each sex. The organ playing when I came in, and they were singing a psalm to the tune we call Old Hundred. Sacrament day. All partook, going up about twenty at a time, men and women promiscuously. The priest and his clerk, or *curè*[2], administered. They all returned very much affected; the women in tears, and many sobbing; the psalm

---

1 Himself, his wife and Madame———, widow of the Portuguese consul, but Italian born (*née*).
2 Burr almost always uses the grave accent for the acute, when it occurs to him to use any accent at all.

going on all the while. I stood in the isle[1], no one taking the least notice of me. The *musa*[2], the principal head-dress of the women. Two very beautiful young women, who were near me, in black, the head *a la mode*[3]. Returned to d'Aries, and we went through the garden to see the Palace, he having engaged one of the keepers as *cicerone*[4]. Just as we entered the Palace met Countess Bunge and Comtesse Löwenhaupt, Baron Wrangle, Captain Dirden, *et al'i.*[5] Went all together into the first *salle*[6]. While I was examining a statue, the ladies and their party, with our guide, went out, but whither we could not discover; and after half an hour of fruitless search and inquiry we returned to the gardens, and to that part called Canton; thence home to dinner at 2. Mr. D. exceedingly mortified and vexed that our chaperon had thus left us in the lurch. He expected several persons to dine, but no one of them came. After dinner walked to see Madame de Castre and her daughter. Both of very pleasant manner. The mother very ladylike; *nè Polonaise*[7]. *Le Mari*[8] formerly in the orchestra of Gustavus III. Both now enjoying pensions. M'lle *tout plein de talents*[9]. Paints in oil in a manner to have attracted notice and admiration at the exhibition. *Pince la harpe superieurement. Danse (comme on dit) comme une ange. Vif. enjouee. 18; jol*

---

1 So in the MS.
2 For *Mossa.* Swedish for bonnet, hood.
3 In fashion.
4 Guide.
5 For Latin *et alii.* And others.
6 Hall, room.
7 For *née*, &c. Polish born.
8 The husband.
9 For *toute pleine*, etc. Very talented.

taille[1] At 4 Madame de Castre came to take tea with us ; but Madame 'd'Aries rather presumptuously told her we were engaged. She went off and we walked out to take tea with Madame———; Madame and all the family abroad. Went then to Dr.———, *medecin du Roi*[2], Gustavus IV.; out also ; but an elderly lady permitted us to see his pictures. *Chez nous* at 6. Brought Madame de Castre to sup with us. Before supper went to the tower ; in ruins ; extensive and picturesque views. After supper saw Madame and M'lle to *chez eux*[3] There are still a few Russian prisoners here ; a small hospital. The situation of the Palace and disposition of the grounds very beautiful. Profusion of statues, principally bronze and *tout nud.*[4] Everything in decay. Two ladies on horseback. One riding *al' Angloise*, the other *en cavalier*[5], with scarlet waist-jacket and white overalls, *a la Turc ou Persé*[6] ; very wide ; a round hat with feathers. She had a very fine form, and made an elegant appearance.

12. *Couche* at 12. *Lev.* at 6. Mr. and Mrs. d'A. breakfasted and with their son August set off at 8 for Stockholm. I breakfasted after they were gone and at ½ p. 9 set off on foot. A very charming promenade, about 6 miles. *Renc. sur chem. Paysan. Prom. ensem. au boi. un heure.* ¾ r. d.[7] Arrive at home at 12 ; undressed, lay down, and slept three

---

1 Plays the harp in a superior manner. Dances (as they say) like an angel. Animated, sprightly (*vive, enjouée*) ; 18 ; pretty figure.
2 Physician of the King.
3 For *chez elles.* To their home.
4 Probably for *tout à fait nues.* Wholly nude.
5 Trooper fashion, astride.
6 After the Turkish or Persian fashion (*à la turque*, etc.).
7 For *Rencontrai sur le chemin une paysanne. Promenade ensemble. Au bois une heure.* ¾ rix dollar. Met on the way a country lass. Took a walk together for an hour in the wood ; ¾ rix dollar.

hours. At 5 to Slade's and Hartshorne's. *Υ:* Hosack
and Heuland; chess with Hartshorne; three games;
won two. Tea at 8 *pour sou. et din.*[1] Note from
Hedboom to dine on Wednesday, to which agreed.

13. *Couche* at ½ p. 12. *Lev.* at 7. Had
scarcely got out of bed when *la Hanoverienne*[2] mentioned on Saturday came in. Being unable to communicate anything by the ear, we tried, successfully,
all the other senses. Passed an hour. After breakfast,
ma bel Mar.[3] came in to try to settle that affair of the
broken glass. *Je voud. mieux* that her vis. had been
defd. till tom. *mais el. est si jolie;* 1 r. d.[4] At 1 to
Dr. Gahn's; all in the country. At 2 came in Caro-
lin. *Cest trop! Mais* ⁵/₄ r. d.[5] *Couche* at 3 and slept
two hours. Dinner *eau et pain.* Tea and four eggs
for supper. *Couche* at ½ p. 12. *Mais ne saurais
dormir*[6]. Just got asleep at ½ p. 4 when Hosack
came and waked me to get his key. I had taken it
to ensure a sight of him. Got asleep at 5 and slept
till 9. Waked by Captain H———, who came to
ask me to go on Saturday next to take tea with
Madame———, who had known Bollman[7] and wished
much to hear of him. I was half asleep and forgot to
enquire who the lady is and where the acquaintance
had been made. Before I was dressed came in Bergström; agreed to go with him to-morrow to take tea

---

1 For *pour souper et diner.* For supper and dinner.
2 For *la Hanovrienne.* The Hanoverian woman.
3 For *ma belle Marie.*
4 I should prefer (*je voudrais mieux*) that her visit had been deferred till to-morrow. But
she is so pretty; 1 rix dollar.
5 It's too much! But ⁵/₄ rix dollars.
6 But cannot sleep.
7 Dr. Erich Bollman, a German, who had distinguished himself by a gallant attempt to
rescue Lafayette from his prison at Olmutz, and who was one of Burr's most trusted confederates
in the Mexican affair.

with Gahn *a la campagne*[1]. At 1 called on Madame de Castre and daughter, who came yesterday to town. *Madame seule*; *3 trappar up*[2]. A bust of M'lle by Bustrom, extremely well executed. Madame took me to see Bustrom (and his *attelier*), who lives under the same roof one story higher, that is, in what we should call the fifth story. The apartments of Madame in the fourth are very handsome. Bustrom was out and his rooms locked. M'lle came; a landscape painted by her, very pretty and showing much talent. The coronation is postponed till the first week in July, that it may be the more brilliant. Mr. de Castre had this morning an interview with the King, who sent for him to solicit him to take part in an opera to be given on the occasion. Note: The opera-house has been shut since the majority of Gustavus IV., and Mr. de Castre has been sixteen years out of practice. *Neanmoins, pour faire plaisir a sa M.*[3] he will attempt. It is not impossible nor altogether improbable, that we may have a Russian audience; for news was yesterday received that the Russian forces on this side of the Gulf of Bothnia had advanced very rapidly. Yet all here is placid, though they are not more than ten or twelve days' march from Stockholm, and neither fortifications nor efficient army in the way. Called on Madame Daily, who is still in town. She is frightened to death about the Russians. The Russian soldiers! It is the universal opinion that, if they come, there will be general

---

1 In the country or at the country house.
2 Swedish. Three flights up. (*3 trappor upp.*)
3 Nevertheless, to please his Majesty (*à Sa Majesté*).

plundering and ravishing. At 2 dressed for dinner and went to Hedboom's. All locked fast; not even a servant. Tried every door, and made a great deal of noise to no effect. Strange! At length discovered from a family on the next floor that Mr. H. and family lived at some distance, where it is expected that I am to dine. About two miles off. Went to hire a boat. Asked 1 rix dollar, which I refused to give. Came home at 4, and took bread and milk at 6. At ½ p. 7 went to the concert, *a la Bourse*¹, where I had engaged to meet Madame de Castre *et* M'lle. The concert began at 6, and was more than half done when I came in. There was, I believe, more than one thousand persons, among them the Queen and the Princess Sophia. Heard three pieces, in one of which " God Save the King " was introduced. The last piece was accompanied by the voice of Mr. de Castre, who has sung here for thirty years. His voice is yet well preserved and really fine. I have great sensibility to music, but no science. Every part was executed extremely to my satisfaction ; but what most interested me was the perfect attention, and the uncommon degree of feeling exhibited by the audience. I have nowhere witnessed the like. Every countenance was affected by those emotions to which the music was adapted. In England you see no expression painted on the visage at a concert. All is sombre and grim. They cry *bravo! bravissimo!*² with the same countenance that they " God damn " their servants and their gov-

---

1 At the Exchange.
2 Superlative of *bravo*.

ernment.   Acerbi is wrong in asserting that *les Suedoises*[1] have no sensibility to music.   The crowd was so great that I could not get sight of the de Castres; but passing their quarters just as they drove up to the door, went in and sat a few moments.   Was introduced to Mr. de Castre, whom I had not before seen, nor did I suspect, till then informed, that it was he who sang, not having seen him while singing.   They engaged me to tea on Friday to meet Baron ————, *Grand Seigneur et fort riche, demeurant en Scanie*[2]. Home at 10.   Read an hour in Captain Barrie Saint Venan's book "*Des Colonies Modernes sous la Zone Torride, particulierement St. Domingo*[3]."   *Imp.* Paris : 1802. *Mangè un morceau de soupè chez Madame D.*[4]

15.   *Couche* 2½.   *Slept sound till 9.   La Hanoverrienne attandoit*[5]; 1¼ rix dollars.   At 11 called on Baron Munck.   Spent an hour in trying to find Catteau without success.   Ordered a bath at 3.   *Il y a rien qui me etab. apres trop de muse comme le bain chaud*[6]   Called at Hartshorne's; found him and Hosack at chess; Heuland and Slade spectators. Brought Hosack home to settle for our two weeks' rent with d'Aries; paid 14 rix dollars.   Hosack gave notice that he should leave his quarters to-morrow *etant mecontent de son demeure coeleste.*[7]   He is in the fifth story.   *An bain a trois h.   Tout pret.   Reste dedans*

---

1   For *les Suédoises.*   The Swedish women.
2   Great lord, very rich and residing in Skåne (an old province of Sweden at its southern extremity).
3   " Modern Colonies in the Torrid Zone, especially St. Domingo."   Printed, etc. (*imprimé*).
4   Ate a bite of supper at Madame D.'s.   (*Mangeai.*)
5   For *attendait.*   Was waiting.
6   There is nothing that restores me after too much *muse* as does the hot bath.   (*Il n'y a rien qui m' établit,* etc.)
7   For *étant mécontent de sa demeure celeste.*   Being dissatisfied with his celestial abode.

*un heure. Tres refraichi. Le dem. qui me servait atten-
dait que, &c. Mais non.* Pai. *pr. bain* 1 rix; *a dem.*
½ rix. *Chez moi* at 5. *En chem. suiv. la plus belle
animal que j'ai vu en Suede. Ignore son nom. Mais nous
saur*[1]. Bergström had promised to walk with me to
Gahn's country house, but came not; went *seul* at 6,
the distance two and a half English miles; walked it
in ¾ hour. A very Romanesque and retired position.
Lake Shreame, locks, hills, meadows, magnificent
forest; on the opposite side of the lake, pretty, neat
country houses. *Y:* The family and four or five
others whose names I did not learn. *Prie a soupè mais
ne veu. pas*[2]. After tea, walked home. Stopped ½ h.
on the way to listen to the band of music. Home at
½ p. 9. Undressed, being *tout mouille*[3] with the exercise. *Morceau de soupè av.*[4] Mr. and Madame d'A.

16. *Couche* at 12. Slept sound till 8. It must
be the milk or omitting tea which produces this extraordinary sleep. Rained hard, which prevented me
from going out. Read in Barre de Venant's book.
Cleared up at 1. Walked an hour *sans accident;* got
very warm; changed. Milk and bread for dinner.
This diet agrees with me exceedingly. Chessed. At
6 to Hartshorne's; all out. "*Parlez vous francoise?*"
"*Pas un mot,*" in very perfect French. "*Adieu,*

---

1 For *Au bain à trois heures. Tout prêt. Reste dedans une heure. Très rafraichi. La
demoiselle qui me servait attendait que,* etc. *Mais non.* Paid *pour bain* 1 rix dollar; *à demoiselle* ½ rix dollar. *Chez moi* at 5. *En chemin suivis le plus bel animal [féminin] que j'ai vu
en Suède. Ignore son nom, mais nous saurons.* To the bath at 3 o'clock. All ready. Remain
in it one hour. Very much refreshed. The girl who waited on me expected that, etc. But
no! Paid for the bath 1 rix dollar; ½ rix dollar to the girl. At home at 6. On the way I
followed the finest she animal that I have seen in Sweden. Don't know her name, but we'll
find it out.
2 Invited to supper but don't want to [go]. (*Ne veux pas.*)
3 Quite wet. (*Mouillé*).
4 Bit of supper with.

M'lle."[1] At 7 to tea *chez* de Castre. *Y.:* The Baron Krame, *arr. de Scanie*[2], *de bon sens et bontè; Chev.* Fauvelet *emig. fr.* 60; Mr. Passi, 19, *nev. de* Desguillon, *tres fort snr le piano;* Mr. ————, *sectr. du roy* Gus. IV.; M'e *et* M'lle d'C.; Mr. *et* M'e d'Ar. *Mus., chant, dans, cartes,* excellent *soupè*[3]. Home at ½ p. 12. Mr. de Castre is deemed the first singer in Sweden. M'lle *pince le harpe superieurment. Elle dansait le schawl; tres jolie ballet*[4], which she executed better than I have ever seen. The evening very pleasant. *La comtesse. Couche* at ½ p. 1.

17. *Couche* at ½ p. 1. *Lev.* at ½ p. 4. *Tro. soupe*[5]. Walked out an hour and on my return got breakfast about 6. Had two hours in the library in "*Les Monuments Antiques Expliquès par la Mythologie*," *par Alexandre Lenoir. En forme de Dictionaire avec gravures en forme de dictionaire*[6]. Vol. 1. Paris: 1806. A voluminous work. At 10 Professor Arnt came in and sat an hour. Much distressed at the prospect of affairs in his country (Germany). Agrees that the nobility is rotten and worthless; would have no hereditary nobles. Slept two hours; walked one; took my milk and bread at 3. Read a ridiculous *roman fr.* "*Gaudriole,*" *conte par*[7] M. D. Paris: 1806. 168

---

1 " Do you speak French?" "Not a word," in very perfect French. (But Burr's French is far from perfect. Should be " *Parlez-vous français?* " etc.) " Adieu, Mademoiselle."

2 For *arrivé de Scanie.* Arrived from Skåne.

3 Having good sense and kindness; Chevalier Fauvelet, French emigrant, aged 60; Mr. Passi, 19, nephew of Desguillon; very expert on the piano, Mr. ————, secretary of King Gustavus IV.; Madame and Mademoiselle d'C.; Mr. and Madame d'Ar. Music, singing, dancing, cards, excellent supper.

4 She danced the shawl dance; very pretty ballet.

5 Too much supper. (*Trop de souper,* or *j'* at *trop soupé.*)

6 " The Ancient Monuments Explained by Mythology," by Alexander Lenoir. In dictionary form with engravings. (Burr's repetition is probably unintentional.)

7 A ridiculous French romance, " Gaudriole," related by (*conte* or *conté*).

pages. Laughed half a dozen times at the most puerile and unmeaning nonsense. Called on Madame de Castre; met her going out and walked with her a few minutes. She goes this afternoon to Drottning-holm, where I am to see her on Monday P. M. Captain Weidenhjolm called at 6 to escort me to the Helvigs. Raining hard; we took coach. Met there Baron Helvig, Madame and two *souers*[1]; Comtesse Posse and Comtesse Hamilton, both very handsome; two gentlemen whose names I did not recollect. Foster came in after tea. Came off at 9 *sans adieu*[2]. It was expected that I should stay to supper, but I had resolved not on that sort of invitation. *M'e H. est literaire, gai, aimable, peut.* 32 ; 2 *enf.; le garcon,* who is the younger, perfectly beautiful ; *sa souer la plus grande,* has a very interesting physiog. *Toutes deux* paint in a very superior style in oil[3].

18. *Couche* at 12. *Lev.* at 8. Slept the whole time sound. Raining. Read till 12. Dressed and walked to Professor Gahn's country house, about two and a half miles. Found there a large circle. Baron (General) Cronstedt (brother of him of Calberg) *et ux.*; she had just performed a journey by land with her three children from Tornea through Finland to ———— and thence across the gulph[4] to Stockholm ; a cheerful, pleasing woman ; *la belle* Comtesse Löwenhaupt, to whom *je feroit l'am.*[5]; M'lle Hoschell, *la charmante*

---

1 For *soeurs*. Sisters. Burr generally misspells this word.
2 Without saying good-by.
3 Madame H. is literary, mirthful, amiable, perhaps 32 ; two children ; the boy, etc.; his sister, the taller, has, etc. Both of them paint, etc.
4 So in the MS. Old-style spelling.
5 The pretty Countess L. to whom I [fain] would make love [*je ferais volontiers l'amour*].

boiteuse[1], who plays on harp *tre. superieurment ;* Colonel Gahn,—we barely saluted and did not speak afterward, *est drole*[2]; M'e————, *fem. du juge et souer cadette de* Hoschell ; *bien belle et interessante ; douce, plein d'am*[3]. A very pleasant day. Came off at 9, declining to stay to supper. Dr. Gahn showed me his ice-house built above ground. Two walls or houses of wood about eighteen inches apart filled in with charcoal. Home at 10. Read various nonsense two hours. Mem Baron Munck's servant called this morning with a verbal message from *le* Baron and *la* Baronne with tickets of entrance and inviting me and Hosack to dine and pass the day at Haga. We were engaged. Hosack did not go to G.'s on account of the rain.

19. *Couche* at ½ p. 12. *Lev.* at ½ p. 8. Slept like a log the whole time. Was to have called on Dr. G. at his house in town at 10, but did not go there till 11. He had waited and gone. Spent an hour hunting for Catteau's without success. Roved about for two hours *sans accid*[4]. Home at 3. Milk and *brot*[5]. for dinner. At 5 set off to walk to Drottningholm, the rain notwithstanding, having a good *pr. de bottes*[6] and a large umbrella. Walked it in two hours, being about 6½ miles ; raining great. At the bridge was overtaken by young de Castre (*le menuisier*)[7] who was returning from town in cabriole (cart). Got in ; my

---

1 The charming lame girl.
2 Probably c'*est drôle.* It is queer !
3 Madame ————, wife of the judge and younger sister of Hoschell. Very fine looking and interesting. Sweet, full of friendship (*amitié*), or love (*amour*).
4 For *sans accident.*
5 The spelling of the German word for bread, but it is probably a misspelling of the Swedish word *bröd.*
6 For *paire de bottes.* Pair of boots.
7 The carpenter.

coat rubbing on the wheel and all mud, which with the aid of the two maids at Drottningholm washed off. Sent out for sugar, coffee, bread, and a pipe; not one of these articles to be had. Consoled myself with a little skimmed milk and warm water and at 9 went to de Castre's. *Recu tres gracieusement.* Supped on *philibonka*[1]. Home at ½ p. 10. *Couche* at ½ p. 11.

20. Slept sound till 9 ! This must be the milk diet which produces such inordinate sleep. Dressed and sent out again for the materials for breakfast. Madame de Castre met the servant, saw her basket, and came over herself for me to tell me that it was vain to try to get a breakfast for me there and that hers was waiting for me. I was then *al fresco*[2]. Made myself up, went over, and found an excellent breakfast. The family had breakfasted about four hours before. At ½ p. 11 Madame and M'lle de Castre went with me to see the Palace. The *wäckmyster*[3] attended us, and we passed two hours in going through the rooms. Not so extensive as the chateau in Stockholm, but the pictures *mieux choisies*[4]. I could pass four hours a day there for a month, with pleasure, to examine the pictures and statues. Of the latter, however, not many. Returned at ½ p. 1. Went to my inn at D. to repose and *fum.*[5] Returned to dine at ½ p. 2. After dinner, coffee. All went to D. at 6. Mr. and Madame D. had just

---

1 *Filbunke* is a wholesome summer dish in Scandinavia and Northern Europe in general. Sweet milk is left to sour in a dish specially made for the purpose. Cream settles thick on top. Powdered sugar and grated ginger are mixed with it. Then it is eaten with relish. Burr spells *filbunke* in seven different ways, but always incorrectly.
2 Spanish. Literally in the cool, i. e., in undress, not presentable.
3 For *vaktmastare*. Watchman, keeper, porter.
4 Better selected.
5 For *fumer*. To smoke.

arrived from town. At ½ p. 6 commenced my march home. The Dev. sent that *U.* after me; walked together two miles. *Ret. en boi;* ¾ r. d.[1] Gave the *wackm'r* who showed us the Palace half a dollar *banco.* Got home at ½ p. 9, not at all fatigued. Milk and *bro.*[2] for supper. Hosack came in at 11 and we played chess till 1. No letter, not a line from any human being nor any other being since I left London. " *Ca ne vaut rien apres dinè. Il gate la digestion*"[3]

21. *Couche* at 2. *Lev.* at 10. One sound nap again! Quarrel with the *blanchisseur*[4], who carried off * * * * and refused to deliver them till I had given some handkerchiefs of another person which I never saw or had; so I must either lose my clothes, enter into a lawsuit or pay for things I never saw. *La vieux* Anna, too, *en mauvaise humeur*[5]. Very cold; still raining, and no wood. Milk and *bro.* at 4. At 6 called on Captain Weidenhjolm; out. Over to Hedboom's, whom I met at his door; made my apology for failing to dine, &c.; all settled. *En ret rencr. gros. blo. noi. che.* 30 *bel. men. che. mo.* 1 r. d. *Tant pis.*[6] Read Kant *par* Villers; 2 hours. *Soup. eau et pain*[7]. *Couche* at ½ p. 11.

22. *Couche* at ½ p. 11. Was waked by a great knocking at my door at ½ p. 9. Heard the voice of

---

1 The devil sent that *jungfru* (maid) after me. Walked together two miles. Returning, in the woods; ¾ rix dollar. (*En retourant, en bois.*)
2 For *bröd.* Bread.
3 That's no good after dinner. It hurts digestion (*gâte*).
4 The launderer; possibly meant for the laundress. If so, it should be *blanchisseuse.* The text is partially undecipherable We should be glad to know what the launderer carried off !
5 Old Anna, too, in bad humor. (*La vieille* Anna).
6 For *En retournant rencontrai une grosse blondine. Cheveux noirs;* 30; *belle.* [La] *menai chez moi.* 1 rix dollar. *Tant pis.* On returning I met a big, fair complexioned woman with black hair. Age 30. Fine looking. Took her to my room. 1 rix dollar. So much the worse !
7 Bread and butter for supper (*souper*).

la bel. Marie, but did not answer. Got up, however, and breakfasted at ½ p. 10. At 12 came into the library Lilly de Castre. *Sor.* at 1 to Catteau's, with whom sat an hour. He is a native of Prussia, where his father *vient de mourir*[1]. *Il ennuye ici*[2]. He is going to Berlin in fifteen days, to take possession of his little heritage, and thence to Paris. Catteau says this is not the country of the Goths, or Ostrogoths, or any Goths; that they all came from Thrace, Asia, Mt. Caucasus, &c., and had been, for centuries before the invasion of the Roman Empire, coming into Germany; that the Swedish language partakes much of the same origin; that there is no reason to believe that any Swedes went south, as far as Italy or France, before the ninth or tenth century; that the application of the term Gotha and Ostrogotha to certain parts of Sweden is the error and stupidity of the geographers of the Middle Ages; that the Romans knew nothing of the Baltic; that it is not mentioned by any of their writers, and that they had no knowledge of Sweden, only that there was a country hereabouts which they called Scandinavia; that Teutons or Teutonic is the true term of the origin of all the northern nations of Europe, including Great Britain; that the Gaelic (Welsh) is, however, of distinct and more remote origin. Met Colonel Gahn; we barely saluted. Called at Dr. G.'s and found him at home (in town). He gave me a letter for his friend and relation Dr. Frederic Schulzen, of Gothenburg, desiring him to take charge of my letters. Not one

---

1 Has just died.
2 For *Il s'ennuie ici*. He is bored here.

has yet been received, which is *suprenante*[1] and embarrassing. Going out this morning *sui. dem. bi. mis. Tour du* Konigl Garden. *Quit. En ret. renc. enc. Me sui. chez mo.* 2 r. d. *Pa. bl. ni. jeu. Tant pis encore*[2]. At 5, milk and *bro.* The weather has been clear, mild, and as pleasant as possible.

23. *Couche* at ½ p. 12. At 9 was waked par *La Hanov.*[3], who staid an hour. *Tres aim. et gent.*; rix[4]. At 1 walked over to Wennerquiest's to answer his note of yesterday inviting Hosack and me to a party Sunday evening. W. out; wrote a note at his desk. Left card at Helvig's. Sent another by Hosack to Count Cronstedt and another to Laing. Called on Captain Weidenhjolm, who was out; stuck card in his keyhole. Home at 2. Read "*Troubadours*," *par* Fabre d' Olivet. *On dit que les Russes ont envoyes passport, pour un min. Soeudois* and that Baron Stedingk *pars demain*[5]. To-day the Austrians are beaten and demolished; yesterday they were victorious. Baron Munck's servant came to ask us to dine there to-morrow, to which assented. Hosack goes out this evening to Professor Gahn's *campagne*[6]. Milk and *bröt*[7] at 6. At 8 walked out along the Blass Holmen[8] over the bridge

---

1 For *surprenant.* Surprising.
2 For *Suivis [une] dame bien mise. Tour du* Kongliga Gård. *[Elle me] quitta. En retournant [la] rencontrai encore. [Elle] me suivit chez moi.* 2 rix dollars. *Pas belle ni jeune. Tant pis encore.* Followed a well-dressed woman. We made a tour of the Royal Garden. She got away from me. On the way back met her again. She followed me home. 2 rix dollars. Neither fine-looking nor young. So much the worse still! (Konigl Garden for Kongliga Djurgård. Royal deer-park. This is a singularly picturesque island of Stockholm, nearly the whole of which is occupied by a public park and the summer villas of wealthy Stockholmers. It is connected with the rest of the city by bridges.)
3 For *la Hanovrienne.* The Hanoverian woman.
4 For *Très aimable et gentille.* 1 rix dollar. Very amiable and pretty.
5 It is said that the Russians have sent a passport (*passeport*) for a Swedish minister (*un ministre suédois*) and that Baron Stedingk leaves to-morrow (*part*).
6 Country house.
7 Notice the umlaut this time, which is an improvement.
8 For Blasieholmen.

to Skeeps Holmen[1], thence by the public (free) ferry to Kongl. Djur Garden, and home by Frederick's Hof[2]. At ½ p. 9, thinking I had need of something *rafraichissant a cause de, &c.*[3], took tea and two eggs. Read Kant and "*Troubadours.*" At 12 Hosack came in. We played chess till ½ p. 1. The tea, the tea!

24. This is St. John's day, the greatest holiday in the year; formerly celebrated with great military and royal pomp, *i. e.*, before Gustavus IV., who abhorred anything gay. It is celebrated throughout the country as May-day and called————. At 10 last evening the cannon were fired, and, at intervals, all night. At midnight, singing and prayers in all the churches. The tea which I had so foolishly taken kept me awake, and, being utterly indisposed for sleep, walked out at ½ p. 2 to see the sun rise, but the sky was clouded. At 3 the streets were full of young people; people, indeed, of all ages and sexes, bearing green boughs, flowers, little Maypoles very prettily ornamented. They had all some good-natured wit at me. I retorted, neither comprehending a word, and we all laughed. Home at 4. Read the last two volumes of Emilie de Varmont through in the course of the night and morning. Prettily written. At 8 Hosack came in and soon after I went to bed and slept till near 11, and before I was dressed Hosack came in with ————, a very amiable and well-informed young Swiss, to make me visit. Sat one-half hour.

---

1 For Skeppsholmen.
2 For Fredrikshof.
3 Need of something refreshing because of, etc.

At 12 took breakfast. From 1 to 2, walked to see what was doing. Little parties of both sexes everywhere. Singing, fiddling, dancing, Maypoles. The day became fine. At 2 walked with Hosack to Haga to dine with Munck. Invited to go with him to his *campagne*, about sixty miles. *En famille*, Professor Arnt, and ourselves. Dinner always good. Greatly pleased with my frankness in telling him that a bottle of *vin*[1] was bad. Refused to sup. Came off at ½ p. 8. Walked with Hosack to see some *U's*[2]; out. Home at 10. Chess till 12. H. to bed. I had again taken both coffee and tea and could not sleep.

25. Read "*Troubadours*" till 4. *Couche* and slept sound till waked by *la vieux* Anna, who came into my room apparently full of anxiety and astonished to find me in bed. She offers me tea, coffee, eggs, and every other thing she could make me comprehend ; all which I refused. Got up and dressed and at 3 took breakfast. Raining all the morning. They say it is always so, both at the summer and winter solstice. At 6 went out with Hosack to call on the young Swiss mentioned Saturday. Sat ½ hour, and went on to Wennerquiest's, about two miles. Hosack, though engaged there also, refused to go, so I went alone. Found there eight gentlemen, mostly musicians, and a pleasant concert. Supper. Very cheerful. He had got Davis's "Travels," in which, it seems, you and I are mentioned.

26. *Couche* at 2. *Lev.* at ½ p. 5. I don't know

---

1 Wine.
2 *Jungfrus*

why, but had slept enough. Dressed. Read a military treatise. At 8, just as I had got breakfast, *la bel*[1]. Mar. came in and staid an hour; 2 rix dollars. Colonel *le* Chev. ————, *emig. fr*[2]. who had served in America with d'Estaing and Bouillé and asked an introduction. Passed an hour. He was aide-de-camp *de* Gustavus IV. Was imprisoned by him two days before his being deposed for having hinted to him that a revolution was meditated to dethrone him. At ½ p. 2 took *phillibonka*[3] with d'Aries *pour din*. At 3 lay down and slept two hours. At 6 walked out to Haga and supped with the Munck's. Home at ½ p. 11.

27. My bed being out of order (*epinasses*[4]) I slept on sopha[5] in d'A.'s parlour. *Couche* at ½ p. 12. *Lev.* at ½ p. 8. *La Han'e*[6]; [5]/4 rix dollars. Breakfast at 10. Walked with Madame ———— to see the church where the coronation is to be performed. *Br.* and milk at 6. At 7 walked to Liston Hill (Wennerquiest's) to take supper and a bed in conformity with his several warm invitations. Found no one at home but a servant, who said he could give me nothing to drink but small beer and nothing to eat but the *brö brû*[7]; so left a note for him on his table and walked home.

28. Your picture was opened and put up in my parlour about ten days ago. It has been very greatly

---

1 For *la belle* Marie.
2 Colonel Chevalier ————, a French emigrant (*émigré français*).
3 His second manner of spelling the word.
4 For *punaises*. Bugs.
5 So in the MS.
6 For *la Hanovrienne*.
7 Burr, who spelled all Swedish words phonetically, was very uncertain about the word *bröd*. Here in despair he writes two incorrect forms.

admired, and given occasion to many inquiries. Thinking it had got a little injured, I took it to Breda's to ask his advice. He has offered to clean it and put it in order. It has suffered no material injury. He says that if a picture must be rolled, you must roll it the paint outside. I had done the contrary; but he gives me good reasons for his advice. I forget whether I told you that Breda is not only the first painter in Sweden, but really one who would in any country be called great. Madame —— walked with me to see the church where the ceremony of coronation is to be performed. Not very spacious, but rich and magnificent. Returning, met the herald going round the city, and proclaiming at different places the coronation intended for to-morrow. He is attended by some troops of horse, by trumpeters, &c., in splendid costumes. Met Slade, Hosack, and —— Agreed to meet them at dinner at the Merchants Society at ½ p. 2. Went at the hour; a very handsome and spacious establishment arranged with perfect convenience. The dinner and wine very good. I prefer this house to that of the Nobles. Baron Armfelt (relative of the other General Armfelt heretofore mentioned) begged me to sit by him, and he amused me much. Says he is 72; very sprightly, and has been over every part of Europe. On my way home met again *la pet*[1]., who was mentioned about a month ago, (we then met at the puppet show theatre). Determined not again to lose so pretty an object, gave

---

1 For *la petite*. The little one.

an arm and we walked to my quarters ; ⁵/₄ rix dollars. Speaks a little French, sings very pretty and dances. General Helvig's card left here to-day. Took tea at 10.

30. After my tea last evening I began to reflect on the folly, and took twelve drops of laudanum, more than I ever before took at a dose, to balance the tea. Read till ½ p. 1 and lay down, but no sleep. At 3 (sunrise) the day was ushered in by the firing of cannon. Gave up the business of sleep, and got up and dressed at 4. Got breakfast by 6, and called Hosack to aid me to get the paraphernalia for the day, viz., hat and sword. Yesterday Baron Munck wrote me a note, enclosing tickets, and telling me how to get introduced. Went to his room at ½ p. 8, where took another breakfast of mutton-chop, wine, &c. At ¼ p. 9 he took me to the room of the *grand maitre de ceremonie*¹; there another breakfast, chocolate, wine, cake, &c., of which partook. At 10 we went to the church. Had a very convenient seat. The public dinner at ½ p. 6. Got home from the church at 3. Took *möjlk*² and *bru* for dinner. Got home from seeing the royal family dine at 8. Took some weak tea and went by appointment to Jacobi's at 10. *Out !*

Stockholm, July 1, 1809. *Couche* at ½ p. 11 and slept one sound nap till ½ p. 7. At 12 to Breda's (he has a charming collection of paintings) to see about the picture and get my chessmen painted ; that is, the heads of the bishops and knights. Breda

---

1 Grand master of ceremonies.
2 For *mjölk*. Swedish word for milk.

was engaged painting the Countess of——— Did
not see him, but his wife and son received me civilly
and would have called him but I forbad[1]. To Wennerquiest's; out. Home at 2. *Mojlk*[2] and *brû* at 4.
Called at Professor Gahn's at 7; out. Home at 8.
Madame d'A. sent me down some *fillibonka*[3], on which
I supped.

2. *Couche* at 12. *Lev.* at 8. Auguste waked
me by appointment to go to the silk manufactory, but
we went not. At ½ p. 9 took Auguste under my
protection and went to Munck's at the Chateau to
view the procession and homage from his windows.
Found there Baron Armfelt and his two sons (13 and
15); Professor Arnt, and several others of both sexes.
The show most magnificent and in the most perfect
taste. The site most happily chosen; perhaps no city
in the world affords so fine a *Plâce*[4] for such a purpose.
Came off at ½ p. 1, though I believe it was intended
I should dine there. Walked about an hour to see
the crowds of all sorts. Home ½ p. 2. Read in
"Anecdotes of the Court of Sweden," anonymous, two
hours. *Fillibonka* at 5. Dressed and went to Helvig's, being Madame's evening; out, all. Left card.
Over to Merchants Society where read the English
papers an hour. No one of my acquaintance. Home
at 9. Two eggs, *Bro.* and *smor*[5], water and sugar *pour
soup*[6]. Read two hours "*Le Voyage au Nord par deux*

1 So in the MS.
2 Notice the variations of spelling in this word and the word for bread.
3 A third misspelling of the word.
4 For French *place*. Square.
5 For *smör*. Swedish for butter.
6 For *pour souper*. For supper.

Francois"[1]. *La pet. Louis. devait sy rendre a 3 h. Mais ne vin. pas*[2].

3. *Couche* at 12½. *Lev.* at 8½. You see I have got up to 8 again. At 10 came in Hosack. He had been last evening to a *bal*[3] at the Park Djurgarden. 11 *un dame parl't fr. et ang. Spirituelle,* &c. *Sur le champ entroit* Jacobi. Then Capt. Weidenhjolm, then Bergström. *Tous s'occupaient beaucoup de la dame qui pretendoit s'amuser dans la biblioth. Restaient un heure. M'e part*[4]. Gave Jacobi a card for Mr. Becker and another for *le Juge*[5] ———— which he promised to transmit. Weidenhjolm says I must have mistaken the *trappur upp*[6] at Helvig's; that they were certainly at home. Received invitation from Comte and Comptesse Cronstedt to dine and sup *jeudi 6 Juliet*[7]; now as *jeudi* is the 7th and not the 6th, what is to be done? Wrote, however, that would come Thursday *jeudi prochain*[8]. Raining all the forenoon. Afternoon clear and fine. Read *Varia*[9]. At 7 walked by the long bridge and Skeeps Holmen; thence boat, the free ferry, to Djurgarden and *au*[10] park, intending to pass the evening at Wennerquiest's. Just before I got there, met Jacobi, who enticed me to return to the Merchants Society to play chess and sup. On the

---

1 " Journey to the North by two Frenchmen " (*Français*).
2 For *La petite Louise devait s'y rendre à trois heures, mais ne vint pas.* Little Louise was to be there at 3 o'clock, but didn't come.
3 A ball.
4 At 11 came in an intellectual lady speaking French and English. Immediately Jacobi entered, then Captain Weidenhjohm, then Bergstrom. All paid a good deal of attention to the lady, who pretended to amuse herself in the library. They remained an hour. Madame left (*partit*).
5 The judge.
6 See Glossary.
7 Thursday, the 6th of July (*Juillet*).
8 Next Thursday
9 Various things.
10 To the.

way met and sat some time with two *U's.* One *jo.;*
nom encor[1] Played chess and supped. Hosack joins
us. Supper and a bottle Moselle wine; 1 rix dollar
chaque[2]. Home at 11. Mem.: Dined on *fillibonka*
at 5.

    4. *Couche* at 1. *Lev.* at 9. Breakfast at 10.
Hosack came in; begins to *demeuble*[3], having taken a
room *au*[4] park, near Wennerquiest's. At 11 walked
out with Auguste to *manf. de soye* to order *bas*[5]. To
Wennerquiest's; find *mais occupè*[6]; not bear telling
about my visit on Tuesday evening. To Breda's to
see about your picture. Nothing yet done; but his
son promises to do it and I am sure he will. The
chessmen done. Home at ½ p. 1. Wrote to Dr.
Frederic Schulzen, Göteborg, to take up my letters,
if any, and transmit them. Wrote Catherine enclosing
the letter to Dumont. Hartshorne and Slade set off
for Petersburg to-day at 2 P. M. At 4 *fillibonka* for
dinner. At 5 came in Bergström by appointment to
walk. To Catteau's to leave my letter. To post-
office. Paid for the letter to Göteborg, 5½ sch.; a
treble letter. *Bon marchè*[7] (A new figure in the
drama. *B. chant. parle tr. bi. fran. et un p. ang. mais nous
en dirons plus* anon[8]). Jacobi joined us at the post-office
and we all went on board a Prussian ship just about to

---

1 For two *jungfrus.* One *jolie.* [*Il faut demander son*] *nom encore.* I must ask her name
again.
2 Each.
3 To unfurnish, i. e., to get things ready for moving (*démeubler*).
4 At the park or in the park.
5 To the silk manufactory (*manufacture de soie*) to order stockings (*des bas*).
6 But he is busy. (*Occupé.*)
7 Cheap. (*Marché.*)
8 For *Belle; chante; parle très bien français et un peu anglais. Mais nous en dirons plus*
anon. Fine looking. Sings. Speaks French very nicely and English a little. But we'll tell
more about her presently.

sail for Pillau ; have a great mind to go on her. A great levee (to which I did not go) at the Palace to-day, 7 P. M. The trouble of dressing and the fatigue of standing prevented ; besides if his Majesty wants me, let him invite me. Met Monsieur Warrendorf who urged me very much to go. A stupid blunder ; Mrs. Brooks and not Madame Baker was the lady for whom the card was intended ; of the other I know nothing. She was astonished at the card. Went at 12 to-day and left one for Madame Brooks. Read this morning *"Playdoyers et Jugement entre un Perro-quet, un Chat et un Chien." Assez ridicule et bien fait pour faire rire*[1].

5. As I was writing you last night, I stopped to hunt for the plays I had read, that I might give them their titles. It happened that the first thing I laid hands on was *"Les Mines de Pologne," melodrame en prose*[2], *par* Guilbert Pixerecourt, which I had not before read. It is very long. One paragraph led to another. I read it through. It was then 2 o'clock in the morning. Being too late to write, went to bed. This melodrama would make a splendid and interesting pantomime. The incidents and scenery extremely well imagined for stage effect. *"La Vie de Chev";* Faublas, eight volumes duodecimo ; a *nouvelle*[3] Well written, rather free and in the manner of Crebillon *fils*[4]. Read only the last volume. The *denouement*[5] is a very

---

1 " Pleadings and Judgment between a Parrot, a Cat and a Dog." Quite ridiculous and bound to cause laughter.
2 " The Polish Mines " ; a melodrama in prose.
3 " The Life of Chev " ; etc., a novel.
4 Crebillon the younger, or junior.
5 The final unraveling of the plot (*dénouement* or *dénoûment*).

incongruous medley, and to me shocking and disgusting. "*Choir Gaure,*" the Grand Orrery of the Ancient Druids, commonly called *Stonehedge*, by Dr. John Smith, 1771, an extremely ingenious work. These last are now mentioned, though read some days ago. At 5 went on board a Prussian ship just about to sail for Pillau. Have a great mind to go in her. Was rowed by two boys, one a Swede about 15, perfectly beautiful, gay, frank, animated; is a sailor at 6 rix dollars per month. Speaks English. Strong affection for his mother, with a laudable pride and ambition. At 7 walked down to Wennerquiest's, having understood that his weekly parties are altered from Sunday to Wednesday. Found there three or four gentlemen sitting with him in the bower, drinking toddy. Hosack came in. At about sunset (9 o'clock) they went off one after another, except H. and myself. We rose to go. Wennerquiest said he could give us no supper, his housekeeper being in town; but offered to go and sup with us at a tavern, which we declined. Note: He has lived several years in England! Home by a most beautiful path through the woods and along the lake.

6. *Couche* at 12. Rose at 6 by force of being waked by my *vielle*[1] Anna, as per order. Breakfast ½ p. 7. *Sor.* at 8 to Bergström's, whom I found in bed, to remind him of Catteau's book. To Jacobi's; in bed, to see about a passage to any port S. side of Baltic. To Captain Weidenhjolm's to settle a time

---

[1] The writer is improving. He is now within one letter of the correct feminine form of the word. It should be *vieille.*

for visiting the *foire*[1] and to advise about the Helvigs.
Read two hours and dressed for dinner. At 2 took
boat to go to Calberg; 28 sch. *rixelt*[2]. We were
thirty at table. Two Count Constredts *et uxs.*[3]; M'lle
Löwenhaupt *et frere* Major L.; the whole family and
connections of Gahn's, including the Colonel. The
Colonel and I just nodded to each other. After dinner came in Count Falkenberg *et ux.;* a very fine
woman; has been about three years married. *Poi.
d'enf.*[4] The Temple in the Woods (eight pillars).
Löwenhaupt sang a great deal; charming voice. Party
on the water; *ramèd*[5] *par* Löwenhaupt. Mrs. Gahn's
present. *Les fleurs. Les souvenirs*[6]. "Don't forget
me." A very cheerful day. Walked home and arrived
at ½ p. 11. There are many pretty little incidents this
morning and evening which will take some hours to
tell. I omit them all. I ought to have mentioned
Mr.———, uncle of Dr. G., a very sprightly, cheerful
man of 77 who has an office in the Department of
Finance and has written a book on the subject. Mr.
Poppius is in the judiciary; both intelligent and communicative and of course interesting acquaintances for
me. , M'lle *la* Baronne *de* Charlotte Heikenskjold
came in this morning and we passed an hour in the
library.

7. *Couche* at ½ p. 1 (was obliged to sit up late,
having supped, &c.). Rose at 7. At 9 called on
Weidenhjolm, who proposes to go with me to the

1 Fair, market.
2 See Glossary.
3 And wives. He pluralizes *ux*. The full form is *uxores*.
4 For *Point d' enfants*. No children at all.
5 From French word *ramer*. To row. A hybrid verb made by the writer.
6 The flowers. The souvenirs.

minister Monday morning. On Jacobi to engage him
to call on me at 10, which he did. Charlotte H. came
in before him; she and *la pet'.* Sang several songs.
Charlotte plays off hand anything you give her, though
she may never before have seen it. Found in the
library a book of Scotch and English songs of which
she played several. At 1 set off to walk to Dr.
Gahn's to dine. Stopped often on the way and arrived
at ½ p. 2. *Υ:* The family; his youngest son, too,
who arrived some days ago from Upsala where he is
at college; Poppius *et ux.* and two *souers*; Colonel G.
Dinner simple. *Un ver de V.*[2] The hay harvest;
four men to mow three acres in a day, but took nearly
one and a half days, being from 3 A. M. to 7 P. M.
Gages[3], 30 sch. per day and *trinka*[4]. Five women to
rake. *Soupè. Point de Vi.*[5] Off at 10. Arrived at
Calberg, met there Löwenhaupt. Her two uncles and
aunts just returning from Drottningholm. Walked
and *caûsed* ¼ hour. *Un secret. Un billet pour le roi
et la reine.* 17th inst. Löwenhaupt *y demeurait*[6].
Chez moi at 11.

8. *Couche* at 1. Rose at 7. Called on Jacobi
at 8. Found him abed. At 10 came in *la* Baronne
Charlotte. Has a very fine voice. She and our little
————sang a great deal for me. Jacobi came in to
confer about modes of traveling through Europe. At
12 to Wennerquiest's; in the country. To Baron

---

1 For *la petite.* The little one.
2 For *un verre de vin.* One glass of wine.
3 Wages.
4 For *dricka.* Home-brewed ale or beer was provided for the harvesters.
5 For *Soupè. Point de vin.* Supper. No wine at all.
6 Walked and chatted [a hybrid verb from French *causer,* to chat] a quarter of an hour. A
secret. A note for the King, etc. Lowenhaupt remained there.

Munck *au chateau*[1]*;* he is at Haga. To Dr. Gahn's ; not in town. To Breda's. *Υ: La* Comtesse sitting for her picture. She consented that I should be admitted. A very cheerful, well-bred old lady. Mother of Baron Wrangle, whom I meet so often *chez* Madame Löwenhaupt. Nothing yet done to your picture, except putting it in a frame. At 5 *fillibonka.* At 7 to Helvig's. Met there *le Genl. et ux. et souer cadette* just going out. They insisted upon my going in to take tea, &c., and I on walking out with them, in which I prevailed. Walked over the long bridge, over Skeeps Island[2], thence by boat to Djurgarden, and so on to the park. Up the rocks ; interesting views. *Waffen, söcre* and *svaatrinka* at the little red *wärdshuset*[3]. Animated debate about the condition and deportment of women. Thought M'lle——— beautiful ; eyes like K. Returned to their door at 10 ; refused to go in ; *bon soir.* Home and supped on three eggs, which was unnecessary. I am better *sans soupè*[4]. Settled this morning with d'Aries for three weeks including this day, at 3½ *rexelt* per week ; 10½ *rexelt.*

9. *Couche* at 1. *Lev.* at 7. *La soupè ne vaut rièn. Lourd*[5] Read till 4 P. M., not going out nor seeing a soul. At 4 came in Hosack. Dressed to call on Poppius. Hosack goes to Dr. G.'s to sup. Captain Weidenhjolm came in at ½ p. 6, and sat two

---

1 At the castle.
2 Skeppsholmen.
3 *Vatten, socker* and *svagdricka* at the little red *vardshus.* Water, sugar and small beer at the little red tavern.
4 Without supper.
5 Supper is no good ! Heavy, dull.

hours and a half. To Poppius's; out. Left cards and walked on to Haga. Baron Munck gone to his *campagne;* a fortnight ago he invited me to go with him, but went without thinking of me. Madame *la Bar., sa niece[1]* and Professor Arnt. Supped at 10. *Beaucoup bû[2]*, Arnt walked with me home. Took circuit through the Calberg woods to avoid the dust, which is excessive. The *marangais[3]* at Haga! Hosack came in just after I arrived and after half an hour went out to his home. Read "*Minuit,*" *comedie en un acte, par* Desandras[4]; Paris: 1798; pretty little bagatelle; "*Le Droit du Seigneur[5];*" *com. en 3 actes, par* M. Desfontaines, 1783; a very dull thing; the music and scenery may have helped it out.

10. *Couche* at 1. *Lev.* at 6. Called on Jacobi at 9. At 10 M'lle Silversparri (not so spelled, however), *dame d'honner[6]; dit la mielleur voix de* Stockholm[7]; but Weidenhjolm coming in to go to the mint, had no opportunity to hear M'lle sing. To the mint. *Υ:* Mr. Hjelm, who being exceedingly occupied and having had no notice begs us to call to-morrow. Returning, called at Gahn's; out. To Wennerquiest's to get some English book to read with Löwenhaupt. Found him in his *contoir[8]* very busy; asked to see his library; he said the key was upstairs and begged me to appoint another day! How ridiculous and rude !

---

1 For *la Baronne, sa nièce.*
2 For *beaucoup bu.* Having drunk much.
3 Probably for *marangouins* [or *maringouins*]. Mosquitoes.
4 "Midnight," a comedy in one act by Desandras.
5 "The Lord's Right."
6 For *dame d'honneur.* Maid of honor.
7 Said to be the best voice (*la meilleure voix*) of Stockholm.
8 For *comptoir.* Counting-house.

Hosack had appointed to call at 1, but came not at all. To Jacobi's; out. *Fillibunc*[1] at 4. At 6 to Calberg; all out. 'Tis court day, which I did not know. Left card, and also one for General Comte Cronstedt, who has rooms with his brother. Went on to Dr. Gahn's. *Y:* The family and Madame ———, niece of the old gentleman who has written on finance. *Sangaree* and cakes, and after an excellent supper, the first green peas I have seen, returned his *Scala* of Thermom'r, which I had copied, and got from him H. Gahn's letter. Engaged his youngest son, who is student at law, to call on me Wednesday to inform me about judicial proceedings. Off at ½ p. 10. Escorted Madame ——— as far as Calberg, where she took boat. Home at ½ p. 11. The watchmen; their Devil's fork[2]; their long speech and prayer. We always sup without candles, the daylight is so perfect at 10 that candles would be ridiculous. Mem.: This morning bought a paper of tobacco for 8 sch. *Voyons*[3] how long it will last.

11. *Couche* at 1. *Lev.* at ½ p. 7. Expected Captain Weidenhjolm to go with me to the mint, but he did not come, *Sor.* at ½ p. 10. To Captain Weidenhjolm's; out. To Jacobi's; deposited with him the watch ring! Don't be frightened; it is only to make inquiries, &c. On my way to the mint, *renc.*[4]; [5]/4 rix dollars. Louis Bruman. Got to the mint at 12. Mr. Hjelm, the director, said he had been ex-

---

1 A fourth spelling of the word *filbunke.*
2 Doubtless referring to the pronged weapons which they carried.
3 Let us see.
4 For *rencontras* [*une demoiselle*]. Met a girl, or [*j 'eus une*] *rencontre.* I had a rencounter.

pecting me since 10 (which, indeed, was the hour appointed), and could then pass but a few minutes with me. Invited me to come on Friday morning, when, he said, the whole will be in operation. Saw a common labourer melting gold; several pounds weight of it; no one to overlook him; all the doors open. Home at 1. *Sor.* again. To Mr. Brook's. *Υ:* Dr. G. (who went out as soon as I came in) and ——, a very handsome young Swede who appeared to be very much at home. Sat half an hour. Madame is sprightly and the young Swede talkative. To Helvig's; all out. Home at 2. *Fillibonka* at 4. At ½ p. 5 walked out to Calberg; both families out again. Walked directly home. Being warm, after changing went to Poppius's. *Υ:* Mr. P., Mr. Lary, and ——. Had a long and interesting conversation with Mr. P. on law subjects. You will be charmed to hear the results of my inquiries on this head. Only to think of a people, the most honest and peaceable in the world, and not a lawyer! No such animal, (according to English ideas of a lawyer), in Sweden! But again and again I remind you that this Journal is only a memorandum to talk from. The most inter esting and amusing incidents are not noted at all, because I am sure to remember them. Mr. P. urged me to stay to supper, which I declined, though hungry. *Vraiment*[1], I was afraid to *gener*[2] them, and I mean to see Mr. P. very often on law subjects, and Madame on other subjects. She is very pretty, speaks French

---

1 Truly.
2 For *géner*. To incommode them.

fluently, and sings charmingly. Home at ½ p. 9. Three eggs and *svaatrinka*[1] for supper. I learn that Hosack called this P. M. during my absence.

11. *Couche* at ½ p. 12. *Lev.* at ½ p. 9. *Ayant dormi profondement toutes les 9 heures. Bian la vielle* Anna *m'appelloit a* 6. *Je l'ai repondu sans m'eveiller*[2]. Dressed and got breakfast with all possible dispatch expecting young Gahn who was to call at 10. *Hereusement*[3] it was near 11 when he called. We went to several booksellers, but the laws of Sweden in Latin are not to be found. To the post-office; no letters! ! At 1 called on Jacobi about the ring; out. On Dr. Gahn to get the address of Engerström,— *a son excellence Mon'r le* Baron d'Engerström, principal *secretaire d'etat pour les affaires etrangers, chev'r des ordres*[4]. *Chez moi* at 2. Read an hour in Catteau's "Sweden" to refresh my memory about the civil administration so that I may question all my acquaintances. At ½ p. 3 to some booksellers. At Ulrick's; *sa fille tres jo*[5]. Found Bentham's "*Principes*"[6]. Home at ½ p. 4. *Fillibonk*[7] *pr. dine. Dom.*[8] *de* Helvig came in to beg me to tea and pass the evening. *Tres volunt.* for M'lle Miriam *m'interesse beaucoup. Aussi sa soeur*, Madame H.[9] They both paint in oil and colours in a very superior style. Walked with them an hour *au jardin*

---

1 For *svagdricka.* Small beer.
2 *Bian* is for *bienque.* Having slept soundly the entire nine hours Although old Anna called me at 6, I answered her without waking. (*Je lui ai*, etc.)
3 Fortunately.
4 To his Excellency Baron d'Engerstrom, Chief Secretary of State for Foreign Affairs; chevalier or knight of the orders.
5 His daughter, very pretty (*jolie*).
6 "Principles."
7 The fifth mode of spelling the word.
8 Helvig's servant, (*domestique*).
9 *Volunt.* for *volontiers,* willingly. Very willingly, for Mademoiselle Miriam interests me greatly. Also her sister, Madame H.

du roy[1] (Vauxhall). Returned to *soupè*. *Tres bi servi. Comblè honet'e.* *Y:* Colonel ——; Mr. ——; Me. ——, *qui poursuit* Gam[2]. Home at ½ p. 11.

12. *Couche* at 1. Having taken half a dish of tea, slept not a wink till past 5. *Lev.* 9. Young Gahn was to have called at 10, but came not at all. *Sor.* at 11. To Jacobi's; got back the ring; nothing can be done with it here. To Ulrick's, bookseller; bought Bentham's "*Principes*," 4½ rix dollars *banco*. He took in exchange for 2½ rix dollars a silly book, "*Sur l' Imagination*[3]," which I foolishly bought on my arrival. Home. At 6 went out with Auguste. To Mesarie, *manufacture de* toys. Nothing done. To Wennerquiest's; out. To Breda's, where passed an hour looking at your picture. I was exceedingly struck and alarmed to see it pale and faded. Why was not this perceivable before? Perhaps it may arise from being placed among his portraits, which are very high coloured. Yet the impression that it is faded is fixed on my mind, and has almost made me superstitious. Home. *Fillibonk* at 5. At 6 to Helvig's; sat an hour; gave to her servant a note to Breda requesting him to bring the picture for her inspection. Passed ½ hour in the cabinet of the General H. *qui est militaire scientifique*[4] Two telescopes for measuring distances where an object of known dimensions (a man for instance) is visible. A beautiful invention. Also a watch for measuring distances by sound; the watch gives the

---

1 In the Royal Garden.
2 Returned to supper; very well served. Overwhelmed with courtesy (*comblè d'honnê-teté*). There were there Colonel ——; Mr. ——; Madame ——, who is pursuing Gamp.
3 "On the Imagination."
4 Who is a scientific military man.

sixtieth part of a second; every artillery officer is obliged to have one. At ½ p. 7 to Poppius's. There was company; was much urged to stay to sup, but refused, though M'lle Hoschell and Madame Yjarta were there and Madame P. is very handsome and amiable. You have before known that I admire M'lle H. But my object was to talk law with Mr. P. and he was at the card table. Home ½ p. 9. Read "*La Destruction de la Ligue ou la Reduction de Paris*," *piece national en 4 acts; a* Amsterdam, 1782[1]. This is *in form* a dramatic piece, but has not any dramatic merit or character. The author, however, has talents, observation, and foresight. It may be read with pleasure and approbation. The preface is 45 pages; the play, 210 octavo. The author advertises that he should shortly publish two other pieces of the same kind—"*La Mort de Louis XI., Roy de France*," and "*Phillippe II., Roy d'Espagne*"[2].

13. (Friday). I must be wrong about the day of the month, but that of the week is right. *Couche* at ½ p. 11. Waked and got up ½ p. 4, having slept enough; but *Som.*[3] begged me so much to pass a few minutes more with him that I consented; lay down and slept profoundly four hours. Note: It was raining very hard. *Tojours abattu*[4] after so much sleeping. *Sor.* at 10. To the mint by appointment with the director, Mr. Hjelm, who very civilly took me through and showed me everything. Nothing very

---

1 " The Destruction of the League, or the Reduction of Paris," a national (patriotic) piece in four acts; at Amsterdam, 1782.
2 " The Death of Louis XI., King of France," and " Philip II., King of Spain."
3 For *Somnus*. Latin for Sleep or the god of sleep.
4 Always depressed.

curious, unless the free manner in which common labourers and workmen handle gold and silver in great quantities, and yet no fraud has been known. To-morrow I am to have coronation medals. To Ulrick's to get the books I bought yesterday, he not having sent them home. Paid 24 sch. for the Laws of Sweden, one small octavo. Home at 12. Then to see Hosack at the mineral springs called ———, about two and a half miles. Still raining. Home at 2. Hosack came with me to do some commissions for me, principally the 6 ducats, but Hedboom could not be found. *Fillibonk* at 4. You can't imagine what an epicure I am with my *filbonk*[1]. At 5 Hosack returned and we played chess two hours. Read " *Kouloup ou les Chinois,*" *opéra comique en prose. 3 actes. Par* Guilbert Pixerecourt. *La musique par* N. Dalayrae, *memb. de la Legion d' Honneur et de l'acad. roy. de* Stockholm. *Imp. et representee a* Paris, 1807[2]. The plot is Shakespeare's beggar made king, but with different draping calculated for stage effect. Sent by Hosack my note to Bergström.

It must be the 15th. By looking back you will see where the error began. *Couche* at 12. Rose at 7. At 8 to Bergström's to get Catteau's book on Denmark ; to engage him (Bergström) to visit the hospitals with me. He promises again. Thence home. Hosack came in at 9 to *breakfast*, as engaged ; no other way to make him punctual. After breakfast he and I

---

1 This, the sixth mode of spelling the word. Note that he spells it in two different ways in two successive sentences.

2 " Kouloup or the Chinese "; a comic opera in prose, in three acts, by G. P. The music by N. D., member of the Legion of Honor and of the Royal Academy of Stockholm. Printed and staged (should be *imprimé et représenté*) at Paris in 1807.

played chess and then Hosack went to hunt Hedboom about the ducats ; not found. At 4 Bergström came in with Catteau's book. Went to several booksellers this morning, but bought nothing. At 6 to Helvig's. *Y:* A Colonel ———, speaking English ; that same Madame ———, whom I met there on Wednesday, and the beautiful Comtesse Posse. Foster came in. All off before 9. I the last and *sans soupè*. Home, *eau et brö*[1]. Read for several days past " *Les Oeuvres Posthum. de Marmontel ;*" 4 vol. duod. *sur Metaphysique, Grammaire, Logique, Moral.*[2] His style is always beautiful and the subjects are treated in a manner new and interesting, except the last (*moral*), in which I find nothing remarkable either of idea or manner. The d'Aries go this P. M. to Drottningholm. Note: The Helvigs engage to meet me at dinner to-morrow at the mineral springs *au Parc*[3].

16. *Couche* at 12. *Lev.* at 8. Bad again. *Sor.* at 11 (though raining) to the Park, three miles ; arrived at 12. Passed an hour with Hosack. The Helvigs did not come. At 1 set off to walk home ; not sorry they did not come *pour des raisons*[4] of state. Home at 2. *Brö et mjolk*[5] for dinner. Read last evening : " *Les Confidences* "[6] *en deux actes*, Paris, 1803. A very pretty little bagatelle. This morning "*Un Tour de jeune Home*" Paris : 1802 ; 1 act (*La, la*. Has the merit of being very short) *par* F. P. A. Leger *et* R.

---

1 Bread and water.
2 " The Posthumous Works of Marmontel ", in 4 volumes duodecimo, on metaphysics, grammar, logic, ethics (should be *la morale*).
3 In the park.
4 For state reasons.
5 Bread and milk. Note how he varies this pair of words.
6 " The Confidences."

Chazet¹. At 6 walked out to Gahn's; all out except *M'lle la gouvernante*² and my beautiful little Eva, with whom played two hours. Passing and repassing Calberg saw no one at the window and did not enquire. Home at 9. Read Catteau's "*Danem'k*³." Just now, 12 o'clock, comes in d'Aries and family. *La belle* —— has been forbidden to speak to Mons.⁴ Gamp. Supper, two eggs. The butter is so bad that *je m'en passe*⁵. Tobacco out; had to buy this holy P. M.

17. *Couche* at 1. Rose at 7. Wrote last evening to Baron Engerström enclosing the letter of H. Gahn. At 12 took the letter to Dr. Gahn, who sent it with my card by his servant. A note of Madame Helvig sent yesterday forenoon has by stupidity of servant come to hand at 1 P. M. this day. The seasonable receipt would have prevented my walk to the bath. Wrote an answer to Madame. Among the wise things, I congratulated her on the appearance of fine settled weather, and since 7 P. M. till 7 A. M. Tuesday morning (the hours at which I write), it has been raining torrents. To the post-office; found there *a* letter, but from Gothenburg saying that no letters had come there for me! On this point I despair, but let us [not] begin a new day with despair. Mem.: On my way home from the post-office an accident *qui me cout.; 1 r. d. Mau. 15*⁶·

18. Yesterday I found * * * *⁷ tea that appeared

---

1 "A Young Man's Tour." Paris: 1802; 1 act (so, so, etc.) by —— and ——.
2 The governess.
3 For "*Danemark.*" "Denmark."
4 For Monsieur.
5 I do without it.
6 For *qui me coûta* 1 rix dollar. *Mauvais. 15.* Which cost me 1 rix dollar. Bad. 15.
7 Undecipherable.

to be good. Bought ¼ pound, and treated myself to
a dish by way of supper. Took two cups moderately
strong. Finding that I should not sleep, I did not go
to bed. Passed the night in reading French plays and
arranging my notes on Swedish jurisprudence. I can't
bear even the smell of tea, though nothing more grateful. But the bare scent would, I believe, keep me
awake. Despairing of letters, I will wait no longer,
but be off. You would never guess whither, nor why !
In December, however, I shall be on your continent.
P. M.——No sort of disposition to sleep. At 4
fillibonka. At 6 to Poppius's to talk law ; out. To
Helvig's ; the ladies had not left town. *Y:* Silversparri, who sang ; deemed the finest voice in Stockholm.
Home at 8 and set to reading plays. This morning
called at Breda's to see your picture. It has been varnished and is perfectly restored. It is very much (and
very justly) admired. How much I wish I could get a
copy made by Breda l Raining hard all day and evening. Read till 12. The plays are : *"Le Judgement
de Midas "*[1], three acts, prose, *par* M. d'Hele, Paris :
1778 ; a very trifling little thing ; the music and
scenery may make anything charming. *"Misanthrope
Repentir"*[2] *traduit de l'allemand de Kotzebu par* Bursay;
Paris *an :* VIII.[3] I like this better than the English
translation under the name of the *"* Stranger." *" Camille ou le Souterrain "*[4], three acts, Paris : 1791 ; *par*
Marsollier. A jealous husband without any reasonable

---

1 " The Judgment of Midas.
2 Should be " *Misanthropie et Repentir.*" " Misanthropy and Repentance."
3 Translated from the German of Kotzebue by Bursay ; Paris : Year VIII.
4 " Camille, or the Vault."

cause confines Camille, a very lovely and virtuous woman, a whole year in a deep vault, lying on the ground, subsisting on a scanty portion of coarse bread and water. He is suspected of having killed her, and being seized by order of the King, the story comes out. Camille is too happy that her honour is justified and she restored to her dear husband. They embrace and all is made up ; not even an apology on his part. Is it possible that a Parisian audience in '91 could relish such a tale ! In the first scene there is something like wit and humour ; afterwards a series of impossibilities and absurdities. "*Le Jeune Sage et le Vieux Fou*"[1]; one act, *par* Hoffman ; Paris : 1793; well enough for a bagatelle "*Raoul Sire de Crequi*"[2]; three acts, *par* M. Monvel ; Paris : 1789 ; well enough calculated for stage effect. "*Felix ou l'Enfant Trouvè*"[3]; anon.; Paris : 1778 ; impossibilities and absurdities in quantity; without wit or humour. "*Jeu de la Fortune ou les Marionettes*"[4]; five acts, *par* L. B. Picard ; Paris : 1806 ; full of rapid reverses of fortune ; love and friendship follow wealth and abandon poverty ; men, women, servants, all rascals, time-serving, cringing sycophants ; the only exception is a little *paysanne*[5] who adheres to her lover through all changes, though he had abandoned her when he became suddenly rich; the design of the play is well illustrated, but gives a most disgusting, probably true, picture of the times.

1 " The Wise Youth and the Old Fool.
2 The actual title is " *Raoul de Créqui.*"
3 " Felix, or the Foundling."
4 " The Game of Fortune, or the Puppet-show."
5 Peasant girl.

19. Instead of going to bed at 10 or 11 as I ought, to make up the arrears of sleep, read till 12 and then lay till 1 sleepless. Slept one profound nap till 10. Yesterday invitation from Wennerquiest to pass this evening; *conviens*[1]. *Sor.* 11 to Hedboom's about the ducats and the list of stages; out; left a note. Paid ½ rix dollar for quire com. paper; 40 sch. for tobacco; 4½ rix dollars for P.'s silk stockings. *Mjolk kokas till middag*[2]. Received this P. M. very civil note from *Grefve*[3] Engerström inviting to an interview at 1 P. M. to-morrow. Walked to Wennerquiest's at 8. *Y:* Hosack; Colloni or Collins; magnificent, fine voice; several other musicians and musical men; Hendrick, a German, settled some time in Liverpool, whom I met at Daily's; Ludert, a very handsome and interesting young Russian; had been only two years in England, but speaks English so as to be mistaken for a native. Supper good. Came off with the young Russian at 11.

20. Hosack called by appointment at 7; the first instance of punctuality. Set him to copying the constitution, of which I have borrowed a French translation. At 1 to Engerström's; *recu tres hon't*[4]. *un bel homme de 55. Madame, polonaise,* who is now in Poland, whence *le Compte* returned on the late revolu tion; has a son, 18, *militaire*[5], now here; two daughters with their mother. Dinner at the Society of Nobles;

---

1 For [*je*] *conviens.* I agree.
2 For *mjolkkaka till middag.* Milk-cakes at noon. Probably a sort of milk-roll.
3 Swedish for Count.
4 For *reçu très honnêtement.* Very courteously received.
5 A fine looking man of 55. His wife a Polish lady who is now in Poland, whence the Count returned, etc. Has a son who is a soldier.

an excellent dinner. A bottle of wine for Hosack and self; paid for both, 2 rix dollars, 12 sch. *Υ:* An *Eveque*[1] of prepossessing phiz.; played billiards well. Home at 4. At 6 to Calberg. *Υ:* Madame and three strangers. L. was out on the lake, in sight, fishing party. Staid an hour and walked to Dr. Gahn's. *Υ:* The family only. Refused supper at both places. Home at ½ p. 9. At Gahn's a kind of strawberry I had not before seen; large, conical, dull red, green, and yellow; dull colours; in flavor like our garden strawberry. This morning called on Mr. Brooks. *Υ:* Klinkerström. *Part. che. lui*[2]. Madame invites me to sup to-morrow evening.

21. Read last evening three more French plays. The best is one which the author announces on his title page had been hissed. The others very silly, unmeaning trash, neither wit nor incident to amuse or interest. Will read no more of them. *Couche* at 1. Waked, and by my watch it was ½ p. 7, but it had run down, and lo, it was 10 l Slept profoundly all that time and, contrary to custom, not the worse for it. Note from Madame B. postponing her party till to-morrow evening, which don't suit me at all, having promised myself to sup with the Helvigs at Drottningholm. *Quoi faire?* To Hedboom's about the ducats and list of roads; out, and nothing done. How that good-natured fellow plagues me! Home at 1. Two more English mails arrived and nothing for us! " *Hist. Naturelle des Femmes* "[3], *par* J. L. Moreau (*de*

---

1 For *évêque.* Bishop.
2 For *Partit chez lui.* He went home.
3 " Natural History of the Women."

la Sarthe)[1], *avec 11 planches*[2]. Three volumes octavo; Paris: 1803, *curiux*[3]. *"Histoire de l'Eglise du Japon," par le* R. P. Crasset, *de la Compagnie de Jesus;* two volumes quarto, *av. planches*[4]; Paris: 1715. The *miracles*, as the compiler, a learned Jesuit, says, are as well attested as any of those in the New Testament. The Emperor of Japan did very right to hang them all, according to their own report. They were bold, daring rascalls[5], and performed wonders, if not miracles. *" Essai sur la Megalanthropogenesie," par* Robert *le jeune des basses Alpes.* Duod. Paris: 1801. *Dedie a l'Institut National de France*[6], showing how talents of every sort may be perpetuated by being transmitted from generation to generation; curious and learned. *" La Guerre d'Espagne de Bavarie et de Flandre, ou Memoirs du Marquis D." Avec plans des bat's,* &c. *Imp. a Cologne*, 1707. Duod. 654 *pa.*[7] A medley of love, politics, and war, tolerably well written and worth perusal, *i. e.*, the historical and military part. Called this afternoon on General Helvig; out. To Jacobi's. *Y:* Professor Phillipson and Luders, the young Russian. They invited me to walk in Kong.[8] Garden, which declined. *Philibonka pr. aftonmilstid*[9] No supper.

---

1 Of La Sarthe, a department of France.
2 With eleven plates.
3 For *curieux*. Curious.
4 " History of the Church of Japan," by R. P. Crasset of the Society of Jesus; two volumes, quarto, with plates.
5 So in the MS.
6 " Essay on the Art of Procreating at Will Men of Lofty Stature and Men of Genius " by Robert the young [or younger] of Les Basses Alpes [a department of France], dedicated to the National Institute of France.
7 " The Spanish, Bavarian, and Flemish Wars, or Memoirs of Marquis D." With Plans of the Battles [*des batailles*]. Printed [*Imprimé*] at Cologne, 1707, duodecimo, 654 pages.
8 For Kungstradgård. Another royal park open to the public. It is Stockholm's great promenade.
9 *Filbunke pour aftonmåltid. Filbunke* for supper.

22. *Couche* 1. *Lev.* 7. Called on Bergström before breakfast and left with him a card to be tendered to his uncle the advocate, which he promised. Home. Hosack came in at 9 and took breakfast with me. Set him to copy the constitution. To Hedboom's; found him and got the list of roads but not the ducats. Dinner, *mjolk köka*[1]. At ½ p. 7 to Brooks's; there were about two dozen of each sex. *La* Comtesse Gyllanstolp *née*[2] De Geer de Finspång; *son mari* colonel in the army *au Nord*[3] and now there; *le* Comte Jacob de la Gardie, a sensible, well-bred, sprightly man. There were some at cards, some walking and chatting when I came in; all appeared content. Madame B. does very well the honours of her house. I came in very late; 6 is the customary hour. Supper at 11; very handsome; came off at 12. It was my *projêt*[4] to have walked after supper to Drottningholm (about eight English miles) and I had ordered matters for my reception at 2 in the morning, the hour I expected to arrive; but this afternoon came the valet *de* Helvig to say that her carriage would call for me at 11 to-morrow. I have, therefore, given up, but with regret, my *promenade a pied*[5], the nights are so lovely. Snuff—" Heavens, Madame, how horrible for a beautiful woman!" " Yes, sir," says she, " and that *I* should offer it!" Aurore[6]—" If I do not mis-

---

1 See Glossary.
2 Born, i. e. her maiden name.
3 Her husband a colonel in the army in the North.
4 For *projet*. Scheme.
5 My walk; literally, my promenade on foot, for the French word *promenade* may also refer to a drive or horseback ride.
6 Aurore de Gyllanstolphe.

take you, that project is only postponed and not abandoned."

23. A supper disqualifies me from going to bed, so sat up till 2. Before 4 woke and feeling no inclination to sleep more, got up. Breakfast at 6. At ½ p. 7 to Breda's, where we talked a great deal of T. "Good God," says he, "pardon the freedom; but can any man on earth be worthy of that woman and know how to estimate her! Such a union of delicacy, dignity, sweetness, and genius I never saw. Is she happy?" He almost shed tears. Thence to Madame Brooks's; not visible. To Comte Gyllanstolphe; out. To Count de la Gardie, who received me very courteously. Not being very certain that I understood the Swedish servant of Madame d'Helvig, went to the town house, where saw the servant, who repeated that he would call at 11. At 11 he did call; took me to ———, where, to my astonishment, saw Madame *l'amie* d'Helvig[1], *seule*. "Do you live here, Madame?" "No; but my husband does." We went, all three, and arrived at 1. Most friendly reception. No company but the family and us. *Tant mieux*[2]. After dinner I walked to my lodgings at d'Aries's, about one mile English. The family of d'H. agreed to meet me at 6 *au Jardin du Roi*. Madame ——— is at my lodgings, and she insists that I lodge elsewhere. Gam. thou. dang[3]. So a room was provided for me in the neighbourhood. Called on Madame d'Castre and

1 The lady friend of Helvig.
2 So much the better.
3 Probably for Gamp thought dangerous.

then went to d'Helvig's. Walked two hours. Returned to *soupe*. Off at 10. *Bien content*[1] with my quarters. The old man cleaned his pipe and lent it to me. Note: I had not smoked since 9 this morning.

24. *Couche* ½ p. 11. *Lev.* 7. Like a log one nap. At 10 to de Castre's. Only M'lle at home. Pursued Madame de Castre to the mineral bath, but missed the way and wandered for two hours in the labyrinth. No Ariadne[2] to help me. To the warm bath, a large establishment, to engage bath at 1. To d'H.; Madame and M'lle sitting on the grass; *ma belle* Mary Ann (only think, your favorite name) becoming daily more interesting. Staid an hour. Refused strawberries and cream. To the bath at 1, but failed from misunderstanding with the *young lady*, and would not wait. Home for an hour, and then to d'C.'s to dine. Dined in the arbour in the garden. *Y:* Madame and M'lle de C., and Madame ———, *un francaise qui ne manque pas d'esprit*[3]. Walked to see the hay harvest and the Castor and Pollux. At 6 to Helvig's. The General had gone early this morning to town. Strawberries and milk. Having mentioned my determination to walk this evening to town they proposed to accompany me to the bridge, but I was obliged to go first to my quarters. We roved through the Gardens and they walked near my residence till I went to change my dress; joined them again and we parted near the bridge. We had ob-

---

1 Well satisfied.
2 In Greek mythology Ariadne was the daughter of Minos, King of Crete. She gave Theseus the clue by means of which he found his way out of the labyrinth.
3 A French woman who does not lack wit, intellect. (*Une Française*, etc.)

served from the house a view of the end of the *2d Pont*[1] and the road ascending the hill towards town; there I paused to contemplate the house of my friends. I could just discern them on the green before the door; a white handkerchief waved and the signal returned, and again and again repeated. I walked on, slow promenade. Presently overtaken by a *paysanne* with whom I walked and was amused for near three miles; ½ rix dollar. Got home a little past 11, not the least fatigued; could have walked back again without reposing. Warm *wattn*[2] to wash my feet and *mjolk kôku*[3] for supper. A most dreadful misfortune and here irreparable! I have mourned over it an hour and more and cannot even now write the details. It happened just as I had finished the preceding and was preparing in good glee for bed. The beautiful little watch of Lepine—both glasses broken ! ! !

25. *Couche* 1. *Lev.* at 8. At 10 to Jacobi's. *Υ:* Luders and another. Asked Jacobi to call on me at 4, which he promised. To the Comtesse Aurore de Gyllanstolphe; out. You will think this a hard name for a beautiful woman. *Neè* Geer de Finspång, where is a sister said to be more beautiful than herself. Thither I was invited. Thither *la* Comtesse goes on Thursday; about 150 English miles. Home. At 1, though called a warm day, walked to the mineral springs *au Parc* to see Hosack. He complained of being weak and unwell. Laughed at him and made

---

1 For [*le*] *second pont.* The second bridge.
2 For Swedish *vatten.* Water.
3 See Glossary.

him walk with me home, two and a half miles. *Filli-bonk* for dinner. Read two hours in Bentham. To General d'Helvig's at 7; out. Home by way of Kong. Garden, where a band of music and much *monde*[1]. Jacobi came at 5. The watch can neither be *sold* nor repaired here. Guineas are 8 ½ rix dollars *Rexelt* cash, which is about 22 per cent. above par. Hosack changed his *last eight* to-day. No letters, nor have I written one since being in Stockholm save the single short one to Achaud on business. I have fifty projects of journeys, all embryos and will be all abortions. No letter. Changed 1 guinea to-day; 8 ½ rix dollars. Paid H. 2 rix dollars 21 sch. in full. The residue shall last me a week. To-day a Russian messenger arrived. The preliminaries, before Russia will even treat, are : 1. that the Prince of ———, the Emperor's brother-in-law, be declared successor to the throne ; 2. the cession of Finland ; 3. that the ports be shut against Great Britain. I have never spoken to you of politics, because I have personally no hand in them, which will be reason enough for you, and for twenty other good reasons. We have every few days news of the advance of the Russian army towards us ; then contradicted. Victories and defeats equally false. Bonaparte one day vanquished, the next victor ; sometimes wounded or killed. Here are French parties and English parties. The former predominate, but nothing of our violence. Calm ; tranquil. The troops in town (here) are all embarking on some expedition ; supposed (indeed known) to aid the army

[1] People.

of Vride on the Gulf of Bothnia. There was a mutiny. Officers knocked down, &c.

26. *Couche* 1. Slept till 9. At 12 to Breda's to see the picture. He has placed it among all the Goth and Vandal beauties and they are really beautiful, but all in the shade by your presence. This and Davis' has given you great *renommé* [2] *here. Au chateau* to see Baron Engerström. He was engaged but gave me rendezvous at 7 this evening. To Hedboom's; out. Returning, seeing Brooks and *fille* [3] at their window, went in for ½ hour. Called on *la* Comtesse ————; out. Breda engaged me this morning to dine *en fam* [4]., to which agreed cheerfully. Went at ½ p. 2. *Y:* The family, *i. e.,* two sons, one in the naval service, the other painter, both fine young men, the latter *un fort esprit* [5]; daughter of 15 plays remarkably well and has a most charming voice. Off at 5. Dined and went for an hour to Mr. Brooks's. *Y:* The Baron; invited to walk; *ne sauroit* [6]. To Engerström's at 7. He never keeps me waiting a minute. Sat half an hour. Mentioned my design of visiting Germany, &c., and he begged that, when my route should be settled, I would inform him, that he might give me letters. To Helvig's at 8, where sat an hour

1 On page 151 will be found another reference to Davis and his " Travels." Possibly Matthew L. Davis is meant. He was one of Burr's most intimate friends, wrote the Memoirs, edited the Journal (see Introduction), and wrote constantly for the newspapers. For a time he contributed from Washington to the New York *Courier and Enquirer* under the pen name of "A Spy in Washington." He also wrote for the London *Times,* signing his letters " The Genevese Traveler." It may be that it was to Davis's letters to the London *Times* that Burr refers.

2 For *renommée.* Renown.
3 Daughter.
4 For *en famille.*
5 A strong mind.
6 For *ne saurais.* I can't.

tête-a-tete[1] in his library. Amused by his military science, and interested by his warmth and frankness. He is a German by birth. Gave me samples of powder which, he says, has more than double the usual force, *i. e.*, that a pistol of fifteen-inch barrel will do effect at 200 yards, and a musket at 600! Samples of *florite*, a *composition*. Showed me a sort of *paper mache*[2] for cannon cartridges, much cheaper and better than linen or cloth. A telescope for measuring distance. The distance required is found by mere inspection of a graduated scale attached to the telescope. An instrument for measuring distances by time, in form of a watch; gives with perfect accuracy the sixtieth part of a second. Every artillery officer is obliged to have one. The cost, $15. Moulds, by which every part of the musket or pistol must be made, so that every part may fit every piece. (Note: The ladies are at Drottningholm; Louisa not arrived.) Home at ½ p. 9. Found on my table the Latin edition of the Swedish laws, which for weeks I had been seeking in vain. It came from the Baron d'Albedÿhll (whom I have never seen), accompanied by a very *honête*[3] note in French. Sat down most greedily to devour *Svenska*[4] law. Read till 1, and now *bon soir*. There is a *bal* to-night at the park, but I went not, for two reasons (which you may divine), though much urged.

    27. *Couche* 1. Rose 7. Before breakfast to

---

1 For *tête-à-tête*. Literally head to head, i. e., in close conversation.
2 For *papier-mâché*.
3 For *honnête*. Civil, polite.
4 *Svensk* is Swedish for Swedish. *Svenska lagen*. The Swedish law.

Bergström's, whom I found. His uncle is a celebrated advocate, whose acquaintance I wish to aid my legal researches. To Breda's; out. M'lle sang and played for me. Home to breakfast. Replied very *honêtely*[1] to the Baron d'Albedÿhll's note To a watchmaker who says he can replace the glasses and that the watch has sustained no other injury. I danced for joy at this news. To Hedboom's, whom I found; got my 6 ducats which are now worth 4 dollars *Rixelt* each. He offered me many civilities. To Breda's again, whom saw only to ask a question. Home to study law. No, I came by Ulrick's, the bookseller, to get a book written by *le* Baron d'Albedÿhll, which got. Read a book before you see the author. Sat half an hour with M'lle Ulrick. She is beautiful, very beautiful; about 15, nearly your size and form. Speaks German and French fluently. Her elder sister keeps a bookstore at Nÿkooping or Noskyping, I forget which. *Dit*[2], that she is also beautiful, knows all languages, ancient and modern, &c., &c. Single; *boit'e*[3]. Home at ½ p. 2. Read the Baron's book. Only about fifty pages, extremely well written in French. The rest of the volume is made up of documents and public letters. The subject is a history of the armed neutrality, the whole merit of which has been given to Catherine of Russia. No such thing! It originated in a treaty made between Denmark and Sweden in 1756; renewed between them in 1779. Catherine,

---

1 A hybrid adverb made from the adjective mentioned in note 3, preceding page.
2 Said.
3 For *boiteuse*. Lame.

during all that year, and till July, 1780, refused to come into it, fearing the effect on the belligerent powers. At length, in that month, by the influence of Count Panin, her minister, she acceded. At 5 to Judge Poppius's, whom, fortunately, I found smoking in his office. He would transfer me over to his beautiful wife till he made his *toilette*[1]; but I sat down and took a pipe, and had an hour's very satisfactory conversation with him. Went in to tea, but took none. *Y:* Madame Djyrta and M'lle ———, her sister. At 8 to Helvig's to see for Louisa; out; not even a servant. Home, and sat to read law. *Filli-bonka* at 4. No supper. I do not report to you my Swedish law; that has a separate department, and many curious things will be found in it. Met Mrs. Daily in the street this morning.

28. *Couche* ½ p. 12. Rose 6. Breakfast at 7. At 8 to the watchmaker's. He has put in both glasses and mended the hinge of the case, which was not broken by accident but actually worn out. Everything wears out; you will wear out. No, alas! you perish joyless in those infernal swamps. I wear out slowly. Really slowly, as you see. But, for all this watchwork, you will be surprised to hear that I paid only 1 rix dollar *rixelt*, nominally 3 shillings sterling, but in fact only 2 shillings and 6 pence. To Baron d'Albedÿhll's just before 9; out; in fact, he was not dressed. To Helvig's, just to inquire for Louisa; she has not come. The impudent huzzy sent me a message of compli-

---

[1] Toilet.

ments. Engaged to pass the day with the family at Drottningholm on Sunday. Propose to walk up Sunday night. Home and went to work at Swedish law. Ludert, the handsome young Russian, came in at 11 and sat an hour. Of Romanzow; Cate; disposition of Russian army toward the French; meeting of two regiments and twenty-six officers condemned to be shot; two actually shot; of Russian finances; copper, paper money, depreciation of. *Fillibonka* at 3. At 5 called on Madame Daily; out. Walked over to Calberg; met *la bel.* Comtesse Löwenhaupt at the door; walked with her toward the park; three ladies followed; asked *la* Comtesse in English who they were; one of them addressed me in very good English and introduced the others. Cakes, tea, &c., a very pleasant drink made of small beer, wine, lemons, sugar. Much *monde* came in. General Cronstedt, *ux. et trois enf.*;[1] Baron or Count ————, who is appointed minister to France; Stul, a young officer, his secretary; *la belle* Comtesse Bönj, *dit* the most beautiful woman in Stockholm, and many others. The two *belles* sang and played, both very fine voices; *c'est trop.*[2] Astonishing that two *belles* should be such devoted friends; very honorable to both and very amiable. Stole off at 8; and have spent two hours in getting the powder out of my hair. Company to supper with d'Aries; invited but decline. My eyes have suffered by much reading; must relax to-night.

    29. *Couche* 11. Slept sound till 8! At 10

---

1 For *uxor et trois enfants.* Wife and three children.
2 Literally, that is too much! Perhaps it might be translated: That caps the climax! That beats me!

called on Ludert. He showed me a collection of
Russian songs, *indegines*[1], and promises to procure me
a copy. Home. At 11 *sor.* with Mr. Gransbom *chez
orfèvrier*[2]. Changed 5 ducats for 4 rix dollars 8 sch.
rexelt cash, which is about 30 per cent. above their
cost in London. Mr. G. has agreed to go with me to
Gripsholm. We pursued our walk to find a passage
by water; found three sloops going this evening, and
resolved to go in one of them. To the bank to get
some silver. To Hedboom's for letter which he
offered for his friend at Gripsholm; out; left note.
Wrote Munck and Gahn for the letters which they
offered me for the same place. Sent Gosse (*poike*[3])
with the letters. Hosack came in at 12 looking better
than what I have seen him. *Fillibonka* at 2. Busy,
busy, busy, preparing for the jaunt.

Drottningholm, Sunday, July 30, 1809. Yesterday noon I told you that I was just setting off for
Gripsholm where the deposed King, his Queen, and
family are now confined. At 6 P. M. (yesterday)
went again to the sloop to see the hour of departure;
it was deferred till Monday P. M. Hosack walked
with me. Resolved to improve the interval by a visit
to this delightful *séjour*[4], now rendered still more interesting by the presence of the d'Helvigs. Set off at
9, a most serene and mild moonlight evening. Passing
the last bridge, which I was very intently measuring
by steps, heedless of a party just passing me, when a

1 For *indigènes.* Native.
2 For *orfèvre.* Goldsmith.
3 For *pojke.* Swedish for boy.
4 For *séjour.* Abode.

man put his hand on my shoulder and stopped me.
It was General d'Helvig, the three *souers*[1], Louisa having arrived from Upsala, M'lle *la* Baronne Silversparri, and M'lle F. I was not the least fatigued;
walked with the Helvigs in the park and gardens till
12. Went to my lodgings; all asleep and fast locked;
tried at d'Aries's; ditto; knocked hard at each; no
movement; resolving not to lay[2] in the street, *j'enfon-
cai le porte*[3] of my lodgings. The old man *et ux.* came
down in some trepidation, got light, and my bed was
ready. Not a mouthful of bread or milk or anything
eatable or drinkable to be had save pure water. Having dined on *fillib.*[4] and walked at least ten miles, a
supper would have been welcome. *Couche* at 1.
Attacked by *epinaises*[5]. Fought hard till 4, slaying
thousands, but the number of the enemy increasing,
resolved on a retreat. The sun had risen; began by
taking the sheets, coverlid, and pillows out doors,
beating and shaking them well; then stripped and
changed my clothes, and laid me on the floor. Got a
sound nap of five hours. Rose at 10. Found note
from d'Aries, inviting me to dine, which declined,
proposing to dine at d'Helvig's. *Sor.* 12 to d'H.; all
out and could not understand where they had gone,
the domestics being all Swedes. Eat cherries and
strawberries in the garden till could swallow no more.
Read a pretty little French *comedie*, " *Un Heure*

---

1 Burr's spelling for *soeurs*. Sisters.
2 So in the MS.
3 For *j'enfonçai la porte*. I broke in the door.
4 His favorite *filbunke*.
5 For *punaises* Bedbugs.

d'ab͜ence[1] " The statues in the garden all crowned with wreaths and garlands ; must be some *jour de fête*[2] Staid till ½ p. 2. No signs of return. *Quoi faire? Ou din.*[3]? To the bath ; took warm bath, ⅓ rix dollar ; cheap enough and everything in excellent order. At 5 to d'Aries's. *Υ* a *grn.* bowl *fillibonca*[4]. *Chez moi* to put up my things, which d'A. takes to town in his *cabriole.* At 7 to d'Helvig's. Found the whole family returned and reposing, having been on a party to the Hat mountain, where King ——————, being dethroned and pursued, lost his hat ; afterwards recovering his throne. The family presently appeared. Tea. Garden. Yesterday was the anniversary, the sixth, of the marriage of Mr. d'H. We played ball. Louisa much more expert than Gamp. Colonel ——————, came in and off before supper. I staid to supper, to which did justice. At ¼ p. 10 came off to walk home, and now at 1 you see me in my room adjoining the library at d'Aries' in Stockholm.

Stockholm, July 31, 1809. *Couche* ½ p. 1 but could not sleep till 4. *Lev.* 9. Having my keys always in my pocket I go out and come in at any hour without disturbing the servants ; have my maches[5] and candle, &c. At 11 to Jacobi's ; out. To Ludert's ; out. To the docks to see about our sloop for Gripsholm ; gone, all gone ! Home at 1. Changed a guinea for 8 rix dollars, 24 sch. Note from Dr. Gahn enclosing letter to his sister

---

1 "An Hour's Absence."
2 Feast-day.
3 For *Quoi faire? Où (peut-on) dîner?* What's to be done? Where may a fellow dine?
4 Had there a large (grand) bowl of *filbunke.* His spelling is the seventh variation.
5 So in the MS.

at Gripsholm. Note from Munck saying that his friend has left Gripsholm and come to reside in Stockholm and he knew no other person at Gripsholm. No letter from Hedboom. Thinking it very proper to have a letter from some man in office, wrote to Baron Engerström, who had offered me letters to every part of the kingdom, that I should set off for Gripsholm on Thursday. Took the note self; saw his secretary; the Baron then very busy, appointed to see me Wednesday 5 P. M. Home. *Mjolk coka*[1] at 4. Went along the docks with Gransbom, but could find no vessel to Gripsholm. Home at 4. Finished reading the mem. of Baron Albedÿhll, *i. e.*, the first volume, the only one I can get. He writes well; sometimes diffuse and declamatory; much political information concerning the periods he was employed; says he now lives on a pension of 200 rix dollars, reduced by ———— to 150. How in the devil can a man live on that? Living with the utmost economy I have spent more the three months I am in Sweden, but here is a French *Cheval.*[2] who lives on $48 per annum, and is always gay. I must take some lessons from him. Took about a gill more than was usual of *mjolk* for dinner *par la toute misplais d'*Anna[3], which has brought on a headache. Have taken *Rhad. Rhei*[4] and go *couche*. Mem.: Went this P. M. to d'H. with a pistol which wants repair. He repeats to me the wonderful *porteĕ*[5] of his firearms. Pistols the same

---

1 See Glossary.
2 For *chevalier*. Cavalier. Knight.
3 To Anna's total displeasure. (*Misplais.* for *déplaisir*.)
4 For *Radix Rhei*. Latin. Rhubarb.
5 For *portée*. Range.

length of barrel as mine, eighty yards, point blank; muskets, 250 to 300 yards point blank. I am almost incredulous, though he is scientific and exact. We are to make experiments some day next week. He showed me at Drottningholm a very curious air pistol of great force. We tried it.

Stockholm, August 1, 1809. *Couche* ½ p. 11. A bad night; troublesome headache, though not violent yet *genant*[1]. Rose at 9; took common tea; *la pauv.* Anna[2] very solicitous. At 11, well and *sor. av.* Gransbom to hunt passage. We discovered that our sloop and all the others in that quarter had been impressed for the public service, but found the King's *yatch*[3] which goes regularly every week to Gripsholm, but she is to go at 4 to-morrow morning. *Quoi faire* with my appointment *chez* d'Engerström and his *lettre*[4]? Breakfast at 2. Tea and salt herring. Again to the yatch. Fortunately she will not sail till Thursday morning; how fortunate! Ludert called this morning and sat an hour; gave me a Russian *rouble* and is to get me more. Says I can readily get a passport from Count Romanyoff. Advises me to write.

2. *Couche* at 1, but insomnia; got up; read, smoked, &c., all to no purpose. At 5 lay down and rose at 7. It was necessary to be up at 7 to give to ————, the Russian messenger, a letter for Count Romanyoff. At 8 to Ludert's who introduced me to

---

1 For *gênant*. Troublesome.
2 For *la pauvre* Anna. Poor Anna.
3 So throughout the MS.
4 Letter.

the Russian messenger; a Swedish officer always present. Thence to Breda to take a look; you had a bluish cast this morning which I didn't like. Engaged young Breda to go with me this P. M. to the Academy to see the exhibition of paintings. Bought a map of the government or district at Stockholm; 1 rix dollar *banco*. Home, expecting Hosack, who ought to write by this Russian messenger a letter on which his very existence depends; have been urging him a fortnight; it could be done in fifteen minutes, but will not be done. Met Lagman Poppius yesterday, who promised to get me Cautzler and Coxe, which he will not do. Jacobi engages me to dine with him to-day. At 1 came in the Russian messenger with his escort; sat ½ hour. *Bien hon*[1]. At ½ p. 2 to Jacobi's to dine. At 5 to Baron Engerstöm's; promises to send the letter this evening. *Dub*[2]. *Bien hon.* To General d'Helvig's, who had promised to send me a small rifle for our amusement on the water, which he has forgotten; out. Met at the door a gentleman whom I had so often met at d'Helvig's but whose name I had never heard. It proves to be the very Baron d'Albedÿhll whom I have been seeking without knowing that I had found him. Mentioned to him my tour to Gripsholm. He begged me to take charge of a letter to his wife, who is, as he sais[3], directly on the route. While at Jacobi's finished my letter to Romaňyoff and gave it to Ludert. It is a great plague to me to write

1 For *Bien honnête.* Very civil, polite.
2 For Latin *dubito.* I doubt it.
3 So in the MS.

in French. Gransbom has been to the yatch. She will go at 4 A. M. to-morrow, pos'. At 7 to d'Helvig's again; out. Nine o'clock, and the letters of d'Engerström not come! Cannot go without. Mr. G. has just gone for them. Heigh ho! nobody punctual. The Russian messenger gone without Hosack's letter. Baron d'Albedÿhll[2] sent servant with his letter and minute directions how to find the house. This is doing things right. Have mislaid Gahn's letter to his sister; *domage*[3]! There are three beautiful daughters, all speaking French. To-morrow shall write you stylographically on the water. *Bon soir.* Curse those swamps and the latitude of 35[4] Now you feel it. Alas, where are those roses which cost an empire to restore! Past 10 o'clock. Messenger from Baron d'Engerström with four letters for Gripsholm and Upsala! *Bon soir.*

Upsala, Thursday, August 17, 1809. This is more legible but less convenient and it makes but one copy. 'Twas a bad calculation to bring only that little book. How could I forget to tell you of a new acquaintance? Yesterday Mr. Turner, who is from good nature the *cicerone* of all strangers, told me that there was a traveler, a Prussian, who had a great desire to see me. He was brought up and presented. A man

---

1 Positively?

2 Baron d'Albedÿhll had great admiration for Burr. In a letter dated September 24, 1809, he asked him for some particulars of his life and said: "*En attendant je vous prierai de me tendre plus que tout-cela, c'est la faveur de votre amitié, et de votre souvenir! et je vous offre en retour l'hommage de la considération et de l'attachement les plus sincères; qui vont vous suivre en tout sens, jusque dans l'autre monde.* (Meanwhile I shall beg you to grant me more than all that, namely, the favor of your friendship and remembrance. I offer you in return the homage of the most sincere esteem and attachment; which will accompany you whithersoever you go, even into the other world.)

3 For *c'est dommage.* It's a pity!

4 Burr refers to the malarial conditions where Theodosia resides. He is alarmed for her health.

of about 34 ; a very intelligent and prepossessing countenance. His name, H. Barth. More I know not,
but we are to meet in Stockholm. He speaks English
fluently, is very chearful¹, and has that amiable German
frankness and *bonhomie*² which I do so love. *Couch.
h. au soi.*³ at 10, but having drank a dish of coffee
*chez le Gouverneur*⁴ could not sleep. Got up and
dressed and walked abroad near an hour very fast to
fatigue myself. I had before walked about five miles,
but all to no purpose, so set me down to read the
Latin edition of the Swedish laws. About 2 got
asleep. Rose at 6. To Turnberg's at 7. Found
him dressed and our coffee was immediately served,
brought in by a pretty maid, with dry bread. Afterwards, bread, butter, pickled eel, and smoked salmon,
both very good, with brandy and cordials. Mr. T.
took no brandy ; we both drank water. He offered
me a copy of his " Travels " in Swedish, which I very
foolishly declined. He answered with great cheerfulness my questions about Japan. I had made notes so
that nothing might be forgotten. Pray read his
" Travels "; they will amuse you much and then you
may question me. You may believe every word he
writes. You are perhaps ignorant that in Japan
women are as free as in any part of Europe and I
think rather more so, but I cannot now (perhaps
never) commit to writing all he says. Staid two
hours. We exchanged abundance of civil expressions

---

1 So in the MS.
2 Good fellowship.
3 For [*je me*] *couchai hier au soir.* Retired last evening.
4 At the Governor's.

and have agreed to keep up an intercourse after my return to America. Home at 10. You know we are to go off this morning to Sigtuna. Called on the Governor to take leave. He was under the hands of his hair-dresser but would see me. Staid a few minutes. Did not see *mademoiselles les baronnes*[1]. Engaged to see him in Stockholm, where he is to be next week. On my return home found Afzelius, Jr. He proposes instead of going now to Sigtuna to make a tour to the mines of Dannemora, which suits me perfectly well. Are to set off at 3 and return to-morrow. Called on Mr. Turner who gave me a great number of pamphlets by the different professors and other matters of curiosity and information. A basket of cherries and a very pretty note from Madame Afzelius *la jeu.*[2] A watchman in the steeple with an immense speaking trumpet proclaims the hour throughout the day as well as the night and immediately after the clock strikes, in a melodious tone of which not a syllable is articulated. No line from Hosack in answer to those which I wrote him on Friday last. The young *etudiant*[3], Mr. Hoxsam, came in again. He has been to the *Läsesällskap i handelsman*[4] Borell, where I shall be always welcome. The newspapers, foreign and domestic, are found there. Afzelius junior has sent me two more books on the ancient laws of Sweden. One, [by] Joh. O. Stiernhöök, "*De Jure Svenorum et Gothorum*

---

1 The baronesses.
2 For *la jeune*. The young; hence the young Mrs. Afzelius.
3 For *étudiant*. Student.
4 Swedish. Reading-circle at the house of the merchant Borell.

Vestuto." *Lib. duo., Holmiæ:* 1672[1]. Second, "*Leges Svecorum, Gothorum*" *per Doctorem* Bagwaldum Ingemvrdi, *Eccle., archid. Ubsalensis, an.* 1681 *latinatate primum donatæ*—a new edition by Johannes Massenius; Stockholm: CIƆIƆCXIV.[2] Third, " Ζαμολξις," (I can't make Greek letters as you can), *Primus Getarum Legislator,* etc., etc. *Carolo Landio.* Upsala: CIƆIƆCLXXXVII[3].

Si Venerem fugias frustra properabis ad arcton
Hoc quoque, quis credat! climate regnat amor[4].

18. The Doctor had sent his horses and servant for our carriage and rode with us to Desubro[5] where is the chateau, &c. Off at ½ p. 2. Separate at 8. Took tea with the *Haradshofding*[6]. *Pas vu M'e. Tant pis*[7]. Home at 9. The whole family seemed rejoiced to see me. Read Zamosis[8] and *Svenscha*[9] law till 12. The distance from Upsala to Dannemora is about thirty miles. Our whole expense, including horses,

———.

19. *Couche* at 1. Much * * * *[10] when afoot. Rose at 7. After breakfast walked to the landing; found two sloops going to Stockholm on Monday. Price for a passage, 16 sch. *banco,* the distance being by water about sixty miles. Yesterday called on the

---

1 Latin. " Concerning the Old Law of the Swedes and the Goths "; in two books; Stockholm: 1672.
2 " The Laws of the Swedes and the Goths." First presented in Latin by Doctor Bagvaldum Ingemurdi, Ecclesiastic, Archdeacon of Upsala, in the year 1681. A new edition by Johannes Massenius; Stockholm: 1614 (An error. He must have meant to indicate 1714, or else the other date should be 1581).
3 " Zamolxis, first legislator of the Goths," etc., etc.; by Carolus Landius, Upsala: 1687.
4 If thou wouldst flee love (Venus), in vain shalt thou hasten to the pole. In this clime, too—who would think it?—Love reigns. (Apparently Burr quotes from Ovid, but there are some suspicious features about the second verse.)
5 Desrutro?
6 For *haradshofding.* Justice of a district; circuit judge.
7 For [*je n'ai*] *pas vu Madame,* etc. I did not see Madame. So much the worse.
8 The Zamolxis mentioned above.
9 See Glossary.
10 An undecipherable word.

Haradshofding. Met him going out. He promised to
call on me at 11, which he did not do. A slight rain.
Called on the Director Afzelius; out. Read law two
hours. My young student called; fine youth. At
12 the Director came; brings me letter from Hosack
with news from the United States of the continuation
of the non-intercourse, &c. An American ship arrived
at Stockholm. Story of the young Dalecarlian¹ who
having by accident shot his wife, immediately shot
himself. Of Adjutant-General Cardell who, when
Gustavus IV. was shipwrecked in 1807 on Rügen,
saved the Queen and an officer by swimming with
them both. The King on first meeting on shore:
" Sir, where is your staff?" The General was confined in prison eight days for appearing before the
King without his staff of office. The King was an
eye-witness to the saving of the Queen. The details
of the revolution of March last, by A. E. A. Took
a sort of supper; ale, sugar-water and *skolpen²*. The
ale of this country is excellent; 6 sch. *Rixelt le bou-
teille³*

    20. *Couche* at 11. *Lev.* ½ p. 4. To the
fontaine⁴. To the landing; no sloop going before
to-morrow. Begin to be impatient to be off. Whilst
I was dressing about 6 o'clock the maid, without
knocking, *a la suedoise⁵*, brought in a stranger who
addressed me in very good English; apologized for
the liberty; that he had a great desire to know me,

---

1 Dalecarlia was an old province of Sweden.
2 Same as *skropel*. See Glossary.
3 Six shillings sterling per bottle (*la bouteille*).
4 Fountain.
5 In the Swedish fashion.

having read much about me in the newspapers. He gave me his address. Mr. Lars Clever, *Huset No. 36 nast Råintmästarehuset vid Skepsbron*[1]; *'en trappur upp*[2]. I give it as a sample of the pretty little names of streets in Stockholm, as another, that in which is my lodgings, is called *Malmskildnadsgatan.* The gentleman tendered me civilities and said he should be in Stockholm on the 24th. It was not till yesterday that I learnt that I have been a subject of newspaper discussion for several weeks. What is said about me I have neither heard nor inquired. At 9 came in my amiable Prussian acquaintance, Barth, on his return from his Northern tour. He took charge of a letter for me for Hosack. At 12 called again at A. E. Afzelius; no one at home. Went on to the landing; no sloop going till to-morrow evening. Shall I wait so long or take a post-horse this evening to Sigtuna? The *Directeur*[3] Afzelius enters; how charmingly he hates the ————, in which we agree, and we curse them by the hour together. He gave me a letter to Baron Hermelin, Nora, where I propose to stay to-night. 2 P. M. All my plans *renversèd*[4]. A. E. Afzelius has been here and proposes to go with me to Stockholm by way of Sigtuna (the ancient and first capital of the country; *dit* the residence of Odin[5]) and Sköklaster if I will wait till Wednesday morning. The further inducements to wait are: First, that I am invited

---

1 Mr. Lars Clever, house at No. 36 next to (*nast*) the treasury (*Rantmastarehuset*) by Skepsbron (*i. e.*, the wharf, quay).
2 For *en trappa upp.* Up one flight.
3 Director.
4 A hybrid perfect participle made from the French verb *renverser*, to turn upside down; hence, upset.
5 The chief of the Norse gods, the same as Wodan in German mythology.

to pass the day to-morrow at the *Landshofdingen's*[1], where I shall see *les belles Baronnes*[2]; second, to attend the territorial court, to be held here to-morrow; third, to assist at the installment of a knight newly erected who, finding it inconvenient to go to Stockholm to be *monted*[3] by the King in person, his Majesty has been graciously pleased to authorize his Excellency the *Landshöfdingen* to perform the cerimony[4] in his name and stead. After the cerimony[4], a dinner. Now, I'm thinking that you'll not scold at this delay because I shall have something to tell you. Remember to ask me to relate to you the history of Baron Hermelin, M'Lean, and Baron Silver. To the *Haradshöfding's* at 4 to talk law. *Reste*[5] to tea. Madame *bien belle*; had been extremely fortunate in her head-dress. Sang a great deal. *Y une jeu. dam. divorcèe*[6]; *la souer et mere de* Madame Afzelius. Off at 7. *Promen.*[7] one hour with the *Haradshofding* and home.

21. *Couche* ½ p. 10. Rose at 6 for the first time in six months. Dreamed engaged to marry a huge ugly beast; name unknown; reflections; Mary A.; delibcrated whether to blow out brains or perform engagement; waked by the striking of 6. Do remind me to give you a dissertation on locking doors. Every person of every sex and grade comes in without knocking; plump into your bedroom! They do not

---

1 The *Landshöfding* is a provincial governor, a lord-lieutenant.
2 The handsome baronesses.
3 Probably a hybrid verb from French *monter*, to raise; here, to raise to knighthood.
4 So in the MS.
5 Remain.
6 For *Y une jeune dame divorcée*, etc. There was there a young divorced lady, etc.
7 For *promenade*. Same meaning as in English.

seem at all embarrassed, nor think of apologizing at finding in bed or dressing or doing—no matter what —but go right on and tell their story as if it were all right. If the door be locked and the key outside (they use altogether spring locks here), no matter, they unlock the door and in they come. It is vain to desire them to knock; they do not comprehend you and if they do, pay no manner of attention to it. It took me six weeks to teach my old Anna not to come in without knocking and leave and finally it was only by appearing to get into a most violent passion and threatening to blow out her brains, which she had not the least doubt I would do without ceremony. I engage she is the only servant in all Sweden who ever knocks. Notwithstanding all my caution I have been almost every day disturbed in this way, and once last week was surprised in the most awkward situation imaginable. So, Madame, when you come to *Svenska*[1], remember to lock the door and take the key inside. At 1 the Director Afzelius came and we walked up to the castle. There were about forty in the drawing-room destined for the ceremony, including the three ladies of the family, Madame ———— from Stockholm, and one *dame* unknown. The order to be conferred was that of *Wasa*[2]; the subject of installation ———— Afzelius, professor of ———— and brother of the Director. He was dressed in the costume of the order, which is black; a short coat (or coatee) rounded at the flaps; the shoulders with ———— of black velvet; a

---

1 The true Swedish name for Sweden is *Sveriga.*
2 Wasa or Vasa. An order founded in 1772 by King Gustavus III.

black scarf round the waist, and black silk cloak *a l'Espagnole*[1]. The dress is rendered graceful by the silk and the cloak. At the upper end of the room was a small table placed before a large chair. M'lle Wetterstedt placed a crimson stool for the knight to kneel and on the table a blue silk cushion whereon was laid the gem, *insignium*[2] of the order. The Governor in full dress stood behind the table. On the stool immediately facing him kneeled the candidate for knighthood, the spectators standing round in a circle at a distance. The King's warrant authorizing the Governor to perform the investiture was then read by a knight. The Governor read the oath, which the candidate repeated. Then the Governor put on his hat, a large cornered hat edged with white feathers. He then drew his sword and laying it three times gently on the shoulder of the candidate said ————. The knight then rose. The Governor embraced him, his relatives and intimate friends did the same; he kissed the hands of the two *baronnes,* and the rest of the company congratulated him. Having never given you an account of a Swedish dinner, I may as well improve this occasion. Of the *forms* I shall only set down so much as is peculiar and invariable. Immediately after the congratulations a small table was set in the same room with bread of two or three kinds, butter, cheese, cut in small slices, brandy and wine glasses. One of the young ladies occupied herself in spreading the small pieces of bread with butter. The

---

1 After the Spanish fashion.
2 A late Latin form of *insigne*.

gentlemen came round, partook of the bread and cheese and each a glass of brandy. The ladies took of the bread and cheese, but not of the brandy. I never on any occasion saw a lady drink brandy. Various travelers have reported the contrary. During this preliminary repast all are standing and walking about without ceremony. In about ¼ hour dinner was announced. The Governor desired me to hand in one of the ladies. I bowed to the new knight, intimating that he should take precedence, the honors of the day being due to him, but no, I was the stranger. I took the hand of the elder M'lle W., but she would not go before the lady from Stockholm ; the Governor led her, the rest followed as they pleased. Arrived in the dining room all stand round and silently say grace ; thus at least the ½ minute of silence is supposed to be employed. You graceless huzzy would, I fear, employ it differently. I was contemplating *la cadette*. What so proper to inspire devotion ! Grace said, you bow to the host, the ladies, and to the company and take seats. The Governor placed me on his right hand ; M'lle on my right ; *la cadette* nearly *vis-a-vis*. You touch nothing ; ask for nothing ; every dish is handed round in succession ; you take or not ; if you see a favorite dish, you must wait till it comes round. The first thing is small slices of ham and salt fish, generally with eggs ; (eggs began the Roman feasts—*ab ovo ad mala*[1])—then *bouilli* ; fish if any, then soup ; (the servants give clean plates at every dish) ; then the *roti*

---

[1] Latin. From the egg to the apples. The Latin proverbial expression meaning " from the beginning to the end " was undoubtedly derived from the courses at dinner.

and other dishes, one at a time and a second not offered till all have done with the preceding and all the plates changed. Bottles of wine and of water, glasses and tumblers are on the table ; during the repast, frequent libations ; much ease and cheerfulness; no healths drank ; in small social parties toasts are often given, in the *odosie*[1], *par example*[2], very often. After the meats, pastry and then fruits. We had to-day apples, gooseberries (large and excellent), and currants. The *moment* the eating is gone through, all rise; everyone carrying his chair back to the wall. There is a sort of emulation in doing this with celerity and slight[3] ; no one turns his back. The servant took charge of my chair. All stand mute another ½ minute, returning thanks, bow and salute each other again. The intimate friends kiss the hands of the ladies ; the children embrace the parents and each other. The ladies are then led to the parlour, where all assemble. Coffee is immediately served on a table at which one of the young ladies presides. It is carried round by the servants, or you may take it standing or sitting by the table. The latter is usually my mode, but on this occasion I was engaged on the other side of the room on the sofa with *la cad.*[4] What a quantity ! Dear soul, you must be surfeited with this feast. I was very glad to meet here the spokesmen or presiding judges of the two courts I had visited and I did not fail to compliment them on the decorum, the simplicity, and

---

1 Possibly for Odyssey, Homer's great epic.
2 For *par exemple.* For example.
3 Obsolete form for sleight.
4 For *la cadette.*

the dispatch which I had witnessed in their tribunals. I forgot to tell you that the dishes were cut up by the young ladies *alternately;* a pretty serious labour when thirty-five guests. It is sometimes done by the servants at a sideboard. The fashionable hour of dining is 2. If the invitation extends only to dine, you are off at 5, which was the case to-day. The new knight engaged me to dine to-morrow, and A. E. Afzelius to supper and pass the evening. You see that my whole time is occupied until our departure, which will certainly be Wednesday morning. The Governor to town the same day; has frequently repeated that he will then have the pleasure of introducing me to his son, *le Chancelier de*[1] ———, in whom he has justly great pride. At 7 to A. E. A. to talk law. The patience and cheerfulness with which he answers (in English, a language not very familiar to him) to all my inquiries. Passed two hours and with great satisfaction. Walked about town an hour *ayant tro. din.*[2] At 10 all is quiet; you meet not a person in the street save the watchmen who sing out the hour and add in the same strain of melody a prayer for your good repose and security from fire and enemies. Note: *La cad.* has lost a little to-day; ουκ νουσ[3].

22. Much eating and drinking requires fumigation and vigilance. *Couche* at 1. Rose at 6. At 10 came the Professor Adam Afzelius to invite me to see his cabinet collected during ten years' residence at

---

1 The Chancellor of ———.
2 For *ayant trop diné.* Having eaten too much for dinner.
3 Greek. Probably means [she has] no mind.

Sierra Leona in the service of English society bearing that name as physician.   He is now one of the professors of botany in this university, is in his sixtieth year, and is the eldest of the three brothers ; a very sprightly man speaking very good English ; might pass for 46. It is to be regretted that his travels and discoveries have not been published and you will participate in that regret when you shall see the short notes which I have made (under this date) of his communications and of a few of the subjects shown in his cabinet. Was obliged to leave it at ½ p. 12 to dress for the knight's, J. Afzelius's, dinner, the invitation being for ½ p. 1.   At ¾ p. 1 *je m'y suis rendre*[1].   I was the last and they had got through the bread and cheese course. *Y:* The Governor; several professors; in all twelve; no *dames*, J. Afz. being *garçon*[2].   He is *bon vivant*[3] and has an excellent *men'ge. et cuisinier*[4].   The dinner such as might be expected.   Rhenish and claret both very good.   Pears, apples, melons, goosberries[5]; currants, four sorts, one of very pale dim red, which we have not; very common here.   The first honors paid to Gamp.   Dishes first presented to him, which I thought wrong, considering that the Governor is, in his government, the representative of majesty.   Off at 5.   Home till ½ p. 6.   Tavern bill for twelve days 12 rix dollars 4 sch.   I always talk in *rixgalt*[6], unless *banco* be named.   One rix dollar to *dom*.   At 7 to

1 For *je m'y suis rendu.*   I went thither.
2 Bachelor.
3 A jolly companion.
4 For *ménagère et cuisinier*.   Housekeeper and cook.
5 So in the MS
6 Burr comes nearest here to the correct spelling, which is *riksgåld*.

Andreas Ericus Afzelius (the name of my friend the *Haradshofding*) to sup. *Υ:* The Governor; his daughter, *la cadette;* Professor Afzelius, *ux.* and daughter, *et autr.*[1]; all thirty. *La cad.* was beautiful; said some smart things which almost redeemed the *νους*[2]. *La Afzelius* also *pas avantageusement mise.*[3] A very luxurious supper and excellent wines. Off at 10. *La jeu.* Madame Afzelius loses nothing. *Les bouches des trois*[4] Further delays. My amiable friend the *Haradshofding* has continued employment for me to-morrow, his business requiring a delay till Thursday. In the Botanic Garden is an American black walnut tree; the body about five inches in diameter; very thrifty; grown from a nut planted here; the only tree of the kind which I have seen on this side of the Atlantic.

23. *Couche* at 12. Rose at 6. Not the better for the intemperance; indeed, I always suffer some slight inconvenience when I depart from my milk diet. At 9 to Professor Afzelius; thence to J. Afzelius to see his cabinet to which he has several times invited me, but I should first have told you that A. E. A. called at 8 to say that his brother would attend me all day and his gig at my service. It was proposed that I should go to ———— to see the place (a parcel of great flat stones with Runic inscriptions) where the ancient Gothic Kings used to be crowned. At 10 called to see this brother; but he was not within. Do

---

1 For *et autres*, and others.
2 Probably meaning the [lack of] mind previously mentioned.
3 Madame Afzelius also not dressed to advantage.
4 The mouths of the three. (The mouths of the three persons evidently appeared peculiar to Burr.)

not regret it, having enough of occupation for the day
without promenades.   Shall stay at home, eat *fillibonk*,
and make law notes.

24   After writing you last evening had 2 * * * *[1]
1½ rix dollars, being exactly one-third of my whole
stock ; there's prudence for you !   Last evening went
to the landing with Mr. Torner as interpreter ; found
two sloops going this morning ; in one a pretty *paysanne* and no other passenger.   The *Häradshofding*
returned and says he will positively go at 10.   *Couche*
at ½ p. 11.   Slept sound till waked by *Haradshofding*
at 7.   It is now 9.   I am ready and waiting for the
Judge.   He has promised that we shall go first to see
the goal[2].   *Dub.*

25.   Yesterday at 10 A. M., A. E. A. called with
his relation, John, professor of chym.[3], greatly distressed that an official duty of which he had no notice
till 8 this morning obliges him to delay his journey till
to-morrow morning.   Invited me to go with him to a
village only two miles off to see the manner of
discharging the duty, &c.   The subject is the division
of a common among the parishioners ; agreed to go,
but went first with Professor J. Afzelius to see his cabinet, his mineralogical cabinet and laboratory.   Two
hours there and much amused.   Complains that he can
get nothing from America.   At 12 with A. E. A. to
———.   Walked ; warm weather ; found there two
priests ; two of the assessors, several peasants.   Whilst

---

1 Undecipherable in the MS.
2 So in the MS   He must mean gaol.
3 So in the MS. Burr did not use the more modern form, chemistry.

they were talking over their business I went to see the tomb of ———— who reigned———— It is a tumulus about the size and the form of that which you saw at Cincinnati. It is placed on a rocky eminence; has a fine view of the castle and cathedral of Upsala and of the *orangerie*[1], which, though about 300 paces nearer than the castle, appears like one of its offices. We were at the house of a respectable farmer. On coming in, brandy, beer, and *skolpen* on the table, of which I partook. At 1, brandy, beer, bread, cheese, another meal. About ½ p. 2 we were called into dinner. Brandy, bread and cheese again; a very good dinner. The first course, as in town, was salt fish, ham, sausages with * * * *[2] beans nicely dressed; then, I forget what; then *fillibonk*; then roast chicken and ham. The business was settled with the utmost good humor. Home at 5. At 6 Mr. Torner invited me to visit the library again; passed there two hours and took note, which you will see, of several books. Home at 8. Read till 11 in Coxe's volume on Sweden. Interrupted by an unexpected visitor; unexpected and unsolicited; ¾ rix dollar. *Couche* at 12. *Lev.* at ½ p. 7. My first business this morning was to examine into the state of finance to determine whether or not Gam. might *dejeune*[3]; found that he could not. Continued reading Coxe and finished the volume. He is more accurate and more intelligent than other of the travelers heretofore mentioned. Please to read him,

1 Orangery.
2 Undecipherable. The word looks like snip.
3 Breakfast. Should be the infinitive *déjeuner*.

for I have been over much of the same ground; seen
the same things and some of the same persons. A.
E. A. came in at 10 and says that he will call at 1
with his carriage and that we shall lodge to-night at
Sigtuna. Adam Afzelius came in and gave me a mem.
in his own handwriting and in English of the several
articles from Africa respecting which I was most desirous to be informed. Then Professor A. with London
papers to the 7th August; offers me, as does Adam,
all sorts of civilities. And now the clock strikes 1
and I am looking out for my eschort[1].

Oeusterly,[2] August 25, 1809. Left Upsala at ½
p. 3 with A. E. Afzelius, *Haradshöfding* of Upsala, in
his coach (phaeton) with post-horses. Rode through
this beautiful plain to Gamla Upsala, ½ miles Swedish; to Ugglesta Vall, 1 mile Swedish. The whole
distance 1½ miles Swedish, or 10 English miles. A
cabin for post-horses and *a cotè*[3] a very respectable-
looking farm-house for lodging, &c., for travelers. In
the garden plenty of currants and goosberries[4] with
which made free. This indulgence is everywhere as
with us. On to ———. Among the pictures are
several said to be of the first masters. Was particularly struck with one of Aurora, Comtesse de
Koningsmare, who frightened Charles XII.; wrapped
in a silk manteau; the bosom, the left foot, and right
knee (and something more) bare; in the open field,
before sunrise, alluding to her name[5] A fine land

---

1 So in the MS.
2 For Österby.
3 For à côté. At the side.
4 So in the MS.
5 Aurora.

scape. A portrait of Anne Bullein[1], *ux.* Henry VIII.;
beautiful and interesting. The chateau a large square
building; twenty-two steps to ascend to the first floor.
Paid ―――― to the old woman. The chateau suffer-
ing for want of repairs; passed 1½ hours here. The
plain narrows; little rocky hills, but always small
fertile spots highly cultivated, and excellent roads, not
a stone as big as an egg. The next stage is 2⅛
Swedish miles or 15 English miles. A peasant's
house; an air of comfort and plenty as in all. Got
horses presently and on to Oerubro; a very neat, comfortable inn; beds, maid, everything neat; were all
abed, but got up cheerfully and got us supper. A
wild fowl, sort of grouse, fish, salad, and *fillibonk.*
While supper was getting, we walked to the furnace.

26. *Couche* at 12. I preferred to lay[2] on the
sofa without undressing. The beds are too soft. At
6 came in the *flika*[3] with coffee. This is *caffè*[4] and not
breakfast, a little *brö.* or *skolpen* is served with it. At
8 walked over to the mines, two miles. (Note: Miles
are always English miles unless I distinguish by S.,
which means Swedish.) This is a most beautiful
village, and like that at Dannemora, is the property of
the owners of the mines. All the streets with rows of
trees; the houses neat. For an account of the mines
see a loose sheet in which the errors of writers of
travels are corrected. The principal director not speaking English or French, he put me in the hands of the

---

1 For Anne Boleyn, mother of Queen Elizabeth.
2 Generally so in the MS.
3 For *flicka.* Girl, serving-maid.
4 Probably for French *café*, coffee, though possibly meant for the Swedish *kaffe.*

sub-director, Mr. ———, who has been in England. The doctor, brother of my *compagnon de voy.*[1], devoted himself to my amusement. The mine is in constant danger of being overflowed by the lake; this has twice happened; the mine about 450 feet deep; from the orifice you see bottom. They insist that this lake cannot be drained, which I deny, and can demonstrate that it can. We talked much of it and they listened to me with great attention. They bore logs (for conduit pipes) by hand with an auger, having no such machine as we used at New York for the Manhattan works. The doctor invited us to breakfast. It was a sumptous feast of chicken, ham, fish, beans, salad, with dessert of preserved ———, a wild fruit which I found delicious; other fruits and bonbons. Excellent ale, which is drank with sugar and water in my own mode. The sub-director played on the peasant's violin for me. The instrument with seven strings and sixteen keys; only three strings are played on. *Polonaise,* the dance of the Norland peasants; it is the waltz with varieties. A dance something like our *contrè* dance[2], whence, probably, the English country dance originated; very pretty and danced with great grace. A young peasant now played. On first coming to the director's house had heard the *jungfru* doing a few notes; begged her to sing a song. Sang several. Marching and dancing in a circle; erect, toes out, *yeux baisseès*[3]. A fine Italian face. Danced with great grace and

---

1 For *compagnon de voyage.* Travelling companion.
2 Meant for contra-dance or country-dance. Burr's accent is wholly wrong, there being no accent over the e even in French, in which the word is *contre-danse.*
3 For *yeux baissés.* Eyes cast down.

agility. Joanna ———; hazel hair parted over the forehead and so just above the eyebrow over the ear, hanging in the neck; ends in *musa*. Gave ½ rix dollar. She took my hand gracefully, kissed it, bowed, and thanked me in the dialect of her country. Quitted with regret to see and hear the blasting, which is always at 12. The reverberations of the sound in this vast vault of solid rock are fine. The steam engine made in England. Makes no more noise than a house clock. The chateau; pictures, faun surprising two sleeping beauties; bear fight. The stables 350 feet long.

26. Sköklaster.[1] We left the chateau at dusk to seek our supper. It was good and abundant; only the hard bread, however. Having eaten nothing the whole day save two very small *skolpen* and some goosberries[2], I did great honor to the supper. *Je mangois comme gourmand*[3]. Beds were provided for us in the house of the *menagere*[4], a house twice as large as Richmond Hill[5]. The rooms spacious and well furnished. *La menagere* a smart, sensible woman, was all attention and civility. *Couche* at 11. Rose at 5. Our coffee was served before we were dressed. It is much the custom to take it in bed; a single cup; far better than the drams and too much with us. I never saw in London a dram taken before coffee. With this coffee nothing is eaten; it is always strong and well prepared; equally well in the peasant's cottage.

---

1 For Skokloster.
2 So in the MS.
3 I ate like a gourmand (*mangeais*).
4 For *ménagère*. Housekeeper.
5 His residence near New York.

We returned to the castle. The library is said to contain 10,000 or 11,000 volumes, chiefly ancient; many are ancient manuscripts. The chateau, the furniture, the books, arms, and manuscripts are all entailed and cannot be alienated. The proprietor, Count Brahe, seldom visits this place, having two or three others, and no person is permitted to visit the library except on permission of the *maitre d'hotel*[1], so that the contents are unknown. We visited also the chapel, which is built on the spot where stood the cloyster[2] whose ruins are still visible. The chapel is about the size of your churches; is handsome without being magnificent; the organist played several tunes for us. The vaulted ceilings give a fine effect to the sound. At 11 we went to seek our breakfast. It was sumptuous. *La menagere*, having learnt that I preferred the soft bread, had made some excellent and had in further compliment to my taste provided fish from the lake which is within 200 yards of the door. Ate as though I had not supped. At 12 embarked to return. A boat had been procured and awaited our orders. It is about three miles hence to the chateau of Rudbeck. The shores of the lake always *riant*[3] and picturesque. Walked to the post-house, ¾ mile and at 1 set off. At 2 P. M. a ferry at which I was obliged to be ferryman and hard work it was. Thence to the main road leading from Upsala to Stockholm, being about five miles. The road a little stony, being not much used

---

1 For *maitre d'hôtel*. Steward.
2 So in the MS.
3 Smiling, cheerful.

and having been injured by the rains and being in the
midst of harvest, the peasants had not yet found time
to repair. Nevertheless that part of the ride is [ren-
dered] beautiful by the varied landscape; lakes,
meadows, rich fields, rocks, hills, forests, all constantly
and charmingly blended.

[26. At Sigtuna.] But I forgot to tell you
that Sigtuna is the most ancient capital of Sweden,
centuries before Upsala. Tradition and what is called
history relates that it was taken, sacked, and burnt by
the Russians about 1,800 years ago. Very fine ruins
of three ancient temples; two of them, at least, are
fine; fifty or sixty feet in height of the turrets are
standing; several of the arches entire; trees growing
on the tops; rude architecture. Of the date and particular use of these temples even tradition is silent.
We visited the church; nothing very remarkable;
much of the material taken from the old temple, which
stands near and is within the same enclosure. On
many of the stones Runic inscriptions so defaced as to
be illegible. The priest asleep kept us waiting two
hours for the key. Goosberries and blackberries in the
churchyard; the latter tasteless. Left Sigtuna at 5,
having taken there a dish of coffee and a *skolpen*,
exactly our rusk. Everywhere, too, you get *wafen*[1];
our wafles[2], and made and eaten in the same way; an
iron cut in diamonds. Sigtuna is now an inconsiderable town of about 200 wooden (log) houses.

Skokloster, August 26, 1809. At 3 P. M. yes-

---

1 For *våfflor*. Waffles.
2 So in the MS.

terday the *Häradshofding* not appearing, went to his house; found all ready; took coffee with Madame. At ½ p. 3 set off; at 5 arrived at ————, where we proposed to traverse the lake. Took boat at the chateau of Rudbeck, formerly Wetterstedt's, who exchanged fortune for titles. An old woman rowed us over, about one mile English, and we walked about 1½ miles to the palace of Skokloster. From Rudbeck's gardener we had got currants, apples, and a melon. They were gathering vegetables for market. Cabbages of uncommon size for 5 sch. each; paid a few sch. for our fruit. Leaving Upsala in this direction you rise the hill on which is the castle and passing over the plain about 100 feet above the more extensive one to the north, you enter the park; fine, lofty pines, about ½ mile; then four miles to the river Sala, which you cross in a scow; three miles more to the post-house. Half a mile before reaching the ferry you are in sight of the lake and after crossing the river the road is parallel to the lake, distant perhaps half a mile. A gentle declivity. The country the whole way under high cultivation, interspersed with those little rocky hills and ledges which make it so picturesque. The chateau now Rudbeck's is very beautifully situated on a promontory extending one-quarter mile into the lake; a long avenue of ancient trees; the body of the house five windows each story, being two stories in front and three in rear. The wings, three windows each story; a plain house; many outbuildings give it the air of a village. Skokloster formerly a cloyster[1] of which the ruins are still visible. The present chateau was built by ———, about ——— years ago. The four turrets about thirty-two feet diameter each; octagon; elevated a full story above the body of the building and again a dome and crowned with a sort of armillary sphere[2]. The main building a square of ——— feet on each side and ——— feet in depth, containing an open court; below an arcade or open gallery all round; beautiful little brass cannon on each side; gallery in each story on the side of the court about twelve feet wide; on each pier, six in each story, the portrait large as life of some distinguished person, companion in arms or in council of Gustavus Adolphus. On the opposite side of the galleries, some historical paintings; all painted on the walls; mottoes in Latin, French, Italian, Swedish. The building is three lofty stories and an attic. The gobelins in many rooms are well preserved and very beautiful; great number of paintings; portraits, battles; historical pieces. Of Aurora Comtesse de Koningsmare, by no means equal to that at ———. Ebba Brahe when a girl and when old woman; General Wrangle in every possible way; a picture of him on horseback large as life, underneath which is inscribed a complete history of his life. An equestrian statue in the apartment in the chapel where is his monument. The attic story is principally a place of arms; ancient armour, spears, swords, bucklers, helmets, hung round with complete suits of armour, looking like so many

1 So in the MS.
2 A globe surrounded with circles.

men in armour. Guns, fusees, pistols, and firearms of all sorts, used 150 years ago; also wardrobes, boots, spurs, &c. Very few of the paintings of much value. The cabinet of ebony and ivory; and another principally ivory with a variety of jewels, trinkets, baubles. Four columns of two pillars each; each column with pedestal and capital of one solid piece of marble. These and many of the other things were brought from Prague when taken by Gustavus Adolphus. The columns, made in Italy, were in the palace at Prague; now supporting the arch of the vestibule. Bones found in Scania, believed to be human. A rib measured eight feet six inches, and is not entire; a vertebra of the spine, ——— inches in circumference; near the same place was found a sword, here also kept, of singular construction; about seven feet long and of a weight which could not be used by men of these days.

Stockholm, August 27, 1809. It was ½ p. 12 last night when we arrived. Being too late to go to my lodgings, *i. e.*, being averse to wake my good old Anna, went with A. E. A. to a tavern in Stor Nyga-tan[1]. They put us three *trappur upp*[2]; that is, in the fourth story. I was so weary and sleepy that I threw myself on the sofa without supper and without undressing and slept profoundly till near 6. Got up quite refreshed. Took one dish coffee at 7. To d'Aries's at 8. He and family *a la campagne*. Mr. Gransbom at home. Wrote Hosack to come to town

---

1 Swedish for Great New street.
2 Up three flights.

and sent messenger with the note. Find here cards
from Poppius and Daily ; met Governor Wetterstedt
and Baron M'Lean ; that is not his name, nor do I
know how to spell it. Hosack came in at 11 and at
same moment my messenger with the letter, having
missed him. Not a letter for him or me from any
quarter ! Two American vessels in this harbour.
The captain of one (Van Alen) *gr. am. de.* Ga.; *tous
amica*[1]. At 1 tea and *skolpen* for breakfast and *middag*[2].
Waited till ½ p. 5 for Hosack who did not come,
though his own appointment. Walked out to Calberg ;
out ; left card. To Eklin ; the ladies and the Hos-
chells ; the Doctor abroad. Took tea and *skolpen* and
off at 7. Home and *couche* at 11.

28. I did lay down at 11 and got asleep, having
slept very little the previous night. At 12 I waked
in a fever and found myself devoured by bugs. Got
up, lighted candle, and saw the bed alive. Being very
sleepy, went into the next room and lay on the sofa.
In a few minutes was attacked in a like manner. Got
up again, lighted candle in despair and read till daylight. Lay down on three chairs, but could not sleep,
so ordered breakfast. At 10 to wait on Governor
Wetterstedt and his son the Chancellor ; out; left
cards. To Baron Engerström's ; out; card. Baron
Munck ; at Haga ; card. To Hedboom's ; went
with his clerk to get guinea changed ; changed one
for 8 rix dollars 36 sch. Home at 2. Found note

---

1 Probably for *grand ami de* Gamp. *Tous amicaux.* (This form is, however, not good
French.) The captain of one (Van Alen) a great friend of Gamp. All friendly.
2 Swedish for midday.

from Hosack that the Americans, Captains Van Alen and Barry and Mr. Robinson, all from New York, had agreed to meet me at dinner at Moysabacke to dine together *al' americaine*[1] on beefsteak, fish, and potatoes; to rendezvous at his quarters; the savage had not the grace to rendezvous at mine. Being very desirous of seeing these compatriots, as they are all said to be very friendly, went and had our dinner. Barry did not come, being unexpectedly called off on some business about his ship. Van Alen is from Kinderhook and connected with the family of Van Ness; an intelligent, friendly young man; the other a fine, handsome, sprightly youth. Our dinner in a saloon in the garden and being elevated about 150 or 200 feet above the mass of the city, affords a most beautiful bird's-eye view of the town, harbour, and country. I had authorized Hosack to propose this dinner, as the Americans had expressed great desire to see me, but he managed so ill that they supposed they came to dine at my invitation and expense, of which I was ignorant till the moment of coming off; paid for the dinner exactly the proceeds of my guinea, 8 rix dollars 36 sch. Besides this, I did not treat them as my guests. Very little wine was called for and they must have thought it scurvy treatment. Alas, Mon. Gamp![2] Took tea at their quarters. Home at 7. Shall go early to bed to make up my long arrears of sleep. These Americans have been eight or nine months from the United States; of course nothing

---

1 For *à la américaine*. After the American fashion.
2 For Monsieur Gamp.

new. Note: Called this morning at General d'Helvig's; the ladies still *a la campagne* and all well.

29. I did go to bed at 10, promising myself a rich sleep. Lay two hours *vigil*[1]*;* that cursed one single dish of tea! Note: My bed had undergone a thorough ablution and there were no bugs or insects. Got up and attempted to light candle, but in vain; had flint and matches but only some shreds of punk which would not catch. Recollected a gun which I had had on my late journey; filled the pan with powder and was just going to flash it when it occurred that though I had not loaded it someone else might; tried and found in it a very heavy charge! What a fine alarm it would have made if I had fired! Then poured out some powder on a piece of paper, put the shreds of punk with it and after fifty essays succeeded in firing the powder; but it being dark, had put more powder than intended; my shirt caught fire, the papers on my table caught fire, burnt my fingers to a blister (the left hand, fortunately); it seemed like a general conflagration. Succeeded, however, in lighting my candle and passed the night till 5 this morning in smoking, reading, and writing this. " *Essai sur le Caractere, les Moeurs et l'esprit des Femmes*"[2]. Par M. Thomas; second edition, Paris: 1772; small octavo, 215 pages. Well written; much historical information; many books, of which I had not heard, are quoted. He meant to be liberal and [a] friend to

---

1 This word, which has been used several times, is a Latin adjective meaning wakeful.
2 " Essay on the Character, the Morals (or Manners), and the Mind of the Women.

the sex, but like all I have read, has set out wrong; has not seen the source of the evil, though the evils are acknowledged, and of course has not found the remedy; this will remain for Gamp. "*Tableau Litteraire de la France pendant le 18me. siecle.*" *Sujet proposè en 1806 par la Classe de la langue et de la litterature*[1]. Paris: 1807. Octavo; 91 pages; close printed; anon. This I presume to be a sort of prize piece. It is well written; his distinctions are pretty good but his eulogies extravagant. "*Le Voyageur Fataliste*"; *comedie en trois actes en vèrs*[2]; *par* Armand Char lemagne; Paris: 1806. I had foresworn French comedies and hate comedy in verse; this, though long, was not found tiresome. "*Rapprochement des Arbres*"[3]. Duodecimo, about 150 pages. Paris: 1807; *par* ———— Where have I laid that book? Will find it to-morrow and give you the author's name. It is a new discovery by which you give to any tree the sap and nourishment of another or of some branch of another, and by this means you may *ehange* and improve the *colour*, size, and flavour of any fruit. The results are curious and useful; pray try it. You see, Madame, I have not been idle; now allow me to attempt sleeping.

29. P. M. Slept very well till 10 when Mr. D. came in *a la souedoise*[4] on some very urgent message, which I answered only by a round of curses. How-

---

1 "Literary Picture of France During the Eighteenth Century." A Subject Proposed (*proposé*) by the Class in Language and Literature [of the French Academy].
2 "The Fatalistic Traveler." A comedy in verse in three acts.
3 "The Bringing Together (Junction) of Trees."
4 For *à la suédoise*. After the Swedish fashion.

ever, I was waked and got up. Took breakfast at 12.
Feuilliéd[1] (rummaged) in the library for two or three
hours (there is an arrival of new books from Paris);
then walked out with Gransbom to try the market for
guineas; changed four at 8 rix dollars 36 sch. each.
Waited an hour for Barth without success. Called at
the post-office; no letters. No doubt my letters are
stopped by the British government! 'Tis impossible
that every human being can have forgotten me for four
months. For my female friends I would swear, but
what remedy. *Me voici*[2]. Post I will go off to Ham
burg or Memel. As soon as I can find Barth will
hunt for passages to ———— everywhere and then
determine. Called at the lodgings of Bar. Ulf-
spasre, for whom I had a letter from London and
just now determined to deliver it; has left town.
Home at 6. On the way called to see Captain Van
Alen. *Mjolk* and *brö.* for *middag* and *afton*[3]. Read an
hour or two in *"L'Itineraire de l'Allemagne"*[4]; Paris ·
1807. You see I am preparing! Read also a
treatise (French) on the authority of parents, *i. e.*,
fathers, for women are not in question. Cannot
now lay hand on it to give you the title, but will find
it. The subject was proposed by the Institut
National and this book gained the approbation and
the prize. In my opinion no way flattering to the
genius of the nation. There is, indeed, a good deal
of historical fact, but much declamation and flourish.

1 Another hybrid verb, and badly formed, from French *feuilleter*, to turn over the leaves of
a book.
2 Here I am.
3 Swedish. Evening.
4 " Itinerary of Germany.

30. *Couche* at 12. Rose at ½ p. 5. Yesterday an officer (*vieux militaire*)[1] called to consult me about seeking employment in the United States, which I flatly discouraged. He wishing a further conversation, appointed 9 this morning. At 8 called on Baron d'Albedhÿll; out; left card. On Governor Wetterstedt, whom found dressing. On Doctor Gahn; engaged to dine with him to-day at Eklin. Home before 9 to meet the Swedish officer. On opening my door found him seated, though I had the key in my pocket, at which I made great eyes. He apologized. Told him that Hosack had served in the United States army and knew more about the subject of his enquiry; gave him the address of Hosack and a line of introduction. At 10 to Breda's to pay my respects to the picture; found it in good order and looking, alas, I fear, very different from the original[2]. Found Barth's lodgings and left card. To Baron Munck's; still at Haga; card. To Professor Arnt's; that, however, was yesterday; at Haga; left card. To Wennerquiest's, but I got to the door, altered my mind. Met in the street *la belle* Mari, of Lil. Nygatan[3]; "*Naen*[4]." Home at 1 and found Barth's card. He had already returned my visit and left word that he would call again to-morrow morning. Walked to Eklin; found, as always, a good dinner and good wine; we were *en famille*. Home at 7 to meet A. E. Afzelius, who left town on Sunday and promised to

---

1 An old soldier.
2 The reference is to the picture of his daughter Theodosia.
3 For Lilla Nygatan. Little New Street—a street not far from Burr's Stockholm residence.
4 Marie said "No." The Swedes say *nej* or in popular slang *na*. Perhaps Marie uttered the German negative *nein*, which Burr spelled phonetically.

call on me this evening, but he has not come (8 P. M.)

31. After quitting you last evening at 8 I *foeul-lièd*[1] in the *bibliotheque*[2] for occupation for the night and brought to my room a new novel and a recent voyage of discovery to the S. Seas, having determined for manifest reasons to read till 2. *"Hotel Garni"*[3], *par* Madame Sur; two volumes, small octavo; about 300 pages each; Paris: 1800; which I read through. It is made up of digressions; stuffed with trite remarks; no novelty in the incidents; in short, a trifling thing. *Couche* at 2. *Lev.* at 6. At 9 came Barth. His plans are altered. He goes to England, which I regret, for I had a secret intention of going with him to Königsberg. I commissioned him to procure me information of vessels going to Wismar. Afzelius not having come last evening as was promised, went to his lodgings; could hear nothing. To the post office! nothing! Strolled about for an hour or two without object. Home at 12. Baron d'Albedÿhll came in and sat an hour. Read in *"Le Voyage aux Mers Australes"*[4]

Stockholm, September 1, 1809. *Couche* at 12. *Lev.* at 6. At 8 came in Barth. Brought list of four vessels for Wismar and gave me the name of a ship broker whom he had engaged to attend to my orders. *Sor.* at 11 with Gransbom. To lodgings of Afzelius; not arrived. To Hedboom's; Mr. ———, his book keeper, returned; gave him the list of the four

---

1 See Glossary under *feuillièd.*
2 For *bibliothèque* Library.
3 For " *Hôtel Garni.*" " Furnished House "
4 " Voyage to the Southern Seas."

Wismar vessels and desired him to go on board, enquire price, see accommodations, &c. He engaged most cheerfully to get the information and make his report to-morrow morning. If he should be punctual he is not *Svenska!*[1] *Rencontre.* Swindled out of 1 dollar *pour rien*[2]. Met Baron Munck's *dom.;* learned that Madame had lain in of a dead child. I do most sincerely sympathize with that amiable [pair]; they have been twelve or fifteen years married and no child; so many fond hopes have been raised on this prospect! Home at 1. Found young Robertson or Robinson of New York waiting to see me. It is an amiable, intelligent, well-behaved young man. Wrote by Barth to William Graves, enclosed duplicate of my letter of July 31st and of the letter to Swartwout introducing Barth to Graves; carried my letter to Barth's lodgings and there left it, he being out. Yesterday gave him my map of Great Britain. At 6 to Popplius's. Took tea *faible*[3] with Madame at 7. Walked till dark. Met Bergström, who invited me to a *bal*; refused. Home and read in my "*Voyage aux Mers Australes*" till 12.

2. *Couche* at ½ p. 12. Rose at 7; at 10 had finished "*Le Voyage de Decouverts aux Terres Australes* in 1800, 1801, 1802, 1803, 1804"; *fait par ordre de l'Empereur; redigè par* M. F. Peron; *tom. 1me.*[4]; quarto; 500 pages; Paris: 1807. Have been amused,

---

1 For *svensk.* Swedish.
2 A rencounter. Swindled out of 1 dollar for nothing.
3 Weak tea.
4 "Voyage of Discovery to the Southern Lands in 1800," etc. Made by order of the Emperor. Edited by M. F. Peron. Volume I. (Should be *tome premier*).

particularly with his account of New South Wales. I mean the English settlements at Port Jackson, Botany Bay, &c. This work will probably consist of many volumes, of which only the first has reached me. Sent Anna to hunt up *la Han*[1] See June 10. It is no easy matter, *ma Min.*[2], to determine how to dispose of myself. Why stay here? To be sure I am unmolested and live at no great expense, but *tem. fug.*[3] and nothing done. When I came here it was with intent to stay till answers should be received to my letters written to the United States. The moment of leaving London, and ———. Just there it was announced to me that a lady in the library wished to speak to me. " What sort of lady ?" " Young and beautiful." In truth, she is very pretty ; not at all a Swedish face ; an aquiline nose, seems a little turned ; blue eyes, very fair, very black hair and eyebrows ; speaking *svenska*[4] and a little French. The pretence (perhaps the real object) of the visit to inquire about certain friends in England and the means of getting there. On my remarking that she could not from her appearance be Swedish, she said she was born in Petersburg, and left me her address. A sad interruption this to the calculations I was about to make ! The summary is that I am resolved to go without knowing exactly why or where. Mr. ———, as was predicted, has not brought me the report of vessels. The facility of getting to a particular place may of itself determine

---

1 For *la Hanovrienne.*
2 Probably for *ma Minerve.* My Minerva.
3 For *tempus fugit.* Latin. Time flies.
4 Swedish.

my course. To be sure the *embarras*[1] of traveling on the Continent is very great, but I am in utter despair of receiving letters through England. Evening: I have been to Hedboom's to see the book-keeper; out, and nothing done. Went on to see *la Russe*[2]; found her *toilette* very prettily made and she engaged on a piece of embroidery; a most convenient visit; too much to write. Home at 7. Have been rummaging in the library and have brought into my room "*La Dot de Gazette*"; a *roman*[3] and Montesquieu's " Grandeur and Decline of the Roman Empire."

3. Couche at 1. Rose at 9. Of this time, however, lay two or three hours without sleeping, having taken some very weak tea in the evening, having dined to-day and yesterday on *brö och wattn*[4]; two days preceding on *mjolk koka*. Went this morning before breakfast with Mr. Gransbom as interpreter to hunt vessels. Went on board several from Wismar and that quarter. Not one would take a passenger by reason, they say, of the great difficulties to which it exposes the ship. The French, they say, are very strict and very suspicious and suffer no passenger to land till after great inquiry. I do not believe all this. Read last evening and this morning about 100 pages in Montesquieu and finished "*La Dot de Gazette.*" It is a small octavo, 237 pages, Paris: 1803. Anonymous but said to be written by a lady. It is a pretty little tale. Read also "*Le Conteur ou Les Deux Post*"[5]; *trois actes*;

---

1 The embarrassment.
2 The Russian lady.
3 " Gazette's Dowry "; a romance.
4 For *brod och vatten.* Swedish. Bread and water.
5 " The Story-teller, or The Two Posts " (*Postes*).

prose; par L. B. Picard; Paris: *an. VIII*; very trifling, but as a trifle, tolerable. Walked out 5.
Swindled out of another dollar *pour rien absolument.*
* * * * with *2 avants; 1, 15; l'aut 22;* 1½ d.[1] *Bru.
oeb wattn pr. din. Ost soc.-watn. koka brü fer afton*[2].
At 6 young Robertson came in. He also had undertaken to hunt passages for Calserona and Wismar and
came to report that there were many small sloops for
Calserona but too small and dirty to be thought of.
To-morrow I will set Hosack at work. Only think,
I have not seen him since Monday last, seven days!
Called this afternoon on Baron d'Albedÿhll to arrange
about a trip to Drottningholm. He objects to my
mode of traveling and is to look out for other and
more rapid means. And now (8 P. M.) I am going to
read any nonsense. You perceive that A. E. Afzelius
has not returned. I much fear that he has gone some
other route to Upsala, which would be a very great
disappointment to me, for I have notes of a hun
dred questions to ask him.

6. It is three days since I have written you.
What is on t'other side this leaf was probably intended
for Sunday the 3d. On Monday went to hunt vessels.
Baron Wetterstedt made a friendly visit. Dinner,
wattn och bru. Tea *l'apresmidi*[3] which, as usual, kept
me awake all night. The bank will give out no more
silver or gold. With difficulty I got the value of 2

---

1 For *Pour rien absolument.* * * * * with *deux aventures. L'une [âgée de]* 15 [*ans*]; *l'autre [de]* 22; 1½ dollars. For absolutely nothing. (Undecipherable word) with two adventures; the one aged 15 and the other 22.
2 For *bröd och vatten pour dîner !. ost, sockervatten, kaka, bröd for afton [måltid].* Bread and water for dinner; cheese, sugar-water, cake [perhaps milk-cake], bread for supper.
3 For *l'après-midi.* Afternoon.

dollars. Hosack called in the afternoon with invitation from Captain Barry to dine with him on board his ship to-morrow. This morning, too, (Monday), I had a visit, unexpected; unsolicited; not unwelcome; 1 rix dollar. Tuesday. Got up late, and, for reasons unknown, in very bad order. Heated, nerves tremor; no appetite for breakfast, which is unusual. Went abroad, however, at 11. Called on Baron Engerström; out. On Mr. Brooks. At 2 to Captain Van Alen's quarters to go with him to Barry's. There were five Americans and three Englishmen. About 5 P. M. came in Major Nordforss *et ux.* and M'lle (*Fruka*[1] being noble) ———; both handsome; the latter an air of delicacy, &c.; the former very lively and speaking French and Spanish. After coffee went with them to a house and garden of their relation about a mile lower down. The garden is extremely picturesque and being on that lofty ridge which bounds the harbour on the right, elevated about 150 feet above the water, affords as fine a view as Morsebaka. Gathered fruits; much romping and coquetry. Went home with Madame N. and engaged to see her at 12 to-morrow. Home at 8. Mr. Dorrell, one of the Englishmen, engages me to dine with him to-morrow. On getting home found all my maladies exceedingly increased. A very quick pulse, agitation of nerves, and burning hot, though the weather is quite cold, and I had drunk very little wine. Withal, a sort of exaltation of *tête*[2], which altogether distressed me exceed-

---

1 For Swedish *Fröken*. Lady. Formerly this title was applied to an unmarried lady of noble birth. In later times it is synonymous with English Miss or German *Fraulein*.
2 The head.

ingly; pains in every bone. The family of d'Aries are in the country. Mr. Gransbom out. No means of explanation with old Anna. Not a lime, or lemon, or anything else to be had at this hour. Ordered hot water and *Sw. trinka'*, of which with sugar drank copiously, but no relief; though lay in bed, exceedingly restless. Took thirteen drops of laudanum, the greatest dose I ever took; and finding sleep quite out of the question, got up, dressed, and read a long, dull *comedie*, "*Le Jaloux*"², 120 pages, close print. About 2 A. M. a little relieved. Went to bed; slept about four hours and got up well. There prevails in this city a malignant fever, which frequently has carried off persons in two or three days. Having been often in the quarter most infected with this disease, no doubt I had caught it, and I have given you this detail to show how very slightly any such disease can affect me. I disclosed to no one that I was sick. A sick man is a very contemptible animal. Owing to very temperate habits, my constitution affords no pabulum to such diseases.

6. Rose at 7. At 10 to d'Albedÿhll's; out. To General d'Helvig's; out. At 12 to Madame Nordforss. Staid an hour. *Ne soutint la 2me Vu.*³; engaged to go with her to the play to-morrow evening. At 2 to Hosack's to get him to show me to Worrell's, who is at lodgings. We were at table five Americans, two English, and five Swedish, among the

---

1 For *svagdricka.* Small or weak beer.
2 " The Jealous Man."
3 Probably for [*elle*] *ne soutint* [*pas*] *la deuxième vue.* She didn't appear so well on a second view.

latter a merchant from Nordkeeping[1] of prepossessing appearance; a brother of Bergström, also merchant; a Finland merchant. Came off at ½ p. 5, the guests appearing disposed to drink *al 'angloise*. Was engaged to tea with Madame Daily, but did not go, being out of order. Passed the evening in reading and project ing my intended journey. Called on Baron Enger- ström to-day. He offered me letters to Prussia, where he had resided as minister.

7. *Couche* at 1. Rose at 6. At ½ p. 8 to Baron d'Albedÿhll's; out. To Madame Daily's, who engaged me to dine to-day *en fam.* precisely at 2. On my way to Hosack *renc. 17. Pas ma.;* 1 r. d.[2] To Hosack. Mr. Robertson has found a vessel bound to Pillau. Home at 1. Passed ½ hour reflecting on the real value of a dollar. To Madame D.'s at 2. Mr. not come in and no preparations for dinner. It seems he had invited two guests, one at 3; the other ½ p. 3. The first came punctually at 3. At ½ p. 3 sat down to dinner. The other guest, purser of a man-of-war, came at 4. They are a couple of pleasant, well-disposed Englishmen. Off at 6. To Madame Nordforss. *Y: La fruk'n*[3] and Captain Barry. To the *com'e*[4]. We were in the amphitheatre, which is the rear part of what you would call the pit, raised and railed; a very commodious place indeed. Sat next a well-dressed man wearing some badge of nobility, who claimed my acquaintance. Was very much amused,

---

1 For Norrkopin ?
2 For *rencontre* [*gigée de*] *17. Pas mauvaise* or *mal ;* 1 rix dollar. A rencounter. Age 17. Not bad ; 1 rix dollar.
3 For *la fröken.* French and Swedish. The lady previously mentioned.
4 For *comédic.* Comedy.

both with the farce and comedy, though all pantomime to me. The farce is first acted. M'lle Vascalia sings well and has a good form; moves with grace and is thought handsome. A little *paysanne*[1], lately come on the stage, pleased me much. The performance closed about 10. Home with Madame, *sans entrer*[2] and then *chez moi.*

8. *Couche* at 12. Rose at 6. At 9 to Baron d'Albedÿhll; out. I want to see him to project our tour to Drottningholm. To Helvig's; no one at home. To Captain Van Alen's; he, Robinson, and Hosack live together. Home at 1. Much heated, the day being warm. Threw off my coat and sat down near the window to read "*Tableaux de la Nature*"[3]; two volumes by A. d'Humboldt. One of the upper sashes of my window is always open. Got much engaged with my book till about 3 found myself extremely uneasy with pains in my left shoulder and breast. Attempted to rise, but unable till after various efforts and much pain. Whilst I had been sitting under the window the weather had changed and become quite cool, and the wind was on my side of the house. Hot water, beer, and sugar, with the application of flannel perfectly relieved me before morning. Take care that you don't commit such a folly !

Drottningholm, September 9, 1809. Rose at 8 perfectly relieved of my rheum. Resolved to go to

---

1 Peasant woman or girl.
2 Without going in.
3 " Pictures from Nature."

Drottningholm.   Sent my little *paquet*[1] by Mr. d'A.,
who goes with his family.   Called to take leave of
Madame Daily who leaves town to-morrow for Goth
enburg, and at 2 marched off with my umbrella, my
pipe and tobacco (having taken about ½ pint of rice
and milk for dinner).   Arrived at ½ p. 5 and stopped
at a tavern near General d'Helvig's to get a messenger
to take the note, *q. v.*   Could not make myself
understood.   Hearing company in an adjacent room,
opened the door and asked if any gentleman present
could speak French.   Several offered and by the
means of one, got a messenger and gave instructions.
This mode of getting an interpreter could not be
practiced in England, but might in Scotland.   My
messenger returned in a few minutes with verbal
answer, that General d'Helvig and *Fruken* Imhoff[2]
were just going to take a ride on horseback and would
call at the tavern door and see me.   I was glad of the
occasion to see M'lle on horseback.   They came
immediately.   M'lle *à cheval en cav.*[3] sat gracefully and
looked very, very well.   They spoke of Madame
d'Helvig as being extremely weak but no longer in
danger.   We talked two or three minutes ; at parting
the General said he hoped Madame would very soon
be well enough to receive her friends !   This was a
shower-bath !   You will recollect that I had walked
eight miles ; that I was then within 200 yards of the
house of General H., which *house* consists of two
buildings quite detached from each other ; in the one

1   Bundle.
2   For *Fröken* Imhoff.   Lady Imhoff.
3   For *à cheval en cavalier.*   On horseback trooper fashion.

are bedrooms, &c.; in the other, the hall, dining room, &c.; company is always received in this last. It is unnecessary to remind you that Mr. H. has two sisters, Mary Ann and Louisa. It is my custom after walking immediately to change my clothes ; but my clothes were at Mr. d'A.'s, six miles off and I had sat half an hour in the tavern ; found stiffness and pain in my hips and loins, otherwise should have gone instantly to Stockholm again ; but went to the bath ; could not have warm water till 8 to-morrow morning. Went on to d'A.'s ; took tea and afterwards supper. In much pain, which aided the reflections of how that pain was acquired, *viz.*, the walk, and what was the walk for? to see my friends, &c. And thus is dissolved all intercourse with a family which I have seen with unusual interest. Mary Ann and Louisa are in different ways very superior women. They would merit distinction in any country ; of the former I have spoken to you much and could have said more, much more. The latter I saw but once ; the day of which I gave you an account (M. A.[1] cannot be to blame) ; at another time you shall have a detailed picture of both. God bless them ! To-morrow, immediately after breakfast, I am off, if able to walk. If not, I shall wait at the lakeside till some boat shall pass.

Stockholm, September 10, 1809. *Couche* at 11 Rose at 7. Could scarcely get out of bed. To the bath at 8 ; staid in ¾ hour and found myself very much relieved. Breakfast at d'A.'s. While at breakfast the beautiful little *dom.* of H. called with a note

---

[1] For Mary Ann.

which he said was from *Fruken* Imhoff. It was an invitation to dine, but not exactly in ordinary terms. I replied that in case of passing the day in Drottning-holm, which, however, was not intended, I was engaged but that I would call before dinner. I was not, in fact, engaged to dine. Went at 12. M. A.[1] received me; considers me in some sort her property; after ½ hour came L.[2] We walked in the garden. They culled fruits for me. Many civil messages from Madame, who is *alitè*[3] (I suppose a *fausse couche*[4]). Announced my determination to leave Sweden, which was approved with politeness and something more. Offered letters to their German friends; urged much my dining, which refused obstinately. Came off at 2. On my way to H.'s called to see my amiable friend Mr. de C., who walked with me through the Kongl. Jurgardn[5] as far as the Palace. To dinner with the d'Aries. Coffee with Madame de C. and then walked home, with stopping to smoke a pipe by the way according to custom. On my arrival at home at ½ p. 6, I learn with surprise that all the ports on the south side the Baltic from Stralsund inclusive west are shut against Sweden. Another interruption to my plans, for it was my project to land at Wismar and thence to Hamburg.

11. Last evening by way of *delassment*[6] took tea. It is very usual here to put brandy in the tea; a sort of tea toddy. It occurred to me that this expedient

---

1 For Mary Ann.
2 For Louisa.
3 For *alité*. Bed-ridden.
4 A miscarriage.
5 For Kongliga Djurgården.
6 For *délassement*. Relaxation.

might prevent its effect on the nerves; so sent out Anna to buy some French brandy, an article to be had only at the apothecary's. I drank my tea, putting in each cup a tablespoonful of brandy. *Couche* at 11. Presently found I should not sleep. Got up, lighted my candle, dressed, took thirteen drops of laudanum and fell to reading; at 3 went to bed again, but no sleep; lay till past 6; then got about two hours' sleep and rose at 8. To Hosack's at 10. Mr. Robinson says that he finds that there is a daily passage boat between Helsingborg in Sweden and Helsingor on the opposite coast in Denmark, distance across being only two or three leagues; that with a Swedish passport there is no difficulty; so at once I resolved to take this route. Home at 1. At 4, rice, which Anna made very good with raisins and plums; then to Robinson's again. He persists in the information given this morning. Thence to Hedboom's to get him to enclose my letters to England, being convinced that my former ones have been stopped. Wrote at Hedboom's to Achaud and to Graves, desiring them to forward my letters under cover to William Gibson, merchant, Göteborg, "*at which place I should be to receive them.*" Home at 6. Read as usual. A wet, chilly day, like our N. E. storms.

12. *Couche* at ½ p. 10. Rose at 8. At 12 to Madame Daily's; she has actually left town. To Baron Engerström's; out; he will be in at 2. To Breda's to see your picture and to talk to him. He is one of the most sensible, well-bred men I meet; his

son, too, only 21, is a youth of extraordinary talents and amiable disposition. At 2 to Engerström's again ; either out or not visible ; am to call at ½ p. 9 to-morrow morning. Home ½ p. 2. A drizzly rain, chilly wind, and to console us they say that two or three weeks of such weather is usual about this season. Rice at 4.

Gothenburg, October 7, 1809. Slept last evening at———, where we arrived at 11, the family all in bed. The maid got up, made us fire, got an excellent supper, and clean beds, and all with a cheerfulness which gave value to our supplies. Our last coachman was again a girl ; a very pretty girl of about 16. She drove us most rapidly, and with boldness and skill. Sam himself could not have done better ; nor here so well, for it was very dark. She returned immediately, having a horse to lead. We had ordered horses at 5 this morning. At 6 we set off, and got here (fourteen miles) at ½ p. 8. Drove to the post-house. Not a room or bed to be had ; not even a place to sit down and take breakfast. We were cold and hungry, and were till 10 cruising about town before we could get admission into a house. We engaged a room, *i. e.*, one corner of it, for it was a public room, for two hours, with promise of breakfast. We ate so enormously that we were charged 1½ rix dollars each for our breakfast, being just three times the usual price. Wrote notes to Lord Nordenschold[1] and young Damon, requesting aid to procure lodgings, as we must

---

1 One of several unsuccessful attempts to spell Nordenskjold.

otherwise go into the street at 12. Neither of them came; but my indefatigable companion found two decent rooms at 27 Torg Gatan[1], two *trappar upp*[2]! at 10½ rix dollars per week, more than double the price of Stockholm. This place is just now very full of strangers, particularly English. There were more than twenty of them in and out of the room while we were breakfasting, God-damning everything that was not exactly as in England. Got settled in our quarters by 1 o'clock, and sent my letters to the Governor and to others, with a card in each, *a la mode soedoise*[3], a mode which I approve. Now, I engage that neither of the three takes the least notice of the letter or card. Sent my card also to the Lieutenant N. Called at Edin's, where I lodged on my arrival here from England in May, to see the family. *La helle* M. is much altered. Very thin and *eruption a la figure*[4] Wrote to Captain Van Alen and to Gransbom *q. v.* by the mail. Took tea at 7, having dined at our enormous breakfast. Our hostess speaks English, being of an English mother. Is neat, active, obliging. In the after noon walked with Lüning to the port, about two English miles. Missed the way and walked double the distance. Laughed at Luning's distress at passing through some ill-looking alleys and streets. Sent card this evening, with my address, to General Consul Gram, who is still here. You may recollect that I saw him about ten days ago, and that he undertook to pro-

---

1 Market Street.
2 Two flights up, *i. e.*, third story.
3 After the Swedish fashion.
4 For *éruption à la figure*. The face broken out.

cure passports for me from the Danish government, to be sent to Helsingborg, so that I might not be detained there.

8, though I think it must be the 9th of October. Will ask some learned man in the course of the day. *Couche* at ½ p. 11. Rose at 8. Mr. Gogle, of Frankfort, a very pleasant, well-bred young man, lodges on the same floor with us ; claims my acquaintance, and is extremely obliging. *Sor.* at 10 to find out Daily. Got his address. Wrote notes to Dr. Shulzen, to Gibson, and to Damm, inquiring for letters. *Verbal* answers that they have none. Our landlord is a bookbinder. Gave him all Bentham's small works and "*Panoptique*"[1] to bind. They had suffered, and were in danger of being *abimed*[2] Yesterday opened your picture. It is in perfect order. Lüning's contrivance had secured it completely from the dust. Since opening it at [Stockholm] I have carried it the whole way (two hundred miles) on my lap. Indeed, Madame, you *gènèd*[3] me not a little. You are now hung up in my room, so that I can talk with you. *Poin. de afton*[4]. Walked to the harbour at 4. Met Daily, and also the captain with whom I came from Harwich. He seemed quite alarmed, and looked about, the few minutes I detained him, to make some inquiries, as if he was afraid of being seen. He has

---

1 The "*Panoptique*" or "Panopticon" was one of Bentham's works, published in 1791, perhaps better known as The Inspection House. It was a plan of making convicts useful.
2 Another hybrid perfect participle made from the French verb *abimer*, to ruin.
3 A hybrid verb which we have already met, meaning bothered.
4 Probably for *poindre de afton*. The evening begins to break. The French might say *La nuit commence à poindre*, although this word is ordinarily used with reference to the dawn. The reader will mark that it is now October, and the night sets in very early.

probably learned how dangerous, &c. The streets of the lower town full of drunken English sailors. Home at 6. Tea. Lüning came in at 7. His whole time seems to be employed in my concerns. He discovers my wants, and, without saying a word to me, makes them his own business. This afternoon he has procured me a traveling companion; a German gentleman, who speaks the Swedish, going to Copenhagen, and to set off on Tuesday, but *will wait a day or two for me* if requisite! He (Luning) has also found Dutch ducats, for which I can exchange the small sum of Swedish paper I have on hand. On our arrival our passports were sent to the police for inspection as the law requires. They were brought back this morning. The bearer demanded 36 sch. each for his trouble. Apropos of passports: On our way from Stockholm at a town a sentinel, rather harsh looking, stopped us and demanded if we had passports. "Yes, sir," says Lüning, and presenting a silver *plote*[1], the face of the sentinel relaxed into complacency. He thanked us with earnestness, and wished us a pleasant journey. At another time we were brought to by a custom-house officer. In every town they have a right to search your baggage for contraband goods. L., who is never at a loss, presented a 12 sch. bill, which satisfied the officer that we had nothing unlawful. Nordenshjöld and Damm called this afternoon; but from the gentleman to whom I sent letters not a word. N.

---

1 For Swedish *plåt*, pronounced plote. A very thin old Swedish coin. One Swedish dictionary says: "Imaginary money nearly of 20 pence English," whatever that may mean.

and D. something cooler. There is something in the atmosphere which I have not yet discovered, and probably never shall.

Göteborg (which is the Swedish spelling), October 10, 1809. *Couche* at ½ p. 10. Rose at 6. At 10 called on Madame Daily. She anticipated the object of my visit (so far, I mean, as regards business), by offering her services to take anything, parcels or letters, for me to England. This is just what I wished, finding that I must still disencumber myself of papers and small articles. On her fidelity and punctuality I can rely. Sat an hour. Home and went to overhauling papers and baggage to see what I could spare. A very embarrassing business. I can never decide what to leave and what to take. If you were here—ah, why are you not?—you would settle all this in a single minute, and all would be right. But I take up a paper and hold it, turning and twisting it, for 10 minutes, and am still undecided. Already I have had occasion to regret the want of a paper which is among those sent off by Barry. This makes me still more cautious and indecisive. If there were an opportunity direct to the United States, I should be at no loss. But there is no such thing, nor can I find any mode of communication to you but through England; a mode to which, you know, I have very serious objections. At 1 P. M. walked to the harbour to hunt up the Americans who are here. Saw none of them, but got the names of six captains, not one of my acquaintance. Left my address for them at the tavern which is their rendezvous, and at the same place consoled myself with bread and cheese, and Swedish ale, 16 sch. which counts for *afton*[1]. Home at ½ p. 2 and went to work again at my papers, but made no progress. Lüning came in at 5, having been running about, as usual, for me. He walked to see Lehman, a Bremener, who is to be my *comp. de voyage*[2]. It won't do. He has a lady in charge, and will travel in a way which will not suit me. He goes at 4 to-morrow morning. Will forward a letter for me to Hauterive. In our walk we met a man of Lüning's acquaintance whose name is Bollman ; a circumstance I did not learn till we got home. Will see him again to inquire. L. and I agreed to treat ourselves to a supper of oysters and Rhenish wine. Sent out for both. Two bottles of wine cost 3 dollars. About a peck of oysters, 3 dollars; rather an extravagant meal. After all was served, L., who had taken all the trouble, and affected to be very keen, acknowledged that he was unwell ; could neither eat nor drink, and must go to bed, which he did at 7. So you see all his zeal for the supper was to gratify me. I made him drink a bottle of warm *sangaree*, made of our wine. Made my supper. The oysters are very small, generally of a greenish colour, and always a strong coppery taste ; just like the English. I tried them roasted and raw, but could only get down nine. Of the wine I drank two-thirds of a bottle. Wrote

---

1 For *aftonmåltid.* Supper.
2 For *compagnon de voyage.* Traveling companion.

my letter to Hauterive, enclosing a copy of that which I wrote him from Stockholm, and at ½ p. 10 took it to Lehman's, but all were abed. Knocked; no answer, and so came off. Must be up at 4 to secure the conveyance of it.

11. *Couche* at 12. Rose at 4. Made my own fire. Waked up the boy (a beautiful lad of 13, son of the landlady) and sent him with the letter. He found all asleep and no signs of traveling. At 5 he went again; still asleep. At 7 found a servant, who said that his master never got up till 9. At 9 sent him, and the letter was delivered. Walked with Lüning, who is quite well this morning, to Todd's (the tavern at the harbour) to see the Americans; not one there. Walked on to the lower harbour, about three miles, and home. Called on Lehman on returning; he does not go till to-morrow. Met in the street Mr. Gibson, who introduced himself to me and said he had no letters. Home at 12. Dr. Schulzen had called in my absence. At 1 went again to Todd's; not one of the captains to be seen. Again took *brö* and *oust*[1] with the addition of *smoeur*[2] and ale; 24 sch. Home at ½ p. 2. A letter, a letter, a letter! At a moment when I had given up all expectation and even all hope! At 5 P. M. this same Tuesday, October 11th, came in a tall, meagre, well-dressed man and asked if I were A. B. "Yes." He handed me a letter superscribed in your handwriting. It is your letter of 1st and 2d August. I could have kissed the

---

1 For Swedish *ost*. Cheese.
2 For Swedish *smör*. Butter.

fellow! After reading it a few times, I went to return the visit of Dr. Schulzen, whom found at home. A modest man, of good sense, and a countenance of goodness. Home at 6. Tea. Lüning not come in, and now, at 10 o'clock, I have done nothing but write this. Your letter has discomposed my projects a little; but I shall persist in them, as you shall see[1].

Helsingborg, October 21, 1809. Supped again last night with the beautiful family of Barque *c. d. Pres. des tribunaux soes. en Pomerania*[2]. Drank *tro. de vin*, seeing that I had dined with the Governor; was, in consequence, obliged to sit up till 3, smoking, and reading, and writing. Having resolved to be up early and off at 9, slept sound till ½ p. 10! *Pas tro. bien*[3] At ½ p. 11 called on Colonel ———, the Commandant, who comports with the utmost politeness. Will order a boat at any hour. Desired it might be at 2; but the passports of Hendrick not having arrived, shall be obliged to go stark alone. At ½ p. 12 got my breakfast, and went to packing up. In the midst of it, came in a very gentlemanly-looking man, who introduced himself to me as the Prussian consul at Elsinore. Gave me much useful information. Had a special favor to ask, to which agreed. Had just done packing, when came in the visiting officer, whose

---

1 Under date of Gothenburg, October 12, 1809, Burr wrote to Henry Gahn, Swedish consul, New York, as follows: "It would require volumes to give you an account of the persons and things which I have seen and thought worthy of notice. An imperfect sketch is preserved in a Journal which I have kept for the amusement of my daughter; and which, if it should ever reach America, shall be offered to your perusal. * * * * * I am indebted to you for the amusement and instruction which I have found in this country; which, but for you, I should not have visited. I leave it with regret, bearing the most pleasing recollections of its hospitalities and with indelible sentiments of admiration and respect."

2 Formerly President of the Swedish tribunals in Pomerania. (*Soes.* probably for *suédois.*)

3 [Feeling] none too well.

duty it is to inspect baggage, &c. Was sent by the Governor, that I might not have the trouble of sending my trunks to the custom-house, or opening them on the wharf. The examination consisted in opening my trunks, and without moving an article, he standing six yards off, and then he received from me ½ dollar; very pleasant. How fortunate is my long sleeping. The Commandant came in at ½ p. 2. "Good news for you. The passport of Hendrick is arrived, and he shall receive mine in fifteen minutes." A few minutes after he brought it, and waited to eschort[1] me to the landing, and see me safe aboard. Heighho! for another, and, nominally, a hostile kingdom. Drizzling, fog, and brisk gale.

Elsinore, October 21, 1809. We crossed in an hour in a small open boat, though the wind was strong ahead; the distance 1,331 *toises*[2]. Before leaving the Danish shore the sky cleared, and the sun shone brilliant; weather mild. At about 100 yards from the Danish shore were met by the Danish flag of truce, another boat like ours; for the Swedish boat is not allowed to approach nearer the shore. Each boat has a white flag to manifest the pacific intent. In the Danish boat we and our baggage embarked, and were presently ashore. Another boat took our passports to the Danish Commandant at the castle. The castle which has for ———— levied tribute on all Europe. We landed, leaving our baggage, and went under guard to the custom-house, where an officer examined

---

1 So throughout the MS.
2 A *toise* is a French measure of slightly more than six feet.

our passports, endorsed them, and transmitted us, *under guard*, to the castle, about half a mile, where we were exhibited to the Commandant, an elderly man of grave but courteous deportment. He asked in French, if I were Colonel Burr. I replied that I had no claim to a military title, but was commonly so called. Ask me to sit; inquired when I proposed to go to Copenhagen. "To-morrow." Said my passports should be transmitted to me that evening. Went then to our proposed lodgings, Madame Jeuel's. At the door saw carts loaded with furniture and much bustle. The good lady had sold out, and was in the act of moving. In this dilemma a sprightly young man interposed; supposed we were Americans addressed to his house; offered to provide us lodgings, and in ten minutes we were splendidly lodged *chez* Oder, a confectioner. Our new friend then went with us to see after our baggage. Found it at the custom-house. Our trunks were barely opened and shut. He paid the necessary (customary) *douceurs*[1] Our baggage being lodged, he ordered tea, at which we had the pleasure of his company. Inquired what hour we should sup, and ordered supper. Told us the wines were excellent, and ordered claret and port. It being a mild, brilliant, moonlight evening, he proposed to walk to the King's Garden and park adjoining the town, and thither we went. The Palace small, but neat and good taste. About twenty or thirty statues in a circular area in front, prettily

---

[1] Literally sweetnesses or softnesses; hence the wherewithal to soften the custom-house officers.

disposed. The hill and terrace in the rear, something higher than the top of the Palace, extends a considerable length, perhaps half a mile, and affords a magnificent and varied view of the town, the castle, the ocean, the Baltic, the Swedish coast, and the town of Helsingborg. Paused at the tomb of Hamlet. It is on this terrace; a square pillar, about four feet high, and without inscription; the only monument. I would willingly have passed an hour alone on this terrace. Returned by another gate. The town very quiet. Our supper served at 9. Eels and mutton, both excellent, and the wines did justice to his recommendation, as he did to them. At ½ p. 10 he left us, first inquiring at what hour in the morning he should call to go and show us the church, which I had expressed a curiosity to see. I appointed ½ p. 8. My companion, Hendrick, went to bed, and I sat till past 12, smoking the segars which our young friend had given me.

22. *Couche* at 12. Rose at 7. The *coverture*[1] of my bed last night was a down (*duvet*) bed, very light, but so intolerably hot that I was obliged to dismiss it and get a blanket. Our friend came punctually at the appointed time. We were at breakfast, and he joined us, not having breakfasted. Went to see the church. The interior is Gothic excessively surcharged with ornament of all colours. The pictures in a very coarse style. Yet there is a solemnity in those lofty arches which renders it the best style of

---

1 For *couverture.* Coverlet.

architecture for temples. The sexton could tell nothing of the history of the church. Saw no date older than 300 years. Went up into the cupola. The fog prevented seeing anything, and we had the pleasure of coming down again a dark, steep stairway, and sometimes a ladder. Thence went to see the Commandant, in which I had several views, one of which was to get rid of the vexatious ceremony of presentation at the police on my arrival at Copenhagen. Was, of course, stopped by a centinel[1] at the outer gate. Sent by a soldier my card, together with a message that I was waiting admission to see him. Was admitted and courteously received. Asked indirectly, and with apologies, to see the apartments in the castle. He informed me that the whole was now a barracks, and the chapel a magazine; that all the furniture and pictures were removed to Copenhagen. He walked with me through two or three rooms, but with evident reluctance; so, pretending that my curiosity was quite satisfied, and having obtained the promise of a letter, which, being shown to the police at Copenhagen, would exonerate me from personal attendance, I took leave. One circumstance, however, did not quite please me. When I was yesterday at the custom-house to exhibit my baggage, the officer asked if I had any sealed letters. I told him I had one of introduction from Baron Engerström to M. Didelot, the French minister at Copenhagen. He made no further inquiry, nor did he ask to see this letter; but, having accidentally

---

[1] So in the MS.

shown it to the Commandant, he said he was bound, by his orders, to retain it, and to transmit it to the King; but assured me that it would be forthwith delivered, unopened, to its address. I had scarcely got home when a Sergeant brought me the promised letter from the Commandant, an open letter to be shown to the police. We had engaged a carriage; a long wicker wagon, with seats on springs, for 5 dollars. The distance is about twenty-six English miles. These 5 dollars are equal to about 1½ of your money. It was near 12 before we were ready to set off, and our young friend thought we had better eat a beefsteak, to prevent delay on the road, and he ordered it. With the steak (which was very good), potatoes, and porter, we made a hearty meal, and he had the goodness to join us. Our bill at this house was 22 dollars and 3 marks. At 12 we set off. The road is broad, straight, elevated, turnpiked, and requires toll; very small, however, about 8 *sti.*[1] for the whole distance. The fog and mist prevented the enjoyment of distant views. There is generally cultivation on each side. Some heaths. Rather deficient in wood. Generally thin soil, of sandy loam. Everywhere piles of turf dug up for fuel. The fences generally of sod, with a small ditch on one or both sides. In some places a substantial bank, like those on your rice-plantations. No rocks or ridges; few stones. Few houses worthy of notice. Gentle swells and hills; none lofty. Frequently in view of the ocean on the left, and several

---

1 Stivers. The stiver was worth perhaps 2 cents.

small lakes. At half way, a small town of about sixty houses in one street; generally of one story and very low, called Amsterdam. Passed two manufactories, one of cotton spinning, weaving, and printing. A palace of the King a little this side of Amsterdam. It was dark before reaching this city. At the first gate our passports were examined. At the next the custom-house officer visited our baggage. It was done with courtesy, and did not detain us two minutes. Arrived at Rau's Hotel, in the Grand Square, at 7. The approach to the city is very pretty; for notwithstanding the fog, the moon (nearly full) gave light enough to show us something. About a mile before reaching the walls of the town, on an extensive plain, you are presented with three avenues through rows of trees. The middle one was our road.

Copenhagen, October 23, 1809. No theatre was opened last evening, nor was there any public amusement. After strolling an hour, during which *mus. mauv.*; 1 d.[1] came home; took tea as my supper; engaged a servant at 3 marks a day; not, however, to attend me exclusively. *Ll. de ch. gro. pas mauv. mus. encore*[2]. My room, a very large and elegant one on the first floor, looks into the square, and it is again my good fortune to have a military parade and band of music under my window in the morning. After breakfast sent cards to Olsen, formerly minister plenipotentiary from this government to the United States,

---

1 For *muse mauvaise*; 1 dollar. Bad *muse*; 1 dollar.
2 For *Fille de chambre; grosse, pas mauvaise. Muse encore.* The chambermaid, fat, not bad; *muse* again.

and to Nailsen, formerly judge in Santa Cruz, who passed some time in New York on his way home. Both were abroad. Olsen at some distance at a country seat. Sent also Baron d'Albedÿhll's letter to M. de Coningk, *conseiller d'etat*[1], with card. Hearing that G. Jay, American consul for Rotterdam, lodged in this house, sent my name by a servant. Walked about town an hour or two. It is regularly laid out on a plain. The harbour artificial. Very few vessels. Houses almost universally of brick, but generally made white or stone-coloured. Had a bowl of soup, with a bottle of Rhenish wine, in my room for dinner. In the afternoon took a servant to pilot me to the Observatory. The height is said to be 160 feet, placed nearly in the center of the town, and affords a most perfect bird's-eye view of the whole, with a prospect of the ocean ; a fine landscape in the interior ; the Palace of Fredericksberg, finely placed on an eminence. The Swedish coast. The ascent to the top is singular ; not by steps, but an inclined spiral plane, paved with brick. It is said that a former King drove up with a coach and four, which is very practicable till you come within about ten feet of the summit, where you have steps, but how he got back is not said, for it is utterly impossible to turn. Paid 1 mark, and one more to my conductor. Home and alone the evening. *La flick*[2] later.

24. Rose at 7. The Prussian consul, Mr. Tutine, called to see me, with Hendrick to introduce

---

1 State Councilor.
2 For *la flicka*. French and Swedish. The lass.

him, and presently Mr. John de Coningk (son of the gentleman to whom I had a letter) on the part of his father who is invalid (a paralytic stroke) and to ask me to dine on Wednesday. Ought to have written a great deal this evening, as Hendrick goes to-morrow and another safe occasion may not soon offer ; but it is now 12 and have not written a line. Yes, I wrote a copy of my letter to Hauterive for the mail to-morrow, and nothing more.

25. Rose at 7. At 10 to de Coningk's ; saw only the son. It is an immense house and everything in a style of great elegance. Thence to return the visit of the Prussian consul, about one mile, being just without the walls on the road to Elsinore ; not at home, but his wife, whom I met in the court, on seeing my card introduced me to her sister and daughter and proposed a walk in the garden. It is prettily laid out, and contains many acres. An avenue extending in a straight line to the sea about ¼ mile. Madame a very pleasing, well-behaved woman. Home at 12. Walked over the ruins, of which a part is the magnificent church of ———, the most splendid in the city, and containing many monuments of kings and great men. The walls and the roof are standing. To a bookseller's, where, on entering, I was called by my name. In a town of this size, about 80,000 inhabitants, a stranger is immediately known. Home. Wrote a short letter to Lüning ; a very short and unsatisfactory one, not having procured for him the mercantile information which I had promised ; but,

indeed, I have tried. At 2 Hendrick actually set off, having been on the point of starting since 8 this morning. Sold a dubloon for 48 rix dollars. The money here, as in Sweden, is paper, but still more depreciated than there. A guinea is worth 16 dollars. Prices have not advanced quite in the same proportion; so that, to one having gold or credit in Hamburg, living is very cheap, as you shall see. Dined in my room and alone yesterday and to-day and had a bottle of wine each day. You see I am making up arrears. After dinner, walked in the King's Garden. It is a garden and park, a beautiful promenade, but did not go over it; having *renc. jo., gent.*, home *ensem.*;[1] 4 rix dollars. In the evening the maid at the usual hour brought tea but in a very unusual style. A splendid tea service of silver and two cups. I asked why she brought two cups (I being alone). She said with perfect simplicity and without any smile or queer looks that she supposed *Madame* would have staid to tea. In the evening walked out, intending to go to the park again, but the gate was locked, though only 8 o'clock. In walking, however, a *renc.;* 2 r. d.; *passab.*[2] How unnecessary and how silly!

26. Sat up till 1 last evening, being a little out of humor with one Gamp; made some pious resolutions. Rose at 7. At 10 to leave a card for the French minister, Mon. Didelot; in the country, not having yet returned to town. Perhaps I have not

1 For having *rencontré* [*une fille*] *jolie, gentille*, home *ensemble.* Having come across a genteel, pretty girl, went home together.
2 For a *rencontre;* 2 rix dollars; *passable.* A rencounter; 2 rix dollars; tolerable or middling.

told you that the Commandant at Elsinore retained Engerström's letter to Didelot. He said he was expressly bound by his orders to do so. I learned yesterday that the letter had been delivered. All letters coming in or going out must be examined by the police. I went there (to the police-office) yesterday with my letter for Hauterive, which was examined and sealed with their seal, which is a warrant to the postmaster to receive and forward it. My letter being in English, and written stylographically, was not very legible, as you know. Yesterday, too, I went with Hendrick to the museum, of which more another time. Paid for the party 3 dollars. Remember, when dollars are mentioned in Denmark, it means the paper dollar, as before explained. At 3 went to de Coningk's to dine. Found there the son heretofore mentioned; a very sensible and well-bred man, speaking perfectly well French and English; his wife *ditto;* her sister; two daughters of Professor Puerari, *Genevois*[1], a man of very prepossessing manners and appearance. The dinner good and abundant. No troublesome stiffness or forms. All rose at once. After coffee and tea, home at 7. Had scarcely got home before Hosack and Robinson came in. I was, indeed, very glad to see them. You may recollect that we parted on the 2d of October. They brought me a letter from Lüning; a most affectionate letter, but something more; enclosing a draught on his correspondent at Hamburg for 1,000 marks! Did you

---

1 For *Génevois.* Genevese.

ever hear of anything to equal this except in novels ? I am quite embarrassed what to do[1]. In the evening, to my great surprise, and uninvited, tapped gently at my door Tempe. You know I never disappoint people if I can help it and so T. was not dismissed ; 4 rix dollars. With great trepidation I opened the picture on Sunday morning. It has suffered no injury. It hangs in my room ; but I am quite out of humour that my visitors have expressed only commonplace admiration. *La jeune* M'lle de Coningk has expressed a desire to see it, and thither you go to-morrow.

27. *Couche* at 1. Rose at 7. You must know, Madame, that the King and Queen are expected to arrive at Fredericksberg to-morrow, and to make formal *entrè*[2] in town on Saturday. There are to be great doings. M. de Coningk called this morning to propose to take me to Mr. de Hellfried's this evening, who would invite me to take my stand at his house on Saturday, as being a most eligible spot for seeing the procession ; agreed. Mr. de H. is commander of the Order of Danborg, and one of his daughters married Schlegel[3], author of a " Treatise on Neutral Rights," which I read some three or four years ago with great pleasure and approbation. Walked about town this forenoon. It is very hand-

---

1 Luning's letter, under date of October 21, 1809, was as follows : " I take the liberty to send you the enclosed letter, at the producing of which Mr. H. Bauer will pay you 1,000 marks, Hamburg currency, which you will please reimburse when you arrive in England or America. I cannot tell you how much I am thankful to Providence for having given me the pleasure to get acquainted with a man whom I admired long ago. I esteemed you before ; now I love you."
2 For *entrée.* Entry.
3 Friedrich Schlegel (1772-1829). The title of the work was " *Sur la Visite des Vaisseaux Neutres Sous Convoi, ou Examen Impartial du Jugement Prononcé par le Tribunal de l'Amirauté Angloise* 1799," etc. " On the Visit of Neutral Ships under Convoy, or an Impartial Examination of the Decision Pronounced by the Court of the English Admiralty."

some, but of this more anon. *Din. seul* and a bottle wine. Have tried in vain to hire a *valet de place*[1], my Mons. Thomas being of no use to me; gets drunk before dinner. At 7 Mr. de C. called, and we went to Mr. de Hellfried's. There was Schlegel. Madame Clements, also daughter of de C., came in and I did not at first recognize her, nor did I afterward atone for it. She staid but a few minutes. A bonnet and a change of dress prevented, and disguised her. At dinner, yesterday, was much pleased with her. Will atone the first opportunity. Staid about an hour. A very pleasant family. Schlegel just such a man as I wished and expected to find; apparently about 44. Sat an hour and home. Mr. Hellfried lent me a book, of which he is the author, " A Survey of the British Attack on Denmark in 1807." I read about one hundred pages. It is written with a genuine patriotic enthusiasm. Omitted: Went this afternoon to see the King's library; 300,000 volumes! Deemed the third in Europe. There are reading rooms and fires. Catteau says this library was burned in 1794. Not a book! The librarian extremely civil; no pay.

28. *Couche* at 1. Rose at 7. Called on J. de C. at 10. Was received by Madame with very engaging frankness and ease. Passed an hour with the family. Got some books, and he sent his servant for others for me from the King's library. Young brother of Mr. J. de C. went to show me Puerari's; out; left card. Had scarcely got home, when Puerari

---

1 A guide for tourists.

a pretty Story to tell you — This
in confined to Nat. hist. & Botany
significant in those
in Care of Professor Zaimis to
these introd — He tendered himself
'th me on Sunday to the Palace
in 2 to shew me the Collection of
2 Medals which is said to be ospten
— I shall make some adn to Gum
take here — you can't thinke what
the little Varlet has brought
— Having on my arrival enquired
some Coins & Medals could be had
noised ab! that I was a
beard Coin hunter & Scientific of
`matique — Puerari introd.
to Ramus, for which I would have
—
ind to S   the   & time at

called on me. We walked to see the library of Classenborg, about which I have a pretty story to tell you. This library is confined to natural history and botany, and is magnificent in those departments. It is in care of Professor Ramus, to whom I was there introduced. He tendered himself to go with me on Sunday to the Palace of Rosen, and to show me the collections of coins and medals, which is said to be splendid. I shall make some addition to Gampy's stock here. You can't think what trouble the little varlet has brought me into. Having on my arrival inquired where some coins and medals could be had, it was immediately noised about that I was a medal and coin hunter, and scientific, of course, in *numismatique*[1] Puerari introduced me *as such* to Ramus, for which I could have boxed him. Dined to-day, for the first time, at the *table d'hote*[2], and am so well pleased with the company that shall dine there henceforth when not engaged abroad. At 6 walked out to see the illuminations and fireworks at the palace of Fredericksberg, about 1½ miles, on occasion of the arrival of the King and Queen. You must know that the Queen has been passing some months (ever since the death of the late King) with her father in Holstein, and has never yet been seen here as Queen, which is the cause of all this stir. And so it happened that we all, about 30,000 of us, came back as we went; the King and Queen had not arrived; there was neither illumination nor fireworks; we were all quite

---

1 The science of coins and medals.
2 For *table d'hôte*. Literally, host's or guest's table. A complete meal regularly served in a public dining room.

sad. The report is that the King cannot get across the Belt *a cause du*[1] British fleet. Called on Schlegel this morning; out.

29. Got another servant (Myer) at 1 dollar per day; but wholly to myself. This partnership in servants won't do at all. Myer is a dignified German of 72; was in the United States war, and has been twenty-five years in England. His last service was with the Russian minister. Sent Myer with a note to G. H. Olsen, brother of the late minister, to inquire of the latter; received a very civil note in reply saying that B. Olsen was in the country, but wife and daughters in town and would be happy to see me. Went off forthwith to see them. Madame is perfectly well preserved; a sensible, lady-like woman. The daughters very well. Mr. G. H. O. tendered all sorts of civilities.

30. Catteau says that it rains usually every day of October in Zealand. Since I landed in Elsinore, I forgot when, but you may see by looking back, it has been every day fine till Friday last, excepting only the day I came from Elsinore to this place. But since Thursday we have not seen sun or moon. A constant fog, and, generally, mist so heavy as to wet you. Called on d'C.'s; the King and Queen have arrived on the Island of Zealand. Will be this night at Fredericksberg, and to-morrow make their *entrè* in town. G. H. Olsen called this morning; and at 12 Professor Ramus, by appointment, to visit the collec-

---

[1] Because of the.

tion of coins and medals at Rosenborg. This palace built by Charles IV. or V., I forget which, and is at one end of the gardens, which are open for the public as a promenade. The palace and garden are in the same enclosure. A wood extending the length of the garden, and about one hundred yards wide. The collection is immense. Ramus says forty thousand, being in value and number next to those of Paris and Vienna. The coins of all times and all nations; Europe, Asia, America, and from the early days of Athens. Several of Alexander and Philip. Most of them are described in a work printed at the expense of the government, three immense volumes in folio, and sold for the inconsiderable price of ———. The *Flora Danica*[1] is published and sold in like manner. Being with the Professor, paid nothing. Hosack and Robinson accompanied me. *Din. a table d'hôte*[2]. Evening to Fredericksberg, a very muddy walk of more than two English miles. The park and gardens must be some hundreds of acres. Water, bridges, fountains; the effect (of the illumination) in some places pretty, but nowhere answering my expectations. Almost total want of music. The crowd such that one was in a constant struggle. The sentinels on each side prevented any one from going out of the walks. Got home at 10 and consoled myself with Tem.[3]

31. It ought to be the 30th. When the blunder began, you must find out. At 11 to Olsen's.

---

1 The Danish Flora.
2 For *diner à* [*la*] *table d'hôte.*
3 For Tempe, a girl previously referred to.

Met Blicker Olsen, who looks as well as when in the United States, though complaining of very bad health. Received me civilly and kindly. Has no establishment in town, and a very plain one in the country. Their house and furniture were burned during the English siege. Madame stayed in the house till it was in flames. Fifty-two balls and shells had come into it while she remained there. Hundreds of families have been ruined by that infernal siege. Dined at J. de Coningk's; about fifteen at table. Nothing very remarkable. The widow Clements has announced her intended marriage with Mr. ————, a gentleman about ten years her junior. She is still handsome and desirable, though a grandmother.

Rochild[1], November 8, 1809. The ancient, not, however, the most ancient, residence of the Kings of Denmark. Though I left Madame Tutine's *et le helle Prussienne*[2] at 8 last evening much against my will and theirs, and without any known or assignable reason, I did nothing all the evening ; was somehow out of order and as I thought unfit for society ; some people thought otherwise. Got tea *a ma facon*[3]. Wrote postscript to my letter to Lüning. At 9 came in the *dom.* of Madame de Wederkop to apologize for the disappointment of last evening and begging to see me in the morning. The apology was something singular. At 12 went to work on the Coest.[4] and wrought

---

1 For Roskilde. Burr pays no attention whatever to the correct spelling of geographical names. Roskilde was an ancient ecclesiastical center. It had at one time a population of 100,000 and was the capital of Denmark till 1443.
2 *Le* for *la*. And the handsome Prussian lady.
3 For *à ma façon*. In my style.
4 See Glossary.

very hard till ½ p. 2. *Couche* at 3. *Lev.* at 7 quite well but more and more out of humor with my brusque manner of quitting *la Prus.*[1] At 9 *sor.* to Madame Wederkop ; gave her in charge my letter to Lüning and received from her two for Sleswick[2]. To A. B. Rothe, with whom ½ hour about committees, councils, &c. A very prompt, intelligent, communicative man about 46. He is to address to me at Hamburg his reply to my queries. To Olsen's ; Blecker O. had left town ; H. G. O. exceedingly civil ; mortified that I will leave town ; offers to devote himself ; assures me of all sorts of respectful attentions. Why, then, do I not stay ? Because I had resolved to go, had announced it, &c., though I do admit that I have had much to encounter to get out. From Olsen's to J. de Coningk's, where ½ hour and thence home. Found H. and R. ready and waiting. I had ordered horses at 11. At 11 I got home and the horses were at the door ; not a thing packed up, bills to settle, servants to pay, *quelle embarras*[3]! We went to work all hands and at 1 were ready and embarked. The mode of traveling is in a long wagon, the body wickerwork ; no springs ; but the seats with cushions and backs, hung on leather. The road is paved with pebbles, like the streets in our towns. Note : At the moment of packing up Mr. Hellfried came in to make a visit ; rather late. The promise of three marks above the customary fee to the driver brought us on

---

1 For *la Prussienne.*
2 For Schleswig.
3 For *quel embarras !* What perplexity !

very briskly. With four fine, large black horses, we performed this stage in three hours ; the distance four Danish miles, about twenty-one English. After rising and descending the hill on which is the palace of Fredericksberg, the whole is almost a plain. Many village churches ; all low, and with a square tower at one end, interspersed with those little hills which are called barrows—places of interment at a period beyond tradition or record. At one time I counted thirteen in view. These, and those I have seen in Sweden, resemble those which *we* have seen on the Ohio, the Mississippi, and the Missouri. We dined at Taastrup[1] (half way). Goose, excellent ; corned pork (ditto), with bread, butter and very fine cheese. Our drink was a kind of light ale. This repast for us three, including drink for our coachman, cost 3 dollars 1 mark, about 1 dollar United States money. Very soon after leaving Taastrup[1] we had in view the turrets of the ancient Cathedral of Rochild[2]. We are lodged in a neat, comfortable inn. A widow lady, two smiling maids, so like Sweden that we cannot believe they are Danes. On my arrival called on Professor Gamberg, and showed him Olsen's note. He returned with me to the inn. He has apprised the *wachmeister*[3] or the sexton to be ready to show us the Cathedral at 8 in the morning. This is the object of my staying here to-night ; I must see the tomb and bust of Marguerite,

---

1 For Höjetaastrup.
2 For Roskilde. There are many interesting tombs at Roskilde, including those of several Kings and Queens of Denmark. The Cathedral, built in the middle of the thirteenth century in the Transition style, is with three exceptions the finest medieval church in Scandinavia. It is 280 feet long, the tower is 246 feet high.
3 For Danish *vagtmeister*. Doorkeeper, porter.

called the Semiramis[1] of the North, and of ———,
but you shall know. That you may judge of the
expense of traveling—we paid for our wagon and four
horses 7½ dollars, and 1 dollar to the coachman; in
the whole about 12 shillings sterling. Having dined
plentifully, we took tea for supper in the evening; a
bottle of very fine claret, and for my part, with hot
water and sugar. The picture has come on my lap.
I could not bear to see you bouncing about at the
bottom of the wagon, but I shall not open it again till
Hamburg. My companions are asleep and now, at 11,
having had my bed warmed, much the mode here, I
am also going to make up the arrears of the last two
nights, having ordered breakfast at 7 and the
pretty maid to wake me at 6. Let me see, how are
you now employed? Probably at breakfast, with
Gampy asking you an hundred of questions about—
God knows!

Golding[2], Jutland, Sunday, November 10 or 11,
1809. We crossed the Little Belt[3] at 8 this evening.
Hosack was so beat out that he would go no further,
finding there a tolerable tavern. R. and I came on
two and a half Danish miles, or ten English, to this
place, where we arrived at midnight. Slept till 8.
Hosack came in about 10. At 11 went to deliver
Lieutenant ———'s letter to Mr. ———; was
received by a very pretty girl plainly dressed but of

---

1 The legendary wife of Ninus, the founder of Nineveh. She reigned after his death and
conquered all Asia except India; built the city of Babylon, with its hanging gardens, etc. She
was said to be endowed with surpassing beauty and wisdom. The Greeks ascribed to this
superlative Queen everything marvelous in the Orient.
2 For Kolding.
3 Strait between Funen and Jutland.

very fine form, which proved to be the daughter. The father a good, kind old man. M'lle sang and played in a very superior style. She has given concerts at Kyholm. The chateau burnt in the time of Bernadotte, Prince de Pontecorvo. Got off at 1. At 5 to Hadersleb.[1], the first town in Sleswig[2], famed for beautiful women. The tavern a very elegant one; fine paintings, &c. The daughter a very accomplished girl, speaking French perfectly well. Were much disposed to stay the night here, but at this rate we shall never get on.

Flensburg, November 13, 1809. Arrived at 5 A. M., having been four and a half hours on the route from ———; very dark. The country appeared to us to be a plain; little cultivated or inhabited and destitute of wood. Passed three small villages; this town the largest since leaving Copenhagen. Plays every night; pleasantly situated on the water. Rose at 9. *Embarras*[3] about money. Changed two guineas at 5 dollars *courant*[4].

Sleswig[2], Monday evening, (I believe), November 13, 1809. Rose this morning at ½ p. 8, having gone twelve miles yesterday, as you already know, and four and a half miles this day, as I now tell you. The story is thus. Our *danske*[5] paper money was exhausted and, indeed, often was worthless; our bills on Humbro[6] could not be sold; fortunately I had reserved a

---

1 For Hadersleben.
2 For Schleswig.
3 Embarrassment.
4 Current money.
5 Danish.
6 For Hamburg.

few guineas, or we must have been on charity. These enquiries and the exchange of guineas which was finally done at 4 rix dollars, (a great loss), took up till 11. We then set off; for the first time a sort of cover on one seat of our wagon. Rose a long hill; when on the height could see no water about the town of Flensburg, as I told you. It must have been some cloud or an optical deception which led me to the error. We then rode among little sandhills; a plain on the right; some towns at a distance. Passed some fine barrows in perfect preservation; only one church. Two very small villages. The whole way sandy and heavy road; were five and one-half hours coming the four and one-half miles, equal to about twenty English. Arrived at ½ p. 4 and ordered horses to go to Redensborg[1]. After this was done we learn that Redensborg is a fortified town, the gates of which are shut at 7 P. M. We therefore countermanded our horses and ordered them at 6. Got an excellent dinner at 7. Soup, fish, ducks, fowls, with cakes and apples for dessert; had two bottles wine, of which I drank my one-third. Changed three guineas at 4 rix dollars 24 sch. The tavern is in all respects excellent, the house, the beds, the maids.

Glückstadt, November 18, 1809. Forever in some trouble about the day of the month, but am never more than one or two days out. Our amiable friend *le* Commandant Donsur took us this morning to see *le haut Chancellier de* Holstein[2], *le Baron de*

1 For Rendsburg.
2 The High Chancellor of Holstein.

quelque chose[1] which shall be found out and told anon. It seems he had already announced us, for his Excellency knew all about us. Received us very courteously and understanding that we are to leave town to-morrow, asked us to dine to-day *en famille*; agreed. Went at ½ p. 2. *Y:* Madame ———; M———, the third Judge, and ———, a literary man of modest, intelligent appearance whose name I regret to have lost. The *Chancellier* appears about 47; small, *maigre*[2], but sprightly, courteous, and sensible; something like Madison[3] in appearance. *A la Soedoise*, we all stood and said our grace; and after dinner all rose at once, and after returning thanks, bowed, &c., adjourned to the drawing-room. The dinner was of several courses. Each dish served in succession, first being carved by Madame, and then handed round by the servant. At each two plates a bottle of wine (claret), tumblers and glasses; each drank as he pleased. Some choice wines were sent round, a glass to each. Madame has four lovely children, the three youngest particularly; the two eldest, girls. Home at 7. Snow and hail. The house at which I lodge is the rendezvous of the Club. The *noblesse*[4] of the town meet every Saturday evening for conversation, cards, and supper. (The ladies' club assemble at the same house every Tuesday evening.) I went in a few minutes, but I declined to join at cards, as well from an aversion to lose as because I must pack up, and so

---

1 The Baron of something.
2 Thin, spare.
3 James Madison, at this time President of the United States.
4 The nobility.

adieu, Madame, till that labour be gone through. *Minuit¹*. Done, even the 'picture; all, all packed, ready for starting at sunrise. I bid you *bon soir* a dozen times before I shut you up in that dark case. I can never do it without regret. It seems as if I were burying you *alive*.

19. (Supposed.) After parting with you last evening H. came in; he had been at the *Chancellier's* table and unfortunate; was willing to go at 8 but had rather not; wished first to see Captain Davis *encore²*, hoping something of *fin.³;* also to see Mrs. ——— of New York, who passed through this place yesterday and proposed to return *cet. aprem'i. Son defunt ami de* Gam⁴. Assented, therefore, to postpone till 5 P. M.; it being near full moon, thought we could go very well the four Danish miles, equal to about seventeen English, to Elmsholm⁵, being the first station. Staid at home all day doing nothing. Mrs. ——— did not come nor has yet come (11 o'clock). Captain D. came about 5. In the meantime I had ordered horses; by 7 no horses had come; sent to the Magistrate (something like our Mayor) whose duty it is to compel the postmaster to give horses. Returned for answer that he would do it forthwith; but as the gates of the town were shut at 7 it would be impossible to go out till the morning. Submitted to the message and have again ordered horses for 8 in the morning.

---

1 Midnight.
2 Again.
3 Probably for finance, or finances.
4 This afternoon (*cet après-midi*). Her deceased [husband] a friend of Gamp. (*Défunt.*)
5 For Elmshorn.

Captain D. sat two hours and *parlè'd*[1] much. Played chess with Hosack till just now and so *bon soir.*

Altona, (what a pretty name), November 20, 1809. We did actually move at 9 this morning. The mode of traveling since we crossed the *sund*[2] is in an immense long wagon, exactly like the great Pennsylvania wagons only not covered and that the body is wicker-work. There are three and sometimes four seats, all open; no springs except that the seats are hung on leathern straps. If you wish a cover you ask for a calash, which is exactly like a chaise-top which falls back. This occupies and forms a seat. As it snowed a little and threatened more, we took a calash. At Kreme[3], one Danish mile, we saw again the beautiful little *demoiselle*[4] of the house. She was very glad to see us, knowing how much we admired her, and was all activity and attention. It was 2 o'clock when we arrived at Elmsholm[5]. There is no getting these people on more than three English miles an hour, though I had promised him a dollar, if he would drive it in four hours. While we were here waiting for horses, came in our French friend whom we left at Korsör and with him a young Holsteiner going to Altona. At Pinnesborg[6], 6 o'clock. Here Hosack and I parted. He went with the Frenchman to Hamburg. I came hither with the Holsteiner. He recommends to me to lodge at Madame Neyl's, *veuve.* We could get no calash at Pinnesborg. There was rain,

1 A hybrid verb from French *parler*, to talk.
2 Strait, sound. A Swedish word.
3 For Krempe?
4 Damsel.
5 For Elmshorn.
6 For Pinneberg.

hail, and wind, and we were in an open wagon. You will shiver to think how I suffered. You may spare yourself the trouble. I did not suffer at all. We were before the wind. My great *paraplui*[1] defended me from the rain, and my feet and legs were covered with straw. We were stopped at the gate to exhibit our passports and have our trunks "visited" (examined). A very courteous old man performed this duty ; and to save us trouble came out in the rain to inspect our baggage. The picture, about which I was most concerned, was not opened. The trunks opened and very slightly examined ; but in the operation some things were a little displaced (you know how my trunks are always packed), for which I *grondèd*[2] the old gentleman. He apologized as if he had really erred ; but, in fact, I did very ill, for he might have unpacked everything, which would have delayed us two hours. I was very sorry afterward that I did not treat him more kindly ; and why I did not, seeing it was my nature and my habit, I have not now time to tell you, Madame. My landlady has a son, 10, and two daughters, 23 and 12. *L'ainèe*[3], a pretty, lively, sensible girl, speaking French fluently, and English a little. They have seen better days. Not a servant in the house. Everything is done by these children, which is embarrassing, for one does not know how to treat them. My room is plainly furnished, but neat and comfortable. Arrived here at ½ p. 8, the distance

---

1 For *parapluie*. Umbrella.
2 Another hybrid verb from French *gronder*, to scold.
3 For *l'ainée*. The elder daughter.

from Glückstadt being about thirty-five English miles.

21. Hosack, as you may recollect, was charged with a certain inquiry of some interest to me, and his report was expected at an early hour this morning; but nothing was heard from him till a line received by the post at 6 this evening. Matters are just as I expected! Sent the letter of Lieutenant Donner to his brother, C. H. Donner, early this morning, with a message that I would call at 11. At 11 I did call. He received me with *bonhommie*[1] and politeness. Staid ½ hour, and home. Changed my quarters, at the request of M'lle, to a larger room. Mist with a little rain and snow all day. Paid for hack to Donner's and to Frank's tavern (to leave my address there), 40 sch., about 3 shillings sterling. All day impatiently expecting Hosack. Walked out several times; saw nothing remarkable. At 5 walked over to Hamburg. The gates are about ½ mile apart. The walk is adorned with fine rows of trees; a plain. Certainly a beautiful promenade. After 5 you pay 4 sch. for passing the Hamburg gate. Did not dare to walk very far for fear of *egarèing*[2]. *Renc.*[3] again, again! Forgot that I should want money to get back. Stopped at the gate and obliged to pawn my pencil. Home to get money, which borrowed of Madame. Back to redeem my pencil, and then walked again about Hamburg. Having redeemed pencil now paid

---

1 For *bonhomie*. Good nature.
2 Hybrid present participle from French *égarer* (*s'égarer*), to go astray.
3 For *rencontre* again and again. It probably means that he met a number of pretty lasses.

Madame. Home at 9, and now was stopped at the Altona gate, an exigence for which I had made no provision. Obliged again to pawn pencil. Took tea. On my first return home, found the letter of Hosaçk before mentioned. I forgot to say that *couched* at 12 *hi. au. soi.*[1] and this morning at 6 lighted my candle and fire with my own flint. You see I go always provided. At 6 this evening the sky cleared and the moon shone out beautifully. I walked at least half a dozen times from one to t'other gate.

22. *Couche* at 1. Rose at 9. This unconscionable sleeping I leave you to account for. *La belle*[2] comes in and makes my fire before sunrise. Tried in vain to get a *dom.*[3]; paying coach-hire is not *jolie*[4] and besides I prefer to walk about. Snowing and raining again this morning and all day till evening. At 3 went over to Hamburg and found my way to *Römische kuijser*[5] where Hosack lodges ; he was out. Left the notes which I had written, *q. v.*, to him and Robinson. On my return called to see *mes am. d'hier. Jeu. est jo. bru.*[6] Home at 8. *U.*[7] took tea with me and at 10 a lesson in English. Omitted: At 11 took coach and went to Donner's ; he had just left home to visit me, so hastened back to meet him but failed. Saw two *dames* at his house, who received me very handsomely ; but I, like a fool, refused to sit, in the hope of finding

---

1 For *couchai (je me couchai) à 12 [heures] hier au soir.* Retired last evening at 12.
2 For *la belle [fille]*.
3 For *domestique.* Domestic.
4 Pretty, nice.
5 Probably for *Gasthaus zum Römischen Kaiser.* The name of a lodging-house. "The Roman Emperor."
6 For *mes amies d'hier.* [La] *jeune est [une] jolie brunette.* To see my lady friends of yesterday. The young one is a pretty brunette.
7 For *la mademoiselle* or *la jungfru.*

mons.[1] at my house. Wrote him a note about a bill of 300 dollars which I enclosed to him to get payment, being *sans sous.*[2]

23. *Couche* at 1. *Lev.* at 8. I did rise at ½ p. 5 and spent ½ hour in vain attempts to light candle, so went to bed again. Having requested both to call at ½ p. 9, which in this latitude is very early; neither came. At 11 *sor.* to Hamburg to the *Romische Kuyser*[3]; Hosack out. To *Kuijser Hoff*[4] to find Netzel; he did not lodge there nor could I find where. Attempted to come home another way and got completely lost; asked at least twenty persons, not one of whom could understand me. At length found one who spoke French and he took great pains to put me in the right way. Nevertheless, got lost again, but seeing a gate through the ramparts and a mile beyond a church, concluded it must be another way to Altona; on I went merrily ; after going round the town, found it to be only a village of about 100 houses but could get no point of view where I could judge of the course, and beside, the weather too sombre to see one mile. On return to that gate through which I had come, met a woman who spoke a few words of French. She told me that Altona was far off, away *t'other side* of Hamburg. Very consoling. Getting into the city again, weary and hungry, stopped at a pastry shop ; there found a pretty black-eyed girl, speaking French fluently. She had no doubt but in five minutes she

---

1 For *Monsieur* [Donner]. Mr. Donner.
2 For *sans* [*un* or *le*] *sou.* Without a cent.
3 See note on preceding page.
4 For *Kaiserhof.* Another lodging-house.

could find me a hack or a pilot. While she was looking out at the door for this purpose, I amused myself,
greatly to my satisfaction, with her cakes and pastry,
and some hot punch. She found a lad to convoy me.
Paid for my repast 18 sch., and 5 sch. to the boy,
whom I dismissed at the gate, recognizing it to be that
at which I had come. Being refreshed by my repast and
by the discovery of my way home, roved about within
limits of which I was sure. At stationer's bought
quire paper for 18 sch. of which this is part. Passing
through the gate met a very ta. *emb. bi. tour. blo. sui.
Mar. M———; 1½ r. d. Pesan. rob. veu. d'un of.
Peut 26. Tres cont.*[1] Home at 5. Robinson had
been here and left me a note. The young rascal staid
an hour, courting my ———. Not a word of Hosack.
Quod mir.[2] Took no further dinner. Mr. Donner's
servant with a verbal message to know whether I was
engaged for dinner on Monday (certainly not), and to
say that he would call at 7 this evening if *chez moi.*
Yes. He did call. Sat an hour and amused me
much. A very curious anecdote of Constantine at
Erfurt. Something of the King of Saxony. Opinion
about the late Swedish revolution ; about the French.
Now I must tell you a great secret. *Ma———*[3] has
a lover whom she has promised to marry. Herself
told me the day after my arrival, and yesterday evening
presented him to me. It is really a young man of

---

1 An excellent specimen of the Burr enigma. Probably for tall, *embonpoint, bien tournée,
blonde.* [*Je la*] *suivis. Mariée. Muse ;* 1½ rix dollars. *Pesante, robuste. Veuve d'un
officier. Peut-être* 26. *Très* content. Tall, plump, well-turned blonde. I followed. Married.
Muse , 1½ rix dollars. Heavy, robust. Widow of an officer. Perhaps 26. Well satisfied.
2 For *quod mirum.* How strange !
3 For *ma* [*belle J.*]. The girl to whom he gave English lessons.

prepossessing appearance, about 22 ; (she is 25). He
is a merchant of genteel manners, and speaking French.
I have pronounced in his favour, which I suspect he
has heard, for this evening he has been extremely
attentive to me. Would himself bring anything I
asked for. Both together, they brought the tea, and
I invited them to take a dish with me. It is luxury
to see people happy. He goes home at 10, and then
————[1] came to take an English lesson. A very apt
scholar. *Plein d'esprit*[2]. *Bon soir.*

24. *Couche* at 1. *Lev.* at 8. Took hack at 10
to go to Hamburg. To Robinson at the *Keyser
hoff*[3]. I find that, among the great number of Americans here and *there*, all are hostile to A. B.—all.
What a lot of rascals they must be to make war on
one whom they do not know ; on one who never did
harm or wished harm to a human being. Yet they,
perhaps, ought not to be blamed, for they are
influenced by what they hear. I learn further that A.
B. is announced in the Paris papers in a manner no
way auspicious. Further, my small stock of money
was in a bill drawn on a house in Hamburg. This
bill was remitted to Mr. F., who, being absent, his
friend and agent got the bill and the money, and "as
he does not know but the money may belong to Mr.
F.," refuses to pay it without his orders! A very
pretty mess this for one day. Went to Netzel's.
You may recollect that I desired Hauterive to trans-

---

1 Janina.
2 For *pleine d'esprit*. Full of intelligence.
3 Note Burr's attempts to spell these German names. (*Kaiserhof.*)

mit his answers to this gentleman. He had no letter for me. Resolved then to go direct to the French Minister to see if he had any orders to give or refuse me passports. Sent in my name, but did not get out of my carriage. After some minutes the servant returned, saying his Excellency was then very much engaged, but would be glad to see me at 3 o'clock. Went to Hosack's quarters, *Romische Keyser*[1], to lounge till 3, then again to the Minister's. Another apology that he was still much engaged, but begged that I would call to-morrow at 12. Went to Hosack's to dine with him, dismissed my carriage and after dinner walked home. Forgot to say that I went to see Lüning's friend, Brauer, who received me very kindly, and asked me to a supper and party on Monday, which declined, being engaged to dine that day with Donner. Did not present Lüning's bill on Brauer, being still doubtful about that. Learned also to-day that the ——— threaten everything, and are taking measures against the peace and dignity of our sovereign self. Intended to have written many letters to-night to the United States. Davis sails to-morrow, and such another opportunity may never offer. But in this state of things, what can I write? To be silent as to my intended movements would be strange, and to tell the true state of things afflicting to my friends. So I will leave you all to your own conjectures. My *bel.* Jan.[2] came up and took tea with me and had then

---

1 See Note 5, page 271.
2 Probably for my (*ma*) *belle* Janina. This is the Swedish and Danish form of Joan, Jeanne, Jennie, etc.

an hour of English lesson. She makes great progress and amuses me.

25. *Couche* at 1. Rose at 8. Slept very sound; ate a great breakfast which little J. got me; very good. Found myself, however, in bad humor. To aid this, waited a full hour for my razors which had given the barber to sharpen, the carriage all the while at the door. At length set off to go to Hamburg and there shave, but met the rascal on the stairs, so came back and shaved. First to Hosack's, where found a letter from Lüning telling me of the prosperous state of his business. One from Graves, full of goodness. One from S. Sw.[1], containing a long bill of untoward circumstances regarding himself. The letter, however, does great honour to his head and heart. L.'s letter determined me to make use of his draft, especially as there was no prospect of getting my own money, and I am penniless. Hosack had just got up, and, of course, had not made further inquiries on this or the other more interesting matter. At 12 to the Minister's; was at once received. He is the transcript of our J. B.[2] only fifteen years older; but marked with the same characters. His reception was courteous, but with a mixture of surprise and curiosity. At once offered me a passport to any frontier town, but has no authority to do more. Passports to go to Paris must come from Paris, and to that end I must write, &c. He advises that I direct the reply to be transmitted to Mayence, where it will be before I get

[1] Samuel Swartwout.
[2] Perhaps J. B. Prevost.

there. At parting he apologized for the delays of
yesterday, and asked me to dine at his country-house
three miles from Altona, to-morrow; agreed[1]. Home
in my carriage and paid 6 marks (2 dollars *courant*).
Dined in my room, J. attending me. Sent word to
Mon.[2] Donner that, if he would be at home, I would
call to pass the evening. He is engaged out. After
dinner, walked to Hamburg to see what news Hosack
had got for me. He was abroad dining, but left a
note and a sack of money, the proceeds of the bill,
200 dollars. In the morning I had called again on
Brauer, presented the bill of Lüning, and got the 1,000
marks, so I am at this moment rich. Left the sacks
at Hosack's and walked home, *i. e.*, strolled about
Hamburg for two hours, doing twenty foolish things,
and spending 2 dollars, but no *mus.*[3] Took care,
however, this time to reserve enough to get through
the gates. *Compag. de voyage* whom I saw home and
was introduced to *son mar*[4]! Home at 9. Took tea.

---

1 This Minister was Louis Antoine Favelet de Bourrienne, (1769–1834). He had been
private secretary of Napoleon I., was now Minister Plenipotentiary in Hamburg, and later served
as Minister of State under Louis XVIII. He wrote the "Memoirs of Napoleon" and therein
gave the following exceedingly interesting account of this visit of Burr's and his application for
a passport: "At the height of his glory and power, Bonaparte was so suspicious that the
veriest trifle sufficed to alarm him. I recollect that about the time the complaints were made
respecting the *Minerva* [newspaper], Colonel Burr, formerly Vice-President of the United
States, who had recently arrived at Altona, was pointed out to me as a dangerous man, and I
received orders to watch him very closely, and to arrest him on the slightest ground of suspicion
if he should come to Hamburg. Colonel Burr was one of those in favor of whom I ventured to
disobey the orders I received from the restless police of Paris. As soon as the Minister of Police
heard of his arrival at Altona, he directed me to adopt towards him those violent measures which
are equivalent to persecution. In answer to these instructions, I stated that Colonel Burr conducted himself at Altona with much prudence and propriety; that he kept but little company, and
he was scarcely spoken of. Far from regarding him as a man who required watching, having
learned that he wished to go to Paris, I caused a passport to be procured for him, which he
was to receive at Frankfort; and I never heard that this dangerous citizen had compromised the
safety of the state in any way."

2 For Monsieur.

3 For *muse*.

4 Traveling female partner (*compagne de voyage*) whom I saw home and was introduced to
her husband (*son mari*). *Compag.* may stand for *compagnon* and *son* may be an error for *sa*.
In that case Burr must have gone home with a man whom he met and have been introduced to his
wife (*sa mariée*).

Lounged till 2 ; and now, while the watchmen are shaking their rattles, I bid you *bon soir.* Mist and fog, with some rain and snow all day.

26. Rose at 9. Though the day has not been cold, and I doubt whether there was frost last night, yet I felt *frileuse*[1], and, for the first time, put on my flannel waistcoat. You recollect that I traveled from Stockholm to Gothenburg, day and night (all night), finding half an inch thickness of ice in the morning, obstinately refusing to put on this waistcoat. Now I am condemned to it for the winter. Sent word to Donner that I would call on him at 11. He was going out, and would call on me. He called about 11. Sat near an hour, amusing me very much. At 5 to Mons. ———, *le Ministre de* France. *Y:* General ———; Mons. Thierry, and three others. *Madame et cinq dem's dont l'ainee se dit 14*[2], finely grown for that age and a very interesting girl ; sweetness and intelligence prettily blended; *blonde, grande, bien faite*[3]. The other four also pretty ; *la cadette* in costume [of a] boy. Mons. occupies a very handsome house on the Elbe about three miles below Altona, for which he pais[4] 1,000 dollars per annum. *Madame sa fem.* is from Leipzig *et par. bien aim.*[5]; a very handsome young man there *partic. attent.*[6] Thierry made me many civilities. "The History of Pitcairn," of whom

1 For *frileux.* Chilly.
2 Madame and five girls (*demoiselles*), the eldest (*l'ainée*) of whom calls herself (or is said to be) 14.
3 Blonde, tall, well made.
4 So in the MS.
5 For *parait bien aimable.* Appears very amiable.
6 May be English, particularly attentive, or French *particulièrement attentif*, with the same meaning.

everyone speaks well. *Bien ri.*[1] Home at 9. *Ayant assez bu.*[2] *Ma* J. amused me for an hour.

27. *Couche* 1. Rose 9. You have not yet been informed, at least by me, that Altona and Hamburg are on the same plain, on the north side of the Elbe. The territory of Hamburg extends to the very gates of Altona. Hamburg is fortified. An immense ditch and parapet. Altona not. The gates of Hamburg and Altona are about one-third of an English mile apart. A beautiful walk through rows of trees, and on the left, going to Hamburg, a wood nearly half way. The plain between the two towns belongs to Hamburg, and the senate do not suffer any houses. A few, however, have formerly been allowed on the side nearest Altona. The city of Hamburg is estimated to contain 100,000 inhabitants, the territory about 35,000 more. Altona contains about 27,000. It is in Holstein now, and for —————— years past, part of Denmark. German is the language of Holstein and of Schleswig as well as of Hamburg. Altona is below Hamburg, on the Elbe. The contribution paid by Hamburg to the French *the last three years* is about 23,000,000 of marks (3 marks to a dollar). This is exclusive of the maintenance of the troops who have assisted the Hamburgers to govern themselves. Now to ourselves. At 5 to dine with Donner. A male party of about fifteen, extremely well composed. De Blucher, General Waltershoff, Lawaetz, Schoenen, Dr. ——————. Every dish is carved at the sideboard,

---

1 For *bien riche.* Very rich.
2 Having drunk enough, *i. e.*, quite a bit.

and handed round by a servant, *a la Soedoise* Sometimes a portion is brought you on a plate. Wine of
different sorts on table, and every one drinks as he
pleases. Now and then one *pledges* another. After
dinner, which lasted at least two hours, all rise
together, bow, and make compliments. The lady is
handed out, and all return to the drawing room, where
coffee is immediately served. About an hour after
coffee, tea was served in the same manner. One
retires without taking leave. Mons. B. proposed
cards, which I declined. Off at ½ p. 8. The mode
of entertaining is easy, and everything was in very
handsome style. Madame is a very lovely little
woman; fair, with very black hair, with blue eyes.
Has three small children, whom I did not see.
Lawaetz, *Conseil d'Etat*[1], engages me to dine with him
to-morrow. I had not been at home this evening ½
hour before I was seized with a tormenting toothache.
This comes of putting on a flannel waistcoat! Being
an under-tooth, and hollow, I thought of my old
remedy, camphor and opium, and have crammed it
full, which has relieved me so far as to allow me to
write this, but still growling.

28. Have had a most uncomfortable night.
Swallowed of the opium enough to stupify and sicken
me. The toothache returned and thus I passed the
night, sleepless. About 7 got asleep, and slept till 11.
Swallowed the juice of three lemons, and afterward
took a dish of coffee, but ate nothing. At 2 walked

---

1 For *Conseiller d'Etat.* State Councilor.

an hour, but found no relief either from the stupor or the pain. Smoking increases it; however, dressed for dinner, and at ½ p. 4 went in a hack. M. Lawaetz's residence is about one English mile below the town, beautifully situated on the Elbe. The house is large, distributed, and finished in very handsome taste. The house is not more than 150 yards from the road in a direct line, but you are taken round a pretty circular or winding road, through trees and shrubs, &c., several hundred yards. On our return this was lighted by lamps hung in the trees and bushes. There must have been near 100 lamps. It was again a male party of about twenty. De Blucher, chamberlain and *premier president*[1], and *le* General Waltershoff among the guests. Also, the amiable young Donner. In short, the grandees of the country. Our host a very sprightly, intelligent man, *d'un certain age*[2]. Madame just such a wife as he ought to have. Both noted for their benevolence and goodness. Among the guests several learned men; the Dr. ———, whom I shall ever be glad to see. I was, unfortunately, in bad order. The toothache, though not violent, was felt, and the stupor and nausea of the opium remained. Stole off at 8. The form of the entertainment was as yesterday, but in more splendor. The rooms are all warmed by stoves; but these stoves are often a very elegant and costly piece of furniture. Pillars, urns, *statues bronzed*, and many whimsical and pretty forms of iron, sometimes bronzed or of porcelain. They

---

1 First President.
2 An elderly gentleman, (*âge*).

put something about the stove, I believe frankincense, which gave a charming perfume to the air. In the country (Holstein) a similar effect is produced by a preparation of dried rose-leaves and other fragrant herbs. Mons. L. is immensely rich, and has no children. Before I had been half an hour home the toothache returned with all its violence. I resolved to have it out early in the morning; but how to get through the night was the first question. The application of pepper and brandy occurred to me. I applied it, and was relieved in ten minutes; but still there is a growling and menacing which alarms me. The opium, too, has brought on a headache. It can be only that, for I did not eat two ounces, nor drink a single glass of wine, though there was a luxurious dinner, and wines of a great variety. Among them champagne and Burgundy. *Bon soir.*

29. It was just as I feared. The toothache returned and kept me in misery all night. Towards morning I got some sleep and lay till 10. Headache; no appetite. Off to Hamburg with my valet (whom I forgot to introduce to you, and now have no time) to hunt a dentist. He recommended to me Mons. ———, from Paris, as *le plus celebre et le meilleur*[1]. Before we got out of the Altona gate the pain left me, and, as the tooth is the most important one of the few I have left, postponed my visit to Mons.[2], and went first to Robinson's; out. Thence to de Chapeau-rouge, for whom I have a letter of introduction from

---

1 The most famous (*célèbre*) and the best.
2 For Monsieur.

Achaud. At his country seat, but will be home to-morrow from 10 to 12. To L. Menard's, for whom also a letter from Achaud. He received me very courteously, and tendered me all manner of civilities. This was unexpected, for he could not hope to make money out of me. He is a man of very pleasing manners and appearance. *Ma J.* has been up, and interrupted me very pleasantly for more than an hour. It is now ½ p. 12, therefore, philosophically speaking, Thursday morning. But to go on with my story. Mons. M. is a merchant of high standing, appearing about 36, of an open, frank, cheerful physiognomy. "Why did you not deliver these letters on your first arrival?" Why, Madame, in the first place, I have a very great aversion to letters of introduction, having everywhere found acquaintances, made accidentally, the most agreeable and permanent, obviously because they are made from sympathy; second, M'lle M. Wollstonecraft, and some other books, had given me a prejudice against Hamburg negotiations. I will never again believe in anything I read in a book (excepting Jeremy Bentham's); third, that matter of M. gave me some little disgust for Hamburg; fourth, the two letters of Achaud to Sweden, you remember, never paid the customary rate of postage. Four such good reasons must, I am sure, have satisfied you. "Yes, but why, in spite of all these reasons, did you deliver them now?" From a certain whim, which I will whisper to you, but dare not write. (Do remind me to tell you how contraband trade is carried on here.)

On my return from town I saw about twenty poor women and girls under guard. From Menard's to the French Minister's. My valet gave my name to the porter of his Excellency, and after waiting several minutes in the corridor, received answer that he was engaged and could not see me. No appointment of any other hour, which I thought odd. Sent back Monsieur Francois with my card, requesting to know when he would be visible, and walked off. Immediately the Minister's valet came running after me, asking me to walk in. It seems that a name totally unlike mine had come to his ears through the mouths of two servants. He received me as might have been expected from his former civilities. Gave me a passport, and, hearing that I was to stay two or three days longer, contrary to what I had told him, gave a general invitation to his house ; engaged to dine with him to-morrow. Thence to see Hosack ; out. Made Francois take up my sack of money. Thence to the Apollo (something, I will learn what)[1]. It is a building containing concert and ball rooms in very handsome style. The concert-room circular, about ninety feet diameter ; vaulted and no pillars. Home by 4 o'clock, having been out five hours, walking the whole time except about thirty minutes. The headache came on about 1, and increased continually. That infernal opium yet! Found the card of the President de Blu cher, which reminds me of a part of the employment

---

1 Salon d'Apollon. Apollo's drawing-room.

of the day which has been omitted ; and, to explain, I must go back to yesterday. Sitting near General W., either yesterday or Monday, I intimated that I should be very gratified to be present at one of President Blucher's courts. He (the General), without any orders or knowledge, mentioned it to the President ; and when we met again at Lawaetz's, the General told me that he was authorized from the President to say that it would afford him [pleasure] to receive me at his court the next audience day (this day). So this morning, when I got to the gate and found the tooth-ache missing, my engagement with *la Haute Chancel-larie*[1] came to my mind, and we turned short about to go to the audience chamber, which is at the other end of the town. On the way, called on Donner to ask some *renseignments*[2] as to how to get in, and to place myself, &c. Mr. D. was in his *comtoir*[3] and would come forthwith. Madame received me. I made her produce her children, a girl and a boy, about 5 and 3. It is impossible to imagine anything more lovely than they are both. I was quite enraptured with them. Then came in the younger Donner, and, finally, Mons. Donner. By the time all this had passed it was ½ p. 11, and too late for the court. Mr. D., therefore, proposed to show me their museum ; but I took for this purpose the younger Donner, and on the way left my card at the President's house, and thus you account for the card returned this evening. The museum is a building of no show, but replete with

1 *La Haute Chancellerie.* The Court of High Chancery.
2 For *renseignements.* Information.
3 For *comptoir.* Counting-house.

convenience. It is maintained by an association of the principal gentlemen of the town, who pay about 16 dollars each a year. The principal gazettes in Europe are taken, and new publications and maps. There are reading-rooms, conversation-rooms, card-rooms. A very convenient ball-room, with parlours and closets, and smoking-rooms. Also a very spacious and well-laid out garden. The associates meet two evenings in the week. Once to sup, and once for conversation, &c. Balls, I forget how often in the season. The rooms always open to the associates, and to any stranger introduced by a member, as now am I. Two o'clock is rattling, and I must be up at 7. You see that my aches are all cured; how, you shall hear to-morrow

30. Had ordered Francois to be here at ½ p. 7. He came, and I rose. Dressed by candle. A very thick, chilling fog. *Sor.* at 10 to Robinson's; settled accounts with him, and received a balance due me from him and Hosack of 45 dollars. (Note the etymology of *Thaler Reichsthaler*[1].) To de Netzel's; he has no letters for me. To Hosack's; engaged Hosack and Robinson to breakfast with me to-morrow. To the dentist's; he thinks he can preserve the tooth for me, but the inflammation must subside before he can do anything. Home at 2. Found card from Menard, and invitation to dine Monday, December 4th; declined, being engaged. "Where am I engaged?" Why, to go out of town, to be sure.

---

1 *Reichsthaler* (German) and *rigsdaler* (Danish) and *riksdaler* (Swedish) all mean rix dollar, or imperial dollar.

What the dəvil do I stay here for? Did not call to-day on de Chapeaurouge ; determined not to deliver the letter for all the reasons mentioned yesterday. At 5 to the French Minister's. He did not return from town till 6. *Y:* General Damasque, General ―――― *de* Westphalie, *Commandant en* Hamburg, the *maitre de postes, le jeu.* daug., *deux autrs*[1]. "*C'est dom. que le roy' e de West'a est si petit.*" "*Mais ça aggrandira. En ıy ajoutant* the territ's of Holst., Hamb., *et* Lubec *il serait beau.*"[2] M'lle Emilie *l'ainee est toujours plus jolie et interessante*[3]. Off at ½ p. 7. To Donner's to sup. *Y:* Schoenbron *et* Dr. Momson *le bon homme que j'aime tant*[4]. Madame came in at ½ p. 9, having been at the play. *Soup.*[5] at 10. Oysters served raw in the shell. The best I had tasted on this side the Atlantic. Then a supper in form of meats, fowl, and dessert. A very pleasant evening. Home at 12. *Ma J. m'attendait*[6]; ½ h. *av. l.*[7] *et* ――――. *Bon soir.*

Altona, December 1, 1809. *Couche* at 1. *Lev.* at ½ p. 7, at which hour one must light candle. At ½ p. 9 came Hosack to breakfast. *Gran dejeunè aprez le caffe et* toast *et* sausage[8]. Wine, cakes, *eau de vie*[9]. Two bottles wine ! Being sunshine for the second time since our advent, invited them to walk

―――――

1 The postmaster (*maitre de poste*), the young (*la jeune*) daughter, and two others (*autres*).
2 "It is too bad (*C'est dommage*) that the Kingdom (*royaume*) of Westphalia is so small." "But that'll grow (*s'agrandira*). By adding to it the territories of Holstein, Hamburg, and Lubeck it would be handsome."
3 Miss Emily the eldest (*l'ainée*) is always prettier and prettier, and more and more interesting.
4 The good fellow that I love so much.
5 For *souper*.
6 My J. was awaiting me.
7 For ½ *heure avec lui* (or *elle*). A half hour with her. If *l.* is for *lui* it is an error.
8 For *grand déjeuné après le café et* toast *et* sausage. Fine big breakfast after coffee, toast, and sausage.
9 Brandy.

out to see Lawaetz's house and garden. Incidents of the day : Lawaetz not at home ; but walked over the gardens and the rooms which were open in the house. The bank appears to be one hundred and fifty feet above the level of the river, and the view, as well from this garden as from many points on the road, is extensive and beautiful. There are still many vessels sailing up and down. A few years ago many, many more. Met General Waltershoff and family. *Chez nous* at 1. Walked to Hamburg with H. and R. Separate at the gate. To the French Minister's, to see the mosaic work, which is truly wonderful. I am incredulous even when I touch it, that all this fine effect is produced by stones and the natural colour of stones. Many civil words. To de Netzel, who offers me a letter to Cassel. To hunt *bijoux*[1]*; 3* rix dollars, *en do. pr. Jea.*[2] Roved with Francois as my guide, and home at 7 *sans accident.* Tea and Jea. filled up the evening. This morning called on Dr. Momson, both going and returning from Lawaetz's, but out. Had this morning a note from de Chapeaurouge, enclosing letter from Achaud, and asking me to dinner to-morrow ; agreed.

2. *Couche* at 1. Rose at 9. At 11 to Dr. Momson's. He gave line of introduction to Madame Sieveken, of Hamburg. Walked with him to see Schoenbron ; out. To Donner's. *Y:* his sister, a very interesting *brun'te, jo.; taille legère*[3]. Headache ;

---

1 Jewels, trinkets.
2 Put 3 rix dollars into ditto, (*i. e.*, the aforesaid trinkets), for Jeanne.
3 For *brunette, jolie ; taille légère.* A very interesting and pretty brunette of a slight figure.

also *la soc. de* Madame D.[1] Home at 1. Thence to Hamburg to see Madame Sieveken. Received with great politeness. It is a lady of very prepossessing appearance. About 50, but exceedingly well preserved. Still handsome, mild, intelligent, dignified. *L'amie de* Bollman, of whom we talked much. Engaged me to dine to-morrow. Hunt *bijoux* an hour and at ½ p. 4 to de Chapeaurouge's to dine. *Y:* Menard *et ux.*, a very amiable, cheerful, well-bred woman, who has traveled over France and England. In all, about twenty-two, of whom five were women. Madame d'C., a small, ladylike woman. Mr. d'C. offered letters and other civilities. Dinner and wines good. A house superbly fitted up, and the company cheerful. Off at ½ p. 8. It is a custom I do not much approve, that the guests give to the servants about a mark or more. To Hosack's ; he and R. had gone to the concert. Home at 9. Francois showed his address when I came down from dinner ; the servant called for my carriage. F. said it was not at the door, but waiting at a house just by, where I was going ! J. and I agreed to drink a bottle of champagne, which we did, and sat till ½ p. 12.

3. *Couche* at 2, having had a rendezvous which failed. *Lev.* at 10. Tooth and jaws plaguing me again. On Saturday (yesterday) Mr. Jacobsen, an advocate of great eminence, called on me and introduced himself. Having heard from President Blucher that I was inquiring into the laws and judicial proceedings

---

1 Had headache; also the society (*la société*) of Madame D.

of this country, he came to offer his services, &c.; so this morning went to return his visit and to have a talk. He has a very neat, pretty little house and large garden in the Pal Maille[1]. Sat an hour. Thence home. At 3 to Hambro[2]. Called on Hosack; thence at 4 to Madame Sieveken's. There were about fifteen, *i. e.,* eight and seven. Mr. and Mrs. Poole, a very sensible couple; Professor Ebeling; Professor Rimarius, father of Madame S.; de Netzel; three or four sons of Madame S., very handsome, and a daughter who will not survive six months. There were several other men of learning. I never saw a party more chearful[3]. I had dismissed Francis[4] for the evening, and at 8 walked off alone to Altona, and quite to the lower end of the town to Jacobsen's, who had invited me to sup. Met about a dozen, equally mixed. Madame is handsome and pleasing. Her elder sister also handsome; somberness; *d'un caract. plus decidie*[5]. Two sets were at cards. I talked law with Mr. J. Played chess with Madame, who plays extremely well. M'lle ———, *juive*[6], played and sang. A fine voice and mistress of music. Off at ½ p. 11. Then an hour with J.

4. *Couche* at 3. Another rendezvous which failed and had nearly done mischief. Robinson came in before I was out of bed, *i. e.,* about 10 o'clock. In bad order; tooth and jaws, but the lip which was

---

1 The Palmaille is the most fashionable street in Altona.
2 For French Hambourg or German Hamburg.
3 So in the MS.
4 Here Burr anglicizes the name of his valet.
5 Of a more decided character. (*D'un caractère plus décidé.*)
6 Jewess.

bitten by a venomous animal on Friday last has swollen, and is very painful. I did not mention it before, because the origin of the thing is so ridiculous that I wished to hush it up; for the bite was given in a paroxysm of great good humour. Hosack came in just after we had done breakfast. At 12 came in Mr. Jacobsen, by appointment, to attend the court with me. Left my young friends and went with Mr. J. to the ——— court. The President not there. His chair vacant. The burgomasters; the police-officers. I was introduced to all the advocates. There are but six. The number is limited. Have no time to detail the proceedings. Home at ½ p. 1. At 2 to Hamburg, to de Chapeaurouge's; out. To Menard's; saw him, Madame, and her brother. Madame had just had a tooth drawn. I was just going to have one drawn. Mr. M. went with me to ———, a society, where are newspapers, new publications, &c. He inscribed my name, which gives admission. We were then to have gone to see the senate and burgomasters *en costume*[1] and in session; but they had adjourned. I called, by appointment, on Robinson, to take him with me on this walk, but he had not come in. Thence to Hosack's, where dined. My tooth still growling. At length made up my mind to have it [drawn], notwithstanding the serious loss it will be to me, to say nothing of the pretty operation of drawing. Went off to the dentist's full of resolution. He was out, and would not be home till the morning. So

---

1 In costume.

that I shall have again to make all this effort to get myself in a tooth-drawing humour. Went thence, by appointment, to Professor Ebeling's. He is a most cheerful, amiable man of about 62. Perfectly deaf. The only mode of communication with him is by writing. He always carries in his pocket pencil and paper; and, when he asks a question, hands them to you to reply. When he has had your answer, he returns it to you; because, he says, persons may not choose to have their free conversations preserved in writing. He speaks, however, extremely well, both French and English. Takes great interest in all that concerns Americans. Is writing a statistical, geographical, political, ———cal, &c., account of the United States. Has a quarto volume for each state, beginning North, and has got South as far as Virginia. I saw twelve of these quartos. The *bruillard*[1] is printed interleaved with blank paper, on which he continually makes his additions and corrections. His library of American books, *i. e.*, books on American affairs, is nearly as large as all the Richmond Hill library. Geography is more particularly his department; and the extent and accuracy of his knowledge is astonishing. A part of his American works were published a few years ago. You will receive a copy, addressed to you by himself, as he understands that you read and write German. Passed near three hours with this amiable man. Home at 9. Omitted: Called on Madame Sieveken this morning, and sat ½

---

1 For *brouillard*. Blotter or waste-book—the first record book.

hour. The state of her daughter's health seemed to depress her. Mr. Menard this morning gave me four letters of introduction for different persons in Germany. Begged that I would advise him if I went to Paris, that he might introduce me to his friends there. Brought home my tooth and my lip, both in bad condition. Tea with J. Will go early to bed and pos.[1] go before breakfast to the dentist's, in Hamburg, about two and a half miles, and get rid of the tooth. You don't believe me, but I will. Mem.: The St. Michael's church at Hamburg; height of steeples. Conversation with Ebeling. A canal now in use from the Elbe to the Drave. You go to the Elbe — miles to ———— and then ascend a small stream to a lake, whence a canal about six English miles to the Drave; down to Lübeck. It is only practicable for very small boats and very narrow. The canal of Charlemagne which joined the Rhine to the Danube by the Main is about to be reopened. *Eh bien, allez vous me deplu mer?*[2] Hamburg funeral; see the plate. No lamps in Altona except Palmaille and near some public build ings. News of arrivals of nine more American vessels at Tonningen. Intercourse with England death[3]

5. I did go to bed at 12 and rose before 7, when it is as dark as at midnight. Dressed in the dark, having made arrangements therefor, and before a creature in the house had moved, sallied forth fasting

---

1 Positively.
2 Well, are you going to displume me?
3 Referring doubtless to the Berlin Decree of 1806, in which Napoleon proclaimed that the harbours of neutrals were closed against British ships under penalty of war with France, and the confiscation of ships and goods.

to the dentist's. He was abed. I had him called up in great haste, and what might not have been expected, he met me with great good humour. He advised strongly against drawing the tooth. Could give me an application which, if I would confine myself for the day, would take out the pain and inflammation, and then he would *plombè*[1] it. How easily one receives advice when it concurs with one's wishes! Like a fool, I listened, and came off with his application, which is flowers of ———[2] and rye meal; a dry cushion applied hot and frequently heated. J. made the cushions very quick and very nice, and has been all day heating and applying them. It has *soulagèed*[3] a little, but still the jaw is not in a condition to travel with or to be *plombèed*. I am very much inclined, not quite resolved, to have the tooth drawn to-morrow. Sent F. to Donner with a note about money matters, and then to town ; *vid.* all the notes, a whole dozen of them. Received a very kind letter from Ebeling, with four letters of introduction to different learned men. *Din.* Soup. Tea with J. Her lover, young———, hearing that I was indisposed, came to see me and tendered his services. He is a very handsome and amiable young man. Have had no other visit to-day. Intended to have written a great many letters to distant friends, but have not written a line. My principal occupation has been in running over a vast pile of American papers which Ebeling sent me. I opened

---

1 Burr has anglicized the French verb *plomber*, to stop a tooth.
2 Possibly camomile.
3 Another hybrid verb from the French verb *soulager*, to alleviate.

your picture yesterday to gratify J., who has the same
taille[1], eyes, and mouth. Got my bill, which frightens
me to death. Seventy-three marks for the last eight
days; equal to 20 species dollars, and Francois not
included! I must, I will be off, if it be only to
Hamburg; but not to-morrow. To-morrow I must
go to President Blucher's court, having been twice
expected there and failed, but next day (to-morrow) I
do think I shall go.

6. *Couche* at 12. Had a bad night. That
bitten lip gave me the most intolerable pain. Very
like the application of a hot coal. The jaw, too, was
not quite silent. Got up at 7, and dressed in the
dark, and without fire, being resolved to attend President Blucher's court. Francois came presently and
helped me. Got breakfast at 8, and, having sent my
greatcoat to the taylor's[2] for improvement, took coach
and went to Jacobsen's (but first I wrote notes to
Robinson, and Hosack, and Netzel, and sent off
Francois to Hamburg with them). Mr. Jacobsen is
author of a very learned treatise on maritime law,
which I shall send out to the United States. Sat an
hour with him; greatly interested by his communications on Holstein and Altona law. Then to court.
The President received me with great politeness, and
gave me a chair at his right hand. Staid in court two
hours, during which time more than forty causes were
despatched in a manner quite new to me, and highly
interesting. In the deportment of the President

---

1 Figure.
2 So in the MS.

there was a happy combination of dignity, courtesy, intelligence, and despatch. Remind me to relate to you the trial between a sea captain and a little girl whom he had enticed from Redensburg, and abandoned here, where he has *fem.* Between a widow lady and her lover; he had lent her money; how the account was balanced. A suit by a girl for breach of promise of marriage. Several cases of debt acknowl edged. Of the manner of giving bail for a stranger (citizens or burghers give none). No imprisonment for debt in Holstein or Altona. Tools of a trade, necessary furniture, &c., cannot be taken in execution. A singular custom called ———, and the manner of executing it. The President in another district, where he presided, at first gave all gratis. No fee for summons, &c. The consequences and the charge; 4 sch. for citation. Having dismissed my coach and paid him 24 sch., walked, *sans* greatcoat, and the weather bleak and raw, to Donner's; out; but his younger brother settled my money affairs. Home just before 1. Found Hosack and Robinson had just gone. I wished to see them, and wrote them this morning as you see, not to come before 1 o'clock. They came at 12 and went off just before 1. I had, with very great reluctance, left the court merely to observe my appointment with them! The President asked me to dine on Friday, which declined. Must, and will go off. At 2 to Hamburg. To Hosack for ½ hour. To *la veu. cap. de Prus.*[1]; 72 sch. To the library

---

[1] For *la veuve* [du] *Capitaine de* [la] *Prusse.* The widow of the Prussian Captain.

to see Professor Ebeling. Passed ½ hour with
him, and always much amused. Received another
letter from him. Then dismissed Francois, and went
to the dentist's with the full determination to have out
the tooth, in spite of his advice or remonstrances.
He was out. To *la veu. prus.*[1] an hour, and home at
5, not having dined nor having any appetite. The
jaw more swollen and very painful. Tea with J.
Sent out for the ingredients of what, in the family, we
used to call Matt's salve, and set Francois to cook it,
which he did very ill. Applied a large plaister[2] to the
place affected. Lay down and got asleep; but the lip,
which is worse and worse, and which I am at a loss
what to think of, waked me after an hour. Found
the jaw much relieved, and now quite in repose; but
the lip gives me such strange twinges that I am afraid
to lay[2] down, for it is much worse. What strange
sort of poison can this be, which does not diffuse
itself, but rankles in that spot? The lip is a little
swollen and quite numb, not painful, except by
twinges, which become more frequent and tough.
Donner called while I was in Hamburg. The President is very like the late Dr. Ledyard. Could
discern the sun this forenoon, but now raining again.
What infernal roads I shall have if I should ever get
out of Altona!

7. *Couche* at 12 and slept very well till 8. Only
two twinges of the lip. The swelling in the face not
having subsided, and a dull pain in the jaw keeping

---

1 For *la veuve prussienne.* The Prussian widow.
2 So in the MS.

me in constant bad humour, immediately after breakfast took a hack, and set off for the dentist's. Francois had been sent to Hamburg early in the morning.
The coachman mistook his directions, or was not
acquainted with the town of Hamburg. I could not
inform him, as he understood not a word of French
or English. He drove about the city a full hour,
stopping frequently to ask questions, probably to get
directions. At length, seeing no end to the journey,
I got out and after walking half an hour, during which
got my feet wet, found ourselves on the north side of
the Lake Alster; whence, however, I could see the
place of our destination, and, having shown it to him,
I got in again. The fellow was so sulky that he
would not get off the box to shut the door, and stood
still full five minutes, till a person passing by shut the
door for us. Finally, got to the dentist's, and went
in with the full determination not to listen to a word of
his advice. He was abroad, and not expected home
till night ! To Hosack's quarters to inquire for
another dentist. The servant knew of one in the
neighbourhood. Sent him to see if he were at home.
After ½ hour's absence, returned with an answer that
the dentist would call on me immediately. This was
exactly what I did not wish, for two obvious reasons,
so drove off to the dentist's house. It is a very
handsome house, and I was received with politeness,
too much for the occasion, by a well-dressed gentleman and lady. The lady came up to me officiously,
and was about to apply her hands to my face. Wish-

ing to get rid of her, I very civilly begged her not to
trouble herself; that I had come to have a tooth
drawn. "*Eh bien, Monsieur, c'est moi qui vais l'arra-
cher.*" "*Vous, Madame?*" "*Oui, moi.*" "*Mais
voyons, est ce que vos petites mains ont la force?*" "*Vous
en serais convainqu et content*"[1]. I submitted, and she
drew the tooth very quick and perfectly well. Paid 1
ducat (two species). Home at 1, in ten times more
pain than I went out. Lay on the bed and slept an
hour. The pain still continues (10 P. M.), though
not so violent, but enough to unfit me for writing
anything but this. Whilst talking with you, I can
forget the pain for half an hour together. Received
this afternoon a note from Ebeling, apologizing that
he could not call on me, having been seized with a
colic. Response, *q. v.* Sent apology to de Blucher
that I could not dine with him to-morrow; indisposi
tion. Received from Jacobsen a message and present
of a book on Holstein law, with explanatory notes in
his own hand; and thus I have passed the day. Alas,
at this rate, when shall I get to Paris; and when to
you! J. and her lover have been very attentive to
me. Looking at the map since writing the above, I
see that I was north of the Binnen-Alster, having
passed over that causeway which divides the Binnen
from the Grosse-Alster[2]. It affords on each side a

---

[1] "Well, sir, I am the one that is going to draw it." "You, Madame?" "Yes, I."
"But, let's see, are your little hands strong enough?" "You'll be convinced of it and satisfied." (*Vous en serez* convaincu *et content.*)

[2] Besides the Elbe, there are two small rivers at Hamburg called the Alster and the Bille.
The former, flowing from the north, forms a large basin, outside the town, and a smaller one
within it, called the Aussen-Alster and Binnen-Alster respectively, and then intersects the town
in two main branches. The Aussen-Alster (outside) being much the larger is often called the
Grosse-Alster.

fine view, but I was not much in the humour to enjoy fine views. Raining all this evening. Twelve o'clock. J. had been to a dinner and party with her lover, and has just been passing an hour with me. Had been very successful in the *toilette.* Simply, but prettily *mise*[1]. Showed her the watch ring, by which you will know that it is safe.

8. *Couche* at 1. *Lev.* at 8. Have found very little relief, I believe none, by the loss of the tooth. The jaw continues in the same state of inflammation, which has now extended to the glands of the throat. A very restless and uncomfortable night. At 10 came in Robinson, and ½ p. 11 H. Great distress about the finances of the latter. Received this morning a very kind note from Ebeling, with some more American papers. Young Wirtz *et sa Dulcin*[2]. Very attentive to me. Not stirred out all day. Determined to try the infallible remedy of fasting. Took no dinner ; nothing. Tea at 8 with J. Wrote to Hauterive a very short and rather morose letter, *q. v.* Wrote also to the Minister of Police in Paris. Sent Francois to Hamburg on sundry errands, particularly to call on de Chap. and de Netzel to ask if any letters. None. Have done nothing more but lounge all day, and went over the *Cests*[3] this evening. The starving has done a *leetle* good. Yes, answered Ebeling's note by his servant. At 11 had wine, hot water, and sugar with J.

---

1 Dressed.
2 Dulcin. for Dulcinea [del Toboso], the lady beloved by Don Quixote in Cervantes's romance. Used here for sweetheart. The Spanish name is made from the Latin adjective *dulcis,* sweet.
3 See Glossary.

9. Worse and worse! All the teeth, neighbours of the departed, have combined in vengeance! Sat up till 2 this morning, and then went to bed because I had no more candle. Wrote H. and R. that I should not go to-day. Might as well write that I shall never go; *vid.* the notes. Wrote also to Monsieur de Bourrienne, enclosing my letter to the Minister of Police[1], &c., *q. v.*, and sent off Francois with them all. Young Donner came and sat an hour with me. Have been laying on the bed half the day in much pain. J., whose attentions are unremitted, boiled figs in milk, and applied them warm to the part most affected in the gums, which has had a good effect. But J., being strongly opposed to my starving system, insisted so much on my eating, that I took a very little (not half a pint) of boiled milk by way of dinner, and in two hours had a violent headache. To remove this took cr. ta. punch, which, indeed, has carried off the headache, but in a way that will keep me up the whole night. At 2 o'clock A. M. of Sunday I write this. The fig application has had a most wonderful effect; the swelling is much reduced, and I am at this moment quite free from pain; but the soreness remains. Think of traveling to-morrow! Will that be prudent? It shall depend on the weather. Have been sorting and burning papers all the evening, *i. e.*, since 11, and

---

1 This letter, dated Hamburg, December 8, 1809, and addressed " To the Minister of Police, Paris," read as follows: " The undersigned, desiring to visit Paris from motives of curiosity and amusement only, has the honour to request that a passport for that purpose may be transmitted to the officer of police in Maycnce, where he (the undersigned) proposes to be in the course of a month. Lest any doubt may arise as to his country, he would add, that his person and his handwriting are known to Mons. le Comte de Volney, to Mons. d'Hauterive, and to many other French gentlemen who have traveled in the United States.—A. BURR."

must now write a letter—not to thee, hussy, but to that good Lüning.

10. *Couche* at 2. The jaws plagued me "*more or less*" all night. Rose, however, with the determination to go. The pain, however, increased, and retarded my proceedings, and by 11 found it utterly impossible to be ready by 1, the hour at which the boat goes. The pain became so violent that I was obliged to muffle up and lay down. It occurred to me that I was just a fit subject for a stool wagon, and fit for nothing else. Got up and fell to packing, which had not yet been begun. Wrote notes to Hosack and Ebeling and sent off Francois. H. C. Donner came in and sat half an hour. Oh, wrote to Lüning the father that I should cross the river to-morrow on my way to his house, and sent letter to the post-office. Francois returned at 5 with note from Hosack. He had done nothing, attempted nothing in his own affairs. Young Wirtz to tender services. J.'s unremitted attention. The application of the cushions at length relieved me. No dinner; no appetite. Tea at 7. J. in the evening; very, very. Adieu; my next will be from the other side the Elbe, once Hanover, now ———

Harburg, December 11, 1809. You see that I have actually got out of Altona! Some tears were shed at parting. After having been so many days confined to a warm room, my head wrapped up with bandages, my first sortie has been to the ferry, and three hours on the water in an open boat, exposed to a very strong gale, and without any bandage; and under this process the pain has left me, though I do assure you I was chilled to the very bone. Hosack and Robinson called on me about 12; at 1 came to the ferry, where waited a full hour. Robinson goes to Leipzig. Hosack stays at Hamburg, so that I shall make this journey without a servant and without a companion, totally ignorant of the language, and in the very worst season of the year. Yet do not be alarmed, we shall get along and find amusement. I have just taken tea and biscuit, by way of dinner and supper. The inn is comfortable and neat. Have been talking an hour with a very intelligent traveler who speaks English. Have written letters to Lüning, to H., and to R.; and this morning before leaving Altona, wrote to Gahn and to Montval, [*le sourd et muet*][1], the deaf and dumb, *q. v.* Your picture gave me a great deal of plague, and but for J., I should never have got it well put up. I have a great mind to roll you up again, and pack you away in the trunk, though your great and good friend, Breda, so strongly remonstrated against it. He also varnished and put you in frame from mere love. And now, at 12, am just going to bed, having ordered horses for 7 in the morning. Written in my bedroom without a fire.

Wille[2], three miles from Harburg, December 12, 1809. Had got to bed and blown out my candle last night, when I found that the sheets were very damp. After laying a few minutes thought I felt some twinges

---

1 These French words appear in the Journal with a line drawn through them.
2 For Welle.

in the jaw, and finding no disposition to sleep, began to apprehend a sleepless and uncomfortable night. Presently in comes Francois with a candle. " *Qu' est ce que vous voulez ?*" " *Monsieur, vous n'avez ordonnè de vous eveiller a sept heures et sept heures vient de sonner*[1]." I looked at my watch and it was so. Thus I had slept six hours so perfectly that I was no way conscious of having been asleep. *Embar.*[2] at getting off. Expenses. Stopped at the Commandant's to show passport. At 8 got fairly out of the town. A fine view of Hamburg and Altona. Clear, windy, cold, not winter cold, but a little ice, &c. Rise a hill of fifty or sixty feet, broken little hills for ¼ mile, then less broken, but sandy, barren, and bleak. Neither trees nor enclosures. Three little clusters of houses, eight or ten each. Some small patches of wood. Houses of plaister; very few of brick, all covered with thatch, which acquires a green moss. The roof, as in Holstein, coming within five feet of the ground. The greater part of the houses without chimneys. There are five or six houses at Wille. It is relieved by the small patches of woods which surround it. My breakfast is tea, bread and butter, boiled beef, and potatoes; all good. The beef slightly salted and a little smoked, is excellent. This is the first meat I have tasted in eight days; 8 *b.* gro.[3] for

---

1 " What do you want ?" " Sir, you ordered me to wake you at 7 o'clock, and 7 o'clock has just struck." (*Viennent de sonner.*)

2 For *embarras*. Embarrassment.

3 For *bons, i. e., Gute*-groschen. The groschen was a silver coin varying in value between 2 and 3 cents. In some German provinces it was worth $\frac{1}{24}$ of a thaler, in others $\frac{1}{36}$ of the same. In Silesia and certain other regions, the former coins of greater value and somewhat large size came to be known as *Gute*-groschen to distinguish them from the *Kaiser*-groschen and the *Marien*-groschen or *Silber*-groschen, which were also called simply groschen.

breakfast ; 2 mar. to dinner ; *Jung.*, 4 gro.; *Wag'm'r* 8[1].
At 9 P. M. arrive at ————[2], being seven miles from
Harburg, and here I stay for the night. While fire is
making in my room, I am in the family room, where
they are making sausages. Four women at a large
table chopping meat. They have knives shaped like
a horseshoe, but larger than half a plate. Each end is
a handle, so that it is held in both hands. Two beautiful little girls, children of the host, running about
and *helping*. Rain and hail soon after leaving Wille.
The wind blew a tempest right in our teeth. Night
overtook us two miles from Wille. The roads are so
very bad that having been thirteen hours from Harburg, I have made only seven miles. The whole way
open, uncultivated, barren plains. The roads very
like those from Bowling Green to Petersburgh, [Va.],
at this season. No trees ; now and then a patch of
wood, which is always the sign of a house ; the houses
being always placed in a patch of forest trees. One
flock of about one hundred sheep, all black, and a
herd of about fifty cattle, is all I have seen. The
country all this distance from Harburg is dreary, and
has a desolate appearance. At this place is the first
church in all the distance (about thirty-two English
miles), and the first village. This contains only about
— houses. This tavern, which is also the post-house,
is very good. My ignorance of the language will cost
a dollar to-night. I told the landlord, who speaks a
little French, to give me my supper in this room,

---

1 Probably for 2 marks to (*i. e.*, for) dinner, to the boy (*Junge*), 4 groschen ; to the carriage-
master (*Wagenmeisster*), 8.
2 Rethem sur l'Aller.

meaning my tea, having thought of no other supper.
The tea was brought in, but without anything to eat.
Asked for bread and butter, and it was brought. He
then asked if I would have my supper now. Yes.
Then was brought soup and beef *bouilli*, roast goose,
bread, butter and cheese. I tasted all and found all
excellent, and asked for wine, which I am always better
without. Had a very pleasant French white wine.
Rethem sur l'Aller. There, I have made the land
lord write down for me the name of this village.

13. *Couche* at 12. Rose ½ p. 6. The supper
did me no good. Off at ½ p. 7. Snow, rain, and
wind in our teeth. Pass into a barren plain about one
mile English. Then woods which had been planted.
A chateau, that is, a coarse two-story brick house ;
two miles and four or five farmhouses. Then plain,
two or three miles, again. Stop for *snaps*[1] at a pleasant little valley through which runs a lively brook.
(Qu.: If all brooks are not lively after a heavy rain.)
The farmhouses are thus : You enter a large barn
door ; on each side cattle in stalls with their heads
towards the middle or passage. At the farther end
you see a fire in a sort of oven, and ranged along on
one or both sides of it, kitchen utensils. On one side
you open a door into the common eating-room, in
which is a stove heated by the aforesaid oven. Here
my postillion took *snaps* and *stuckey*[2] for which I paid
4 bon-gros. Was glad to stop, being very cold.

1 Burr's spelling of *schnapps*, a popular drink.
2 Probably for *schnapps* and *Rundstuckchen*. The latter were small round pieces of well
baked bread, like buns without the sweetening. They were much eaten in Northern Germany.

There are four or five such farmhouses in this valley.
Rising very gently the plain for one mile English to
the right or west, an extensive view. On the summit
of this plain, woods, in which are a great number of
buildings about fourteen feet square. Roof-boards
and sides wickerwork. No chimney or window;
what can they be for? Descend gently, a village
and church to the left on the low plain now before
us. A rope ferry (the river Aller); land on an island,
¾ English mile on a raised causeway; trees on each
side. A bridge which brings you to the station and
town of ———, whence this is written, at a most comfortable house. Two beautiful *flik.*, one *blo.*, one *bru.*[1],
both speaking French, not sisters, but too busy to
speak much. Got breakfast; coffee, two portions of
sugar, three portions of milk, three eggs. At the last
stage I was told that there were four regiments
(French) in Nionsborg[2]. Here the lady says there
are none at all. We shall know presently, being only
2½ miles off. The stoves. A gallant horse, going
on at a great rate. A hand, issuing from a cloud and
holding a wreath, crowns the horse. Motto: "*In
recto decus*"[3]. Paid 3 dollars 20 gro. to postillion, 2
gro. to *dom.* I forgot to tell you that while we were
at the valley mentioned on the preceding page, the
storm ceased, and the sun came out. In the ferry-
boat with me were five *paysans*, or *bourgeois*[4], all in

---

1 For two beautiful *flickas*, one *blonde*, one *brunette*. Burr is still using the Swedish word
for *lasses*.
2 For Nienburg-on-the-Weser.
3 Latin. Honour in rectitude.
4 The *paysans* are country people, peasants, while the *bourgeois* are city people of the middle
or trading class.

the same costume, viz., a long blue coat, straight before, worked worsted buttons, three-cornered hat, black neck-cloth or silk handkerchief, &c.

Nionsborg, 6 P. M. Almost a dead plain the whole way. Either wading in mud and water or ploughing through sand. We were three and a half hours coming these two miles, and I cannot complain of the postillion. The lady was right. There are no troops here. It is a smart little town, but here no calash is to be had. I must either go in an open wagon more than three miles, or wait till morning. I'll go!

Sulingen, December 14, 1809. I did come on in an open wagon last night, and was from 7 till 1 o'clock—six hours coming a little more than three miles! You who love so to ride fast would die to go at this rate. I could walk much faster; but then, how transport my little *malle*[1] and the picture? A little before entering Nionsborg, and for half a mile this side, the country enclosed with hedges and ditches. Then a small village of half a dozen farm-houses; a few very small hills. Then more than a mile without a house, save one, which appeared uninhabited. All the way open plain. Some pretty forests, however, planted by the late sovereign, George III., both oak and pine. Near Rethem, too, is also a small forest of fine old oak trees. At 1 arrived at Mr. Lüning's, the father of my young friend. The *madgen*[2] made me fire and got tea. *Couche* at 2, but hating to give more

1 Trunk.
2 For *Madchen*, *i. e.*, *Dienstmadchen*. Maid-servant.

trouble, slept under the down (*duvet*) bed, the universal covering in this country and in Denmark and
Holstein. In twenty minutes one of these things
heats me up to about 150° of Fahrenheit; then I
throw all off till I got cooled down to the freezing
point; then heat again, and so on, repeating the process.
Not very refreshing. At 7 was very glad to see the
madgen come in with candle and fire. Mr. Lüning
came in and invited me to take breakfast with him
below, which did. Exceedingly mortified that I had
passed at Nionsborg a brother of Dr. Bollman, a
merchant, very handsomely established there. Another
brother, well settled in trade at Hoya, three miles from
this. A sister, Madame ———, married to an apothecary at Lüneberg, also well. I cannot now go to see
any of them. Mr. Lüning offers to go with me
anywhere and everywhere. Insists on my staying a
fortnight, &c., but I'll do no such thing, though
nothing can be more kind than every member of the
family. There are eight children, three girls and five
boys, of whom all are at home except the two elder
sons. You shall have some account of them another
time. I am now planning how to pursue my journey.
The post extra is horribly expensive. It has cost me
18 dollars from Harburg to this. The diligence goes
day and night, and at the rate of about one mile in
three hours. An open wagon. Think of trying it to
Hanover!

15. At length I yielded to the solicitations of
Eleonora and Doris and opened the picture. No

small labour; for, to secure it more perfectly, I had covered it with cartridge paper, sealed down to the edge of the box, and over that the lid tied by an hundred cords. It is in perfect order, and was greatly admired. Of course, a thousand questions about you. The girls did it up again without my aid. Lest I should lead you into error as to the soil and means of subsistence in this country, observe that the cattle are not seen abroad, because they are housed. Though the soil be thin, yet cultivations are seen more or less extensive, and where you see a house there is an air of comfort and even abundance. Though no enclosures are seen except in and near the towns and villages, yet, as cattle are not allowed to run at large, this is no impediment to cultivation. The meat is very fine. Everywhere good bread; both wheat and rye are as cheap as on our seacoast. The common fuel is turf, which is very pleasant for stoves, and so very cheap that Mr. L., who has a very large family, and a house as big as six of yours at the Oaks', told me that his fuel cost him but about 12 louis (about 50 dollars) per annum. Taxes are light, even now under the French administration. The tax on land is about 2 cents per acre. The French government derive a revenue of about two millions per annum from this country (Hanover); but this is the mere conjecture of those I conversed with. I cannot perceive the sources of one-half that sum. Whilst this country was held by George III., he made a point that the whole reve-

---

1 Theodosia's residence near Georgetown, S. C.

nue drawn from the electorate should be expended within it. It was not, however, appropriated, that I can learn, to useful purposes. After leaving you last night, I weighed again the merits of going to Bremen, to Hoya, whither Mr. Lüning proposes to eschort me with his carriage, or of going on my route. The different projects preponderated alternately. At length I resolved to go on, and to go with the diligence, the most detestable, the slowest, and the cheapest of all modes. Went to work, packed all up, and lay down at 12, expecting every minute the diligence. Slept sound till the *madgen* came in to make fire at 7, for I had got rid of the down covering, and had a light warm quilt in place. Hearing nothing of the dili gence, took another nap till 8, and now at 12, it has not arrived. While I am writing, *le bon* L.[1] has been up to offer new parties and allurements to detain. Eleonora and Doris, too, have used some pretty arts; but I shall resist all and go. Walked over the village this morning with Mr. Lüning, his mills, houses and farms. It is a wealthy establishment, in that style of simplicity which leaves one at ease. Doris is manager this week. She is a beautiful creature of 15; more natural grace, and sweetness, and modesty, without *mauvaise honte*[2], I never saw. Played chess last night with Eleonora; then she gave me a number of songs, accompanied with the piano. Her voice is very fine, and just enough formed to leave a little of the wild-ness of nature. Just now school is out, and I counted

---

1 The good Lüning.
2 Bashfulness.

passing my window 104 children of each sex. It is fair to conclude that as many went the other way, for we are adjoining the priest's house, opposite the church, in the center of the village, which appears to have about sixty houses. Not one mean. But let me tell you how we got on from Nionsborg. There was a cold wind in our face. Took away the seat; filled the wagon with straw; sat down on the straw, with my back to the horses; made the postillion sit right against me. Being a full-blooded fellow, his back served as well to lean against as to keep me warm. In five minutes I could feel him through all my clothes, like a heater. He had his flint, steel, and tinder, and we kept our pipes going the whole day. During the six hours, from 7 to 1, I did not get out of the wagon, nor did I suffer. Every minute some one of this amiable family is offering me some kindness or civility. One brings me a fine apple, another a pear, another a new pipe or better tobacco, and they are all in constant good humour with each other. All the children, except the youngest (Christopher), speak French fluently.

Nieustadt', December 16, 1809. The diligence came into Sulingen at 3 P. M., and at 4 I got in and we moved on towards Nienburg, which is again my route. Arrived there at 11. Two passengers in the diligence. A pleasant Frenchman, and a German who speaks only German. They were going to Hamburg. So that at Nienburg we parted; first having taken tea together, for which paid 10 bon-gros.—very dear. I

1 For Neustadt.

am quite satisfied with the diligence. It is spacious, warm, well cushioned, and, as we never go off a walk, for a good nap. But, alas, from Nienburg to Hanover it is an open wagon. Submitted, therefore, once more to the experiment of post extra. The fellow charged 6 bon-gros. additional for a covered calash, which is an imposition. Left Nienburg at 12 and arrived here at 6, the distance being two miles and a half. Think of such a rate of traveling! Not quite twelve English miles in six hours. The calash, too, was badly closed, so that I suffered with the cold. Nevertheless slept three hours, and find myself refreshed and well. The family all asleep when we arrived. In five minutes had a good fire, and in fifteen minutes excellent coffee, bread, and butter, served by a girl, the model of good humour. There must be good humour naturally, when it is exhibited after being waked, &c., on a cold frosty morning. Neustadt is on a little river, a branch, I suppose, of the Aller. An excellent stone bridge; gates, but no walks. Has about one hundred and fifty houses.

Hanover, December 16, 1809. Arrived at 11 this morning, my last postillion being much better than his predecessor. From Neustadt to this place you are the whole day between rows of trees planted on each side the road, which is also ditched on each side and raised in the middle; but it is only the sand thrown up, so that the road is very pretty and very bad. On leaving Neustadt, saw to the right a range of blue hills (the first I have seen since crossing the

Elbe), distant, apparently, about four leagues. There are hopes, therefore, of getting off this tiresome plain. Had two letters from Lüning to Hasse and to another person. Took lodgings with the former, a cheerful man of 70. The letter procured me a good room and good attendance. The other, Mr. Menzzer, is quite a young man. He has been running about with me all day. It is a beautiful little town, containing 16,000 inhabitants. The river, a branch of the Aller, is made to surround it. Promenade and extensive rows of trees everywhere, but nothing of its former splendour. Many valuable and curious things taken to Paris. Many of the first families removed to England. The only garrison here is a small regiment of Westphalians; very fine men. Sent my card to Salcette, and left another for *son Excellence*[1] Madame de Decken. Mr. Menzzer procured me a ticket to the concert, and thither we went at ½ p. 6. It is given and executed by the gentlemen of the town, amateurs and performers. No tickets sold. Admittance only to those invited. There were, I think, near thirty performers. The room appears to be about 120 feet by 40 or 50; well lighted by seven *lustres* pendant from the ceiling; ornamented with eight or ten statues, large as life, nearly plain; ceiling horizontal, and about sixteen feet high. The room was very full. At the intervals between the pieces or acts, they walk about and talk. Mr. de Spilcker, *conseiller de la cour de justice*[2], got introduced to me, I

---

1 Her Excellency.
2 Councilor of the Court of Justice.

don't know how; a well-bred man of 30, speaking
French and English. He ciceroned me about the
room; presented me to General St. Simon, *commandant de la ville*[1], who had served with Moreau[2] and
spoke of him. To Madame de Decken, who immediately proposed some parties, dinners, suppers, &c.,
and when I announced my intention of leaving town
to-morrow, absolutely forbade it. I yielded, and
agreed to be at her command Monday evening.
There were several handsome women, and many
comely, with very fine complexions, hair, &c. The
young ladies put up their hair in various simple and
pretty ways, no caps or headdress; married women,
generally hats or caps. Of particulars I dare not
attempt any. The music pleased me, particularly two
songs. But Madame de Decken, who is scientific,
and from whose judgment there is no appeal in any
matter of taste, was not satisfied. She introduced me
to her daughter-in-law, Madame *la Baronne* de Wan-
genheim, handsome, graceful, ladylike woman; *tres
belle taille*[3]. Home at 9. No supper, having had tea
before I went out. For dinner, took a small bowl of
soup, finding myself heated by the journey. Learning
that the diligence, a covered wagon, leaves this for
Brunswick on Tuesday morning, resolved to go with
it. The difference of expense is some indemnity for
the delay.

1 Governor of the town.
2 Probably Jean Victor Moreau, (1761-1813), a French general. He commanded in Holland
in 1795 and was at the head of the army of the Rhine and the Moselle in 1796. He commanded
in Italy in 1799 and in 1800 was appointed to the command of the army of the Rhine and gained
a decisive victory over the Austrians at Hohenlinden. Because of intrigues he was exiled in
1804 and lived in the United States (near Trenton, N. J.), from 1805 to 1813, when he entered
the Russian service. He was mortally wounded at the battle of Dresden, August 27, 1813, and
died on the 2d of the following September.
3 Very fine figure.

17. Waked this morning, and found myself in a high fever, with a difficulty of respiration. Threw off the bedclothes, but no relief. A strong smell of burnt wool led me, at length, to suspect the cause of this strange malady. The door to my stove is in the entry or hall, so that the fire is made without coming into my room. The boy, in great kindness, had, at an early hour, heated the stove to that degree that a pair of woolen stockings (my fine Edinburgh knit stockings) and a pair of *culottes*[1], which I had hung at least three inches from the stove, were so burned as to be ruined. Got up, opened the window, and found I could breathe well enough ; but I assure you I have been all day much the worse for the baking. At 10 came in Mr. Menzzer, and at 11 I went to Mons. de Spilcker's. Having early received a card from the Governor, General La Salcette, called on him and sat a few minutes. A man of prepossessing physiognomy and pleasing manners. He engaged me to dine with him to-morrow. Just before I had engaged myself to de Spilcker, but he very kindly agreed to let me off. Mr. de Sp. then went with me to the Commander General St. Simon, who asked me to dine either to-day or to-morrow; being engaged both days, was obliged to decline. To Mr. ———, first librarian, a very amiable old gentleman, who received me most kindly. To Madame de D.'s, who was out; sent up my card to Mr. de D., who received us. A very dignified and courteous man. *Actuellement premier*

---

1 Breeches.

min.[1] Home at 1. Found the card of Madame de Decken. At the moment of my return came in Mr. de Patje, *president des*[2] ———, who introduced himself to me. Hearing of my arrival, and wishing the honour of my acquaintance, &c., &c., which is certainly civil and hospitable in a high degree. An intelligent and well-bred man. At 2 to dine with my friend Menzzer (who had invited me also yesterday), *en famille.* ϒ: besides *ux. et mer.*[3], Mr. Palm, an interesting young man, *bailie du* ———[4], great *am. de* E. Boll.[5]; this at once made us acquainted; also Madame ———, *vraiment belle femme*, whose *mar.*[6] is at Demar, or somewhere thereabouts. *Theatre*[7]— "Hamlet"—Theatre Philosoph.[8] *al' dir.*[9] Sleight of hand. Ventriloq. I admire very much the Theatre au Palais[10], where I was to see "Hamlet" in German, translated from Shakespeare. There is *paterre*[11] and five rows of boxes; no gallery, as in Edinburgh.

1 At this very time Prime Minister (*Ministre*).
2 President of the ———.
3 For *uxor et mère*. Wife and mother.
4 For *bailli du* ———. Bailiff of the ———.
5 Great friend (*ami*) of E. Bol., meaning Eric Bollman, a most interesting character, who was one of Burr's associates in the affair of Mexico and to whom there are frequent references in the Journal. Mr. Bollman was born in Hoya, Hanover, in 1769, and died in Jamaica, W. I., December 9, 1821. He studied medicine at Gottingen, and practiced in Carlsruhe and Paris, where he settled at the beginning of the French Revolution. He accompanied Count Narbonne, who fled to England in 1792, and in London fell in with Lally-Tollendal, who induced him to go to Austria and endeavor to find out where General Lafayette was kept in confinement. He established himself as a physician in Vienna. Learning that Lafayette was a prisoner at Olmutz, he formed a plan to rescue him with the assistance of Francis Kinlock Huger, a young American. Communicating with the prisoner through the prison surgeon, the two fell upon his guards while Lafayette was taking exercise in a carriage, and succeeded in getting him away on a horse; but he rode in the wrong direction and was recaptured. Dr. Bollman escaped to Prussia, but was handed over to the Austrian authorities, who kept him in prison for nearly a year, and then released him on condition that he should leave the country. He came to the United States and was well received; but in 1806 was implicated in Burr's conspiracy. He was Burr's agent in New Orleans. In 1814 he returned to Europe, and after another visit to the United States, took up his residence in London. Burr and Bollman corresponded regularly and were firm friends to the last.
6 Truly a beautiful woman, whose husband (*mari*) is, etc.
7 For *théâtre*.
8 *Théâtre Philosophique*. Philosophical Theatre.
9 Probably for *au dire*. According to the saying, *i. e.*, as they call it.
10 The Palace Theatre.
11 For *parterre*. On the Continent, the pit.

There is a place assigned for *les courtisannes*[1]. The curtain is of the ornament of the theatre the thing most worthy of notice. I will endeavor to get a description for you. It is about the size of that in Philadelphia; but in every part of the house you hear distinctly. I saw nothing very remarkable in the performers. The style of acting a good deal like that in England. Staid only two acts, having engaged to go to the Theatre Philosophique (sleight of hand). Here met Madame de Decken and *la belle* K.; with the latter went home. The tricks and sleight of hand were very fatiguing to me, but I was indemnified by the ventriloquism. I am satisfied, however, that it is an acquirement, an art, and not, as many have supposed, a natural gift.

18. *Couche* at 2. Rose at 8. For fear of another baking, had forbid any fire to be made till I should be up and order it. At 10 came in Mr. Palm. He has exactly the features, the profile, and character of countenance of John Swartwout[2], about his height, not so lusty; more blonde; younger by ten years. Went at 11 to see President Patje; out. To Menzzer's; out. Home. Found the card of *le Conseiller* Feder. Visit from *Commandant le* General St. Simon, very handsome young man. From Mr. Meyer, *le ministre*

---

1 For *les courtisanes.* This word may here have two meanings; ladies of the court or courtesans. Burr probably refers to the latter.

2 The Swartwout family was well known in New York. Abraham Swartwout was a Revolutionary soldier. His son Robert (1788-1838) became a Colonel of New York militia and after the war was a merchant at New York. He wounded Richard Riker, recorder of New York city, in a duel. Another son of Abraham, Samuel (1783-1856), accompanied Burr in his expedition in 1805, fought in the war of 1812, and afterward became a merchant in New York city. He was a captain of a city troop called the Iron Grays, celebrated by the poet Halleck, and was appointed collector of the port of New York by President Jackson. John Swartwout, another son, was a Member of Assembly in 1798-1799, 1800-1801, and 1820-1821, and United States Marshal at New York in 1801 and 1802, while Burr was Vice-President.

de police[1]. Walked out, and seeing the door of church open, went in. Surcharged with gilding and ornament. Two galleries. The panels between the first and second gallery, a suite of paintings; forty or fifty. Scripture history. Nothing remarkable.

Evening. No, indeed! Looking at my watch, it is ½ p. 1, and, therefore, philosophically speaking, Tuesday morning. Mr. Palm promised to call on me, and I waited from 12 till 4, but he came not, which I very greatly regret. Something has prevented, for I am sure he wished the interview. Took hack to go to dinner, and on the way called on Menzzer. Saw also Madame, but *la belle* ———— not there. Thence to La Salcette's. There were three French ladies and about a dozen gentlemen, of whom only *le* President Patje appeared to me to be German. *Le Commandant* was there, and offered me letters, which I very gladly accepted, particularly one for Mayence. Now, if you have not forgotten your geography, that would tell you where I am going, which has hitherto been kept secret. At that moment came in Mr. Menzzer, to give me my ticket for the diligence, which he had procured (and now it occurs that he must have paid for it), and to take leave. It is too late to give you an account of the party at Madame Decken's, or to relate the affectionate letter and present of caravan tea received this afternoon from Mr. Lüning, the father. Mr. Menzzer tells me that the diligence goes at 5, and that he will send a servant to call me at ½ p. 4. So good night, or morning.

---

1 The Minister of Police.

Bronswig[1], December 19, 1809. I was up at ½ p. 4, and we were off at 5. As I got into the diligence, saw by the light of the lamp a very pretty youth, apparently 17 or 18, whom but for the dress I should have supposed a girl. *Le caval.*[2] and his lover are two itinerant musicians. They amused me much on the road. At parting, each of them slung a box on the back, and marched off chearful[3] as birds. We arrived at 11 this evening. We have been very industrious. Eighteen hours to make this eight miles. The country for about half way is the same sandy plain with which you have been so fatigued. Then less sandy, and, perhaps a little more fertile, but still a plain. Pänet[4] is the first town in Westphalia ; but we had no *visites* of *douanniers*[5] nor of police-officers. It will be matter of curiosity to you to see a bill of the expenses of this mode of traveling, say for the eight miles :

Bon-gro.

Paid at Hanover, I don't know for what, to the *wagen-meister*[6],
4 bon-gros. 4
Douceur[7], now established by law, to each postillion, 4 bon-gros. ;
three postillions, ... 12
To the other two *wagen-meisters*, 2 bon-gros. each, ... 4
Fare of passenger, 7 bon-gros. German mile, ... 56
Breakfast, coffee, bread and butter, ... 7
Luncheon (bread, butter, cold beef, and beer), ... 4
Pipe and tobacco, ... 1
                                                    ⎯⎯
Bon-gros., ... 88
Twenty-four bon-gros. to a dollar[8] ; 88 bon-gros. = 3 dollars and 16 bon-gros., or 3⅔ dollars.

---

1 For Braunschweig, or Brunswick.
2 For *le cavalier.* The cavalier or gentleman.
3 So in the MS.
4 For Peine.
5 Inspections of custom-house officers (*douaniers*).
6 Wagon-master; in more modern parlance, conductor.
7 A gift, a bribe.
8 He means a thaler, which was about three-fourths of an American dollar.

Saw now and then a little appearance of blue hills, still to the right. We seem to be riding parallel to them. Passed through the burnt village of —— Among the ruins a fine, large, ancient, stone Gothic church. The poor people are very busy rebuilding. Walked over the town of Pänet. Everything looks old and decaying. It seems to have been formerly fortified, at least —— *Lettre de* L. Menard *et Co.*, *a* Messrs. *Freres* Lobecke *et Co.*, Brunswick[1]. *De* Professor Ebeling, a *Herrn Etats rath* von Zimmerman[2], Braunsweig. Sent the above with my card *chez* Brendecke; also *lettre de* C. H. Donner, a *Mons. Conseiller d'Etat* de Zimmerman[3], Bronsvic.

Evening, *i. e.*, ½ p. 12. I wrote Zimmerman a note that I would call at 11, and went with it myself at 10. Sent in the letters and card. He, hearing that I was below, invited me up, and I sat ½ hour. Mr. Zimmerman is the author of that statistical account of Europe which you have seen. He wrote it in England and in English. Author, also, of many things which you have not seen, but which you will see. He is about 72, cheerful, animated, and extremely frank; of prepossessing countenance and manners, simple and courteous. Talking on American affairs, I happened to express a sentiment not usual. He turned to one of his books and read me the same idea.

1   Letter from L. Menard & Co. to Lobecke Brothers & Co. (*Co.* for *compagnie*).
2   [Letter] from Professor Ebeling to State-Councilor Von Zimmerman. This was Eberhard August Wilhelm von Zimmerman (1743-1815), a well known naturalist and philosopher of Germany. He was for some years a professor at the Carolinum, the great technical high-school of Brunswick. He published, among other things, "France and the Free States of North America" (1795), and "A Political Abstract of the Present State of Europe" (1788). The latter work was in French.
3   Letter of C. H Donner to State-Councilor Von Zimmerman. Note the variation in spelling of Brunswick, the German name of which is Braunschweig.

You know how such an incident advances an acquaintance. Thence to the *Hotel d'Angleterre*[1], where found Hosack and Robinson. We were very glad to meet. Hosack had got out of his trouble. Agreed to dine at my quarters. Strolled about the town. Went into St. Michael's and another church; both Gothic. The latter has a splendid and beautiful altarpiece. Neither of them very large; also the cloyster[2] (nunnery), which always fills me with the most painful reflections. Returned to my quarters, and while we were at dinner two of the Lobeckes came in. (Note: The usual dining hour in this place is 1 o'clock.) One of them invited me to pass the evening and sup, and seeing my two friends, whom I mentioned as my countrymen and companions, he invited them also. At 6 he sent his carriage for me, and we went. He resides with his father-in-law, Mr. ———, the Prefect[3] of this district, being, of course, the first in point of rank. The house is a very spacious building, on the square by the cloyster, and is called *La Prefecture.* There were about twenty-five present, and nearly an equal number of either sex. Several pretty women. *La Veuve* ———, very handsome. Madame Lobecke, wife of the elder partner of the house (I believe uncle of the other), is the handsomest and youngest woman I ever saw having a son 23 years of age. On the first floor, which you call the second story, there were a suite of four large rooms, which we occupied. Then

1 The English Hotel.
2 So in the MS.
3 The title in French is *Le Préfet.* His house is *La Préfecture.*

a ballroom about sixty or seventy feet square, and twenty or thirty high, finished with taste and expense, which is the center of the house. Of course, the same rooms on the other side. The company were easy and social. Cards, conversation, cakes, lemonade, *sangaree*, &c. At 11, hot supper. I played chess with *le fils de* Madame[1], &c. Home at 12.

21. *Couche* 2. Rose 7. At 10 came in Rob inson ; soon after, Hosack, with *le* Baron de Schale, *gouv. du Palais*[2]. He proposed to go with me to the mint. As we were going out, met Monsieur Mercier, *commissaire general, de la haute police a* Bronsvig[3], to make a visit. He agreed to join and walk with us. The mint is not a very large establishment ; about fifty men employed. They coin for their neighbours, also. Said that the mines of Hartz produce about ———— of silver annually. Got sample of their small silver coins, new and shining, to add to Gamp's collection. The Baron left us at the mint. Mercier walked about with me. I like him much. At 3 de Zimmerman came to take me to dine, and he had had the politeness to invite, also, Hosack and Robinson. It was at a *restaurateur's*[4] that we dined. *Y:* Professors Emperius *et* de Florincourt, both speaking English ; very intelligent. Hosack and Robinson went off at 6 to go to the concert. I sat till 9. Much conversation on American and German affairs.

22. *Couche* 2. *Lev.* 7. *Sor.* at 10 to Zimmer-

---

1 Madame's son.
2 For *Gouverneur du Palais.* Governor of the Palace.
3 Commissary General of the High (the Correctional) Police at Brunswick.
4 Keeper of a restaurant.

man's. To Mercier's, who engaged me to dine to-day. To Baron de Schale's where introduced to *M'lle la Bar.*[1], a pretty, genteel, amiable girl. To museum by appointment with Emperius, who has the charge of it. Mr. Denon had taken to Paris some of the most curious articles; but much remains. Several heads, real antiques, Grecian and Roman. Collection from Herculaneum. Ditto from Egypt; amulets. Called at the Prefect's; being near 2 they were at dinner; left card. Strolled an hour. At 3 to Zimmerman's. Home at 4. Took coach to go to dine with Mercier at 5. *Y:* Mr. d'Escalonne, *cont'r des postes*[2], and Dr. Valentine, (*emig.*[3]). Burgundy and champagne. Off at 8. Mr. M. would attend me. On the way *muse. Tres bien.*[4] At 9 came in Robinson and sat till 11. Engaged to breakfast with Mercier. Costume of the *paysans* a very long white coat of canvas (sail duck), lined with red flannel; waistcoat various colours, generally striped, red and green predominant; large hat, cocked before and flapped behind. Women—The cap generally white, close to the head on the back, reaching not quite to the ears; huge baskets, not like the pretty little Altona baskets. No public women, but great plenty who grant favors *a bon marchè*[5]. After leaving the mint Mr. Mercier went with us to the lacquered ware manufactory of ————. The most famous in all

---

- 1 *La Baronne.*
- 2 For *contrôleur des postes*. Controller of the postal service.
- 3 For *émigré.* Emigrant.
- 4 On the way, *muse.* Splendid.
- 5 For *à bon marché.* Cheap.

Europe for that ware. He has upwards of twenty painters employed. Am very sorry that I cannot stay here long enough to get your picture put on a small box, for here are artists of the first merit.

Bronswig[1], December 23, 1809. *Couche* ½ p. 1. *Lev.* 7. At ½ p. 10 to Mercier's to breakfast *a la fourchette*[2]*;* fearing there would be only wine and meat, took coffee before I went. *Y:* Dr. Valentine, Mr. d'Escalonne, *controleur des postes*, and a young man supposed *commis*[3] *de* Mercier. Home at 12, when Dr. Zimmerman came in and sat ½ hour. Story of Archentloiz, a gambler and swindler. His fraud on Baron Berkley of Zurich, for which the Baron, Archentloiz, *et sa demirep*[4] put in prison at Berlin. Robinson sat with us. Received note from Mercier that the gentlemen proposed for *comp. de voyage*[5] for me to Cassel had made a different arrangement. Thus I am condemned either to wait till Monday night for the diligence or to take *Post Extra*[6]. Saturday night —Since writing the above which was at about 2 P. M., I have been deliberating on the important point just mentioned and have at length resolved once more to submit to the horrors of *post extra tout seul*[7] as far, at least, as Göttingen. As usual, therefore, I have everything to do, everything to pack up, the most dire of all labors, and twenty letters to write, having not yet begun. Have been employed as follows:

---

1 For Braunschweig. Brunswick.
2 A *déjeuner à la fourchette* is a meat breakfast, at which forks must be used.
3 Clerk.
4 And his woman of questionable chastity. (*Demi-rep* from *demi* and *réputation*. The English word demirep is similarly formed.)
5 For *compagnon de voyage.* Traveling companion.
6 A private conveyance at greater expense.
7 Entirely alone.

At 3 to Zimmerman's by appointment. (Note: Took no dinner, my breakfast *a la fourchette* sufficing); sat an hour with Zim. He is a most interesting man; at the age of 71 he has the animation, the ardor, and the sensibility of youth, replete with science and a mind really vigorous and correct; withal, frankness and cheerfulness which render him a very interesting social companion; would have staid longer but had engaged to meet Robinson and Hosack at ½ p. 4. R. and H. came and with them Zimmerman *fils*[1]. They all sat more than an hour and till I wished them gone, as I expected Mercier at 6, but the young Zimmerman entertained us very much with anecdotes of various personages. The Duke of Brunswick; Captain Helvig, son of the Professor of this place; of the late Dr. Zimmerman, author of "*Solitude*[2]," &c. He died insane at Hanover; his son is now mad; my friend here is no relation, or a very distant. At 6 came in Mercier; he is native of the island of Martinique; educated in Philadelphia; has served eleven years in the French armies; is here *commiss. 'gen. de la haute police*[3]; does not look more than 30, has a wife, *francoise, alitee*[4], and supposed incurable. While we were talking, Zimmerman *le pere*[5] came in to bring me letter for a friend of his in Weimar (you will find out presently all where I am going, which I did not intend); these two men, though living in the same town, had never before met. Zimmerman lives

---

1 The younger Zimmerman.
2 Same meaning as in English.
3 For *commissaire général*, etc.
4 A French lady (*Française*). Bedridden (*alitée*).
5 The elder Zimmerman.

retired, continually writing. He went off and left Mercier, who sat till 9. Gave me two letters to his friends at Cassel. There is rumor that the King will not be there till the 30th, though he had appointed the 25th. The incident of the breakfaster, who called while Mercier was here.

Göttingen, December 25, 1809, (Monday). I was too busy yesterday to write you a line and we must therefore go back to Sunday morning. I rose at 7. At ½ p. 9 went to Mercier to prevent his calling on me. He had already got out and gone to my lodgings. Fortunately we met in the street and he came home with me. *Sor.* again to Baron de Schale; out, but my servant and pilot who spoke only German, hearing me also ask for *M'lle la Baronne*, brought her pell-mell down stairs into the court in dishabille[1] and to see, she knew not whom nor for what. Went up and sat ½ hour with M'lle, a very pleasing, pretty, amiable *personne*[2]. Thence to Lobecke's. He had gone that day to Cassel, but saw the *beau pere*[3] *le prefect*[4]. Thence to Zimmerman's, where ½ hour; he gave me a letter for the celebrated astronomer, Mr. ———. Home and met going in to see me Mr. d'Escalonne, *l'inspecteur des postes*[5]. He had got me a carriage, that of Monsieur Otto, *l'inspecteur General des Postes*[6] de Westphalia, and would take me with him to see Mr. O. Went and

---

1 A word anglicized from the French *déshabillé*, in undress.
2 Person.
3 For *beau-père*. Father-in-law.
4 If Burr meant this for a French word he should have spelled it *préfet*.
5 D'Escalonne is called both *contrôleur* (controller) and *inspecteur* (inspector).
6 Inspector General of the mails, *i. e.*, Postmaster-General.

found him and his wife, an English woman, a very sprightly, charming Yorkshire girl. They begged me to take breakfast with them, *a la fourchette*, at ½ p. 1 ; agreed. Mercier came in and walked home with me Talked of X matters and thinks the moment favorable. Home. Wrote Menard & Prathes, the booksellers at Hamburg; also a note to Robinson to tell him to call at 3. To breakfast at the *Hotel Roi de Prusse*[1] (Natalis). Sat down at 2. Three courses of meat, variety of wines and coffee. It was to me exceedingly like dinner, having breakfasted at 8. *Y.*: d'Escalonne, Mercier, and Mr. O. Sat till 4, all very gay ; all talking English except Escalonne. A good deal of X again. All want a hand. Monsieur O. gave me a circular letter to all the postmasters on the road ; something to expedite me ; being in German, I could not read it, but it made the postmasters amazingly active and civil ; every one after reading it made me a most profound bow. Got home a little past 4. On the way met *M'lle la Baronne* and walked with her. Found Hosack and Robinson at my quarters and they helped me pack up. The horses came before I was ready, punctually at 5 as I had ordered, with the handsome carriage of Mons. O. Off at 6 and arrived here about noon this 25th of December, being Christmas day. The first three miles flat as before ; then more and more hilly, better settled and cultivated. Nothing very remarkable except about one mile back saw on a hill the ruins of a romantic castle on the summit of a hill on my left ; find on inquiring of

1 The King of Prussia Hotel.

Professor ——— that it is one of those enchanted castles where was held in durance a lady who was finally delivered by the valiant knight, R———. I regret exceedingly for your sake that I did not go to see it ; you do so love enchanted castles ! One of the towers is almost entire and is very lofty. The distance from Braunschweig (all these different spellings are from authority) to this place is about fifty English miles. The road very bad, though the greater part of the way *chaussè*[1] (turnpike). Immediately on my arrival sent my two letters to the Professors Heeren[2] and Gaus with my card. Monsieur H. came in almost immediately and found me dressing ; agreed to call in an hour, which he did. Walked to Professor Gaus, *l'astronome tres celebre ; un juenhomme peut-etre* 25 to 32[3]. Will relate to you an anecdote of his history very honorable to him and to Zimmerman, who *discovered* him. To the Observatory. The largest telescope is about ten feet long and one diameter. The observatory is one of the castles (rotundas) of the old walls ; thence to the library, 200,000 volumes. Took tea with Professor Heeren. Home at 6. Took tea again and have ordered my horses for 4 to-morrow morning. Snowed all yesterday and till near noon to-day ; not fast ; now chiefly melted ; only evidence, the cold and the mud ; was very chilly

---

1 For *chaussée.* Same in meaning as causeway, with which it is connected philologically.
2 Arnold Hermann Louis Heeren (1760-1842). German historian and scholar, who lectured on philosophy at Gottingen.
3 The very famous astronomer ; a young man (*jeune homme*) perhaps 25 to 32. Karl Friedrich Gausz (1777-1855) was director of the Gottingen Observatory from 1807 to his death. He published numerous works well known to mathematicians and astronomers all over the world. He was also one of the pioneers in the study of magnetism and electricity, and one of the discoverers of the electric telegraph.

last night, so resolve to take a sleep to-night. Five hundred students here.

Cassel, December 26, 1809. Now capital of the kingdom of Westphalia. Notwithstanding my resolutions, did not get to bed till 11 last night. At 4 was waked, but so imperfectly that I turned over and slept till 5. It had been snowing all night and there are three or four inches of snow on the ground, which makes the traveling even more tedious than usual. Snowed hard, always wind ahead on land. Was glad to keep myself close; scarcely looked out till we got to the end of our first stage, three miles (sixteen English). Münden is at the confluence of the Werts[1] and the Fulda, which together form the Weser. As you approach Münden, the north banks of the Weser become very high. I should suppose 300 feet, and very steep. A road for some hundred yards is cut in the side of the mountain. To your right a ridge and a fine view of the river and town, which has the appearance of great antiquity and may have ———— inhabitants. Cross the Werts on a very solid stone bridge. Stopped at the post-house, where were several pretty children and two pretty and genteel-looking girls. The youngest about 16, Louisa, tall, graceful, had just received *cudot*[2], a very handsome *guitarre*[3], but I could not persuade [her] to give me a tune. Got breakfast and off at 12, having been detained an hour to get my carriage mended. On leaving Münden you have the Fulda on your right and a like mountain on

---

1 For Werra.
2 For *cadeau.* Present.
3 For *guitare.* Guitar.

the left, into which a road is cut as before. This hill is cut into walks and laid out into whimsical gardens to the very top, within ½ English mile or more of the town. There you leave the river and ascend by a gentle acclivity. It appeared to me to be an English mile from the bottom to the top of the hill. Much such an one as that you rise in coming from Fishkill to Peekskill. Woods on each side till you approach the summit, which is a plain whereon is a village and church. After rising and descending several considerable hills, you open at once on an extensive valley surrounded by mountains, the Fulda winding through the valley, and in the center of it Cassel, of which you have a perfect bird's-eye view, being, I should suppose, 200 feet above it. From the first view of Cassel till you reach it may be about two English miles, following the road. The approaches are extremely picturesque. Cross the Fulda on a very handsome stone bridge. At 3 I was put down at the *Hotel de Westphalie*[1] where I have an indifferent room and a prospect of bad attendance. Rising that long hill we overtook a very old man evidently exhausted by the storm and the fatigue, with a younger one (about 30) by his side, aiding him. The young man addressed himself to the postillion to ask a place for the patriarch. The postillion referred him to me. The young man turned to me, made me a speech with an accent the most pathetic and a countenance full of sweetness and solicitude. The pantomime was eloquent, for I understood not a word, though every syllable was

---

1 The Westphalia Hotel.

perfectly intelligible. The old man cast a pensive look of humble expectation. I did not wait to hear out the speech. The drama spoke most feelingly. We all assisted the old man to get in and we put him down at the door of a decent house in the village. Three comely young women ran out in all the snow and seemed to strive for the first embrace. An old woman at the window partook of the joy of his return. He told them that he was indebted to me and I had an hundred curtsies and *bedanke mich's*[1], and might, if I had [got] out, have had as many kisses. I never saw the scene half as well acted on any stage. That man, thought I, has lived happy and will die happy. While dressing, sent out my letters (with cards) to the following : From Mercier to : *Le* Comte de Fursten-stein (formerly Camus[2], who was with the King (Jerome), in United States), now *prem. min. d'etat*[3]; *a* Mons. de Bercagny, *prefet de police*[4]; *a* Mon. Allèye, *employè dans le depart. d'af. Etrang*[5]. From General St. Simon at Hanover : To *le* Col. Wolff, *Chev.* &c., *Com't le chev. leg. du Garde Royale*[6]. From Professor Zimmerman (or his son *ne scais lequel*[7]), to *le* Baron de Nordenflycht, &c., &c. From ———, *chargè des affaires de S. M. le R. de Suede a* Han.[8] to *le* Comte de Levenhjelm, with three lines of titles. Enough surely

---

1 The Germans say *Ich bedanke mich*. I thank you.
2 The word *camus* is a French word meaning flat-nosed. It may have been a sobriquet of Count Furstenstein.
3 For *Premier Ministre d'État*. Prime minister.
4 Police prefect.
5 For *employé dans le Département des Affaires Étrangères*. Employed in the Foreign Office.
6 For *Chevalier*, etc. *Commandant le Chevalier de la Legion de la Garde Royale*. Knight &c. Commanding Knight of the Legion of the Royal Guard.
7 For *ne sais lequel*. I do not know which.
8 For *Chargé d'affaires de Sa Majesté le Roi de Suède à Hanovre*. Chargé d'affaires of His Majesty the King of Sweden at Hanover.

for the four days I have allotted to this place. There was no theatre open at Bronsvig. Here is both a French and a German, there being an opera at the French to-night. I am going to take a seat *incog.* in the *"Paterre Noble"*[1]. The theatre is small but very beautiful. The King's boxes, crimson and gold ; gilt lattices. The house lighted by a *lustre* suspended from the middle of the ceiling containing forty argand lamps. The auditors may see each other very distinctly. There was not a performer remarkable for beauty or voice or diction. M'lle Delêtre, much in the style of Mrs. Johnson, but more animated, the best. Got near a sensible, *convenable*[2] man. Upon the whole was much amused and got the worth of my 16 bon-gros.—exactly half a dollar, which is the highest price for any seat in the house. The bill is enclosed to save me the trouble of answering a dozen questions. The orchestra good, about thirty performers. The whole house (four rows of boxes) may be able to contain 600 or 800. Did not see a single striking face, (though there might have been fifty which I did not see). The side boxes not brilliant. The King not arrived. The convocation of the states postponed till the 10th of January. Won't stay here, that's pos. Zimmerman fond of cats.

27. *Couche* 1. Rose 8. Off before breakfast to the stage house (post-house) to see about the ways and means of getting off, whither I have not told you. Well, now I'll tell you. To Gotha and Weimar.

---

1 For *Parterre des Nobles.* The nobles' pit.
2 Agreeable.

And for what? Aye, that you'll know when I get there! A diligence goes at 1 P. M. Friday, the 29th, the day after to-morrow. In that I go. No more *extra post*. After breakfast called on Mr. Mylart with my letter of credit for the enormous sum of —— No matter! It shall carry me to Paris happy. Then took coach and went to see the celebrated Palace of ——, now called Napoleon Höhe.[1] Went through the buildings. The main building all new furnished from Paris; the right wing with the furniture of the late Prince. The old Palace, higher up the mountain, mod.[2] ruins, with ancient arms and furniture of the Middle Ages. Had not time to go to see Hercules on the top of the mountain[3], nor the immense *oran 'gerie*[4]. Two statues and two pictures of the King, not one of the Queen. The *maitre*, keeper, or *prem. valet*[5] who shows the house, was in the same capacity to the expelled Prince. Much like a gentleman. Amused me greatly. The bedrooms; the Cyprian alcove lined with mirrors; not, however, for her Majesty to see her royal *face*. Home at 3. Paid 2 dollars to one and 1 dollar to another (shewer)[6] at the two Palaces. Instead of dinner walked out to see the town. It is really unique in many particulars. I will endeavor to buy some *tableau*[7], for I am bad at description, nor is it possible to afford the time.

---

1 Height. (It is in more modern times known as Wilhelmshohe.)
2 Modern?
3 An immense statue of Hercules rises from the castle on the height.
4 Orangery.
5 The master, keeper or chief valet (*premier valet*).
6 The form shewer is archaic for shower, one who shows.
7 A picture or picturesque representation. (Should be the plural, *tableaux*.)

Bought *bru.*[1] Home at 5 and had tea. Gave up the opera that I might write to you and make notes. Only think, not one of my cards returned, nor any message! A gentleman in regimentals (a sub.[2]) has called and inquired for me, but left neither message nor card! Mon'r said: *"Je suis trop* * * * * *dav. vu un om. lab."*[3] Streets badly lighted. At Bronswig not at all. No *trottoir*[4] anywhere. *Dit 19,000 habit.*[5] in Cassel. Are building a new penitentiary and work-house here. What pity they know nothing of Panopticon[6]! Snowing all day and about six inches on the ground. These mountains are parts of the Hartz, of which Bruken' or Broken[7], famed in legend, is the highest, about the height of our Alleghanies. The Giant's Mountain, another of Hartz.

28. *Couche* 12. Rose ½ p. 7. Mr. de Martens[8], celebrated as the author of a book on the law of nations, *" Relations Exterieures"*[9], being the only man in this place whom I had any real wish to see, sent him my card with a message that I should call on him at any hour he would be at leisure in the forenoon. Replied that he would be happy to see me from 11 to

---

1 Burr seems to be still using the Swedish word for bread, but it should be spelled *brod.*
2 For subaltern?
3 Possibly for " *Je suis trop* * * * * *d'avoir vu un homme laborieux.*" " I am too [happy?] to have seen a laborious man."
4 Sidewalk.
5 For *habitants.* Residents. Said [to have] 19,000 residents.
6 Referring again to Bentham's work, which discusses the question of what to do with convicts, how to make them useful.
7 For Brocken.
8 Probably Georg Friedrich von Martens, born at Hamburg in 1756, died at Frankfort-on-the-Main, 1821; a German publicist and diplomatist; he became professor of law at Gottingen in 1784.
9 This was a work in three volumes published at Berlin in 1801. Its full title was: " *Cours Diplomatique ou Tableau des Relations Extérieures des Puissances de l'Europe.*" " The Course of Diplomacy or a Picture of the External Relations of the Powers of Europe."

12. *Sor.* 10 to Mylart's about money. He appointed to call on me at 2. To several booksellers to get map and *tableau* of Cassel. Bought you a beautiful map of the Napoleon Höhe and its environs, for which paid the enormous price of 1½ dollars. The bookstores here are humble things. Thence to the post-house again to be sure of the diligence. The man put me quite in a fever by telling me that it had just gone! Only think of the horrid alternative of waiting here a week or taking *post extra* for fifteen German miles! It put me quite out of breath. Fortunately the man was mistaken. The diligence goes at 3 P. M. to-morrow. At 12 to Mr. de Martens. A tall, handsome man about 42. Dark hair and eyes; very sprightly in his manner. Received me with very great politeness and thanked me over and over again. Expressed great regret at my determination to leave town to-morrow. Home at 1. Read *Moniteur de Westphalie*[1] till 2. *Diner a tab d'hote*[2]. Of six at table not one who could speak French. A very young professor from Koningsburg[3] was the only one whose countenance strongly invited acquaintance. At 3 (Mylart not coming) sent again to the post-house and actually paid for a seat in the diligence so that you will no longer dare to doubt whether I go to-morrow. To convince you, huzzy, here is the ticket! On my way home with my High Dutch valet for pilot and counsel, *muse, tres bo*[4]; 1½

1 The Westphalia " Monitor."
2 For *diner à* [*la*] *table d'hôte.*
3 For Königsberg.
4 For *Muse. Très bonne. Muse*, very good.

336

marks. Oh, I forgot to tell my dear little Gampy[1]; he would have jumped out of his skin to see it; such a family and such music, bnt I must give him the particulars. The principal personages were : 1, a jackass; 2, two monkeys dressed in regimentals, one in green, the other in scarlet; 3, an enormous bear; 4, drummer and bagpiper. But they did dance in such a style, and the monkeys played so many tricks to the poor bear and Herr[2] Bear did so growl and Gamp did so laugh, but I'll tell him all about it next time. Yesterday I must have been possessed by the devil. A pretty little girl about 15 years old came into my room with a little *guitarre* in her hand and muttering a few words in German began to sing and play. Could you imagine anything more calculated to fascinate me? I drove her rudely out! To be sure, I did give her a *goodengroshen*[3], which was probably much more than she expected; but I was unkind. One minute after, I was sorry and sent for her, but she was not to be found; and I have been all day looking out for her in vain. There are troops of these singers and players of all ages and sexes. Several of them have amused me very much. One in particular, a girl of about 11, has a very fine voice which she accompanies with her violin in a charming style. Have a great mind to bring her out to United States for you. She will teach Gam'y German and would presently serve him

---

1 Meaning his grandson. Notice the extraordinary manner in which Burr throws in a reference to one of his amorous escapades between a remark to his daughter and one to his grandson !
2 Mr. Bear.
3 For *Guten*-groschen. Good groschen.

other purposes. She is quite decently dressed but, as all the girls of the lower order are here, bareheaded ; snowing all the while and very cold, yet playing out doors and of course without a glove. She must be as tough as a little white bear. I will bring her out for little Gamp. I am to-day more civil to all these little creatures to atone for the barbarity of yesterday. How truly English that was ! Not a visit from any one of my six addressees. *Tant mieux.* I have seen de M. and all I wish to see, and shall get off the sooner and henceforth you will see fewer delays. *Ecoutez*[1]. At Göttingen Professor Heeren told me two very important articles of news. First, the divorce of Emperor and Empress, the manner of it is noble and worthy of him; second, the Emperor's assent to the independence of Mexico and the other Spanish colonies ! Now, why the devil didn't he tell me of this two years ago ?

Bischausen (four miles west from Cassel), December 30, 1809. Saturday. Sat up till 2 on Thursday night pretending to write and get ready for setting off on Friday. Rose at 8. At 9 sent to Myart, who came over with 23 *Fred. d'ors*[2] which I had agreed to take. *Deus nobis hæc otia fecit*[3]. At 11 received card of Mons. Allèye, who sent word that he had not sooner been able to find me, as my card was Brendecke's, Bronsvig, instead of my Cassel address. At 12 came in de Martens and sat ½ hour. He offered many allurements to change my determination of leaving

---

1 Listen.
2 A Prussian Friedrich d'or was a gold coin worth about $4.
3 God made this leisure for us. (Quoted from Vergil's first Eclogue.)

town. The most powerful, which, indeed, made me hesitate, was his conversation. He resembles Gallatin with more of fashion and animation, and something younger. Happening to mention the resemblance, it came out that his *belle-mere*[1] was born Gallatin and *genevoise.* Mr. de M. is *Hambourgeois* by birth. At 2 came in Bercagny, *la com. gen'l de police.* I was in my traveling costume, my trunks packed and ready. He apologized over and over again for the delay of his visit (business was the burthen of it), asked me to dine, proposed various parties. It was too late, I had really determined to go. Mr. Bercagny is a very gay, cheerful man of about 40 ; looks too good-tempered for his office. He sat till I wished him gone and gave signs of impatience, for I feared to lose my passage in the diligence. At 3 punctually went to the stage office with my baggage. There were no signs of going. It was blowing and snowing violently. After pacing the court yard about twenty minutes I fortunately found the *conducteur*[3] and *veny* fortunately he could speak French. Told me the diligence would go a little after 5 and begged me to be very punctual. I was punctual ; then it would certainly go at 6. By way of consolation, went to my quarters and took dinner. Was in the field again at 6 and determined not to quit it. At 7 we set off. The storm had risen to a tempest. Our road lay right through the mountains, something like those between Croton and Peekskill.

---

[1] Mother-in-law.
[2] A Hamburger.
[3] Conductor.

The snow had become deep and in places excessively drifted. We were six in the wagon. I had the worst place, which is everywhere the lot of the stranger except in Scotland and Sweden. The storm in our face; the wagon badly covered. We were all covered with snow. Every half hour we got fast in some snowdrift; were once obliged to send back a postillion an English mile for additional horses to drag us up a mountain, and at another time to send as far forward to get men and tools to dig us out of the snow and open a path. These operations took up about two hours each between 12 and 5 in the night. We arrived here at 2 P. M. this day, having been nineteen hours indefatigably employed in getting over four miles, about nineteen English! And what do you do here and why don't you go on? *Infandum regina jubes.*[1], but I will tell you. The diligence goes no further on my route till 6 A. M. to-morrow. Having resolved against post extra, here I wait with all imaginable patience in a humble inn where I am received with extreme good humor and filth, and having dined on potatoes and drank beer and, since, some execrable tea, which was unnecessary, I am now at 10 about to undergo the operation of stewing and freezing, as heretofore described, there being no sort of covering except the down bed. I suffered a good deal with the cold last night. My companions appeared quite at ease. They were in constant good humor, sang a great deal, two of them having very fine voices.

---

[1] Latin. Queen, thou dost order an unspeakable thing. (Quoted from Vergil's "Æneid," II. 3.)

Among them all during the whole nineteen hours I did not hear a single tone or expression of ill humor or impatience.

31. Up at 6 and ready to move, so soon, at least, as I shall have swallowed my coffee which is on the stove by my side. Take notice, Madame, that I never again get under one of these infernal down beds. It has been a night of extreme fatigue and I had great ————[1].

Gotha, December 31, 1809. At the moment of writing the last line above the *wagon-meister*[2] came a *third* time to inform me that the diligence was waiting, and added that the passengers, I had before understood there were none, were growing impatient. Disposed of my coffee, paid my bill, 32 *gooden groshen*, and packed up my loose articles with all possible dispatch, and at ½ p. 7 we were under weigh. You must divine how that sentence would have been concluded. The passengers were three *paysans* going to Eisenach. They strove to amuse me by details regarding the country through which we were passing and the incidents of modern times. If my pipe were out, would run through the snow 100 yards to fetch me fire, &c. We had six horses to drag us up the mountain. These mountains are no more than great hills. At every ¼ mile a village. The soil is better here than in the plains of Hanover. At three miles we changed horses and postillion. Our new postillion was an angel, quite inspired. We went on fast more

---

1 The sentence is unfinished.
2 For *Wagenmeister*. Conductor.

than half the way and once he actually galloped for near 200 yards. At 4 we were at Eisenach, having made five miles in 8½ hours, a most wonderful transit for this region. Eisenach is in a valley of three or four leagues circumference and several hundred feet below the surrounding *mountains*, one of which conceals it from your view till you enter the *suburbs*. May have about 10,000 inhabitants. The plain, however, is in view, and the salt-works for ½ hour before, and ornamented with rows of trees. Eisenach was (is) a walled town. The walls of stone, now in decay. On the right as you enter, a castle about 100 feet above the town, walled in and capable of defence (before cannon invented). It is a neat town; has a theatre open this very night, formerly the residence of the —— no, that must be mistake. These little walled towns are a great nuisance to travelers; searches and questions. The theatre would not have detained me, but I did wish to examine the noble ruins of a castle on the very summit of the mountain immediately beyond (on this side) the town. It is exactly the scene of a fairy tale. Here, no doubt, many a fair damsel has been confined by diabolical enchantments and delivered by valiant Christian knights. But a matter nearer home engages my attention. The postmaster, who speaks French, informed me that the diligence must wait till that from Frankfort arrived, which was not expected till midnight; might be after. Having been two nights without rest—— (Happy New Year! The clock strikes 12; a band of music is playing near my window, guns firing, as with us, &c.)— without rest and undergoing great fatigues, I determined to take post horses to Gotha. Went to a tavern, took tea, and at 5 was in my calash. The postillion was a slow-motioned rascal who was 5½ hours bringing me to this place. My first business was to go personally to the diligence office and secure a place for the morning. The expense of post extra is beyond all bearing. Before Eisenach we enter the *kingdom* of Saxony (Ch's Loss' kingdom)[1]. (Note the bridges over the ———— at Eisenach.) And here I am in a great *auberge*[2] where no creature speaks a word of French or English. Have had a supper brought which I did not want and did not order and twenty other *mesintelligences*[3] which I will tell you another time; but expecting to be called at ½ p. 5, must bid you good-night. Good-morning! this 1st of January, 1810. It has been snowing all day and is now raining very hard. Having a bed with *couverture* and *a chauf lit*[4], promise myself a few hours' comfort. (Note : the infernal *douaniers* and *commissaires de police !*[5] I wish Mercier[6] were police officer over the whole world. For your amusement I enclose a copy of the paper I have signed. It will puzzle their Highnesses.)

Gotha, January 1, 1810, 7 A. M. Was really up at 6 and have breakfasted. Not the better for the

---

1 Who was Charles Loss ? Further on, under date of February 4, 1810, Burr mentions him again.
2 Inn.
3 For *mésintelligences.* Misunderstandings.
4 With quilt and bed-warmer (*chauffe-lit*).
5 The infernal custom-house officers and police commissaries.
6 It will be remembered that Mercier was the highest police official of Brunswick, Germany.

wine. Raining very hard. How sorry I feel for the lower orders of people when it rains on a holiday! They have so few enjoyments, in Europe especially, nowhere so few as in England. It is now said that the diligence will not go till 9. At Eisenach saw the first sleighs I have seen since leaving America. They were pretty little things; fine horses ornamented with cords and tassels and bells; gentlemen and ladies. Saw a great number of pretty faces the hour I was there among the servants and *bourgeoise*[1] disfigured by a strange head-dress and all false hips, even girls of 5 years old. At the tavern I caught one to examine those hips; she screamed as if I was going to eat her, to the great amusement of twenty spectators. The fountains at Eisenach and Gotha; all the bells ringing since 7 o'clock. (Forgot Kreutzberg, a little town in a plain (a hollow) in the midst of the mountains, where are extensive salt-works; a pretty scene as you descend the mountains; it is three miles west (the other side) of Eisenach.) 9 A. M. The Frankfort stage (in which I am to go to Weimar) not yet arrived. Determined to wait for it. Will go out in all the rain to see if there be anything to amuse you. There are plenty, I know, but not visible at this hour; besides I dare not be long absent. Just as I had finished the last sheet a message from a lady now somewhere in this great house that she was going alone in a carriage to Weimar, and a proposition that I should take a seat with her, to go immediately. *Voluntiers*[2],

---

1 For *bourgeoises*. Middle-class women.
2 For *volontiers*. Willingly.

Madame! I understood this to be an overture of economy and not of gallantry. She may be deformed and 90 for aught I have learnt. From Weimar you shall know the result, Weimar, Weimar, for which I have gone seventy miles out of my way, have expended so much time and money! and all this for thee, lovely d'Im.[1] I shall at least have the satisfaction of having performed my engagement; perhaps the only reward, but how little did I know how much I should regret the time. Something I told you a few days past has inspired this impatience; a little, *leetle* ray of light. Adieu; 6 miles to Weimar, we shall arrive about midnight.

4 P. M. *toujours*[2] Gotha. The Frankfort stage not arrived! The *postmeister*[3] now says that it is probable the rain and melting of the snow may have so swelled the rivers as to render them impassable (Dumfries)[4] and that of course there can be no conjecture about the arrival. Very pleasant, Madame, to be a whole day in a place where there is no being (* * * *)[5] who can understand a sentence I say nor be understood by me. This is not the worst. I would amuse myself very well, could *go* (*have gone*) to church or to see some of the fine things, or, as at Glückstadt, could make acquaintances, but my great apprehension of losing the damned diligence keeps me

---

1 For d'Imhoff. In Davis's abridged reprint the last words of this sentence are "and all this for the lovely D'Or." This means nothing. The reference is doubtless to Lady Imhoff, whose acquaintance Burr made in Sweden. She is mentioned under date of September 9, 1809, as Fruken Imhoff. As the reader proceeds it will become plain that Burr has come to Weimar to meet a certain aristocratic lady of whom Lady Imhoff had spoken.
2 Gotha still.
3 Postmaster.
4 Dumfries is a city of Scotland in a county of the same name. Does Burr mention it here because he had a similar experience there with impassable rivers?
5 An undecipherable word.

from being abroad more than ½ hour at a time. Nevertheless I have been all day roving; have made some acquaintances, some discoveries about those false hips, which, to be sure, cost me 1½ dollars. Several little adventures; know the town. Every lady you look at sitting in her window nods to you. I drew strange conclusions at first; but how dangerous are rash inferences! Have seen only one beautiful woman. Lo, the diligence arrives, I saw it from my window! "But what has become of the lady?" Too long a story to tell and worth nothing when told. Have been over to see the diligence. It goes at 7. The price to Weimar is 2 *ecus*[1], about $1.75 of your money. There are two passengers, of whom one speaks French. A very forbidding phiz, but not worse than my own. The weather mild.

Weimar, *a la fin*[2], Weimar, Tuesday evening, January 2, 1810. At 6 last evening at Gotha went to the *stage-house*. These post-houses are not always taverns, but there is always a room with fire for the passengers. Here sat with my two companions till 8. I was amused by the *bourgeoises* who were continually coming in to visit one belonging to the house. A vigorous, active, athletic race; reminded one of those German women spoken of by Tacitus and Cæsar. Their laugh might have been heard a mile. At 8 we embarked and moved. (But Gamp is tired and must go to bed. He will try to devote a few moments to you to-morrow.)

---

1 An *écu* is commonly called a crown.
2 Finally.

3. *Couche* 11. Rose 7. Had a fine sleep. Have breakfasted and am refreshed. Now to go back to the waggoning[1] at Gotha. Going in and out of these towns you pay a toll for passing the gate, 1½ gro. It was warm. The wagon well cushioned and our very slow motion relieved us from the jolting, though we were without springs. At the end of a mile the postillion stopt[1] at a tavern to take *snaps*[2] and I went in, as I always do, to see &c. The hostess is the picture of Megara[3]. She asked me if I would have brandy. No. Beer? No. She then turned to her husband and the postillion, the only auditors, and abused me with a profusion of curses. A fellow who would come in and warm himself by her fire and drink nothing! The postillion informed her that I was a Frenchman who understood not a word of German and I affected to understand nothing. At going out I very civilly bid her good-night. She threw back her head with the most malignant expression and demanded 1 groschen for having warmed myself by her fire, which I paid her and again bid her good-night. The wagon being closed, I saw nothing. Arrived at Erfurth[4] at 2 in the morning. Took a servant to show me the houses where the Emperors Napoleon and Alexander lodged while forming the treaty in 1806. Got coffee after an hour's delay and without undressing lay down to sleep till called to continue our journey. Was waked by the servant at ½ p. 6 to know if I

1 So in the MS.
2 For *schnapps*.
3 For Megæra, one of the avenging goddesses, the Erinyes or Furies.
4 For Erfurt.

would have breakfast; again at 7 to know if I would have my boots cleaned; these inquiries being answered in the negative, and *with great good humor*, I rose and after two hours delay we moved about 9. An open country with gentle swells and extensive plains of rich soil and highly cultivated. No enclosures; the cattle are not suffered to go at large. Destitute of wood. Two English miles before reaching Weimar you are on an elevated plain terminated by hills more distant. An extensive horison[1] on every side. You do not suspect a valley till, within ½ mile of Weimar, you discover the town in a vale 100 feet below you. I was not deceived in the phiz of my *compagnon*. He was morose to rudeness, a merchant from the neighborhood of Frankfort, and being bound to Leipzig, left us at Erfurth. The other, who came with me hither, a most amiable youth, a sub. in the *chasseurs*[2] of *Saxe*[3], devoted himself to me with constant assiduity. At 2 arrive and put up at the Elephant, not a creature in the house speaking a word of French. Was shown into a very, very small triangular room, coarsely furnished and no bell. " Have you no larger room ? " " No." So I found this very good. Let me see, I don't recollect where I breakfasted. In fact, I think I had not breakfasted at all. Ordered tea. Opened my trunks, sent out the following letters with my address :[4]

At 4 came in the Baron de Schrade[5], who introduced himself to me as the brother of *la* Baronne

---

1 So in the MS.
2 The *chasseurs* were originally infantry or cavalry soldiers in the French army trained for rapid maneuvers. In Germany they are called *Jager*, and are practically sharpshooters.
3 French for Saxony.
4 Here there is a break in the MS.
5 His true name was Von Schardt.

de Stein[1]; presently a message from *la* Baronne de Stein, asking me to call and take tea. Message from M. de Bartuck[2], apologizing that he could not call till morning. From *la* Princesse Caroline, requesting to see me in the morning at 11. Then in came my landlord, expressed his dissatisfaction with my room and asked if I would not prefer a larger. "Most certainly." In five minutes myself and baggage were transferred to a large, handsome, well-furnished room, with every convenience. (*On fait peu de cas des voyageurs en diligence[3].*) At 6 to *la* Bar. de Stein. *Y: Sa fille, grande, belle, bien fait, chev. no., blonde[4];* Madame *la* Bar. d'Egglestein; *la* Bar. de Knebel, *dame d'hon.[5] de la Princesse* Caroline; all in calico and *en famille.* Tea made at the table of which and biscuit (rusk) I partook. Sat about an hour, then home and engaged in fifty nameless occupations the remainder of the evening. The Elephant is on one of the principal squares. Looking out of my window just at dawn this morning saw great numbers of people, principally women, erecting tents and slight sheds all round the square. It must be a great market day or a fair. After breakfast went out for an hour to see the show and the people. It is a kind of fair. Made one pleasant acquaintance. At 10 came in Mons. Bertuch, a frank, sprightly, sensible man, of much learning and

---

1 Frau von Stein was one of the best known ladies at the Weimar court. She is especially noted in German literature because of her close intimacy with the poet Goethe and her remarkable influence upon his poetic development.
2 Friedrich Justin Bertuch (1747–1822) was a book and art dealer in Weimar. He was also an author of some note and a councilor in the government of the Duke of Saxe-Weimar.
3 Stage-coach passengers are slighted.
4 Her daughter, tall, beautiful, well formed (*bien faite*), black hair (*cheveux noirs*), blonde.
5 For *dame d'honneur.* Maid of honor. Frau von Knebel was the wife of Karl Ludwig von Knebel (1744–1834), who was a close friend of the poets Goethe and Herder, and himself an author.

in *liason*[1] with all the *literati*[2] of Germany. Appears about 55 but says he is 67; has promised to announce me to Wieland[3] and Goethe[4] and gave me some *renseignments* as to my duty toward the court. At 10 to *la* Princesse Caroline, a very lovely, interesting woman. *Υ:* M'lle *la* Baronne de Knebel, Madame *la* Baronne de Stein. They inquired with great interest about the Imhoffs; about America. At 12 to Bertuch's to get further instructions. To *le* Baron de Schrade, where ½ hour. *Υ* Madame *la* Baronne. To Baron ———, *marèchal de la cour*[5]; he was indisposed and invisible. *Υ* Madame *sa femme* whom I met the first evening. *Chez* Madame de Stein and her *belle soeur*[6]. Madame d'Egglestein told me that M'lle Gore would be glad to see me. (An English lady of fortune, resident here for many years; sister of Lady Cooper, now in Italy.) Went there and sent in my address; denied ! To Madame de Stein's; out, which was true, for I met her on my way home. Just after I got home came in an elderly man superbly dressed, with sword and *chap. bra.*[7] I supposed he must be a Baron at least. He very formally delivered me a message from *S. A. le Duc Regnant*[8],

---

1 For *liasson*. Intimacy.
2 Latin. Men of letters.
3 Christoph Martin Wieland (1733–1813) was one of the best known of German authors. In 1772 he was called from his chair of philosophy and literature, at the University of Erfurt, to become tutor of the young Duke, the Crown Prince, at Weimar. There he remained until his death, some forty years afterward.
4 Goethe (1749–1832), the greatest of German poets and the author of " Faust," settled at Weimar in 1775 on the invitation of the Duke of Saxe-Weimar, Charles Augustus. Here he was the great center of attraction, not only as a poet, but also as a scientific investigator and a very high official in the ducal government. The friendship between him and the Duke was one of the most notable in history.
5 Marshal of the court.
6 For *belle-soeur*. Sister-in-law.
7 See Glossary.
8 For *Son Altesse le Duc Régnant*. His Highness the reigning Duke.

requesting me to dine with him the same day at ½ p. 2. There was no refusing, so made my *toilette*, got a sedan chair (much used here) and went *au Palais*. But just before going, the valet who attends me repeated to me an hundred times, with great impatience and emphasis, something which I could not comprehend, nor could any way conceive to be of the least importance ; but there happening to be below a gentleman who spoke French, with his aid I discovered that the valet wished to inform me that before going to court it was indispensable that I should send cards to two of the *great* officers of court, in which, the gentleman said, the valet was right. Gave him two cards and he went off very happy. Arrived *au Palais* was shown into a drawing room where was nobody. Presently came in maids of honor, two very pretty girls and *au fait*[1] to their duty. They led me into an adjoining room where was presented to *S. A. la Duchesse Regnante*[2]; to *S. A. la Duchesse* ———, sister of Emperor Alexander ; *au Prince Hereditaire*[3], a very amiable, well-bred young man of about 25, and finally came in *le Duc Regnant*[4]. The gentlemen led each a lady to dinner. I was placed on the right hand of *le pri. hered.*[3], *vis-a-vis la* Comtesse de Peyster, *dame d'hon. au* Princess Marie (de Russie[5]), a very interest-

---

1 Acquainted with.
2 Her Highness the reigning Duchess.
3 For *au Prince Héréditaire*. To the Crown Prince.
4 Karl August, Duke, and from 1815, Grand Duke, of Saxe-Weimar-Eisenach, was no ordinary ruler. His reign was the most brilliant epoch in the history of Saxe-Weimar. He was a gifted and intelligent patron of literature and art, and is especially notable as having been the patron and friend of Goethe. During his reign Weimar became a modern Athens. He was also the first of the German rulers to grant a liberal constitution.
5 For *dame d' honneur à la* Princesse Marie de Russie. Maid of honor to the Princess Marie of Russia.

ing face *et les plus belles mains*[1]. Marie is very handsome and does credit to her rank and birth. But I must stop with details and only make short notes to talk from. *La* Baronne Knebel, *dame d'hon.* a Princesse Caroline asked me to tea to-morrow (invitation of the Princesse). Baron d'Humbold[2]; *la* Princesse Caroline. Home at ½ p. 5 and at 6 to the theatre. No *grille* or *jalousie* before *les loges*[3] of the royal family. Much amused at theatre. Young Bertuch explained to me. Home at 9. Left to my valet to get *mus.*[4], which he did of his own taste. *Pas mauv.*[5] But white and white. It is so *fade.*[6] Tea, which was unnecessary. The battle of Jena terminated in this place ; in the town, gardens, houses, parks ; disorders and incidents of ditto. Major ———— riding through town without his head.

4. *Couche* ½ p. 12. *Lev.* 7. Note from Bertuch that he would call at 10 to take me to Weiland's[7] and Goethe's. At 10 *pere et fils*[8] called. Went first to Wieland's, 77. To Goethe's, 58[9]. *Y* Humboldt. *Les medailles*[10]. To *la* Baronne de Stein's ; *tete-a-tete* ½ hour. Promenade through the park ; crossing the little Ulm ; the summer house ; the fountains ; caves ; ruins ; walks and views. *Din. chez moi.* *Vin* Johan-

---

1 And the most beautiful hands.
2 Probably Wilhelm von Humboldt. Both he and his great brother Alexander bore the title of baron.
3 No railing or screen in front of the boxes, etc.
4 For *muse*.
5 For *pas mauvaise*. Not bad.
6 It is so insipid.
7 For Wieland.
8 Father and son. Probably Goethe and his son.
9 Goethe was actually over 60. Wieland was 76.
10 The medals or medallions.

nisberg[1]. At 6 to *la* Baronne Kneble *chez la Prin.*[2] Caroline's. *Y: La* Baronne de Stein ; *la Prin'se ;* a gentleman, and another *dame.* Tea and cheerful confab. M'lle Gore, who began an apology. " *Mad., tout belle femme a le droit de faire la coquette"*[3]. *On rit*[4]. Tea, bishop, cakes. At ½ p. 7 Bertuch sent his coach for me to take me to ———. *Y* a circle of about fifteen, very gay. Saw but one ; de Reizenstein, *souer de la* Comtesse de Peystre. *"Obstupui"*[5]. Rendezvous for to-morrow. *Helas*[6] Mary Ann! This day would make about 200 pages if written out. T.[7] would have been *cont.*[8] Home at 10.

5. *Couche* 2. *Lev.* 8. At 10 by appointment to Bertuch's. *Y: Le pere, le fils et fem.;* Mons. de Müller, *conseiller privè de la Regence et env. ext. de* Weimar *a* Paris[9]. To Madame Wollzogen, *souer de la veuve de* Schiller[10]. *Y ent.* Madame de Goethe[11], *c. d.* housekeeper. *Un fils 17*[12]. *Encore chez* Bertuch. *Alors av. un carte d'Amerique chez la belle* de Reizenstein[13]. *Y: Mere et* Com'se[14] de Peystre *sa souer.* M'lle has lost no ground to-day. We ran over United

1 For Johannisberger wine.
2 For *la Princesse.*
3 *Mad.* probably for *Mademoiselle.* " Mademoiselle, every (*toute*) beautiful woman has the right to coquet."
4 Laughter. Literally, one laughs.
5 Latin. I was stricken dumb.
6 For *hélas.* Alas !
7 Theodosia, Burr's daughter.
8 For *contente.* Pleased.
9 For *Conseiller Privé de la Régence et Envoyé Extraordinaire de* Weimar à Paris. Privy Councilor of the Regency and Envoy Extraordinary of Weimar at Paris. The word *régence,* regency, must refer here simply to the ducal government, and not to the regency of the Duchess Amalia, which had lasted from 1759 to 1775. Friedrich von Muller was born in 1779 and died in 1849. He was a close friend of Goethe.
10 Sister of Schiller's widow.
11 Madame Goethe entered (*y entra*). This was Christine Vulpius, whose acquaintance Goethe made in 1788 and who lived with him as his mistress until their public marriage in 1806, on the day of the battle of Jena.
12 [They have] a son of 17.
13 To Bertuch's again. Then with a (*une*) map of America to the beautiful de Reizenstein
14 For Comtesse.

States. Her remarks charmed and astonished me. *Din. chez moi.* Soup. At 4 to Madame de Wollzogen by her own appointment; denied, but why, could not comprehend. Her *dom.* told me in German a very long story and with great animation and zeal of which I understood not a sentence. Home. Note to Bertuch's that I would call to see him if at home and disengaged; *dèsolè*[1] to be engaged. Then sat to reading the details of the battle *de* Jena, &c., when Mr. de Müller, whom of all men in this place I wished most to see, came in.

6. I had a baking this morning and lay in a torpid state till 8. Before 10 came in Bertuch *fils*[2] (a young man of talents and learning). Went together to the *attelier de sculpture*[3] *de* Mr. ———, a young man of extraordinary talents. Thence to Madame *la* Marechale d'Eglefsstein[4] by invitation delivered by Mr. Müller last evening. *Y: la* Baronne Reizenstein (*la conqu. est finie*[5] and Gamp is ready for any romance); Mr. Müller, and about half a dozen of each sex and of the most distinguished. *Le poete*[6] Falk would have amused me much had it not been for Reizenstein. Staid till near 1. Chocolate, biscuit, and cakes are the repast on these morning parties. Madame *la Marechale* made an apology on part of *la* Duchesse; she supposed I had bid *congè*[7] to the Court and there-

---

1 Very sorry (*dèsolè*).
2 Bertuch junior.
3 Sculptor's studio. (*Atelier.*)
4 For Madame *la Maréchale* d'Egglestein, the wife of the Marshal (of the Court).
5 For *la conquète est finie.* The conquest is complete, *i. e.*, she has entirely won me over. I am her slave.
6 Falk, the poet (*poète*). This was Johannes Daniel Falk, a German philanthropist and writer, the founder of the Falk Institute for abandoned and neglected children at Weimar.
7 Taken my leave of (*congé*).

fore had not invited me. To Madame *la* Baronne de Stein, where ½ hour; a very sensible, well-bred woman. She told me what I did not know nor suspect, that *la* Princesse Caroline would be glad to see me any morning. Home at 2. Found note from Madame de Wollzogen inviting me to tea this evening, to which replied *desolè*[1] that I was engaged with Bertuch. At 5 to Bertuch's. He is full of all sorts of information and seems to take pleasure in communicating. Revenue of Weimar about 800,000 *ecus*[2]. Territory 40 square miles German; about 700 English miles. Five branches of Ernest[3]. Weimar, Gotha, Eisenac. At 6 Bertuch *fils* went with me to the play. The Duke *y* in plain dress and in his little open side box without an attendant. Duke pays about 3,000 *ecus* per annum to support the theatre. A serious comedy, of which I will send you a copy, was performed perfectly to my satisfaction. Near me in the ————; Professor Weisser; M'lles Goldacker, *deux souers.*

7. *Lev.* 7. At 10 to Bertuch's to have 100 *renseignments*[4]. To M'lle *la* Baronne Knebel; out. *La* Baronne de Stein; out. M'lle Reizenstein; out. *Chez* Goethe, where found them all. Also *les deux souers* Goldacker, *la* Com. de Peystre, and a *belle assemblage*[5]; a musical party *a midi*[6]. (But going in the

---

1 See note 1, preceding page.
2 An *ecu* or crown was worth about 88 cents in United States money of the time.
3 In 1485 the grandsons of Frederick the Valiant, Ernst and Albert, divided the inherited countries of Saxony, so that Ernst received Thuringia, and Albert, Meissen, and two lines were thus formed, which still flourish, the Ernestine and the Albertine, of which the former reigns in the Saxon duchies, the latter in the kingdom of Saxony.
4 To have or get a hundred pieces of information.
5 For *un bel assemblage.* A fine assemblage.
6 At noon (*à midi*).

street met Madame de Schopenhauer[1] who asked me to meet a small party at her house at 6.) De Reizenstein said she would be at Schopenhauer's, so resolved to go; walked with her and sisters. Early in the morning one of the *huissiers*[2] called with invitation from the Duke to dinner at ½ p. 2. Yesterday did a *betise*[3]. Saw in the street a girl of 3 years old making a stand and refusing to move. Two ladies trying to prevail on her to go, but no. Went to see the child; very lovely. One of the ladies *la* Com. de Peystre, whom I recognized. Spoke formally; the other I did not recognize nor notice. It was *la* Grand Duchesse! Relating the story to Madame de Stein, told her I had met the little Princess with *la* Com. de Peystre and a *jolie fille de chambre*[4]; all which was repeated to the Grand Duchesse. Had to settle this when we met at dinner. About thirty at table; *le grand salon*[5]. Message just before coming off that *la* Grand Duchesse asked me to pass the evening. Tea and cards. *Voila plein d'aff's*[6], for there is a ball to-night to which I am resolved to go. At 5 came home for dinner. Off directly to Bertuch's and thence to Schopenhauer's; there were two brothers and a sister from Jena, a most charming family. Was obliged to leave it at ½ p. 6 to attend *la* Grand Duchesse. De Reizenstein had not come in but understood I should meet her at

1 Madame Johanna Henriette Schopenhauer, the mother of Arthur Schopenhauer, the celebrated German philosopher, the chief expounder of pessimism. She was herself a writer of novels, books of travel, etc.
2 Ushers, door-keepers.
3 Stupidity, tom-foolery (*bêtise*).
4 A pretty chamber-maid.
5 The large drawing room.
6 For [*me*] *voilà plein d'affaires*. I'm full of business.

court, but she was not there! *La* Grand Duchesse engaged me at her table at whist. *Υ* Mr. de Stein de Lensihoten, *Hollandais*[1]. *La* Princesse speaks English extremely well; French like a Parisian. Fine hands and arms. Elbow perfect. Very intelligent questions. Lost 28 gro. At ½ p. 9 *au bal.*[2] *Υ: Le* Doctor Holberg; *les deux souers;* M'lle John (*fig. Espan.*[3]); Madame Goethe, about thirty or forty *dames* and a most beautiful assemblage; *contre danse*[4]; *valse;* *grandpere*[5]; *soupè.* Mr. Wolff *l'acteur et fem.*[6] Staid till 1. Bertuch *fils toujours*[7] *et le* Doctor Holberg *et* Müller. The Americans known here are Smith and Poinsett, both of South Carolina; the latter particularly intimate with Dr. ———, the physician of Clarke, now minister of war.

Erfurt, January 8-9, 1810. Felicitate me, my dear T., on my escape from the most critical danger of my life! I have been, as you know, in a pretty many dilemmas and jeopardies, but in no one that called for so much effort and determination as this, and even now, at the distance of fifteen English miles, I do not feel myself quite safe. Yet having ordered post-horses for 6 in the morning, not choosing to hazard the lapse of two or three hours to wait for the diligence (for possibly I may be pursued), my escape may, I think, be considered as accomplished. How

1 A Hollander.
2 To the ball.
3 For *une figure espagnole.* A Spanish face.
4 For *contredanse.* Quadrille.
5 Grandfather. What the reference is is not plain.
6 Mr. Wolff, the actor, and his wife.
7 This word has here the meaning of still, *i. e.*, Bertuch junior was still with him.

shall I apologize to *la* Baronne de S. to whom I was engaged for to-morrow (Tuesday) evening, when she promised that I should see all that is beautiful and brilliant in Weimar and its vicinage? How to the good and amiable Wieland whom I had promised to meet this evening? How to Dr. H. whose friendship has been so disinterested and may be so important? At this [hour] probably enough, he is writing letters for me. But I have escaped, that is my consolation! I do verily believe that de Reizenstein is a sorceress! Indeed, I have no doubt of it and if I were President of the secret tribunal she should be burnt alive to-morrow. Another interview and I might have been lost, my hopes and projects blasted and abandoned. The horror of this last of catastrophes struck me so forcibly and the danger was so imminent that at 8 o'clock I ordered post-horses, gave a crown extra to the postillion to drive like the devil, and lo! here I am in a warm room near a neat good bed, safely locked within the walls of Erfurt, rejoicing and repining. If you had been near me I should have had none of this trouble. The history of the day must be deferred till my head is more *posèd*[1].

Gotha. As I was writing the concluding line of the preceding page last evening (about 1 o'clock) an ill-looking fellow opened my door without knocking, and muttering in German something which I did not comprehend, bid me put out my candle. Being in no very placid humor at the moment, as you see, I cursed him and sent him to hell in French and

---

[1] Staid, sedate. See Glossary.

English. He advanced and was going to seize the candle. My umbrella, which had a dirk in the handle, being near me, I seized it, drew the dirk, and drove him out of the room. Some minutes after I heard the steps of a number of men and looking out at my windows saw it was a corporal's guard. It then occurred to me that this Erfurt, being a garrison town with a French governor (de Vismes), there might probably enough be an order for extinguishing lights at a certain hour, and I had no doubt but the gentlemen I had just seen in the street were coming to invite me to take a walk with them. So I bundled up my papers and put them in my pocket to be ready for a lodging in the guard house. It was only the relief of the centinels[1] going round and who the impertinent extinguisher was I have not learnt. At ½ p. 7 I was off without breakfast. Ascended a very long hill; a small fort on the left; stopped by the guard as usual at the gate to give your name, &c. After rising the hill, a plain the whole way, about fifteen English miles; an open plain; not a fence, not a grove, not a house save two small toll-houses; many villages on the right; you pass through only one, about two English miles before reaching Gotha, a parcel of poor-looking houses; a row of immense trees are each side the road the whole way. Very cold. Arrived at Gotha at 11. After getting breakfast and dressing, sent Mons. B.'s letter to Mr. Reichart[2] with my card; also cards to

---

1 So in the MS.

2 Heinrich August Ottokar Reichard (1751-1828), whose entire life was lived in and about Gotha. He was an author of considerable repute, a statesman, being war councilor at the time of Burr's visit, and was for many years director of the court theatre at Gotha.

————, and walked out. Charl.[1] came running full speed and in spite of all I could do, joined me and walked with me. *Le* Baron de Strick arrived at 2. At 5 din. *chez moi.* Reichart, *conseiller de guerre et auteur de*[2] ———— came in and sat a few minutes, and whilst I was dressing Mons. *le* Baron de Salish, *merechal de la Cour*[3], on the part of the Duchesse to ask me to pass the evening. Sup. *au Palais*[4]. *Y* a small select party. Cards (boston) with *la Duchesse* and won a ¹/₅ *ecu* which I have wrapped in paper and marked for you. About 9 the Duke[5] came in; a very handsome, tall, graceful *blond, bein blond*[6]. Engaged me in conversation so that I could not again join the card table. At supper was on the left and the Duke on the right of the Duchesse. Very cheerful. M'lle *La* Baronne de Dalwigk, *dame d'hon., a del' esprit*[7]. Much of United States. Was greatly astonished by some of the remarks of the Duke, manifesting sensibility and sentiment. Of cannibals. He has flashes and detached, solitary ideas which are extraordinary and admirable. He detests the English, though nearly allied to the British family. Of Napoleon. Showed a ring with his hair. Of presentiments; omens; superstitions; of his brother Frederick, now in Italy; singular disease, *roideur*[8]; showed me the boudoir beautifully fitted up;

---

1 Probably for Charlotte.
2 War councillor and author of ————. Burr may have meant to refer to Reichard's " *The-ater-kalender* " in twenty-five volumes, or to his guide books for travelers, especially those appearing in French, *e. g.,* "*Passagier auf der Reise in Deutschland*," " The Traveler Journeying in Germany."
3 Court Marshal; in German *Hofmarschall.*
4 At the Palace.
5 Ernst I., who began to reign as Duke of Saxe-Coburg in 1806. Gotha was his capital.
6 Blond, very (*bien*) blond.
7 M'lle de Dalwigk, lady of honour (*dame d'honneur*), has intellect (*a de l'esprit*).
8 For *raideur.* Stiffness, rigidity.

the designs given by himself. But the most interesting subject to me was the little Princesse Louisa in her tenth year; his only child; born of a former marriage; a fine, healthy, frank, animated child, very handsome. I did very humbly express my admiration for her. At coming away the Duke asked me to dinner to-morrow. Home at ½ p. 11 and somehow quite fatigued, of which not sensible till I got home. *Bon soir.* Mem.: Paid 18 groschen for the hire of a hat and sword.

11. It must have been very late when I went to bed for I rose with reluctance at ½ p. 7. Wrote note to Reichart requesting his company to see the *Cabinet des Medailles*[1], said to be the third in Europe. At 9 a *hussier*[2] of the Duke to ask me to dine to-day at 2. He came back after five minutes to say that the dinner was to be in the Duke's apartments. Called on Reichard at 10 and went to the *Cabinet des Med.*, which is in a wing of the Palace. It is, indeed, very rich. The list and description is in sixteen volumes folio; that sounds very large, but I am pretty sure that I had the XVIth in my hand. A great many of Alexander; of the Roman coins a complete series from the first Consul to the last Emperor. Passed three hours in the cabinet and library. Home at 1 and *au Palais* at 2. The *salon à manger* is *magnifique*[3]. Placed as before. About thirty at table; only one lady besides the family.

---

1 Cabinet of Medals (*des Médailles*).
2 For *huissier*. Usher.
3 The dining saloon is magnificent.

Much talk about X and of *la Princesse* for Queen.
How he does hate the English ! Of Coxe who married M'lle de Schale "Men are fit to educate
nothing but horses and dogs." After dinner *la petite
Princesse* came in ; her destiny announced. She very
frequently declared that she loves Charles ; was sent
to show me the pictures of the late Duchesse and of
the present Duke and other matters. About two
hours at table. Adjourned to the ———— and after
coffee continued ½ hour. Conversation. The Duke
and Duchesse retired and then the rest. The same
usage prevails at Weimar. The only lady beside the
family was M'lle Vidonie de Dieskau, who is with her
uncle, Baron Hardenberg, from Altenberg[1]. Agreed
to be of the party but embarassed at learning that no
maids beyond 18 would be permitted. M'lle V. de
D. 40; fat; willing; cheerful but not gay; *disp.*,
la la[2].

12. Rose at 7. At 9 ran in to see Reichard,
who is next door. *Veuf, Auteur de*[3], etc. At 10 *le*
Baron de Tummel called with his carriage to take me
to the *Observatoire*[4] The old building being in
decay a new one has been constructed under his direction. The *local,* is *magnifique*[5]; 300 feet above the
city ; distance about one English mile. Extremely
well supplied with instruments. But the most interesting object to me was Bernard de Lindenau[6], the

1 For Altenburg. A considerable city of the duchy Saxe-Altenburg.
2 Probably for *disposée, là là* ! Disposed, ready. Now then !
3 A widower, author of, etc.
4 The Observatory. This was at Seeberg, near Gotha.
5 The premises are magnificent.
6 Bernhard August von Lindenau (1780-1854) was both a very prominent Saxon statesman
and a well-known astronomer. From 1804 until 1817 he was director of the Observatory mentioned above.

Professor, the occupant; already, at the age of 25, has celebrity as an astronomer and mathematician throughout Europe. His appearance is in the highest degree prepossessing. Sensibility, modesty, intelligence, finely blended. His story is quite a romance; was gay, extravagant, dissolute; got in love and was beloved; his mistress died; he shut himself up, went nowhere, saw no one; devoted himself to science; was known to *le* Baron Tummel, who procured for him the place he occupies. He presented me a copy of the book he has lately published, " *Tables Barometriques*"[1]. [Read] the introduction with great pleasure. You will see that he is not merely mathematician, but a man of thought and sentiment. The son of the Baron, a fine lad of about 17, was with us. Home at 1. Yesterday sent my card to M. de Kunkel, *conseiller interne de S. A. R. l'Electrice de Hesse, nee Princesse de Dannemare*[2]. Received message that her Highness would be glad to see me after dinner this day. At 2 *au Chateau* to dine. A party of more than thirty. One stranger, a Prussian general. *Le* Com. de P.[3] begged[4] me to cede to him *ma plac*[4] next *la* Duchesse, as he was a stranger just arrived. The table is always cheerful. *Le Duc* extremely gay. Having said that I had your picture, after dinner he insisted that I should send for it, which was done by one of the *huissiers.* You were exhibited and suffi-

---

1 " Barometric Tables."
2 Interior Councilor (*i. e.*, Secretary of the Interior) of her Royal Highness (*Son Altesse Royale*) the Electress of Hesse who was born Princess of Denmark (*Danemark*).
3 Probably for *Le* Commandant de P.
4 For *ma place*, My seat.

ciently admired. *S. A.*[1] was quite gallant to you. *La Prin. reg'te*[2] asked me to her concert this evening at 7. Home at 5 and went out with Reichard to see Gallati[3], professor of history and author of a history of Germany which is esteemed the best of its kind, being, as he said, a mere summary in ten volumes quarto. It has gone through six editions and has been translated into French and Russian. He presented me a small statistical book, having heard that I was making inquiries on such subjects. Home at 6 and learned that a servant of *S. A. R. l'Electrice* has been to say that she was expecting me! Now, to say the truth, I had totally forgotten *S. A.* and her condecension in giving me audience. Off I went, however; was received by M. de K. and announced; then passing through several rooms was presented. After saluting, she sat on a sofa and begged me to be seated on a sofa chair by her side, which I obeyed. M. de K. and M'lle de ————, *dame d'hon.*, stood. She is mother of *la D. reg'te*[4], aunt of Gustavus IV. and the King of Den.[5] Much conversation about Sweden, especially as I had seen Gustavus IV. and his family After ½ hour came in *S. A. la Duchesse reg.*[4] and a few minutes after, I retired. *S. A. R.* thanked me and said many civil things. Her Palaces, &c. are now occupied by King Jerome. Her husband in

---

1 For *Son Altesse.* His or her Highness.
2 For *la Princesse Régnante.* The reigning Princess.
3 Johann Georg August Galletti (1750-1828) was the author of numerous historical works on Germany, France, and the world in general, none of which has stood the test of time unless it be his "History and Description of the Dukedom Gotha" in four volumes, published about 1781. A few years after Burr's visit he was appointed ducal historiographer and geographer, as well as court councilor.
4 For *la Duchesse Régnante.* The reigning Duchess.
5 Denmark.

Bohemia with his mistress. Home and then to the concert. Besides the ducal family, there were eight ladies and about twenty gentlemen; about thirty musical performers; many of them have salaries from the *Duc.*[1] Madame ———— played the violin and her daughter the piano extremely well. After the concert an elegant supper. I was seated between *S. A.* and M'lle de Dalwigk. With the latter much conversation about her lover, who has behaved like a true Englishman. She is a very charming woman; will tell you the story at large. *La petite*[2] Louisa was at the concert. I demanded a souvenir, to which she agreed and would think what it should be. Proposed a garter. A deal of laughter, &c. Home at ½ p. 10, having been asked to dinner to-morrow in case I should stay. (It must have been Wednesday evening that I called with Mr. de Reichard on *le* Baron de Falkenberg; the most extraordinary [man] of 83 that I ever beheld. He is Prime Minister and attends to all the duties of the office; works generally till 12 and 1 o'clock; reads without spectacles, is cheerful, animated; fine teeth and features well preserved; his voice as firm as at 40. Madame a very charming, lady-like woman about 55; she presented me *l'* "*Almanac de Gotha*"[3] in a very beautiful form, as you shall see.)

Gotha, Friday, January 13, 1810. (That's

---

1 The Duke.
2 The little.
3 For *l'* "*Almanach de Gotha.*" An annual register containing lists of government officials, genealogies of German princely families, necrology, diplomatic intelligence, statistics, etc. From 1764 to 1804 it was published in the German language. Since that time it has been published in both French and German.

impossible, for Monday was New Year's. You must look back and see where the error commenced.)

Gotha, Friday, January 12, 1810. You will suspect that I have taken winter quarters at Gotha. Not quite so, nor is the delay mere *nonchalance*[1], but I have no time to reason or explain or comment or apologize; mere notes of facts is all that I can attempt. We will dilate and fill up the canvas with the interesting details (it is only minute details that interest), *viv. voc.*[2] Rose at 7. At 9 to Reichart's. At 10 came in Mr. de Kunkel to thank me in the name of *S. A. R.* and in his own and to make compliments, &c. I gave him yesterday a small Swedish coin having a good likeness of Gustavus IV. which he gave to *S. A. R.* and whereon they had the politeness to set great value. It is one of Gampy's collection, but I've got the like or would not have given it to any Prince or Princess in Europe. At 12 to M. de Tummel; out; left card. The brother Tummel is author of many pretty and very gallant things. The *hussier* came in to know whether I would stay to dinner; yes. At 2 went to dinner *au Palais*. *La Duchesse* indisposed and did not appear; had my place. Dalwigk proposed to me to pass a few minutes in her room after dinner; did so; showed me the picture of her lover, which I very honestly (not very kind, however), told her I did not like at all. Gave me address of him and her. Home at 5. At 6 to the comedy as agreed with M'lle D. The *dramatis personæ*[3] you

---

1 Heedlessness.
2 For *viva voce.* By the living voice, orally.
3 The cast of characters.

will see in the bill attached to this. The parts were well cast and played to perfection. I laughed a great deal, as did M'lle D. Everything expressed in the bill was really performed and perfectly well performed. Just at this moment, 10 o'clock, comes in a *huissier* with compliments of *la petite* Louisa and a bouquet of her own drawing as "souvenir" The bouquet is really wonderfully executed for her years. The border in handsome taste. You shall see and judge, but on examining I find no name or inscription to verify this important transaction. 12 o'clock. Have been two hours about *mus.*[1] affair which failed. Saw Miss W., a most lovely *klin. demir., Carol. Charl. Wilhelm.*[2]; say 16. Have done nothing toward packing. But the most interesting part of the evening has not been told. At the comedy met *le min.*[3] *le* Baron de Tummel. He insisted that I should take a seat in his coach with his brother the author and visit *le Prem. Min.*[4] *le* Baron de Falkenberg. Agreed, though I had put off my court paraphernalia and was in my traveling costume, having *bona fide*[5] resolved to leave Gotha to-morrow. Met *le* Baron de F. in full dress and in the *salon*[6] lo, the Duke himself and Madame de F l We five were all. Sat round the tea table and took tea. The Duke perfectly amiable ; renewed the subject of your picture ; found a great deal of

---

1 For *muse.*
2 For a most lovely *kleine demirep,* Caroline Charlotte Wilhelmina. A most lovely little demirep, etc. Note the mixture ot French, German and English.
3 For *le Ministre.* The Minister.
4 For *le Premier Ministre.* The Prime Minister.
5 Latin. In good faith.
6 The drawing-room.

fault with the painter. (He has taste and skill in all the fine arts.) In the original, said he, there must be dignity, majesty, genius, gentleness, sensibility—all discernible in the picture, but imperfectly expressed; would have had a copy if there had been time; promised to send him one. He wished very much that a friend of his in Paris, *S. A. S.*[1] *la* Duchesse de C., etc. should know me; asked if I would take a letter; most certainly. *Le Ministre* Baron de F., hearing that *I was a coin and medal hunter*, (see again, you little villain, oh, I could choke you!) offered me several of the coins of Gotha, which are not now seen in circulation. These I peremptorily and constantly refused, though I did really wish to add them to my collection. Sat about two hours and home just before 10. The Duke took a most affectionate leave of me.

13. *Couche* 1. Rose 7. I shall really go this morning; have been very hard at work packing. Your picture took me ½ hour at least, you huzzy, you! Last night after writing you, passed an hour with the Baron Strick. It would seem that every incident of my life is known throughout Germany. Duels, treasons, speeches, gallantries. Le Baron Str., a young, handsome man, formerly minister plenipotentiary from Holland to ——— and now chamberlain

---

1 The reader will note the variation. This is not *S. A. R.* There is a difference. The following explanation is taken substantially from Larousse's great French work. When about the time of Louis XI. the Kings of France had adopted the title of *Majesté*, that of *Altesse*, Highness, was given at first to their brothers and their children only. In Germany the sovereign princes, secular as well as ecclesiastical, also took the title of *Altesse* at the epoch at which that of *Majesté* came into vogue for kings. The princes invested with the electorate were called *Altesses Électorales*, Electoral Highnesses. To-day, save a few exceptions, the title of *Altesse Royale* or *Impériale* belongs to all the princes issuing directly from a king or an emperor and that of *Altesse Sérénissime*, Most Serene Highness, to their collaterals.

du roi de Prusse[1], *accablès*[2] me with all sorts of attention. Introductions to his friends at Eisenach, Paris, Holland. Indeed, more in this way than I can tell. He has *nous et connaissances*[3], speaks French, German, and English; knows everybody and is everywhere well received. Showed him Bollman's[4] letter to Jefferson; B.'s *congè au Sen.*[5] he had seen before. Wrote early this morning to *la belle* Baronne de Dalwigk requesting that she would prevail on *ma Princesse*[6] to add a name and date to the bouquet, *q. v.* Just now a very kind note from *S. A. S. le Duc.* with a letter addressed *a S. [A. S.]*[7] *la* Duchesse de C., *q. v.* Too full of business to write you any more.

Eisenach, January 13, 1810. You see, Madame, that in spite of all your predictions to the contrary I did leave Gotha to-day ! For once you were out. It was at ½ p. 1 that I got into a chaise with horses *post extra;* was here at 5. An exceptionally cold day, snowing a little, very little, all day. It does not know how to snow fast in this country. We can snow more in four hours than they in four days. All yesterday from 2 in the morning it snowed what they call hard and there is not yet four inches. At leaving Gotha after passing the gate and bridge, (thanks *Mons. le Ministre* de Tummel, these walls are now prostrating and filling up the ditch), you rise a hill, a gentle

1 Of the King of Prussia.
2 A hybrid verb anglicized from the French verb *accabler*, to overwhelm.
3 He has brains and understanding. *Nous* probably stands for the Greek $\nu o \nu \sigma$, mind.
4 Eric Bollman. See Note 5, page 317.
5 For *Congé au Sénat*. Aaron Burr's farewell to the senate of the United States upon the expiration of his term as Vice-President, a wonderfully eloquent production. It is said that nearly every senator was in tears when Burr concluded.
6 My Princess.
7 For *à Son Altesse Sérénissime*. Her Most Serene Highness.

declivity. It may be called an inclined plain for 1½ English miles. We were forty minutes getting to the summit and then we were not at the summit, for after descending a very little, we rose again still higher. The distance to this place is about fifteen English miles. The first ten or eleven you pass through three villages. The last two or three miles (English) are almost a continual village and the country extremely romantic and picturesque. The preceding part is quite an open country; not a tree, fence, or house except in the villages; gentle, bold, swells; all the way under cultivation, but let me go back for a moment to Gotha. Gotha! I bear thee in kind remembrance. The bouquet was sent back with the addition of a name and date by the fair hand of Louisa, accompanied by a very pretty note in English from *la* Baronne de Dal wigk. Answered the note of *S. A. S. le Duc.* Received a letter from de Reichart to his son-in-law *le* Baron de Goekhausen at the *Place*[1] ———. More letters from *le* Baron de Strick. Put up *a La Demi Lune*[2]. Ordered dinner; fish and potatoes, and sent letters with my cards to Madame *la* Baronne de Bechtolsheim *née* Baronne de Koller[3]; to M. de Streiber, *conseiller de legation de S. A. S. Mons'r le Duc Reg't*[4] *de* Saxe-Weimar-Eisenac; to M. *le* Baron de Goekhausen *b. fils de* Reichert[5]; to M. ——— de

---

[1] ——— square.
[2] For à *la Demi-lune.* At the Half-moon.
[3] Julie Freifrau (Baroness) von Bechtolsheim (1751–1847), whose maiden name was Keller. Her husband was Vice-Chancellor at Eisenach. She was well known in Germany as a poetess under the name of Psyche, and was a great friend of the poet Wieland.
[4] His Most Serene Highness, the reigning Duke (*Le Duc Régnant*). There may be a question as to whether the abbreviation *Mons'r* stands for *Monsieur* or *Monseigneur*. The latter title, meaning My Lord, was often applied to the princes of a sovereign family.
[5] Reichard's son-in-law (*beau-fils*).

Massovius. The three gentlemen above named called within an hour and proposed various things for my amusement. Agreed to meet the club to-night and to visit ———— to-morrow. M. de Streiber has passed six years in Great Britain and speaks perfectly good English. Passed an hour with the club ; about twenty gentlemen. The Prussian General whom I met at Gotha ; quite another animal here. *Y* also *le* Baron de Bechtolsheim, son of *la Baronne* above mentioned. It is most unfortunate that the mother is absent on a visit to some friends near Erfurt ; very unfortunate. She is one of the most distinguished personages in Germany for learning, wit, talents, grace, &c.—*la* de l'Enclos[1] of the age ! Stole off from the club at 9 ; walked the streets ½ hour ; no accident[2]. A beautiful little town ; all white ; walled and fortified. What nonsense ! This has been much the coldest day this year, and really cold ; would be called cold at Albany, but perfectly calm.

14. Rose 7. Could not keep myself warm in bed, having ordered a mattress, thin and hard, and two thin quilts (called *couvertures*) ; added my great coat. At 10 to the post-house to see about diligence ; none goes to Frankfort before Tuesday P. M. and then not direct, but some miles about, and is between three and four days, going day and night, from this to Frankfort, which by the direct route is twenty-one miles

---

1 Anne, called Ninon, de L'Enclos (1616–1706) was a noted French woman of pleasure who, though leading a free life, was never a public courtesan. She retained her beauty and charms to a very old age. In her salon she received the highest society, which has been compared for its tone with the Hôtel de Rambouillet. Some of the most noted men of the day were among her lovers. If we are to believe Voltaire, Richelieu was the first of these.

2 Here and elsewhere Burr uses the word accident to mean that he sought an amorous adventure.

German. What's to be done? Thence to *le* Baron de Goeckhausen *beau-fils* de Reichart, a sensible young man ; staid but a few minutes. Thence to Massovius's and he and I went together, as invited, to breakfast *a la fourchette* with Streiber. Met there Mr. M'Intosh, a Scotsman, who had been many years in North America and in Asia and Africa ; had an immense fortune which he lost by the French Revolution ; a very intelligent, amusing man. After breakfast Mons. Streiber took me in his sleigh to Wilhelmsthal, *chateau de plaisance*[1] *de Duc de* Weimar (we are here again in his dominions). *Y:* Mr. Roese and M'lle ———, *amie de sa femme*[2] ; Madame ———. They all spoke French very well. The road is exceedingly romantic. For 1½ English miles in a very narrow valley, the locks and mountains hanging over us ; then about one mile English rising the mountain. Descending about the same, the chateau, &c., in a valley of half a mile diameter below. Fires had been ordered and we had coffee and cakes. M'lle de ——— is cheerful and pretty. Home at ½ p. 4. The cold most intense. I was almost perished and had to bake an hour before I got thawed. Mr. Roese, seeing that I admired a picture of the Duke of Weimar which we saw *au Chateau*[3], procured and presented me one. At 7 to Mr. de Streiber's ; a small club ; five of each sex. *Y:* Madame Roese, who is very handsome; she and M'lle ——— are both from Gotha. Cards ; whist ; won a

---

1 Literally castle (*château*) of pleasure of the Duke (*du Duc*); hence his villa.
2 Friend of his wife.
3 At the castle.

thaler[1]. Supper with variety of wines. Home at 4 11. I much wished *for ιyour sake* to have visited *l'ancien. chateau de* Wartzbourg[2], which is on the summit of the mountain overhanging this town. You can imagine nothing more romantic than the site. It has been famous in story more than 800 years. It is a fine ruin but part habitable and inhabited. The singer[3], the battles, the enchantments, the imprisonments, &c., render it very famous. Luther, too, was there and had some squabbles with the Devil; threw his ink-stand at his Majesty's head and the marks of the ink still visible. But the snow and ice have rendered the mountain impracticable and the castle absolutely inac-cessible. Mr. M'Intosh came in this morning and sat an hour. I admire his constancy and his loyalty. He is prisoner on parole as being a British subject; has corresponded with Washington ; one of the letters now in the museum at Weimar. Met many very pretty faces in the *streets.* The lamps here are sus-pended on wire attached to the houses on each side. The same in several other towns and in the Pall Maille[4], Altona. Eisenach has 9,000 inhabitants[5].

15. *Couche* 1. Rose 7. Still colder than yes-terday but perfectly calm. Called on Mr. Roese ; saw his beautiful wife and her *jolie amie*[6]. Madame has lately lost two children ; has left a very fine boy about 3 or

1 A German silver coin worth 3 marks or between 70 and 75 cents of United States money.
2 The ancient castle of Wartburg. It was founded in 1067 by Ludwig the Leaper, Land-grave of Thuringia, and was for several centuries the residence of his successors. Many histori-cal remembrances attach to this spot. Here took place, for instance, the famous contest between the Minnesingers about 1206. Luther was kept concealed in the castle from May 4, 1521, to March 3, 1522, during which time he finished his translation of the Bible into German.
3 Probably for singers. See the foregoing note.
4 It will be remembered that Palmaille is the most fashionable street of Altona.
5 To-day it has 24,000 inhabitants.
6 Pretty friend.

4 years old. Thence to General L. This is the
General whom I met *chez le duc a*[1] Gotha. He is
now in the service of the King of Naples. Yesterday
he sent me card of invitation for this evening, which
accepted. Thence to *one* of the manufactories, &c.
Mr. de Streiber. Home to thaw and then walked
about the town and environs for near an hour ; inscription on an old building, " *Hic sunt pulvis, umbra,
nihil*[2]." Got home frozen stiff, though I had on my
great coat and calashes. Baked an hour and then dinner *seul.* *Mon hote*[3] is native of Hanover and speaks
French freely and is very communicative. He sus-
pects that I am an Englishman and has intimated how
much, &c., &c. This duchy separating from Weimar
paid a contribution of 150,000 *ecus en argent*[4]*;* more
than 200,000 troops have passed through ; always
maintained by the inhabitants ; free quarters, which
must have been more than double the contribution.
Recollect that the Duke of Weimar was in arms
against the Emperor at this time. At 4 came Mr. de
Streiber to inform me of the best means of getting to
Frankfort. The best will be the expense of about 25
dollars. The worst, *i. e.,* diligence which goes a
circuitous route and is *three days and three nights on the
way always going,* would be about 12. Truly, as the
weather is and is like to be, I should not like to hazard
my precious carcass in a wagon without springs and
badly covered, three days and nights. At ½ p. 6 to

---

1 At the Duke's at Gotha.
2 Latin. " Here are dust, shade, nothing."
3 For *mon hôte.* My host.
4 150,000 crowns (*écus*) in money or silver.

General Letocq's ; a very elegant party ; the rooms in very beautiful style. It is the house, the rooms, the furniture, and the taste of Madame *la* Baronne de Beckholsteim[1]. Her son was of the party, a very accomplished young man with a lovely wife to whom he was married a few months ago. *Y* also *la Gotharienne*[2]. Cards, chess, supper. I played two games chess with the General and won both. It was a very cheerful party. Mon. ———, a young man of fortune, of talents and learning, would bring me home in his carriage. *Chez moi* at ½ p. 11. Not so cold. Mon. ———, who keeps regular meteorological notes, told me this evening that the thermometer (Reamur's[3]) was at 7 o'clock this morning at 20½ below o and at 8, 19½, and that for ten years the cold has not been so intense by many degrees.

Hünnefeld, January 16, 1810, 12 at night. Rose at 7. Went early to the post-office to see about diligence. It is expected at 2, but after much deliberation resolved to take post-horses to Fulda, whence a very convenient diligence goes on Thursday to Frankfort. Called on Streiber at his manufactory and sent card of *congè* to General Letocq. At 2 set out. About two English miles winding round the mountains along narrow valleys. Ascend mountain and descending the same, pass a small town. At two miles German from Eisenac to Berka, where changed horses and car. Two miles to Vach[4], where change again. Three miles more to this place,

---

1 For Bechtolsheim.
2 The lady from Gotha.
3 In the Réaumur thermometer the freezing-point is marked zero, and the space between this and the boiling-point is divided into 80 degrees. Hence 20½° Réaumur is about 14° below zero, Fahrenheit, 19½° Réaumur being about 12° below zero Fahrenheit.
4 For Vacha.

frozen to an icicle and so resolve to thaw and bake till 7.

Hannau, January 17, 1810. Laid on a sofa last night without undressing. Rose at 7. Got breakfast and at 8 continued my route; bitter, bitter cold. Arrived at Fulda at 10 ; formerly the sovereignty of the Bishop of Fulda; beautifully situate in an extensive valley on the small river Fulda. Though a small town of about 10,000 inhabitants, it exhibits much magnificence. You see twelve or fifteen steeples or towers as you approach; in every direction chateaus, rows of trees. There are many things here worthy of notice, but the distressing intelligence that no diligence goes hence till Sunday left me the sad alternative of either waiting here four days or continuing in the same expensive way. Resolved on the latter and ordered horses immediately. While they were getting, walked about the town. This being a Catholic bishop everything is stamped with that character; crosses, &c., on the houses ; the mile-posts a crucifix ten or fifteen feet high with a wooden Christ as large as life ; some lines carved on stone. The Bishop still resides here with a provision of 40,000 florins from the great Emperor. The Bishop was dethroned some years ago by the Prince of Orange. *"Sic vos non Vobis"*[1].

---

1 Burr refers here to a celebrated tradition, which is worth taking entire from Brewer's " The Reader's Handbook." The tale is that Vergil wrote an epigram on Augustus Cæsar, which so much pleased the Emperor that he desired to know who was the author. As Vergil did not claim the lines, one Bathyllus declared they were his, This displeased Vergil, and he wrote these four words, *Sic vos non vobis* (so you not to you) four times at the commencement of four lines, and Bathyllus was requested to finish them. This he could not do, but Vergil completed the lines thus :

Sic vos non vobis nidificatis aves;
Sic vos non vobis villera fertis oves;
Sic vos non vobis mellificatis apes;
Sic vos non vobis fertis aratra boves.
Not for yourselves your nests ye song-birds build ,
Not for yourselves ye sheep your fleeces bear ,
Not for yourselves your hives ye bees have filled ;
Not for yourselves ye oxen draw the share.

Arrived here at 11 and after giving my name and other particulars am allowed to go to bed and write this while I am thawing. You will see from your map that Hannau is on the Main about two or three miles English before arriving here. Looked out and found we were on a perfect plain. Till then or thereabouts it was continual mountain and hill; but the road excellent and at every ¼ mile German a town or village, but I ought not to omit that at ——, but Gamp is stiff and tired. Will do something at Frankfort; about vineyards and the beautiful *fille de m'r. de poste*[1].

Frankfort, January 18, 1810. Arrived at 10 this morning. A continued plain; a ridge about one English mile off on the right (scarcely visible by reason of the fog and mist which is eternal). Have not seen a clear American sky since left the United States; (something like it in Sweden). Approaching the ridge as you approach the town, it is seen covered with vineyards and beautiful little houses. I took quarters as advised by Reichard, *a l'Empereur Romain* (*Romische keyser*)[2], and as usual, was shown into the third story; the room, however, is decent and comfortable; those on the first floor (second story) are all occupied. Sent letters to Mons. de Bethmann, *consul de Russie*[3] and ——; to *Messrs. freres* Bestina, *nég't et banquiers*[4]; to *Messrs.* Bansa *et fils, banquiers,*

---

1 For *fille du maitre de poste.* Daughter of the postmaster.
2 For *à l'Empereur Romain zum Romischen Kaiser.* At the sign of the Roman Emperor.
3 Russian Consul.
4 To Bestina Brothers (*Frères*), merchants or brokers (*négociants*) and bankers.

and cards to Chiron, Sarasin *et Co.*, *banquiers* (my bankers ! !). To *le* Comte de Beuste *beau pere de la belle* Comtesse de Beuste *a* Weimar *dont je vous ai parle sur le nom de*[1] de Peystre, which is the *allemande*[2] pronunciation of de Beuste. M. *le* Comte de B. is *Premier Ministre* and in the absence of the Prince Primate, who is now at Paris, represents royalty here. To Mons. *le* Gen'l. Com. Sweyer. To ———— *Commissaire de Police*[3]. These *commissaires de police* are fellows very formidable to strangers. Presently came in the valet *de* Mr. de Bethmann to request that I would dine with him to-day at 1. This was doing things right— *al' allemange*[4]—but the hour surprised me. Went at 1 to dinner. A magnificent establishment. He is *garcon*[5]; his mother (60) lives with him and does the honors of the house with great civility and real hospitality. There were about fifteen. A mother and daughter of the celebrated name of Euler[6] and nearly related to that distinguished man; another young lady; the French intendant of all *the French provinces in Germany*, a very intelligent, well-bred man; Mr. ————, a young man much resembling Otto. Sat, but the two Eulers and the mother recommended to me to talk to her daughter, who, she said, spoke French much better than herself. I obeyed her and

---

1 Count de Beuste, father-in-law (*beau-père*) of the handsome Countess de Beuste at Weimar, whom I have mentioned to you under the name of, etc.
2 The German pronunciation.
3 Police Commissary.
4 For *à l' allemande*. After the German fashion.
5 For *garçon*. Bachelor.
6 Leonhard Euler (1707-1783) was a celebrated Swiss mathematician whose long life was divided about equally between Switzerland, Germany, and Russia. Although blind for many years he wrote a multitude of treatises on mathematics. Indeed, it is said that he wrote more than half of all the forty-six quarto volumes published by the St. Petersburg Academy between 1727 and 1783.

was much amused. A sensible, amiable girl of 17. Home at 5. Immediately after my return home received under cover from Bethmann tickets of admission to the Casino, to the *Musèe*[1], and to the *Cabinet Literaire*[2], three charming lounging places ; the first and last under the same roof; a most elegant establishment ; the other opposite and appropriate to its name. The receptacle and place of exhibition of the productions of *Frankfort artists.* Mr. Bethmann called in the P. M. and we went to the Casino and *Cab. Lit.* where you meet persons of the first grade and no others. The nature of the establishment and how maintained must be explained verbally. You find here a library ; new publications ; all the gazettes and periodical publications of Europe ; maps, ditto. Can have any refreshment and any meal. To the *Comedie Alemande*[3]. The opera of " Camilla." Being perfectly acquainted with the story, having read the French translation while at Stockholm, of which you will find a note and a comment, " *La Souterrain*"[4], I was much amused. The theatre is convenient and handsome without being splendid. The parts well performed ; the orchestra excellent ; one superior male voice and two good female ; the best a lady from Vienna who has married and left the stage, but loves the business and performs when she likes. She was ———, the nephew, and was quite at her ease *en cavallier*[5] Madame ———, formerly M'lle ———. Left the

1 For *Musée.* Museum.
2 For *Cabinet Litéraire.* Literary rooms (or quarters).
3 For *La Comédie Allemande.* German Comedy, a theatre.
4 For " *Le Souterrain.*" " The Vault."
5 For *en cavalier.* As a cavalier. See Glossary.

Comedie at the second act, being very cold and having an engagement proper to warm me. All this is written; no, not all, but this and the preceding page with a personage in the room. My tea is ready, the good Lüning's Caravan tea, and other matters claim my attention. *Bon soir.*

19. I have none but this great thick ugly paper which you hate so and it is now too late to get other, so this or nothing. Very pleasant night. Rose at 7. Received cards from *le* Gen. Comt.[1] Baron de Sweyer and *le* Comte de Beuste, who ought to have been first named. Card from Chiron & Sarasin. My landlord sent to know whether it would please his Excellency to have a larger room and on first floor. Yes, certainly; but not to-day. The *embarras*[2] of moving to-morrow morning. You see how things go. Mr. Elsinger, " *libraire tres celebre*"[3], sent a clerk with a civil message tendering his services, new publications, etc., this at the instigation of Bethmann. A man of grave appearance, *d'un certain age*[4], dressed and powdered, presented himself. I supposed him to be *marechale de la cour.*[5] He undeceived me by saying that he understood I wanted a *commissionaire d'affaire*[6]. Then I concluded he was merely a broker and told him it was a mistake, that I had no sort of business to transact. He bowed and said he had been sent to me by the landlord, and " Pray, sir, *qulques especes d'affaires*

---

1 For *le Général Commandant.* The commanding general.
2 Embarrassment.
3 For *libraire très célèbre.* Very noted bookseller.
4 An old French expression meaning an elderly man (*âge*).
5 Court Marshal.
6 For *commissionnaire d'affaires.* Messenger, servant.

est de votre Etat." Pour faire vos petites commissions de Mon'r. Apportez ses messages, nettoyer ses habits et bottes"[1]. Mr. Käyser was received as *valet de place*[2]. To Bethmann's at 12 ; out. Saw Madame *sa mere.* To Casino ; read newspapers and saw and was introduced to many people. Staid till 3 to avoid the hour of dinner which is at 1 ; an hour at which it would be useless to me. Bethmann engages me to dine with his sister on Sunday and with himself on Monday. Young Mons. Bansa, who is nephew of de Streiber, came in this morning to offer civilities ; a very pleasant young man. At 6 to Casino, it being ladies' night. There were perhaps 100 people, about equal of each sex. The ladies who most caught my attention were *la* Princesse de ————; her *compagnone*[3] *la* Baronne de ———— , and M'lle *la* Baronne de Ende. There were many very handsome ; several handsome men there. " Sir, allow me to interrupt you to ask who is that beautiful creature with the black bonnet !" " That, sir, is my dauhgter ; shall I have the honor to present you ?" " Pray, Count, what fine, voluptuous woman was that you were just now talking with ?" " Who, the very one with the *bon. rouge*[4]?" " Exactly her, a most striking figure." " That, sir is my wife." " *Ha, ha! Venez ici ma chere. Mons. le* C. B. *desire vous connaitre"*[5]. This was rather too much for one evening. Having two other

---

1 " Pray, sir, some kinds of business belong to your station (*quelques espèces d'affaires sont de votre état*) ; to do Monsieur's little errands ; to bring (*apporter*) his messages, clean his clothes and boots."
2 Courier.
3 For *compagne.* Female companion.
4 For *bonnet rouge.* Red bonnet.
5 " Ha, ha ! Come hither, my dear (*chère*) ; Colonel Burr wants to make your acquaintance " (*désire vous connaître*).

engagements was obliged to go at 7 to *la Musèe*[1], which is open every other Friday evening for exhibition and declamation and, as I presumed, on subjects of science. On entering, a very comely and very young lady was on the rostrum declaiming with much grace and animation, at which made great eyes. It was an actress; her manner was very pleasing. To the concert *au maison rouge*[2]. *Y:* Mons. Elsinger, who introduced me to Mr. Gerning, author of " Travels in Italy " and *Legations Rath*[3]; also Madame ———, *la cel. actrice de Vienne*[4], who sang. The music really fine, *surtout*[5] the horn which was played in a style I had never witnessed. *Y* also Mr. ———, a man of fortune and consequence, with his mistress, a very pretty, modest-looking girl to whom everybody spoke with civility and respect as to other *dames.* Back again at ½ p. 8 to the Casino, to which the principal inducement was d'Ende. There were perhaps a dozen card tables; some backgammon, but all the most beautiful women were walking the floor in the suite of rooms, five or six, well lighted and perfectly well warmed and perfumed. " Prey, M'lle, is there any law forbidding a gentleman to walk with a lady?" "*Poh! folie! Comment peut y avoir un tel loi.*" "*Mais donc, nestce pas, contre les bienseances?*" "*Tout au contraire.*" "*Alors cest permi que je marche avec*

---

1 The word *musée*, museum, has been degraded somewhat in most languages from its original Greek signification of a temple of the Muses, a place for study. Here it seems to possess somewhat, at least, of the better signification.
2 To the Red House (à *la*, etc.).
3 For *Legationsrat.* Councilor of Legation.
4 For *la célèbre actrice*, etc. The celebrated actress from Vienna.
5 Especially.

vous?" "*Certainement*"[1] So I did an hour. No other male walked with a lady. *Le* Baron d'Ende, who is *charge d'affaires de la cour de* Saxe-Gotha[2], told me he had received a letter from the venerable Falkenberg about one A. B.[3], requesting his attentions, &c., &c. Very good in Mons. de F. Met also General Baron Sweyer, *Comm't*[4] and *le* Comte de Beuste; *le* Baron de ———, *marechal de la Cour de* ———, which is only a mile off, *et mult. al.*[5] Forgot to get paper and so you must receive another of this *grossiere*[6]. Home at 10. *Le* Baron de ——— came in and gave me a very pressing invitation to visit him *au chateau de*[7] ———. Went in to see the *table d'hote. Madame et sa fille; tres gentille*[8]. A French Colonel; German Major *Hussard*[9]. Nothing very remarkable, but told me they had expected me to dinner.

20. *Couche* 1. *Lev.* 7. Wrote General ———, *commandant* at Mayence, enclosing the letter of General St. Simon and requesting that he would enquire whether my passport had been sent from Paris. Note to Chiron & Sarasin about exchange of money. *Sor.* at 11 to Elsinger's to *fouiller*[10] in his library. Think to buy you a dictionary and something for Gampy to be sent to Hamburg. At 12 to Casino. At 2 to the *Musée*, which is open from 2 to 4 P. M. once a

---

1 " Pshaw! Nonsense! How can there be such a law (*une telle loi*)?" " But all the same it's contrary to decorum (*les bienséances*), isn't it (*n'est-ce pas*)? " Quite the contrary." " Then it is allowable (*c'est permis*) for me to walk with you?" " Certainly."
2 Of the Court of Saxe-Gotha.
3 Aaron Burr.
4 For *Commandant*. In command.
5 For *et multi alii*. And many others.
6 For *ce papier grossier*. This coarse paper.
7 At the castle of ———.
8 Very pretty.
9 A German major of the hussars.
10 To rummage.

fortnight to see the paintings. None but the works of Frankfort artists are admitted. The day being cold the company was less than usual. A few ladies. Madame Calvina and her sister; M'lles are both handsome; the former striking, a *veuve*[1]. M'lle Koch, an *artiste*[2], is very pleasing, and many others handsome, but I have not yet a decided preference. Home at ½ p. 4. After dinner walked the streets an hour. Some folly, not expensive. Tea at 7 and at ½ p. 8 by appointment, Lisette. Sent card to-day to Baron d'Ende, which was immediately returned by visit in person. Mr. Sarasin called this afternoon and sat an hour.

21. *Couche* 1. Rose 7. *Tro. fa.* ½ gui.[3] *Je vous dem., 1,000 pardons*[4]. At 10 to Mons. *Legations Rath* Gerning. Happening to mention *les* d'Imh.[5] he avowed himself the lover *de l'ainee*[6]. He has some choice paintings and some very curious antiquities from the Herculaneum and other places in Italy. Among the things brasses and iron stamps with letters and names; evidently for marking things, which ought to have led to the invention of printing. Some fine Etruscan vases. At 12 to d'Ende's. *Le* Baron out, but *les dem's*[7] received me; sat ½ hour. *Ma belle* which is the *cad.*[8] has lost nothing at the second inspection; pleasing, not dangerous like that infernal

---

1 A widow.
2 A female artist.
3 For *trop fatigué*, too tired, or *trop faible*, too weak; ½ guinea.
4 I beg a thousand pardons. (*Je vous demande* mille *pardons.*)
5 For d'Imhoffs. A family whose acquaintance Burr made in Sweden.
6 For *de l' ainée.* Of the elder or eldest.
7 For *les demoiselles.* The girls.
8 My beauty, who is the younger. (*Cadette.*)

Tinte[1]. Home. Note from Bethmann that he would call at 2 to take me to dinner. To Madame Hohlweg's. *Y:* her daughter and child; two sons; *la helle Viennienne, actrice*[2], a modest, sensible, amiable woman, also pretty. *Y* also Mons. ———, whom met at the concert *au sall*[3]. At 6 to Mr. Sarasin's; having met him in the street to-day he asked me to dine; being engaged was obliged to decline, so went this evening. A pleasant family party of a dozen. Came in also Madame Dumont *et M.'lle sa soeur de* Mayence[4]; *M'lle bel.*[5] *Y* also a very sensible, sprightly, well-informed young lady, *pas tro jeu*[6] but pleasant. Tea, &c. Home at 9. Smoked and wrote your Journal.

22. *Couche* 1. *Lev.* 8. At 11 took hack and went to Eisenbourg[7] to see le Baron de Wallschmitt, *marechal, de cour du Prince* d'Eisenbourg[8]; out, but sat ½ hour with *la baronne*. A very pretty promenade. Home at 1 and at ½ p. 1 to dine with Bethmann. *Y encore*[9] Madame ——— *et sa fille*; Madame———, whose *mari*[10] is partner of Gogel[11] whom I saw at Göthenburg, a very charming woman, speaking French and English; l'Abbe ———, *editeur du "Journal, de*

1 Does he not refer to de Reizenstein, "the sorceress of Weimar"? Was her name Tinte or is there a reference to her character in the word *Tinte*, which means ink in German?
2 The beautiful actress from Vienna.
3 Possibly for *dans la* (or *à la*) *salle de spectacle*. In the show room, in the theatre.
4 Her sister from Mayence [on the Rhine].
5 For M'lle *est belle*.
6 For *pas trop jeune*. None too young, *i. e.*, rather old.
7 Eisenberg is a city in the duchy of Saxe-Altenburg From 1675 it was the capital of the duchy of Saxe-Eisenberg, which afterwards was merged into that of Gotha, and later into that of Saxe-Altenburg.
8 Court Marshal of the Prince of Eisenberg.
9 There again [were], etc.
10 Husband.
11 Here the name Gogel is spelled correctly by Burr, but when in Sweden he spelled it Gogle.

Frank"[1]   *On trouve beaucoup de* A. B.[2]   After dinner much and *bizarre* about America[3].   Home at 5.   At 7 Mr. Fuchs, who had sent me a ticket for the ball, called with his carriage to take me.   There were about 100 ladies, a great many very handsome, and many dancing very well.   *Les deux souers* d'Ende[4] were there. Princesse Marie *et*[5] beautiful; two Mayerhoffs (*baronnes* or *comtesses*), very handsome; a little ————, in blue, lovely; M'lle ———— *le ainet*[6] black, elegant, striking; forms a resemblance stronger than I have ever seen to a person once dear to you and me; Mons. ————, brother of the Elector of Hesse, very civil; *le* Prince de Hesse *pere de* Marie; *la* Duchesse de ————, *les chev. jaun.*[7]   But my attention to beauty was interrupted by a communication from young Bansa that he had answer from Mayence and that my passport *had not arrived*!!   No answer from Meynier, which looks black, also.

23.   Certainly, Madame, you owe me great obligations for writing you at all, at this moment, lo! the catastrophe of my hopes.   Mr. ———— called at 10 this morning and with an air of mystery, with hesitation and unaffected embarrassment, said that he had a letter from his friend at Mayence advising not only that no passport for me had been received, but there were advices from Paris concerning me extremely

---

1   Editor of the Frankfort " Journal "?
2   This may mean, Many Aaron Burr's are found, or else it stands for *on trouve beaucoup à redire à* A. B., which means, Much fault is found with Aaron Burr. Possibly he may mean that people find much in Aaron Burr.
3   Much strange talk about America.
4   The two D'Ende sisters. (*Soeurs.*)
5   For *est*. Is.
6   Probably for *l'ainée*. The elder.
7   For *les cheveux jaunes*. Yellow hair.

unfavorable, and requesting I might be advised by no means to hazard my person within the territories of France. After thanking him for the communication, I told him I should go to-morrow to Mayence, which you know is now in France, and asked a line of introduction to his friend. He seemed to consider my resolution as madness and very delicately declined giving a letter from the danger which might ensue from any apparent communication with me. At 11 to Bethmann's. Saw him in his *com.*[1] house, a vast establishment, and after, his mother *au chateau*[2]. Some current conversation ; thence to Sarasin's to whom I told the story. He is not frightened and voluntarily offered a letter to his friend at Mayence. To Abbe ————, where sat ¼ hour. Thence to Casino, where, among others, saw Mon. Conertagen Farci ; engaged to dine with him at the hotel where he lodges. Went at 1. A very pretty sensible landlady *au Cygne hlane*[3]. He came home with me to smoke a segar in my room. Engaged to meet me at the theatre *au paterre*[4] and to show me a beautiful woman. At 6 *au theatre*[5]. The orchestra was the best I ever heard ; the scenery very fine. M'lle was there ; really beautiful, but engaged. Two gentlemen near me successively addressed me by name and in French. One voluntarily served me as interpreter with M'lle, who spoke French imperfectly. Finally * * * *[6] her from her

---

1 For *Comptoir*. Counting-house.
2 At the castle or mansion. (*Château*)
3 At the [sign of the] White Swan—the name of the hotel.
4 For *au parterre*. In the pit.
5 For *au théâtre*. To the theatre.
6 An undecipherable word, possibly intended for took or tricked.

paramour and home to sup with me. But first to her lod.[1] Mons. attended me thither lest some mischief might befal[2] me. Jean't[3] returned home at 12, perhaps to fulfill an engagement. Really beautiful and extremely *bizarre*[4]. On entering my room this evening found on my table a very polite letter from General Meynier; too polite. "No passport has been received nor any notice of the application," but nothing further. Continue in the determination to go to Mayence to know the state of things, but must stay to the masquerade ball to-morrow and to sup with ———, on invitation of Sarasin, who promises there shall be *helles*.[5] *La bel.*[6] Calvina was at theatre and witnessed all the maneuvres of bu.[7]; probably 100 others; so reputation ruined. Written from 12 to 1 Tuesday night.

24. At 10 *chez* Sarasin; 12 *à* Casino. *Y: Le* Comte de Rode, *c. d. min. plen. de Prus. a* Madrid *et* Lisbon[8]; *le jeune* Comte de Westphalen[9]; Alexander Goutard; *le* Prince Frederic de Hesse. *Pas din.*[10] Alexander G. invited me to pass the evening on Sunday. At 4 Comte de Rode called with his carriage to take me to Prince Frederic's. *Y sa fem. et six dam. d'hon.*[11] Home and dressed for evening. At 6 *le*

---

1 Lodgings.
2 So in the MS.
3 For Jeannette.
4 Same meaning as in English.
5 Beauties.
6 For *la belle*.
7 For Burr.
8 For *ci-devant Ministre Plénipotentiaire de Prusse à* Madrid *et* Lisbon. Formerly Minister Plenipotentiary of Prussia at Madrid and Lisbon.
9 For Westfalen, the German name of the province Westphalia, since 1815 a part of Prussia, but from 1807 to the Congress of Vienna in 1815 a kingdom. Napoleon formed it out of various German provinces and gave it to his brother Jerome.
10 For *Pas de diner*. Or *Je n'ai pas diné*. No dinner.
11 For *Y sa femme et six dames d'honneur*. His wife and six maids of honour were there

Comte called again and took me to see *Son Altesse la Duchesse de ———. Y sa fl. divor. Bel. embon. yeu. noi.*[1] Home at 7 and soon after Mr. Sarasin called with his carriage and took me to pass evening and sup *chez sa parente*[2] Madame ———. *Y an assemblè de 50*[3]. Cards. Conversation. A *famille interressante de Vienne*[4]. Madame ——— *nèe* Goutard; *3 dem. et 1 fils. L'ainèe*[5] speaking fluently English. A very elegant supper and very cheerful. At 11 *au bal masque*[6] given at the theatre. Holbein's *"Danse"*[7]. Staid with Sarasin till 4 this morning (Thursday).

Mayence, January 25, 1810. *Lev.* 9. Headache. Took no breakfast, but paid for one. Message from Elsinger that Madame Van ——— claimed me as relation, she being the granddaughter of Daniel Burr of Harwich. Called on Elsinger to apologize for not seeing *ma chere cousine*[8] till my return. Home. Invitation from Bethmann to dine, which could not. *Embarras*[9] of packing up. A bill of 47 florins and 17 kreu.[10] to my *valet de place!* At 12 took diligence; being the last, went outside and was nearly frozen. At the ½ way house a civil young man gave me his place inside. A soldier's widow who had served fifteen campaigns and still handsome. Went over the

---

1 For *Y sa fille divorcée; belle; embonpoint; yeux noirs.* Her divorced daughter; fine looking, plump, black eyes.
2 At the house of his kinswoman, Madame ———.
3 An assemblage (*assemblée*) of fifty.
4 An interesting family from Vienna.
5 For *trois demoiselles et un fils. L'ainée* (the eldest daughter) speaking, etc.
6 For *au bal masqué.* To the masquerade.
7 Among the works of Hans Holbein the Younger is a series of designs, fifty-three in number, for wood engraving, representing the Dance of Death (*la danse des morts*)—an allegorical representation of the power of death over all classes and conditions of men.
8 For *ma chère cousine.* My dear feminine cousin.
9 The trouble.
10 For Kreuzer. One hundredth of a florin; in Germany one thirtieth of a mark.

Rhine on *traineau*[1] drawn by two men with m.[2] Took qu'rs at the 3 *Couronnes*[3]. Card to General Meynier and to *le Prefet*[4] *le* Baron Jean Bon St. Andrè. To Kayser, to whom had a letter from my very kind friend Sarasin. Mr. Kayser called immediately and invited me to go to the theater with him; agreed. He called at 6 with his carriage; met there his wife, a very beautiful woman who is a grandmother; her daughter; a French gentleman and wife. The comedy "*Les Deux Ionnèes*" or "*Les Journèes*"[5], and the afterpiece, ———; both in French, amused me very much; laughed a great deal. Home at 10. A *rendz.* with *ma com. de Vay.*[6], but failed.

26. At 10 went by appointment to see General Mayence, *un brave franc soldat*[7]; unfortunately just now *gouteux*[8]. Thence to the *Prefet le celebre* Jean Bon St. Andre[9], now Baron, &c. His appearance justifies the character we had had of him. Met accidentally a young man of very intelligent countenance; exchanged looks and made acquaintance, but not a word said. The *Prefet* cannot give me a passport for Paris; must write and get one from the Minister of Police at Paris. About an hour afterwards received a

---

1 For *traineau*. Sledge.
2 It is not plain what the letter m stands for.
3 Took quarters at the Three Crowns (*aux Trois Couronnes*).
4 The Prefect.
5 This reference is obscure. Does Burr mean "*Les Deux Yonnées*," "The Two Women of Yonne" (a department of France)? Possibly it should be "*Les Deux Dionées*." In this case it might mean Venus the goddess of pleasure and Diana the chaste, for the name *Dionée* is applied to both of these divinities. Hence the title might refer to two women possessing these opposite characters. The title "*Les Journées*" means "The Days."
6 Probably for a *rendez-vous* with *ma Comtesse* de Vay———. A rendezvous with my Countess de Vay———.
7 Burr may mean here either a brave, sincere soldier, or a brave French soldier. In the latter case *franc* would stand for *français* and should follow the noun.
8 For *goutteux*. Gouty.
9 For *le célèbre* Jean Bon Saint André. The celebrated, etc.

note from the young man requesting permission to call and introduce himself. It seems that in order to discover my lodgings he had gone to the guard who watch the gate and enquired of the officer. He dined with me at the hotel lest I might want interpreter or countenance. Presently my indefatigable friend brought a girl; one made for the purpose, speaking French and German; a fine animated, intelligent countenance; pretty and well made. All was instantly arranged.—Never take the advice of one who is agitated or alarmed.—To the *Prefet's* for my passport; *bureau*[1] shut. To the Secretary; he had not the passport. I might call at the *hureau* in the morning, but told me that I should not have to come to Mayence unless I meant to stay there till the answer should be received from Paris and that I must remain in Mayence under *surveillance de la police*[2]. Now, this will not be very convenient for I am engaged to-morrow evening at Goutard's (not Sunday as supposed), and to dine on Sunday at Mons. de B's. To a coffee-house; took coffee and played chess, while the young man was preparing for me. Evening at d'P.'s. *Y.* Two ladies and three gents. Chess. Was beaten by the lady. Herr Von Borg, *de Soede*[3]. But had scarcely left the door of my friend when I was stopped by two soldiers. After some parley, understood from them that it was not permitted to walk the streets at that hour without a lamp and that I must go with

---

1 Office.
2 Supervision of the police.
3 Mr. Von Borg, of Sweden (*la Suède*).

them to the guard-house. There are various ways of getting along in this world. After some explanations, they agreed to eschort[1] me to my lodgings. Home at ½ p. 11 and am now going to *couche.* That matter of the passport sticks in my throat. There is no possibility of going one mile without a passport.

27. Rose 8. Waited till 10 very impatiently for P., who had promised to call on me very early. Then sent to him to know whether he would be at home if I should call. Yes. Called and passed ¼ hour. Thence to *Prefet's.* Received in the most polite and amiable manner; compliments passed and returned. I might stay at Mayence or go to Frankfort, or wherever I pleased, save the interior of France. Returned my passport. Handed him the other which I had addressed to him, requesting that he would apply for me to the Minister of Police at Paris. All right. Thence to Mr. Kayser's; saw him and his *bel. fem.*[2] To a *libraire*[3], where bought Gray's poems for *la jol. Viennienne*[4] (whose name I will try to get for you). To P.'s.; *fem., deux char. garc's.*[5] *Auberge*[6]; paid bill, 7 fl. 16 gro. and 6 liv.[7] to *mon valet de place.* The moment you arrive at any town if to stay six hours you are saddled with a *valet de place*, whose pay per day is from 3 liv. to a dollar. Wrote note of *conge* to P. Crossed the Rhine *en pet.*

---

1 So in the MS.
2 For *belle femme.*
3 Bookseller.
4 For *la jolie Viennienne.* The pretty lady from Vienna.
5 Wife and two charming boys. (*Charmants garçons.*)
6 Inn.
7 For livres. The livre was 20 sous or a franc.

traineau[1] and got to the diligence office just at 12, the hour of setting off. Got No. 9, being the last place and again outside. Met again *la guerre*[2]. Exceedingly cold and suffered much. Arrived at *Frankfort* at 5. Went first to Sarasin's to hear the news and inquire for private lodgings, as I must necessarily be here at least a week. As I got to the *Rom. kayser*[3] eight or ten carriages drew up. It was the *c. d.*[4] King of Sweden, Gustavus IV., with his family and attendants. My room on first floor was taken, of which I was very glad, for I got one as good on second floor for ½ the price. Dressed and at ½ p. 7 to A. Goutard's. It was a mistake; that little huzzy the *Ven'e*[5] led me to the error. The ball to-night is at another Goutard's with whom have no acquaintance. Very glad of it, for I was but half thawed and had much to do, *i. e.*, to think what and how and where in case I am excluded from France, of which there seems little room to doubt. This is probably the work of the United States minister, for certainly I have claims to protection if not to hospitality from France, and then I had hoped to do the Emperor and myself so much good.

28. *Couche* 1. Rose 8. At 10 to Sarasin; went with his young man to look at rooms, but could not be suited. Determined, however, to take the

---

1 For *en petit traineau.* On [a] small sledge.
2 *La guerre* means war. Possibly Burr refers to the hard time he had outside in the cold, somewhat as we say, "I had a regular siege of it." Or he may mean that he again met the soldier's widow, mentioned on page 389.
3 For *Gasthaus zum Römischen Kaiser.* The Roman Emperor Hotel.
4 For *ci-devant.* Heretofore, former.
5 For *la Viennienne.* The lady of Vienna.

worst of them rather than endure longer to the expense of this hotel and my *v. de pl.*[1] At 1 to Casino ; saw no acquaintance who chose to recognize me. Read the papers and off. *Pa. din*[2]. Called this morning on *le* Comte de R., who received me very kindly and said many things for which I am greatly obliged to him. Sat over com. of wa. and m * *[3] till 7 P. M. Dressed and went to Goutard's. An immense party of all that is titled and much untitled good matter ; perhaps sixty *dames*. The young ones are in a room by themselves ; a very bad arrangement. Perceived a wonderful coldness and after making half a dozen bows came off. My host, however, was most polite and attentive. To Casino, where read newspapers an hour. Home ½ p. 9. Tea *a la* Gamp[4]. Ruminating on the *statu quo*[5] till 1, and now *bon soir*.

29. Rose ½ p. 8. At 10 to Sarasin's to see about lodgings ; looked at several, but a new difficulty occurs ; no *burger*[6] can receive a stranger in his house without the license of the police. S. recommends that I call on Comte de Beuste for this purpose, which I shall do to-morrow. At 11 Comte de Beuste gave me some clue to the coldness "I thank you very much." Resolved to wait here the result of my application for passport. To Casino at 1. Walked a mile out of town. Still very cold. *Renc.* on ret.; 1 fl.;

---

1 For *valet de place.*
2 For *Pas de diner*, or *Je n'ai pas dîné.* No dinner.
3 Probably for Sat over a composition (or compound) of water and * * * *. The undecipherable word may be *mel* for *miel*, honey ; or milk.
4 After Gamp's fashion.
5 For *status quo* or *status in quo.* Latin. The state in which anything is already.
6 For *Burger.* Citizen, burgher.

pa. bo.[1] Home at 3. Ruminate till 8, then to the Casino ball, my good friend S. having furnished me with a ticket. *Υ* about thirty ladies, noble, not one *bourgeoise*[2]. The three Swedish officers who attend Gustavus IV. all claimed my acquaintance and was amused to talk over Sweden. A few other acquaintances. (Mr. Bethmann sent his *dom.* this evening to offer me ticket for the *bal.*[3] but I was provided.) Home at 11. Same symptoms this evening as before. Ruminating till 1.

30. *Couche* 2. Rose 8. I sleep always but a single nap and without dreaming; have not had a dream in six months. Walked round with my *valet de place* to look at rooms. Think I shall fix on the bookbinder's. To Comte de Beuste. He had gone to Mayence for a week. To Sarasin to know what was to be done. He advised me that as soon as I had fixed on my lodgings, for they must be designated, he would apply to the police for me. Received letter from my cousin John Carnad de Rön giving a history of his branch of the family of Burr and inviting invitation on the part of his sister, Madame Van ————, to call and take chocolate with her some morning. Response and proposed to call on Madame to-morrow at 11. Called on C. de R., who is to leave town to-morrow. Gave me friendly invitation to come and pass a day with him. Mr. Bethmann's *dom.* to invite me to sup to-night after the play is

---

1 For *Rencontre* on returning; 1 florin; *pas bon* (or *honne*). A rencounter, etc. Not good.
2 Woman of the middle or shop-keeping class.
3 For *bal masqué*. Masquerade.

over. Ruminated till 8, then to the Casino. At 9 (play over) to Bethmann's. *Y:* The three Swedish officers; Madame Euler; Madame ———, her daugher and son-in-law; no others. Very good supper and wine. Home at 11.

31. Hail me in my new lodgings in a little back-yard! The access is a perfect labyrinth. Two neat small rooms and a lumber room, pretty furnished for 3 florins per week, about 1⅛ dollars. Did you ever hear anything so *bon marchè*[1]? Rose 9, heavy, heavy, headache! No breakfast. At 11 to *ma cousine*[2] Madame Von ———. *Y:* Madame de Rön and M'lle Wickelhausen, daughter of a niece of Madame V.; both pretty and speaking fluently French. Swallowed a dish of chocolate. Might as well have swallowed arsenic. At 1 to Sarasin. Had fixed on the bookbinder's; the mistress, the maid, and the boy being all cheerful, good-natured faces. He, S., sent to the police and the license was granted without hesitation. Paid my bill at *Rom. Kays*[3], 16 florins 20 gro.; 1 duc.[4] to *madg.* and *garc.*,[5] 10 florins to my *v. d. p.*[6] and at 5 was installed in my new quarters. I am really more than content. Madame and all the household have that promptness to oblige that forestalls one's wishes. The mistress and servants speak French enough for my purposes. Madame says she has a charming friend who speaks English perfectly whom she will bring to see me.

---

1 For *à bon marché*. Cheap.
2 My feminine cousin.
3 For *Gasthaus* zum *Romischen Kaiser.*
4 For ducat. A ducat was worth nearly 2 dollars in Germany.
5 For *Madchen* and *garçon.* Servant girl and waiter.
6 For *valet de place.*

My new *style* will put me out of society, but in the first place, Madame, that I am already, and in the second my ducats will be of more use to me than their dinners. S. and C. D. R. approve the arrangement. I have had my tea in my own fashion and have not felt so much at home in many months, except at Lüning's. The juice of *four* lemons carried off my headache, the infernal chocolate notwithstanding; for this remedy, thank you.

Frankfort, February 1, 1810. Mr. Bansa's clerk came in before I was out of bed this morning with a letter from M. de Streiber, enclosing one of introduction for Bethmann. Sent it with a note, and also E. B.'s letter for perusal. At 11 to Mr. de Rode. Sat half an hour; he was packing up to return to his *chateau*, about five leagues from town; a magnificent establishment, as is said. Home. Mr. Sarasin came in, and after, young Bansa. To Casino at 1, where an hour reading newspapers. Home at 2. *Bro. cas.*[1] for *din.* The French louis which I bought at Hamburg are all right. A loss of 3 florins on each. *Fortunately* have but three left. At 3 to Sarasin's. Much confab; naught new. This P. M., my hostess, who is always thinking of something to oblige me, brought in Madame ———, a sweat[2], sprightly, comely English woman, who staid and took tea with me. Projects for the amusement of Kam.[3] and Gamp advance.

---

1 Probably for *Brot und Kase.* Bread and cheese.
2 So in the MS.
3 This word is somewhat illegible in the MS. The reference is obscure. *Kam.* might be an abbreviation of the German *Kamerad.* Comrade.

Ruminating all the evening. A new essay to change the state of affairs will be made to-morrow. Invitation from Bethmann for Tuesday evening, February 6, to sup, &c. Birthday of ———.

2. My rooms are so small and the ceilings so low, that when the stove is heated I am suffocated, the hot air being above ; while my head is in an oven, my feet are in an ice-house. Got up this morning later than usual, stupid, and choaked[1] with a cold. At 12 to *le ministre*[2] Hedouville. He was engaged, but appointed 1 o'clock. To Casino to pass the interval reading newspapers. Cut all my friends to be beforehand. At 1 to the *Ministre*, an amiable, intelligent, well-bred man. Received my communication with courtesy and engaged to transmit it forthwith to Paris. A reply cannot be expected within twelve days. Have a great mind to go to Weimar. *Pa. din.*[3] At 3 to Elsinger, *le libraire*. He has caught the infection. Passed an hour looking over books, but bought nothing. I wish to send you so many that it will end in sending none. Yes, a good French dictionary, if one there be, I will send. Tea at 6, and at 7 came in Sarasin to take me to the museum. The music very fine. Two airs by the enchanting voice of Schonberg. A handsome young man introduced himself to me as from Hanover, and bearing a civil message to me from the beautiful M'lle Karsaboom ; not quite so spelled, however. This is ladies' night at Casino, but did not

---

1 So in the MS.
2 The Minister.
3 For *Pas de diner.*

go. Home ½ p. 8. *Ma hotesse*[1] invited me to partake of her supper ; agreed. The party was Madame, her seamstress, another woman, and one of the jour neymen. Invitation to-day from Bethmann to dine on Sunday. Doubting whether I will not go to de Rode's on Sunday.

3. Rose very late. The maid makes my fire, that is, heats my room at 7, but I get stupified by the heat ; for this I see no remedy, unless I could muster force enough to get up before any heat was introduced. But there is no exigence requiring this effort. After the answer from Paris, which may be expected on Tuesday, the case will be altered, whatever may be the tenor of that answer. At 12 to Casino. Met at the door Mons. de Wickelhausen, who, having married the niece of Madame Vandervelten, has thus become my cousin. He talked to me ½ hour about family matters, &c. Read newspapers an hour. Home an hour ; then to the Musée, this being the day of exhibition. *Y :* Sarasin and family ; *mon aimable cousin, mais pa beaucoup de monde*[2]. Was amused with the pictures and the visitors. Among the paintings was a Cleopatra ; as usual, *blonde et grande,* though in fact, she was *petite et brune*[3]. *Mon cousin* proposed to me twenty different parties and promenades, all of which I declined. At length one to which I acceded. It was very kind and very hospitable, but failed in the result, the parties not found. Home at 5. Dressed

---

1 For *ma hôtesse.* My hostess.
2 My amiable [male] cousin, but not (*pas*) many people.
3 Blonde and tall, though, in fact, she was short and dark.

and waited for Sarasin, who came at 7. To his brother's, Mons. Lars, a name of adoption (these adoptions are always attended with fortune), he being born Sarasin. There was a very handsome and gay party. Mons. and Madame Schonberg; she sang for us; *la fam. Venetienne*[1]; M. Chaumont *et souer fem. de* ———; Madame ———, *helle et superbe femme, soeur de ces deux de* Mayence[2], whom I met at Sarasin's; *la jolie pit.* Cloison[3], or something thereabouts, who pleased me so much at the Casino ball on Monday of last week. *La* blue. Not *princesse ni noble mais merite d'etre; est par nature*[4]. Une fem. *interressante de* Konigsberg[5], now Madame ———. *Les dem.* Sarasin, *bel. bru.*[6] We had a great deal of charming music. *La Prussienne* sings delightfully; so Cloison *mere* so *pet. guitarre*[7]. A suite of four rooms well lighted. The supper elegant and the guests extremely gay. Somehow thought more of *Many Ann*[8] than of all the present. Home at 1. My stove cold as ice. Took one hour to make fire, get warmed, and smoke my pipe. Now at ½ p. 2 Sunday morning and I shall smoke another pipe before *couche.*

Frankfort, S. M., February 4, 1810. I have not

1 This is probably a slip of Burr's pen. He undoubtedly means *la fameuse Viennienne*, the celebrated lady from Vienna, instead of *Vénitienne*, the lady from Venice, as the reader will soon see.

2 For *et soeur, femme de*, etc. And sister, wife of ———. Madame ———, a handsome, superb woman, sister of those two of Mayence

3 For *la jolie petite* Cloison. The pretty little Cloison.

4 For *la fille miso en* blue. (*Bleu.*) Not *princesse ni noble mais mérito de l'être; elle l'est par nature.* The girl in blue, neither a princess nor a noble, but she deserves to be; is so by nature.

5 For *une femme intéressante de* Konigsberg. An interesting woman of Konigsberg.

6 For *les demoiselles* Sarasin, *belles, brunettes.* The Sarasin girls, fine-looking brunettes.

7 The Prussian lady sings delightfully; so the mother (*mère*) Cloison; so *la petite fille touche très bien la guitare.* So the little maid plays the guitar delightfully.

8 Mary Ann must be a pet name given by Burr to his daughter. Under date of July 24, 1809, he writes: " *Ma belle* Mary Ann (only think, your favorite name ").

before put S. M. which means *sur* Mein[1], to distinguish it from Frankfort, S. O., (*sur* Oder). Rose late.
Did nothing till 1 ; then to dine with Bethmann. *Υ:*
La mere et deux filles, Brevilliere ; *la fam. Viennienne*[2],
of which I have so often spoken ; M'lle D. M. is one
of the finest women I meet; Mons. de Brevilliere,
brother of the deceased father ; *la mere* was Goutard.
Euler *mere et fils.*[3] In all we were twenty-one at table.
The dinner handsome, but the rapidity with which
things were done is inconvenient and unsocial ; you
would think we were eating for wagers, such is the
velocity with which the courses are served. The
moment the last course has gone round (everything is
handed round by the servant), all rise and go off to
the drawing-room, where coffee is served. A sprightly
young *Genevoise*[4] merchant pursued me a great deal,
and was very civil. Had also, to-day, an invitation to
dine *chez* Madame ———— *souer de* Sarasin ; but Bethmann's was first. Off at 5, and to Madame ————,
who lives under the same roof with her brother, where
passed an hour very pleasantly. Home at 7. *Ma
hostesse* invited me to her party, *i. e.*, the English
woman ; another English woman, native of Pennsylvania, where played lottery till 9. Had my tea.
Wrote a long letter about Charles Loss[5] and family,
to be transmitted to the parents of Mr. and Mrs.
Loss, who live seventy or eighty miles hence. Wrote

1 On the Main, the river on which Frankfort is situated.
2 For *la fameuse Viennienne.* The celebrated Vienna lady.
3 Mrs. Euler and son.
4 For *Génevois.* Genevese.
5 Under date of December 31, 1809, Burr spoke of Saxony as being Chas. Loss's kingdom.

also to General Meynier, and to Dr. Perkins at Mayence, requesting each of them to inform me if there
was any news about my passports.

    5.   *Couche 3.*   Rose 8.   At 9 to Sarasin's with
my letters.   Home to breakfast; then to work to
assort papers, &c., and prepare for locomotion, which
I *feel* will soon become *necessary*.   But whether to
Paris, or to prison, or to Russia, or to the United
States, is known yonder above, but they won't tell
Gamp.   Wickelhausen promised to call between 4 and
5 to go *al chas.*[1] but did not.   At 5 *sor.* (*Pa. di.*[2]).
Renc. Dougan. Jo.jeu. amin. Tre. cont.; 4 fl.[3] Home
at 6.   Wickelhausen had called during my absence.
Tea.   Laid on the *canop.*[4] to smoke my pipe and
slept an hour.   At 9 to the Casino ball *au Maison
Rouge*[5], Sarasin having sent me a ticket.   *Υ* · The
Endes : M'lle Brevilliere, who introduced to me her
cousin, Dr. Schlosser, LL.D.   I was just wishing to
know some lawyer.   *Ma. pet.*[6] Ende looked very well;
Cloison not there.   The *assemblè* was very full and
very brilliant.   There seems to be a sort of tacit accord
among the *bourgeoises* to go only every other week.
Le Baron d'Ende, Mr. de B., and the Sarasin family
were my principal associates.   Off at ½ p. 11.   Yes,
there was also that fine, imposing form and countenance, M'lle de ——————, who resembles Emilie de

---

1 Probably for *à la chasse.* To go hunting.
2 For *Pas de diner.*
3 For *Rencontre.* Dougan, *jolio, jeune, amincie. Très content ;* 4 florins. A rencounter;
[by name] Dougan, pretty, young, thin. Very well satisfied, etc. (*Amin.* may stand for the
noun *amincissement*, thinness, just as Burr uses the noun *embonpoint*, plumpness.)
4 For *canapé.* Couch.
5 For *à la Maison Rouge.* At the Red Mansion.
6 For *ma petite.* My little.

Visme. "Suspense," says Swift, "is the life of a spider."

6. *Jour mem'r pour nous aut.*[1], because two and two make four; so that, according to some logicians, twice 27 make 54, and so on *ad inf.*[2] Sat up till 3, smoking and assorting scraps. Rose about 10. To Casino at 1. *Υ:* Bethmann, and the *m. g. fr.*[3], resembling Gallatin, but not the front nor the stable nose. An amiable phiz. G. always meet *monde*[4] there; but go off about 1, that being the unusual hour of dining. Gamp is more sought and spoke to these some days past; *pas tout a fait le mon'r ter.*[5] Bethmann, who wrote to Paris about ten days ago, has, as he says, no answer. Perhaps they care nothing, think nothing about us. The moment the Rhine is open, will be off, if suffered. Saw from the Casino windows two regiments French cavalry, on march to France. The horses and men small, but the men handsome, sprightly youths. Did not see a horse that would have sold at Philadelphia for 100 dollars. Much talking among the men. Swords not very long; nearly straight; light. Written at 3 P. M. You will have a word more on my return from Bethmann's to-night. Got home from Bethmann's at ½ p. 12. It was a very handsome party of about thirty. The

---

1 This is an interesting riddle. The French abbreviations stand for *Jour mémorable pour nous autres.* Day memorable for us folks. The reader will note that the date in the Journal is February 6, 1810. Burr was born February 6, 1756, being therefore 54 years old. Theodosia was born June 20, 1783, and was therefore 27. So the riddle " twice 27 make 54 " becomes clear. Of course this day is memorable to both.
2 For Latin *ad infinitum.* To infinity.
3 Probably for *monsieur grand français.* Tall French gentleman.
4 People.
5 For *il n'est pas tout à fait le monsieur terrible.* Literally, he is not entirely the terrible man !

supper *com. il faut*[1]. Conversation, cards, billiards, music, filled the interval before supper, which was served about ½ p. 10. The same rapidity as at dinner. The company retired about an hour after supper. The party was wholly of citizens, except General Sweyer, two young French officers, and a Russian envoy. Many of my particular acquaintance of both sexes were there. Was most occupied with Madame ———, who, to many *agreements*[2], adds that of speaking English. She very wickedly led me into dilemma by exciting remarks on her brother and his *ux*. It happened that she was a beautiful woman, and that I pronounced very favorable on both. The evening passed off very well. Mr. Bethmann has no news for me, but expects a messenger to-night. To-morrow, too, I shall have answers to my letters to P. and M. at Mayence to-morrow night.

7. *Couche 3. Lev. 8.* At 10 to Bethmann's for news. He had none. *Pour me distraire*[3], walked an hour to find *la* Doug.[4], but could not find the place. Home and got my bill, the week having expired. *Voici les details*[5], and then you will know how I live ·

	Florins.	Kreutzers.
Rooms and furniture	3	00
Bread	0	35
1 lb. cheese	0	28
1 lb. butter	0	16
1 bottle wine		36
1 lb. sugar	2	04
Wood	2	00
	8	59

---

1 For *comme il faut.* As it should be.
2 For *agréments.* Accomplishments. Possibly Burr meant this as an English word.
3 In order to entertain myself.
4 For *la* Dougan. The girl mentioned on page 402.
5 Here are the details (*détails*).

Eight florins and 59 kreutzers is about 4 dollars. Not extravagant. But then the contingencies :

	Florins.	Kreutzers.
A decanter broken by the stove heat	1	12
Washing	1	2
To the servants	2	30
To servants when dining or sup-ping abroad	4	00
Mus.[1]	6	00
	13	44
	8	59
	22	43

Twenty-two florins and 43 kreutzers is about 8½ dollars. At the hotel for one week it cost me 82 florins, and I had not half the comfort. Now for the Casino to read the news, of which I am told there is much by this mail regarding the interior The moment of entering the Casino a gentleman took me aside ; told me he was secretary of Mr. ———; that his Excellency was ready to give me a passport when I should please, and would be glad to see me at 11 to-morrow. This was what I least expected to meet at Casino, or at all through that channel. At ½ p. 2 to see our cousins, Madame Vandervelten & Co. Found there a pleasant little party. Three pretty girls, all cousins, sitting round a large table drinking coffee. It is a very respectable old lady. Her husband a *comte*, but she does not assume the title. At 4 to Sarasin's to counsel. Always frank and kind. Home at 5. Tea at 7. Sarasin came in and sat ½

---

1 For *mus.* See Glossary.

hour. Agreed to go to the *bal masquè.* Said that there will be many *honêtes gens*[1].

1 A. M. Wednesday night. Have returned early from the ball. It was very full, and much more brilliant than the first. It seems that the *honetes gens* (*dames*) are resolved not to be *chassèd*[2] from their favorite amusement by the *demireps*[3]. The latter were, however, the great majority. For want of the language I was a mere spectator. I conceive that it *may be made* very charming. My head, however, is full of other things. That message, and the channel through which it comes! but to-morrow (to-day, being near 2 in the morning), will develop. *Je t'embrasse*[4].

12. Reichard[5] and maps being locked up, and the *conducteur* refusing me access to them till we reach Metz, which will be to-morrow P. M., can give you no account of my route, but we are 44 *lieue de poste*[6] from Mayence, about 110 English miles. But, as you have heard nothing from me since Wednesday [the 7th], it is necessary to go back. On Thursday paid visit of *congé* to Bethmann's, to Baron d'Ende, to Gerning. Saw not one of them. Mr. B. was in his *comtoir*[7] and sent message by the servant asking me to dine to-morrow (Friday), which declined, having resolved to leave town. Sat a few minutes with

---

1 For *honnêtes gens.* Virtuous, genteel people.
2 Another French verb, *chasser*, to expel, anglicized by Burr; hence, driven out.
3 See Glossary.
4 I embrace thee.
5 Burr refers to Reichard's guide-book for travelers entitled " *Passagier auf der Reise in Deutschland.*" " The Traveler Journeying in Germany."
6 For *lieues de poste.* Post leagues. A *lieue* was about two and a half English miles.
7 For *comptoir.* Counting-house.

Madame sa mere. Dined with Sarasin *en famille* at ½ p.
1. Thence to Madame Vandervelten, our cousin. *Y*
½ hour. Yesterday sent for her inspection the picture,
of which many pretty things were said. Sent also the
miniature of Caroline as of a niece. Home at ½ p.
4, but not finding disposition to go to work, went out
to see Doug.; out, but consoled self with *la maitr. de
mais. Encore* not being satisfactory, roved an hour.
Y ca mou. p. Gamp fully; 2 *j. U.* Home at 9 quite
tranquil. 'Tis the sole rem. in such cases'. I forgot
to say that before dinner I went to see if the Com.
de R. had returned to town. He had just arrived.
We met like old affectionate friends. He was
engaged to dine with Com. de Beuste, to cele-
brate the birthday of the Prince Primate, and so
we arranged an interview at 10 at his house. At 10
went *y* and passed nearly two hours. Much information and *renseignments*² about Paris. Talked to
him of X, in which he entered warmly and predicted
success. Home at 12 and worked like a beaver till 3.
Made a long list of letters to be written before leaving
Frankfort; of which I wrote not one. Did nothing
but what had a direct reference to my object. Oh, if
they will only hear me, and Hedouville says they will.
Rose at 7 Friday morning. Worked hard, but did
not get through the assorting, transcribing addresses,

---

1 Went out to see Dougan; out, but consoled self with the mistress of the house (*la
maîtresse de la maison*). [It] still not being satisfactory, roved an hour. That move (*ce
mouvement* [-*la*]) paid (or pleased) Gamp fully; two pretty maids (*deux jolies mademoiselles* or
jungfrus). Home at 9 quite tranquil. 'Tis the sole remedy in such cases. (In Davis's abridged
reprint of the Journal, see Introduction for the explanation, all this is translated " and walked
half an hour.")
2 Much information and intelligence (or inquiries).

&c. Had visit of *congé* from Sarasin, Fuchs, his son-in-law, and from Com. de R.; no others. Got to the stage office at 12, and, for the first time, got inside. Most alarming account of the rigid visitation at Cassel[1] (opposite Mayence) and at Mayence. At Cassel the search was very slight; and at Mayence, where I supposed my pockets would be *fouilled*[2], met a good-natured looking fellow, who asked me where I would lodge. *"Au trois Couronnes"*[3]. *"Allez y et votre baggage vous suivra en cinque minutes"*[4]. In effect, in five minutes my baggage came, not having been opened and no *douceur*[5] paid. Went direct to the *Prefet's* to get my passport *viséd*[6]. He was out, and would not be home till 10. Gave a livre to the servant to deliver him a message, requesting that he would *visè* my passport to-night. Called and left card at Kàyser's. Then home. The diligence was to go at 6 next morning. Little chance of seeing the *Prefet* to-night, and so went off to hunt his secretary. He received me civilly, and agreed to do the business, which he was half an hour doing, while I played with his two beautiful children. At 10 came in D. and sat an hour. Gave me memorandum of a lady who might be an agreeable acquaintance. *Couche* 2, having spent two hours in assorting, &c., which got through to my satisfaction. Was called at 6. Went to take place in the diligence. The inside full; four *dames;* but as

---

1 Kastel, a town of a few thousand, is meant.
2 Another French verb, *fouiller*, to rummage, anglicized by Burr. Searched.
3 For *aux Trois Couronnes*. At the Three Crowns.
4 Go thither (*Allez-y*) and your baggage (*bagage*) will follow you in five (*cinq*) minutes.
5 Tip.
6 A French-English verb now used in English, from French *viser*, to inspect. To *visé* a passport is to inspect it and endorse it officially.

two were to be received eight leagues on our way, got the privilege of riding inside so far. The two *dames* were an officer's wife, very pretty, and a soldier's wife. The two we took in were a lady and a pretty daughter. Took my station outside, with a young man of very decent appearance, who was going as conscript to join the army. He says that a substitute costs 100 louis[1], and if he deserts the principal must replace him. Got to our quarters at 10, and to bed at 12. Called up at 4 this morning, and arrived here at 6. Ordered a room and fire, with which all this is written at 12 o'clock. Seven leagues back is the beautiful little town of ———— on the Saar, formerly the residence of the Prince of Nassau. His elegant palace being manfestly an aristocratical structure, was burned by the democrats[2] when they carried war here early in the Revolution. The palace was then a hospital, and there being no time to remove the patients, they were also burnt. The church (one of them) is a very elegant little thing. Just t'other side of this town saw along the banks of the Saar broad fields of the stubble or stalks of Indian corn, the first I have seen since leaving the United States, but have not yet seen on this side the Rhine a single vineyard. They say it is too cold, though on the other side, even in the neighborhood of Fulda, nearly one hundred miles north of this, all the hills were covered with vines. No interest or amusement of any sort with the *dames.* Am supposed a Swede. All the country I

1 The louis was a French gold coin worth about 4 dollars.
2 Meaning Jacobins?

have passed through since crossing the Rhine till within a league of this place where I now write was formerly subject to different German princes, and has been conquered by and incorporated into France since the Revolution. Hitherto, of course, everything has been German. Here all is French; the language of the family; the manners. The hostess, a very handsome young woman (minus a beard), extremely attractive and polite. Our *conducteur* is French by birth, but not by manners. He is in all respects the chief of the party; does the honors of the table, &c. At ———— met an interesting young sub-officer, speaking perfectly good English. I am very bad company and unsocial, my head being so full of X matters.

Paris, February 16, 1810. Hotel de Lyon, Rue Grenelle No. 7, St. Honore. Left Chalons at 5 yesterday. The day, yesterday, was fine spring weather. The atmosphere tolerably clear. I rode outside to enjoy the beauty of the scenery. We breakfasted at Epernay, the centre of the fine *vin Champaigne*[1] country, and we drank of several sorts. Thence along the Marne for ———— leagues. The mountains on each side are covered with vines, but the land on the north side of the valley is of ten times more value than on the south. An *arpent*[2] of the former is said to be worth 2 to 4 thousand dollars. Rode all night, and arrived here at 12 this day. My room (the only vacant one in the hotel) is up two pairs of stairs, about fourteen feet square; paved with brick, very coarsely

1 For *vin de Champagne.* Champagne.
2 An old French measure of from one to one and a half acres.

furnished ; a large, very large ill-constructed fire-place. No quantity of wood can warm the room. The wood is brought, five sticks at a time (such as Gampy would take in one hand), for 30 sous. The sou is about equal to our cent. *This room is 40 sous per day.* My *comp. de voyage*[1], Major Thomas, took me to a coffee-house to dine. The expense with two bottles of wine was 60 sous each. Thence to a coffee-house *au* Palais Royal[2]. A dish of coffee, 10 sous. Walked an hour under the arches, which is the evening promenade. Saw not one beautiful or very fine woman. The best, you know, is always good. *M'aime*[3]; 2 *Eo.*[4] Home at 9.

17. My first business this morning was to address a note to the Duc de Cadore, *min. des rel'ns ext.*[5], which sent by a messenger, 12 sous. Thence to Hauterive ; out, left my name. To Mr. Schoel, *libraire*, with letter from Bertuch ; out, left the letter, but no card. To Dr. Swediaur, with letter from Baron Strick. Sat half an hour with the Doctor. A man of sense and science ; frank and cheerful. Gave me very kind reception. Home at 4. A bowl of soup in my room for dinner, 8 sous, with bread. Tea in the evening, 30 sous. A note from the Duc de Cadore, appointing Monday, 2 P. M., for an audience. Home and alone all the evening.

1 For *compagnon de voyage.* Traveling companion.
2 At the Palais Royal. This was originally, as its name denotes, a royal palace Richelieu built it, 1629–1634, and gave it to the King. Louis XVI. presented it to the Duke of Orleans, in whose family it remained for many generations. The Duke of Orleans, known as Philippe Egalité, surrounded it with houses and galleries which are still used for purposes of trade. In one of its angles is the Théâtre Français.
3 Burr may mean this for *mon aimée*, my beloved, or for *elle'm'aime*, she loves me.
4 Another riddle. Perhaps the apparent o is meant for u, in which case the word may be meant for *écus;* hence 2 crowns.
5 For *ministre des relations extérieures.* Minister of Foreign Relations, like our Secretary of State.

18. Breakfast, tea, brought from the *lemonadiere's*[1], 30 sous. The tea very bad; coffee rather worse. At 12 to Comte de Volney's; out, left card. Having heard nothing from Hauterive, wrote him note, requesting information about several of my acquaintances; out, and got no answer. Much trouble about outfits for presentation to-morrow. Tailor, *chaponier*[2], &c. About 5 with Major Thomas to dine at any coffee-house or *traiteur*[3]. Seeing *affiche*[4], dinner of four courses for 24 sous, went in to make experiments. Had for 24 sous a very good dinner and a small caraffe[5] of *vin* each. Took another bottle of *vin Bourg. blanc*[6] at 30 sous in honor of the house. The waiter expects nothing from you at these places. On the way went into a shop, *vingt cinque sous le piece*[7], and bought each a couple. A most curious collection of all manner of things, each being 25 sous. Thence to a coffee-house and took coffee. Thence *au* Coffee-house *des Aveugles*[8], *i. e.*, a cellar vaulted, eighty or a hundred feet square, well furnished. Music, an orchestra of blind performers. Entrance gratis. We were four, and took beer and biscuit, 3 sous each. Ladies of all sorts. Will talk with you, sit, eat, drink; but no further than solicitations unless you make overtures. I found one of them very amusing. Thence *au Coffee des Milles Colonnes*[9], celebrated for the

---

1 For *limonadière.* Coffee-house keeper.
2 For *chapelier.* Hatter.
3 Eating-house keeper.
4 Placard.
5 Old spelling of carafe.
6 For *vin blanc de Bourgogne.* White Burgundy wine.
7 For *vingt cinq sous la pièce.* Twenty-five sous for each article.
8 To the Blind Men's coffee-house. Burr probably confuses coffee-house with *Café.*
9 For *au Café,* etc. To the Café of the Thousand Columns.

beauty of the mistress. The rooms are supported by
colonnes, and every pier filled by mirror. The reflections give the idea of boundless space and numberless
colonnes. The lady at one side, elevated about two
feet ; a kind of throne, from which gives orders and
receives money most graciously, and for 20 louis—but
that must be a lie. We had a hot *sangaree*. Thence
au Coffè des Varietiès[1]. Pantomimic and dramatic per-
formances are given. Entrance gratis. It was so
crowded that we could not get in. Left my companions and got home at ½ p. 9.

19. Rose late, which always stupifies me.
Wrote a note to Hauterive requesting an answer.
Got an answer, *q. v.!* He knows nothing of Delage
or Senat, or of any one of the subjects of my inquiry.
Being dressed by 1, and having an hour to spare,
went to *Son Alt. Seren*[2]. *la H.*[3] *Duchesse de* Courland
and Semigalle[4], to whom had a letter of introduction
from Duke *Reg.*[5] *de* Gotha ; out. Left letter and
card. To *le* Prince de Benevent[6]; out, left card. The
porter said if I wished to see him, I must address him
a line and get his hour. Thence to *le* Duc de Cadore.
Here I was denied, not being on the list of receiva-
bles, and not having brought with me the Duke's
note. Fortunately, the porter of the day was a woman,

---

1 For *Café des Variétés.* To the Café of the Varieties.
2 For *Son Altesse Sérénissime.* Her Most Serene Highness.
3 H. may stand for the Duchess's name, or possibly *Haute*, high.
4 Courlande or Kurland is a government of Russia, one of the Baltic provinces. Semigalle
or Semigallia was a Russian dukedom formerly united with Kurland.
5 For *Régnant.* Reigning.
6 Charles Maurice de Talleyrand-Périgord (1754–1838), Prince de Bénevént, commonly
known as Talleyrand. He was Napoleon's Minister of Foreign Affairs until 1809, when he
quarreled with him, being opposed to the Emperor's Russian and Spanish policy.

her husband being sick. After much negotiating got admission to the antechamber. Sent in my card and was received. Had an hour's conversation; all in French, and I was in bad order. Home at 4. *Soup. au riz et boeuft au naturel*, &c., for dinner, 14 sous, bread included. Nothing is furnished at the hotel where I lodge but rooms, wood, candles, and wine. At 6 *au* Theatre Francois². It was full, and no admission could be had. Told my valet to take me to the nearest theatre. Paid 3 livres for a place. It was a rope-dancer. The first performer, a boy of about 7 years ; the second, a girl of 5 or 6 ; the third, a lad of 12 ; the fourth, a pretty girl of 16. Then successively three men who did wonders. You would think these fellows were made, like Bentham's tongs, of air and steel. Made a very pleasant acquaintance, who was in the adjoining box. We walked ½ hour. *"Vous parroisses plein de genie ; la quelle de toutes vos talents vos fier vous le plus ?"* *" Je n'ai cultivè que celle de plaire"*³ She gave me her address and invited me to sup, which I declined. How wonderfully discreet ! But then I engaged to call on her to-morrow. How wonderfully silly ! Home at 9.

20. Rose again very late, and, of course, very stupid. The first thing I did was to call on my valet, and tell him I would discharge him if I was abed one minute later than ½ p. 6 to-morrow. He swears by

---

1 For *soupe au riz et boeuf au naturel*. Rice porridge and beef cooked plain.
2 For Théâtre Français. To the, etc. This theatre was in one of the angles of the Palais Royal.
3 For " *Vous paraissez pleine de génie ; auquel de tous vos talents vous fiez-vous le plus !*" (Asked by Burr). " *Je n'ai cultivé que celui de plaire*" (answered by the woman). "You appear to be full of genius ; upon which of all your talents do you rely most *?*" " I have cultivated only that of pleasing.'

all the saints that I shall be up at ½ p. 6. At 1 to
Lepine's, to whom I committed your watch to be put
in perfect order. He knew it immediately, and by
turning to his book told me the day it was sold. He
showed me many superb clocks and timepieces. Several of curious construction and his invention.
Thence to my rendezvous, Madame d'C. Choosing
to go without my valet, it was ½ p. 2 before I found
the street. The rooms are elegantly fitted up. A
young lady and a beautiful little boy urged me very
much to walk in and wait the return of Madame, but
my fit of discretion returned and I came off congratu-
lating myself on my escape from a dangerous siren.
The Major laughed at me most heartily and swore I
should introduce him, but he has a security which God
forbid I should ever [have]. "*Ah! Mon ami, je ne b.
Plus.*" "*Que vous etes heureux*[1]*!*" He is about my age
but more youthful and fresh in appearance; a very
handsome, well-made man of six feet; a full *chevelure*[2]
of fine chestnut hair. Went to several shops to hunt
for American maps, but found none of any value.
Called again on Schoel, whom I met. A most charming, prepossessing, frank, open German face. Full of
bonhommie[3]. We shall be good acquaintances. Gave
me some useful information, and an address to Mons.
de Valkenaer, who is to give me more. At 3 came in
le Comte de Volney[4]. He had peruke, and I did not

1 Possibly for "*Ah! Mon ami, je ne bois plus.*" "*Que vous êtes heureux!*" "Ah, my
friend, I drink no more." "How fortunate you are!
2 Head of hair.
3 For *bonhomie*. Good nature.
4 Constantin François de Chasseboeuf de Volney (1757–1820), a French scholar and author.
He traveled in Syria and Egypt in 1783–87, and in the United States; was a member of the Constituent Assembly; and was made a count by Napoleon and a peer by Louis XVIII. He was a
prolific writer His most famous work is, "*Ruines, ou Méditations sur les Révolutions des
Empires*" (1791).

recognize him. Turned his profile; still *méconnoisable*[1].
Gave me his name, and we embraced. Sat an hour.
Have not been out since 5, and have made but one
meal. Tea, bread, and butter.

21. Still hard winter. With my great chimney
and small room ventilated at a thousand crevices, and
wood at 25 sous for five small sticks, I suffer and
freeze. Lay abed till near 10 this morning to keep
myself warm. Sent my valet to hunt Barnett, late
United States consul. He is out of town and Adet[2],
whose address he brought me. At 1 called on
Scherer and Fringestin, with the letter of Sarasin.
Saw Scherer, who invited me, in the name of his wife,
to a party this evening, which declined. His establishment is vast and splendid. To Schoel's to get
Volney's new book. Home by way of P. R.[3] Took
a room on the first floor; wooden floor, something
better furnished than the other, but I fear no warmer,
at 50 livres per month, with liberty to quit sooner on
paying a little more. Being out of humor with my
thé[4] at 30 sous, and very bad, bought for 6 livres.
Had the satisfaction to make my own slop in my own
way. I have by this means learned the prices following: Butter, 36 sous per lb.; coffee, 110 sous per lb.;
bread is reasonable; for 4 sous I got my day's allow-
ance and more.

22. Last evening, after writing the preceding

---

1 For *méconnaissable*. Not easy to be known again.
2 Pierre Auguste Adet (1763–1832), was appointed minister from France to the United States in 1795. Two years later he broke off his diplomatic relations and before returning to France issued an address to the American people intended to make them dissatisfied with their government and its policy.
3 For Palais Royal.
4 Tea.

page, read three hours in Bentham's notes on Judiciary. It answered the purpose of talking with him, and I caught a ray of illumination from his genius. This ray regards my own immediate concerns. At 10 went to hunt Adet, whom I found. He recognized me immediately. Made an appointment to meet him *au Corps Legislatif*[1] at 2. Hence to Volney's; out. To Bovet and Bourdillion. Saw Bovet, who told me that young Bourdillion of Frankfort had announced me several days ago. Thence home, and at 2 *au Corps Legislatif.* The building is so immense and so intricate that I was a long time finding the right way. Mons. Adet met me, and we walked through the building and talked for ½ hour. Home at 4. After dinner walked two hours in and about Palais Royal, where the eye and the ear may be always amused, and the other senses, if you please. Wrote a note to Duc de Cadore. While I was dining a gentleman came in with a written message from the Rev. Mr. I. Burr, *Chanoine du Chapitre Collegial. de Rheinfeld en Suisse*[2], inquiring if I were not son of Zacché Burr, mer.[3] d'Ostende, and hoping that we were very nearly related. I regretted that I could not claim the honor of any very near relationship, but shall write a line to my coz.

23. There is no end to this winter. By way of variety, there is now a sort of sleet. Yesterday we had a little snow. Don't know at what hour I go to

---

1 At the Legislative Assembly. This body originated in 1791 and existed under one form or another for many years.
2 Canon of the Collegiate Chapter of Rheinfelden in Switzerland.
3 For merchant?

bed or get up, for your watch is in the hands of Lepine himself, who told me when it was sold, to whom, and for how much. He promised that it shall be put in complete order. At 12 to-day came in the celebrated Captain Haley. The first American I have seen. Told me that Vanderlyn¹ is in Paris, and hunting for me. I thought him in Rome. How glad! Major or Colonel Hunt and Barnett are on a tour to sell lands. At 1, the weather notwithstanding, to Mons. ————, the celebrated geographer. Was received. Showed the maps I wished to examine. Offered to lend me any and to give me several. Passed an hour with him much to my satisfaction. A sensible, cheerful man of about 45; I believe a German, but speaks French and English. Home at 4. Before going out this morning, sent my note to the Duke de Cadore. Have no answer yet. This evening a card from Mr. and Madame Scherer, to pass the evening on Thursday.

---

1 This was John Vanderlyn, a celebrated painter. He was born at Kingston, N. Y., October 15, 1776. At an early age he attracted the attention of Burr, who invited him to New York and received him in his own house. Vanderlyn studied painting with Stuart, and in 1796 went to Europe through the assistance of Burr, where he remained five years. He came back to the United States in 1801, but returned to Europe in 1803, remaining until 1815. He made many admirable copies from the old masters; painted the picture of Marius Seated Amid the Ruins of Carthage, which gained the Louvre gold medal in 1808; the Murder of Jane McCrea by the Indians, and other original works, which gave him a high reputation. Returning to the United States, he painted the portraits of Calhoun, Clinton, Madison, Monroe, Jackson, and other distinguished men. In 1832 he was commissioned to paint a full-length portrait of Washington for the hall of the House of Representatives, and in 1839 was commissioned to paint the Landing of Columbus for the Rotunda of the Capitol. The later years of Vanderlyn's life were spent in poverty. He died at Kingston, N. Y., September 23, 1852.
  The following is the letter of introduction which Burr wrote for Vanderlyn to Thomas Morris (son of Robert Morris, the financier of the Revolution), residing at the frontier settlement of Canandaigua, N. Y. It is dated New York, September 18, 1801:
  " Mr. Vanderlyn, the young painter from Eusopus, who went about six years ago to Paris, has recently returned, having improved his talents in a manner that does very great honour to himself, his friends, and his country; proposing to return to France in the spring, he wishes to take with him some American views, and for this purpose he is now on his way through your country to Niagara. I beg your advice and protection. He is a perfect stranger to the roads, the country, and the customs of the people, and, in short, knows nothing but what immediately concerns painting. From some samples which he has left here, he is pronounced to be the best painter that now is or ever has been in America. Your affectionate friend, A. BURR."

24. Did not go out of my room yesterday after dinner. *Voila huit jours* in Paris[1] without having been to a theatre or place of amusement, though I am in the very center of theatres, *bals masquè et non masquè*[2], and shows of all sorts. I had set my heart on one object, and that one sufficed for occupation and amusement, but two days having now elapsed since my note to the *Duc* and no reply, I may conclude that my hopes of business are at an end. Though *couche* at 1, did not rise till near 10. At 1 to Captain Haley's, whence sent a note to Vanderlyn, requiring him to present himself. Roved two hours. Home at 4. *Potage au ris pour din., 8 sous. Sor. 6.* Bo't *bru.* and *cas., 20 sous. Rencon. 2, 1 bonne; encore,* 3d; *13 fra.! Voila de l'econ.*[3] Home at 9. Bo't b'd, 8 sous[4]. At 12 Major Thomas came in to take leave. He goes to Portugal.

25. *Couche* 1. Rose 9. Perhaps this great torpor may arise from having left off my evening tea, which was a very great luxury, but certain objections which you can divine. Waited till ½ p. 11 in hopes of seeing Vanderlyn, but he came not. Is it possible that he, too, can have turned rascal? *Sor.* 12 to Comte de Volney. *Y: Le Chev.*[5] de ———. Sat ½ hour. Gave him several commissions, which he undertook cheerfully. The sessions of the *senat*[6] are always

---

1 For *Voilà huit jours que je suis* in Paris, etc. Here I have been eight days in Paris.
2 For *bals masqués et non masqués.* Masquerade balls and balls without masquerade.
3 For *Potage au ris pour diner, 8 sous. Sors à six heures.* Bought Brod and Kase, 20 sous. *Deux rencontres, dont l'une fut bonne; encore une rencontre, la troisième; 13 francs. Voilà de l'économie !* Rice soup for dinner, 8 sous. Go out at 6. Bought bread and cheese. Two rencounters, one good ; another, the third, 13 francs! That's economy for you !
4 Bought bread, 8 sous.
5 For *le Chevalier de* ———.
6 The senate.

secret; no one admitted. The treaty with Sweden proclaimed in all form yesterday. Forgot to tell you that I met one of the processions yesterday on the Pont Neuf[1]. The carnival must have commenced, for I meet in the streets persons in the most *fantastique*[2] attire. Some covered from head to foot with slips of various colored paper, imitating plumes; others *a l'harlequin*[3], &c. The weather has become mild. Two days of strong south wind, with mist. Dinner ½ p. *mjol.* and *bru.*[4] but first *au bain*[5], 30 sous. On return from *bain* found card of V. D. L.[6] Went at 6 to find him, a full league. The address must be wrong, for at 71 Vaugirard he was not known. Called on Captain Haley on return. He tells me that S. Broome is here, and desirous of seeing me! Home at 8. Did not go out again. Resol.[7] to make further attempt to get hearing.

26. *Couche* 1. Rose 7. At 9 to Captain Haley's to get him to show me Vanderlyn's quarters. He had given me the wrong number, 71 instead of 72. They were ½ mile distant. Found Vanderlyn. He is the same as *ci-dev.*[8] Took breakfast with him. An hour looking at his pictures. Marius on the Ruins of Carthage obtained the gold medal in 1808. I see nothing in that line to exceed it. Other admirable things, both original and copied. Then walked

---

1 One of the great bridges over the Seine; literally, new bridge.
2 Fantastic.
3 For *à l'harlequin.* In the manner of a harlequin.
4 Probably for ½ pint *mjolk* and *brod.* Milk and bread.
5 To the bath.
6 For Vanderlyn. It is in this way that Burr usually abbreviates the name.
7 For resolve.
8 For *ci-devant.* Heretofore.

to his shoemaker's. Thence to St. Mar. Gate[1], where Madame Senat lately lodged, that is to say, six years ago. No person at the house had any recollection of her, so that matter must be given up. Thence to the Louvre[2]. The statues and pictures; the Venus de Medici, Apollo de Belvidere, Laocoon[3], &c. The gallery containing the paintings is 1,400 French feet long, about 1,550 English, besides a very large hall. Home at 4. *Pot. au ris.*[4] At 6 to the little Vaudville[5] Theatre, where were performed "*Le Mar. de ————*"[6], "*Le ————*", *et le fandango*[7], each about an hour long. Home ½ p. 10. The theatre is small and very plain. No scenery but a change of rooms. *Paterre*[8], orchestra, and five rows of boxes. For the first and second row of boxes and orchestra you pay *un ecu de* 6 francs[9]. All the parts extremely well acted.

27. Vanderlyn came in about 9 and took breakfast with me, and went with me to Fonzi, the *dentiste*[10].

28. Fruitless tour to find Fonzi. Visit from Comte de Volney. Visit to Adet. To Fonzi. A

---

1 Saint Martin's Gate, one of the well-known gates of old Paris. It was a triumphal arch erected in 1674 in honour of Louis XIV.

2 The Louvre is one of the most extensive and historically interesting buildings in the world. It was a castle for the kings of France from or before the thirteenth century, and the chief royal palace until Louis XIV. built Versailles. It has been changed and enlarged in the course of the centuries. A great deal of the interior has been occupied since 1793 by the famous museum.

3 The Venus of Medici, now in the Uffizi Gallery in Florence, and the Apollo Belvidere and the Laocoon, now in the Vatican at Rome, were among the many celebrated works of art which fell into Napoleon's hands about 1796 and were transferred to the Louvre, where they remained till 1815.

4 For *Potage au riz*. Rice soup or porridge.

5 Meaning probably *le Théâtre du Vaudeville*, the Vaudeville Theatre near the Louvre.

6 Probably for " *Le Marquis de* ————," or " *Le Mariage de*————.

7 The fandango is a Spanish dance in triple time, usually accompanied by castanets.

8 For *parterre*. Pit.

9 Literally a crown of 6 francs.

10 Dentist.

note from *min. rel. ext.*[1] appointing M. Roux_z to treat with me. To Piquet's, where bought map of the United States and of Mexico for 9 francs.

Paris, March 1, 1810. To the *chaponier's*[3], the greatest rascal in Paris. Paid 15 francs for using a hat and sword one hour, and 27 livres for a round hat *hors du mode*[4]. But, thank God, I am quit of him. To Comte de Volney at 11; out. To Hauterive's; out. To Vanderlyn, with whom left the picture to be put into the hands of an engraver. Home at 1, and at 2 to Roux, with whom an hour. A sensible, amiable young man. Home at ½ p. 3. At 4 came Vanderlyn; at 7 Mr. B. At 8 to Scherer's. Was the first arrived. They were coming till past 10. Danced till 2. *Le gr. Suisse*[5] *Le beau fils*[6] de Coninck. Mr. La Cas[7] *et sa jo. fem. espag.*[8] General Waltershoff. Bar. ———; *min. de Socd.*[9] General Valleme. Madame ———, *che. am. de* Mirabeau[10].

---

1 For *Ministre des Relations Extérieures.* Minister of Exterior (*i. e.*, Foreign) Relations.
2 Louis Roux (1759–1817). At the beginning of the Revolution a priest. He was a deputy to the Convention and voted for the death of Louis XVI. He was one of the committee which prepared the constitution of 1793. Afterward was a member of the Committee of Public Safety, then a member of the council of 500. After 1797 he became archivist to the ministry of police under Fouché. He went over to the ministry of commerce during the consulate and empire and sat in the chamber of representatives during the Hundred Days. In 1816 he was compelled to leave France as a regicide.
3 For *chapelier.* Hatter.
4 For *hors de mode.* Out of style.
5 For *Le grand suisse.* The tall Swiss guard. This word has a history. Mercenaries from Switzerland were used as a species of bodyguard by foreign sovereigns of France and Naples and also by other monarchs. The proper noun became a common noun, synonymous with bodyguard. The guards at the Vatican are still so called.
6 For *beau-fils.* Son-in-law.
7 Meaning Las Cases, mentioned further on.
8 Mr. L. and his pretty Spanish wife (*sa jolie femme espagnole*).
9 For *Ministre de la Suède.* Swedish Minister
10 For *chère amie de* Mirabeau. Dear friend of Mirabeau. There were several Mirabeaus, but the reference is probably to the celebrated Gabriel Honoré Riquetti, Comte de Mirabeau, (1749–1791), the greatest orator of the French Revolution. The lady hinted at by Burr but not named may have been Madame de Nehra, whom Mirabeau met during his flight into Holland and whom he later sent to Paris to make his peace with the authorities. For years she exercised a wholesome influence on the headstrong, passionate Mirabeau.

La Russe.[1] *La Portug*[2]. Tea, cakes, ices, lemonade, *sangaree*, finally soups; all served round. Home at 3. Carriage hire, going and coming, 4 francs 10 sous.

2. *Couche* 3. Rose 7. At 9 to Hauterive's. The porter said his master was abroad, which was a lie, and that Madame was too indisposed to see any one, which was another. That he was charged by Monsieur to say to me, in case I should call, that, if I had anything to communicate or require, it ought to be by letter, as his engagements, &c., did not allow him the time to see me! There's for you! To Mr. Roux's house at 10, to make supplementary communication; passed ½ hour. Home at 11. Coach-hire, 4 francs. At 1 to Baron d'Alberg, Minister of Bade[3]; out; left letter and card. To Scherer's to get sundry addresses, and to get him to find Louisa Marlow. To hunt General Waltershoff, but could not find the house. To Comte de Volney's; out. Home at 3. Coach hire, 3 franc 10 sous. *" Un bon. consommation"*[4] which was scarcely *mangable*[5] for *din.*, 8 sous. At 4 to de Zauche's, the geographer. Bought two maps for 4 francs. To Vanderlyn's; out. A little stupid or so. At 9 came in Mr. Bro. Ate bread and smoked and sat till ½ p. 11.

3. *Couche* 1. Rose 7. Again to Scherer's to get the address of Waltershoff, but did not get it.

---

1 The Russian lady.
2 For *La Portugaise.* The Portuguese lady.
3 French name of Baden, Germany.
4 For *une bonne consommation.* Literally, a good consumption. As here used the word *consommation* is somewhat vulgar. The phrase represents the English phrase, " good feed."
5 For *mangeable.* Eatable. *Din.* for *diner.*

To Volney's; out. To Mons. la Case[1], whom saw; very civil; has been in the United States. Is int.[2] with Carmg.[3] *un hom. qu. veu. fai. chem.*[4]

P. M. Note from Baron d'Alberg to dine with him on Monday, *Au* Theatre François[5], where saw the new tragedy of " *Brunehart,*" and after, the " *Barbier de Seville ou Figaro*[6]," *par* Beaumarchais. I thought M'lle ———— better in tragedy than Madame ————[7], who is the Siddons of Paris. Sat next an English lady. The Emperor came in during the fourth act, and was *vis-a-vis de moi.*[8] Had a good view of him. There was clapping in the pit when he entered and when he went out. He made a slight bow on going out.

Paris, March 10, 1810. Just one week since I have written you a line, for which I have no apology to offer. The Emperor attends service (mass) every Sunday at his chapel. He also attends frequently reviews in the Tuileries[9]. To assist[10] at either requires

1 Comte Emmanuel Augustin Dieudonné de Las Cases (1766-1842) was a French historian of considerable repute. In 1808 Napoleon made him a baron and gave him a position in the council of state. He is best known to the world as the companion of the fallen Emperor at St. Helena, to whom Napoleon dictated a part of his memoirs, which he afterwards published. As a young man Las Cases had been several times in the United States.
2 Probably for intimate.
3 The name *carmagnole* was originally applied to a wild dance and song popularized by the French revolutionists of 1789. It also came to be applied to the extreme revolutionists. Burr may mean that the man named was intimate with the most rabid revolutionists.
4 For *un homme qui veut faire son chemin.* A man who means to make his way; an ambitious man. Perhaps there is in these words a squint at Burr's own plots, for he was constantly on the outlook for persons whom he might use in realizing his dream of Mexico.
5 For Théâtre Français.
6 Beaumarchais wrote two very famous comedies, the most famous of their class since those of Molière. Their titles were, " *Le Barbier de Seville* " (1775) and " *Le Mariage de Figaro* " (1781). Figaro is the principal character in both plays.
7 Burr does not give the name. Perhaps Duchesnois.
8 For *vis-à-vis de moi.* Opposite me.
9 The Tuileries, properly speaking, no longer exists, having been demolished by the Communists in 1871. It was an old palace, built originally in the sixteenth century. Before the Revolution it had been used at times as a temporary residence of the kings, but after that epoch it became the permanent abode of the French rulers.
10 This verb is at best a Gallicism. An authority says : " Assist for ' be present ' still has foreign air about it." Lord Macaulay and Dr. Newman used the word.

a ticket, and I have not yet had influence enough to procure one for either. Sunday, Monday and Tuesday I was very busy preparing a letter intended to be presented to the Emperor. When it was nearly done, something occurred, which altered my mind. On Monday dined with the Baron d'Alberg. There was a Count Louis (*senateur*[1], I think), General Vallance, two ladies, and five other gentlemen. Gamp was of so small account that neither chair nor plate was provided for him, and he stood a minute after all were seated. Mons. *le* Baron d'Alberg is a man of about 32, Madame about the same. He has been created a Duke by the Emperor. While I was preparing my letter I had occasion for some maps, which, on my first visit to Valkenaer, he had offered to lend me, but which I then declined. On Wednesday went to him to ask the loan. He denied having made such offer, and treated me rudely. Monday had a note from Madame L., requesting an interview. After leaving d'Alberg's, called on Madame. A sensible, well-bred woman. Has a daughter about 16. The husband of Madame has been in America six years, having, as I take it, abandoned wife and daughter. Adet has not returned my visit. On Monday evening with Vanderlyn at the opera. The scenery, and ballets, and decorations are charming, and that is all. On Tuesday *a minuit au grand bal masque*[2] at the Theatre Imperial. There were very few characteristic dresses, and about one thousand people. It appeared to me

[1] Senator.
[2] At midnight to the grand masquerade.

that at least 900 *ennuied*[1] themselves. I was without mask. Took seat in the boxes, promenaded a little the room, and came off at 2 o'clock. A gentleman remarked that the English had no word to express *ennui*[1], which he thought the more remarkable as they were so subject to that evil. No, replied *le* Comte de L. In England it is conceived to be the natural state, and synonymous with existence, and, therefore, no word requisite. This P. M. wrote note to Adet, to remind him of the ticket for the chapel. He answered that he had applied, and it had been refused. Thursday called at Fonzi's to take Vanderlyn to the Theatre Comique. There were Madame F. and Mr. de Castro, and we staid and passed the evening there. De Castro is very charming. The other sensible and amiable. I have been running all this week to booksellers to hunt something, particularly dictionaries, for you. There is no good dictionary of the French language. The National Institute[2] are now occupied in that affair, and their work may be expected to appear about the year 1835 ; so a distinguished member of that body informed me. Yesterday called on M. Roux to know if any answer. None ; but the Minister hoped I would not be impatient to leave Paris. To-day called again on Mr. R., and, after conversation, agreed to take dinner with him *en famille*.

---

1 This word is certainly English in our day, although it still has a foreign sound. Caleb Colton says "Ennui, perhaps, has made more gamblers than avarice, more drunkards than thirst, and perhaps as many suicides as despair."

2 The French Academy (*L'Académie Française*) was founded by Cardinal Richelieu in 1635 for the purpose of controlling the French language and regulating literary taste. Among the objects provided for in its constitution was the preparation of a dictionary of the French language. The first edition of the celebrated "Dictionnaire de L'Académie" appeared in 1694 while the seventh came out in 1878. The "French Academy" is but one of five academies comprised in the National Institute of France.

There were, besides him, Madame, and *fils*, two gentlemen and a lady. Was amused and something more.
Home at 9. My friend, Captain Haley, has left town
for a fortnight. *Le* Comte de L——— also for eight
days. Cannot hear of Delage, Senat, or Marlow. At
this late hour, am going to make a slop tea.

11. The tea kept me awake till 4, and then I
locked my door to prevent the coming in of the servant as usual at 7. Slept till 10, which have had
reason to regret. First, D. Swede, whom I wished
much to see, called at 9, and I was reported out.
Second, at 8 came a note from Mons. R., informing
me that Mr. M. would conduct me to the Tuileries,
and procure me admission to see the reviews at ½ p.
9 ; that, too, was lost. I did, however, call on Mr.
M. about ½ p. 11, and he was still waiting for me ;
but the Tuileries gates were shut, and there was no
entrance. We were turned off very rudely. Thence
to Schoel's. Saw Mr. and Mrs. ———. Met several
regiments passing the bridge, coming from the parade.
At 3 to Madame Loigerot's. She tells me of several
ladies of my acquaintance ; among others, Mrs. Robertson (*c. d.* Reid) whom you knew at New York ;
now a widow, he having died six months ago. Am to
meet Madame R. at Madame L.'s on Tuesday evening. Home at 4, and have not been out since.
Vanderlyn came in at 8, took tea, and staid till 10.
Have a vile sore throat since four days. It grows
worse and yields to nothing. *Din. fillibonka*[1].

---

[1] Even in Paris Burr likes to return now and then to his favorite Swedish dish.

12. The tea kept me awake till 4. Rose at 9, quite choaked[1] with sore throat. Walked out an hour before breakfast, though a chilly morning, to hunt your dictionaries, but have not purchased. There is not yet any very good dictionary. A new edition of the Academy, by Moulardier and Le Clerc, not being issued under the proper authority, has, I am told, been condemned. It is, however, in one shop offered for sale at the enormous price of 80 francs, in two volumes quarto. The "*Dic. Critique*"[2] of Feraud, not pretending to be a complete dictionary of the language, in three volumes, may, at the same time, be had for 36 francs. That of Gattel, in two volumes octavo, for 14 francs. The last two I shall buy for you, and the new edition of the "*Dic. des Synonyms*"[3]. But how they are to be got out to you is a circumstance not yet foreseen, all commerce on both sides being prohibited. Home, and took some tea and bread, which swallowed with difficulty. At 1 to Swediaur's, and gave him a louis[4] professionally, the first cent spent in this way in ten years. He tells me nothing new, but with the ordinary remedies thinks I will be able to speak and swallow in three or four days. The latter is of little consequence to me, you know; but the former may be of very great, having yet a hope of being called on for explanations, &c. The Doctor gave me the address of another bookseller, Madame Paschaud, *genevoise*[5]. I was very agreeably surprised

---

1 So in the MS.
2 For "*La Dictionnaire Critique*." "The Critical Dictionary."
3 For "*La Dictionnaire des Synonymes*." "The Dictionary of Synonyms."
4 The fee seems extremely high.
5 For *Génevoise*. A Genevese lady.

to find a beautiful, sensible, well-bred woman. Sat ½ hour, and engaged to call again as visitor, though I am yet *incog.* Called on my shoemaker, who is as faithless as any American mechanick[1]. Home at 3.

28. Looking over my scraps, I cannot find that I have written you a line since the 12th inst., nor have I any sort of apology to offer for the negligence. Not want of leisure, for of that I have but too much. It was on that day that I saw Madame Paschaud, and I have been there regularly twice a day. Have passed every evening with her save one. Have walked with her; been to the opera; dined there two or three times *en fam.*[2] She introduced me to her sister, who is married and settled here; also to the very venerable and interesting Mons. Suard[3], eminent for his literary talents and acquirements. My principal rival is Mons. Cha———, who comes very often with a very elegant equipage. Madame is about the size and form of Dolly[4], though some ten years younger, still larger. Very black hair and eyes. A fine, clear, fair brunette, with the complexion of full health. Her husband is at Geneve[5]. I rather think that she must be the cause that I have not written you. This evening she goes to a ball, so that I am at home at 10 (having just now left her), which is at least one hour earlier than usual. Have dined once with Swediaur. A pleasant, social party of eight; among them Oelsner,

---

1 So in the MS.
2 For *en famille.*
3 Jean Baptiste Antoine Suard (1733–1817) was a very voluminous French writer. For many years he was theatrical censor at Paris. In 1803 he became perpetual secretary of the class of language and literature of the French Academy.
4 The reference may be to Mrs. James Madison, known to her intimate friends as Dolly.
5 For Genève. Geneva.

to whom he had introduced me some days before. Oelsner introduced me to a very singular and amiable man, *d'un certain age*[1], *le* Comte de Slubrendorf. There met the celebrated Abbé Gerard[2] and a Polish nobleman. Yesterday called on Mrs. Robertson, *the widow* of Dr. Robertson, who has here a very elegant establishment. She is amazingly well preserved. She told me that young T. Butler and one of his sisters are here for his health. Called on him, but they were out. Was at a ball at Scherer's on Thursday. There were several fine women. A young Swiss of the name of de Rham introduced himself to me. He has been five years in the United States. Left New York in December last. Intimate with the Laights, &c. A young Frenchman, *nommè*[3] Paul, also just from Philadelphia. He met me in the street, and claimed my acquaintance. Madame ———, author of the " *Orphelins* "[4], sent me a copy of her book, with a pretty note, which cost me a louis. Very silly. On Friday last wrote to his Majesty the King of Westphalia[5], asking an audience, but he had gone to Compiègne[6]. Have had several interviews with M. Roux, and once dined with him. Have no reason to believe that my business advances, or that I shall do

1 An elderly gentleman (*âge*).
2 This was probably Philippe Louis Gérard (1737-1813) who was a well-known French ecclesiastic of the period. His work on " The Errors of the Reason " was for many years widely read in France. There was another well-known churchman of the time named François Girard (1735-1811) who assisted Marie Antoinette during her last moments, and subsequently became canon of Notre Dame in Paris.
3 For *nommé*. Named.
4 " The Orphans."
5 Jerome Bonaparte was King of Westphalia from 1807 to 1813.
6 Compiègne is a town on the river Oise, northeast of Paris. It is notable as having been in former times a favorite royal residence. There was an ancient palace from the Merovingian times which was rebuilt in the time of Louis XV. and beautifully fitted up by Napoleon I. It was at Compiègne that Joan of Arc was taken prisoner in 1430.

anything here. On Monday called on Mr. Ferris, an Irishman, related to Blennerhasset[1]. Visit returned yesterday. Called on Schweitzer, who has returned the visit. He is little changed. Yesterday wrote the Prince de Benevent, asking an interview, but have received no answer. Have seen Volney several times. Have bought you dictionaries, &c., to the amount of 9 louis. Dined once at a *restaurateur's*[2] with Vanderlyn, 3 francs 6 sous. He calls on me almost daily. What's next to be done, Madame?

Paris, April 6 or 7, 1810. Eight days more without a line! Paschaud takes up all my time. On Wednesday wrote a letter to the King of Westphalia, desiring an audience. Left the letter in person. Within two hours after, a note from his chamberlain, giving me rendezvous at 5 P. M. same day. Went. Passed ½ hour in private with him. Was received graciously. *Y* the Count de Furstenstein (*camus*)[3] claimed my acquaintance. By order of his Majesty, the Comte is to aid me to translate; for this purpose rendezvous *chez lui* at 9 next morning. Thence to Paschaud's to dine. They had waited an hour for me. In the morning of the same day called on the

---

1 Harman Blennerhasset, who has gone into history as " a victim of Aaron Burr." He was born in Hampshire, England, October 8, 1764 or 1765. He was liberally educated and removed to the United States, taking up his abode on an island in the Ohio river below Parkersburg, where he erected a magnificent house and devoted himself to scientific recreation and luxury. Burr met him there and the two embarked in the Mexican scheme, both supplying money. Upon the failure of the joint projects, Blennerhasset became involved in litigation and confiscations; he tried in vain to recover his fortune and died in Guernsey, February 1, 1831. His wife wrote some books and died in this country while trying to recover losses from the government. Blennerhasset went into a dangerous and difficult enterprise with his eyes open; he lost, and spent the remainder of his life in whimpering. Burr lost far more, and bore his losses like a man, never complaining and never condescending to explanations or excuses.
2 At a restaurant keeper's.
3 The word means flat-nosed, but it may be intended here as a nickname.

Duke d'Alberg, who always receives me kindly. Told him that I wanted access, &c. He gave me note of introduction to *le* Comte de S., which I transmitted forthwith, requesting an interview. Have no reply from this Comte. *Q. mir.*[1] At an early hour, same morning, called on Comte de V. by appointment. Seems frightened. Passed the evening of Wednesday with Paschaud till 9, and then home to write. Wrote a short let. *a S. M., l'E., et R.*[2] At 9 next morning to Furstenstein's, to whom explained my business, and left him my letter to translate. At 5 P. M. called and got the translation. Thence to Paschaud, where copied and sealed it, and sent it under cover to the Comte, to be delivered as he or the King of Westphalia should see fit. Staid with Pash. till 11. Rose this morning at 6. My barber comes at that hour, and I have taken a barber for no other purpose but to be waked regularly. Eight sous per day. To Fonzi's at 10, where was detained three hours. At 2 to *La Monnoie*[3], but was too late. *Au bibliothec.*[4] *et au Mon. des Medailles*[5] to see for medals for Gampy, but had no success. Did I ever tell you that Lepine charged me 3 louis for repairing your watch? Worse still, he says, and refers to his register, that he received for the watch 26 louis only! To Paschaud's at 4.

1 For Latin *quod mirum !* How strange !
2 For *à Sa Majesté l'Empereur et Roi.* To His Majesty the Emperor and King. Does Burr mean both these titles for Napoleon ? Or does the title of king refer to King Jerome ?
3 For *La Monnaie* or *L'Hôtel de la Monnaie* or *L'Hôtel des Monnaies.* The Mint. This was an old institution. The present great building was constructed from 1771 to 1775.
4 For *à la bibliothèque.* To the library. It was probably *La Bibliothèque Ste-Geneviève,* one of the very old libraries of Paris.
5 For *à la Monnaie des Médailles.* At the medal mint. Long after the founding of the mint mentioned in Note 2, Louis XV. caused to be constructed a separate mint for medals, medallions, etc. This was discontinued as a separate establishment in 1832.

To Roux at 5. He has nothing to communicate! This morning I've called on *le* Comte de Slubrendorf, who always amuses and interests me. About a fortnight ago that called on Madame Robertson. Refused to go to Paschaud's this evening. The only one (save one) since the 12th of March. Called on Madame Loigerot. Home at 9. Raw, chilly weather, and I keep no fire.

19. Rose 7. Raining and chilly weather. This climate is worse than ours. At 11 to S. P. B. to talk of various projects. At 1 to Madame Paschaud's. ϒ Pelough *et ux.* Home at 3. Dressed, and at 5 walked to Mr. Stone's to dine. ϒ: Miss Williams¹ *tres celeb.²*; le Harpe³ *èt ux.;* Madame Gretanius, of South Carolina; Madame a Swede and now *veuve* and her beautiful daughter *dit*⁴ 13 but might pass for 15; Mr. Smith, *emig. d'ecosse c. d. assoc. de Muir⁵;* le Cheval. Boufflers⁶ *et ux.;* two others. Easy and elegant hospitality. Staid till ½ p. 10. This day paid my monthly bills to landlord and porter;

1 Helen Maria Williams.
2 For *très célèbre.* Very celebrated. In Davis's alleged reprint of the Journal the abbreviation *celeb.* is printed Coeleb!
3 Frédéric César de La Harpe (1754–1838) was born in Switzerland. As a young man he met at Rome Catherine II. of Russia, who invited him to St. Petersburg to take charge of the education of the two young Grand Dukes, Alexander and Constantin. He accepted the post and was given the rank of colonel in the Russian army. When the French Revolution broke out, La Harpe wrote revolutionary letters to Switzerland, which made him an exile. He took refuge in France. Soon the Swiss Revolution broke out and La Harpe went thither with the French troops. He became a member of the directory of the new republic. He attempted a *coup d'état* after the French fashion, but failed. In 1820 he went to France again, but was coldly received by Napoleon. He lived in retreat in the vicinity of Paris until about 1815. In that year he again saw his former pupil, then Alexander, Emperor of Russia, by whom he was made a general in the Russian army. La Harpe was present at the congress of Vienna, and it is said that it was due to his influence over Alexander that Switzerland, La Harpe's native land, fared better than other countries at the hands of the congress. He passed his last days at Lausanne, Switzerland.
4 Said to be.
5 For *émigré d'Ecosse, ci-devant associé de* Muir. Scotch emigrant, formerly Muir's associate.
6 Catherine Stanislas, Marquis de Boufflers (1738–1815)called Abbé and afterwards Chevalier de Boufflers. He was a French *littérateur*, soldier, and courtier, and for three years was Governor of Senegal. His best-known literary work was "Voyage en Suisse," ("Journey in Switzerland "). He was a disciple and friend of Voltaire.

together 80 francs. *Non. Voici*[1] : Doprez, 58.11 ; porter, 16.1 and *etrennes*[2], 12 ; equal 86 francs 13 sous. Story of Le Roy *Mar'd de Modes et l'Emp.*[3] Yesterday, 18th, rose 9. To Fonzi's at 10 and till 11. To the *imprim. de fayance de Stone et Co.*[4] with ————, the young German introduced to me by Madame —— *c. d.*[5] Langworthy. Mr. Stone asked me to dine tomorrow, 19th. At ½ p. 2 to Paschaud. Thence to *le Musè des Antiq.*[6] The tombs and monuments for 1,400 years ; Gabrielle[7] of Henry IV. ; Marie de Medici. To Paschaud's till 4. Thence to Vanderlyn's, but he had company and did not stay to dine. On way home bought *bru.*[8] and called at Rochetti's. Home ½ p. 5. Tea for *din.* At 8 to Paschaud's and till ½ p. 10. *Mus.* 10 francs. *Mauv.*[9] Much * * * *[10]

17. Rose 7. To Paschaud's at 11 ; asked to dine, but was engaged with young German, Gerhard Oncken. At 5 went with him to the *hotel de*————[11] *Bu. tro.*[12] Home at 8 in bad order. *Couche* 11 and laid till 9.

---

1 No, this is the way it is : Doprez (probably the host's name), 58 francs 11 sous, etc.
2 For *des étrennes.* Literally, New Year's gifts ; here probably meant for ordinary presents or tips.
3 Le Roy, may be the merchant's name, or else it may stand for *le Roi*, the King. Then *Le Roy marchand de Modes et l'Empereur.* Le Roy (or the King), fashion merchant and the Emperor.
4 For *l'Imprimerie de Faience de Stone et Compagnie.* The faience printing establishment of Stone & Co.
5 For *ci-devant.* Here the equivalent of *née.*
6 For *Le Musée des Antiquités.* The Museum of Antiquities.
7 Gabrielle d'Estrées (1571–1599) was a mistress of Henry IV. of France and was famous for her beauty and notorious for her scandalous life and luxury. She acquired the titles Marquise de Monceaux and Duchesse de Beaufort
8 Is it not strange that Burr so persists in using this misspelled Swedish word for bread ?
9 For *muse 10 francs. Mauvaise. Muse,* 10 francs   Bad.
10 An undecipherable word. It looks like *potts'c* or *patis'c.*
11 Possibly tor *L'Hôtel des Monnaies.* The mint, which he attempted to enter a few days before, but was too late.
12 For *J'avais trop bu.* Had drunk too much.

20. *Couche* 12. *Lev.* 7. Read an hour in Weiss. *Sor.* 11 to the umbrella-mender; nothing done To *bottier* to leave pair of boots to *racom.*[1] To Paschaud's. *Y* till ½ p. 2. To Loigerot's, where found invitation from ———— to concert to-morrow evening. Think I shall not go. To Fonzi's; to Madame P.'s at 4 and went with her to her sister's to dine *en fam.*[2] After dinner walked with her along Boulevard to Port St. Denis[3], and returned *chez elle*[4] at 10. Home very *las*[5]. Made tea to *refraich*[6], and now, at ½ p. 11, *bon soir.*

21. Rose 6. At 9 to Fonzi's and till 11. Thence to Loigerot's. M. had told that Gamp had related various things of her *mar.*,[7] though Gamp never saw, never heard, nor spoke of him. *Y* received invitation of Mr. ———— to concert this evening, which declined. To Duc d'Alberg's. Always receives me with civility, and gives me the best advice in his power. To Madame Gretanius's. Saw her and her beautiful daughter. To M'lle H. M. Williams; out. To the *magaz.*[8] of Mr. Stone to see him; out; not there. Very *las.*[5] Home to rest an hour. At ½ p. 3 to Madame P.'s, where was engaged to dine at 5. Mr. La Salle; Mr. and Mrs. Pelough. Staid till 8. Came home expecting Bro., but he came not.

---

1 For To the *bottier* to leave a pair of boots to *raccommoder.* To the bootmaker's to leave a pair of boots to mend.
2 For *en famille.*
3 The St. Denis gate was, like that of St. Martin, erected in the seventeenth century in honour of the triumphs of Louis XIV.
4 To her house.
5 Tired.
6 For *pour me rafraichir.* To refresh myself.
7 For *mari* Husband.
8 For *magasin.* Shop.

Took tea, contrary to custom and to reason. Had this day card from Captain Lawson, note from Vanderlyn, and a very civil invitation from H. M. Williams to dine on Tuesday, to which agreed.

22. Rose 7, having been kept awake almost all night by the tea. At 8 to Vanderlyn's to breakfast. Off at 10. Your picture goes on slowly. At 12 to see Lawson. ♈ ½ hour. To Fonzi's to get my hat, but had not left it there. To Duc d'Alberg's to see for my hat; not there; so must be finally lost, *i. e.*, exchanged for a very bad one. To *le* Comte de Furstenstein's. He nor his Ki.[1] not returned to town, nor expected these ten days. To Dr. Swediaur's ; out. To Madame P.'s ; out. Home at 3. At 4 came in Vanderlyn. *Din. bro. mjolk. Sor. 5* to change money. Get 20 francs 14 sous for *Fred. d'or*[2] and 26.10 for English guinea. To the Theatre Francois to hear Talma[3]. Obliged to wait forty minutes in the crowd, nearly squeezed to death. Heard the tragedy of " Manlius." Did not wait to see the after-piece. For the characters, see the gazette *ci joint*[4]. M'lle —————— is very unjustly condemned. She had more of truth, of nature and feeling, but less of vehement action, which is the taste of the day.

23. Rose 7. At 9 came in Lawson and sat an hour. He will take charge of all I can send you. Eight louis in dictionaries ! I think you will be

---

1 Probably for King.
2 For *Friedrich d'or*. A former gold coin of Prussia, worth about $4.
3 François Joseph Talma (1763–1826) was the greatest tragedian of his time. He was a favorite with Napoleon and accompanied him to Erfurt in 1808 and to Dresden in 1813.
4 For *ci-joint*. Literally, here joined, hence, herewith.

rasassied[1], yet I am greatly tempted to add Moreri and Bayle, twelve volumes folio, for 4 louis! At 11 to the *Prefecture de Police*[2], to demand passport for Compiègne. What business have I at Compiègne? Why, hussy, there is the Emperor, and the King of Westphalia, &c. But they had nothing to do with it, and said I must send a petition to the Duc. of ———[3] To Paschaud's ½ hour. To Loigerot's, and walked an hour with Madame and M'lle in the Thuleries[4], where left them. To a bookseller's, Rue des Noegres[5], and bought the *"Codes Napoleon"*[6], five volumes, and a book for Gampy, in all 13 francs. Home. *Bro.* and *mjolk* for *din.* To Paschaud's at 7. Mr. Chabaud came in. Told my troubles about the Compiègne expedition, and he very kindly gave his advice and offered his aid, he being personally acquainted with the Duc of ———. Home at 10. Br. came in and sat an hour. Sleepy. *Bon soir.* Had to-day invitation from Madame Robinson[7] to dine on Thursday, which accepted.

24. Slept till ½ p. 7. At 10 to Paschaud's, with whose aid wrote my petition (a letter) in French to Duc d'Otrante, and an English letter to Chabaud,

---

1　Another hybrid perfect participle made from the French verb *rassasier*, to satiate. Hence, I think you will be satiated.
2　To the office of the police prefect.
3　Otrante?
4　So in the MS. For Tuileries.
5　This word is doubtful, being very obscure in the MS. Could it stand for *Rue des Nègres*, Street of the Negroes?
6　Napoleon pushed forward the work begun by the National Assembly of collecting and fusing the laws and usages of the nation into an organic code, employing a body of eminent jurists. The "*Code Civil*" was published in 1801, but the "*Code de Commerce*," the "*Code Penal*" and the "*Code d'Instruction Criminelle*" occupied the commissioners till near the close of Napoleon's career. What is known as the "*Code Napoléon*," which was made up of these four parts, at once took rank as one of the foremost legal productions of history. Napoleon declared that it would outlive his victories.
7　For Robertson.

q. v. Took them myself to Chabaud's, who, being out, left them. Lounged two hours at P.'s, and then we walked by thuleries[1] and boulevards to Madame Pelough's. Invitation to the marriage of Madame Pelough's daughter, on Thursday, to dine, &c. *Malheureusement*[2], am engaged to Madame Robertson, but will go and see the ceremonies. To Fonzi's ½. Home at 4, and at 5 to M'lle H. M. W.'s to dine. *Y le* Baron de Humboldt[3]; Mons. Haase, *employee a la bib. imp. aux manuscripts*[4]; a French gentleman not named. Others came in after dinner. A very pleasant day. Mr. St. and M'lle Williams engaged me to go to their country seat at Montmorency on Sunday Home at ½ p. 10, and now at ½ p. 12 am about to *couche.*

25. Rose ½ p. 7. Breakfast and lounged an hour. To Paschaud's at 11 and till 1. Thence home and to *Bib. Imper.*[5] to see Haase, who promised to aid me about medals. What running I have had about that little rascal's[6] medals. Haase conducted me through the departments of *gravures*[7] and of manuscripts. Showed me the most ancient Greek and Latin, which are of the fourth century. The original love-letters of Henry IV. to various of his mistresses. Patents, &c., by Charlemagne, &c. No medals can

---

1 For Tuileries.
2 Unfortunately.
3 Friedrich Heinrich Alexander, Baron Von Humboldt (1769–1859), the distinguished German scientist, one of the greatest of the world's great scholars. At this time he had returned from his remarkable journey through the Spanish colonies of Central and South America, and was engaged in writing and publishing a wonderful series of books, twenty-nine in all, which made his fame secure. In 1827 he removed to Berlin.
4 Probably for *employé à la Bibliothèque Impériale aux Manuscrits.* Employed in the Imperial Library for Manuscripts.
5 See Note 4.
6 Meaning his grandson.
7 Engravings.

be had there but antiques, and those in *soufre*[1] *;* too fragile and too dull of appearance to suit Gampy. I got, however, an address to one from whom, it is said, something in *his way* may be had. But my reputation is gone. Everywhere announced as a numismatician. I shift it all on you. It is you, and not me, who are scientific in medals. Home for ½ hour, and to the bath, 36 sous. *Bro. mjolk* for *din.* To Vanderlyn's to tak. sh. to *lav.*[2]; thence to Pelough's to meet Paschaud. They were all so busy preparing and signing contracts, &c., for the marriage, which is to take place to-morrow, that I stole off, for which I shall have a quarrel with P'd[3]. Home at 8. Went out and bought 15 francs of writing paper. Hungry and took four eggs raw. Cocoa with water made supper.

26. *Lev.* 7, but very sleepy and heated, as if I had drank two bottles *vin,* though I had drank nothing but water. It must have been the four yolks of eggs. At 10 came in Mr. ——, the *commis*[4] of Madame Paschaud, to see about packing up your books. I was astonished to see the mass when put together. At least four cubic feet. But alas! the greater part worthless stuff, which has been imposed on me in different places. We resolved, at length, to transport the whole to Paschaud's, and there have the inventory and the packing. At 11 to Paschaud's; there learned that

---

1 Sulphur.
2 *Lav.* for *laver*, to wash. The sentence may then mean: To Vanderlyn's to take shirt to be washed.
3 For Madame Paschaud.
4 Clerk.

Mr. *le* Chev.[1] Chabaud had not made my application
for Compiègne, learning the arrival of His Majesty of
Westphalia. Posted off to see the Comte de Fursten
stein; out. To the King of Westphalia; out. But
there was the Count de F., who gave me rendezvous
for 9 to-morrow morning. The King leaves town
this day! Back to Paschaud's, and thence with the
Chev. and Madame P., in his *voiture aux noces*[2], *i. e.*,
to the house of Madame Pelough, *mère de M'.lle*
Thelusson, *la fiancees*[3]. To the Mayor's office, where
the civil marriage was performed. Very simple.
Thence to the pastor of the Protestant church, Mr.
———, a man of very prepossessing appearance and
manners. The *cerem'y relig.*[4] was performed in a most
impressive manner. M'lle is Protestant. Thence left
the parties and went home. Was asked to the wedding dinner, but engaged to Madame Robertson. To
Mrs. Robertson's at ½ p. 5. *Y:* M'e Tone, widow
of the Irish general, an interesting woman; Mr.
———, *senateur*[5] and *sa nièce*; *le* Baron de ———,
and Mr. Vanderlyn. The family of Evans detained
by an accident to the father; a fall and broken knee!
A very pleasant party, Madame Robertson engaged
to dine on Monday. Off at ½ p. 9 and to Pelough's,
where found the whole party, about twenty-five, still
at the dinner table. Very gay. Songs, music, and
afterward dancing. Off at ½ p. 12; and now, at 1,

---

1 For *Monsieur le Chevalier.*
2 In his carriage (*voiture*) to the wedding (*aux noces*). Possibly meant for in his wedding
carriage.
3 For *la fiancée.* The affianced lady.
4 For *la cérémonie religieuse.* The religious ceremony.
5 For *sénateur.* Senator.

you ought to be much obliged to me for writing, seeing I must be up at 6.

27. Rose at ½ p. 6, quite refreshed. At 9 to *le* Comte de Furstenstein. He was with the King, and not visible. Asked at the King's for the *chamberlain du jour.*[1]; not yet visible. Home, about 1½ miles. On the way, left note for Loigerot and called at Menutzi's; not visible, and could make no rendezvous to-day. At 10 to P.'s, and thence to Comte de F. He was still with *S. M.*[2] Went there. A crowd of grandees; was nevertheless received by *le* Comte de F., who told me that he had delivered my letter to the E. and K.[3] That all hands were going to Anvers[4], and no reply could be expected till their return, 15 May. *Voilà*[5], twenty days more of spider life. Thence to Paschaud's for ½ hour and thence to Loigerot's. A tale of distress. Home at 1. At 2 to Pelough's to see the new pair. All very well. Asked to dine, but am engaged to Swediaur. On way home *recon. Mus.*[6] 12 francs but good. Watc. *perd.*[7]; not discovered till got home. *Back again* in the utmost distress. It was restored *sans façon et sans* reward[8]. *Deschams, je te sçai grè*[9]. To Paschaud's at 4. *Y* Picard *et ux.*, the new pair. On to Swediaur; *y* Lelande. Off at ½ p. 8 and to the Theatre des

---

1 For *chambellan du jour.* Day chamberlain.
2 For *sa Majesté.* His Majesty.
3 Emperor and King. See note 2, page 432.
4 The French name of Antwerp, Belgium.
5 Behold!
6 For *rencontre. Muse.* Rencounter. *Muse.*
7 For watch *perdu.* Watch lost.
8 Without ceremony and without reward.
9 For Deschamps, *je te sais grè.* Deschamps, I am pleased with thee.

Varietès[1] to meet the family Peloughs, &c.; but the theatre being full, no place;/came home. Visit to-day from that amiable man *le* Chev. Chabaud L'atour[2] M. Arnold, *le commis*[3], carried all my (*your*) books to Paschaud's. Shall move to-morrow.

2. *Din. chez* Swediaur. Broke elec. apparat. *Chez* Paschaud at 9 *pour un moment*[4]. Home to pack up.

28. Ran about on brief errands several hours. *Din. bro. mj'l*[5]. At 7 to Pelough's. *Υ* Paschaud. Reproaches for *non din.*[6] Home. Took *voit.*[7] and transported *y* my baggage and took my quarters.

29. *Tres cont.*[8] with my new quarters. *Din. chez nous.* *Υ* uncle of Adelle[9]. The snuff-box which plays a tune of fifteen minutes; soft, sweet music. *Promène la soirèe*[10].

30. *Din. chez* M'lle Williams. Paris, May 1, 1810. *Din. ehez* M'lle Williams.

2. *Chez* M'e Robinson.

3. *Chez nous.*

Bury, Val.[11] de Montmorency[12], May 4, 1810.

---

1 For le Théâtre des Variétés. To-day this theatre is called simply Les Variétés. The Varieties, as the name implies, a vaudeville theatre.
2 For *le* Chevalier Chabaud-Latour. The reference is to Antoine Georges François, Baron de Chabaud-Latour (1769–1832), a French politician and statesman.
3 The clerk
4 For a moment.
5 For *diner, bröd et mjolk.*
6 For *non diner*, which is bad French for *de n'avoir pas diné.* Not having dined.
7 For *voiture.* Carriage.
8 For *très content.* Much pleased.
9 For Adèle.
10 For *Je me promène la soirée* (or *pendant la soirée* or *le soir*). Go walking in the evening.
11 For *vallée.* Valley.
12 Montmorency is a town in the department of Seine-et-Oise, about nine miles north of Paris. On account of its magnificent site and its forest, it has long been one of the favorite promenades of Parisians. Its celebrity has come largely from the fact that Jean Jacques Rousseau, the French philosopher and writer, lived near there for a few years. The Countess d'Epinay, a great friend of Rousseau, had there offered him a cottage in order to hinder, if possible, his return to Geneva. This place is well known under the name of the Hermitage.

Arrived at 3 *en voit av*[1] M'lle W. and Mr. and Madame La Harpe. *Din. 5 Ap. din. prom. seul. le village de ——— jusu' a le foret*[2]. *Couche* 11. 5. Rose 6. *Prom. seul. le village de ——— jusqu'*[3] *a 8 h.* At 11 *prom. av* Mr. S. *par le village de ———*[4] to the side of the mountain, where met M'lle S. and Mr. and Madame La Harpe. Ascend the mountain and walk till 3. M'lle W. much fatigued. Mr. Froissart arrives this P. M. and dines. 6. Rain in the morning. Cold northerly wind three days past. Mr. *et* Madame La Harpe *part.*[5] to Paris. This is the neighborhood in which Rousseau lived and died[6]. The trees where was given *le baiser fatal*[7]; the house of Eloise ; the walks they frequented. Every spot hereabout is consecrated by his memory.

1 For *en voiture avec.* In a carriage with.
2 For *après diné je me promenai seul au village de* ——— *jusqu' à la forêt.* After dinner I walked alone to the village of ——— as far as the forest.
3 For *Je me promenai seul au village de* ——— *jusqu' à huit heures.* Walked alone to the village of ——— until 8 o'clock.
4 For *At 11 je me promenai avec Monsieur S. par le village de.* At 11 walked with Mr. S. through the village of.
5 For Mr. and Madame La Harpe *partirent,* etc. Mr. and Mrs. La Harpe left for Paris.
6 This statement is hardly true. Rousseau lived and wrote for some time at Montmorency, a place about nine miles north from Paris, but he died at Ermenonville, a town further north of the capital.
7 Literally, the fatal kiss. The allusion is to the novel entitled " *La Nouvelle Héloise* " (" The New Heloise," for it will be remembered that the celebrated Peter Abelard, 1079-1142, had had his beloved Heloise who fell and rose again), which Rousseau wrote during his retirement at the Hermitage. This novel is written in the form of letters and describes the amours of a man of low position called Saint Preux and a girl of rank named Julie. This romance is one of the significant works in the history of French literature by reason of the immense vogue which it had and the remarkable influence which it exerted on feminine Europe in the eighteenth century. The first part of the romance may be said to center about what Burr calls *the fatal kiss.* Saint Preux and Julie meet one night under the trees, not of the valley of Montmorency as Burr intimates, but rather on the shores of Lake Geneva in Switzerland, and Julie loses her virtue. But she regains it as had Abelard's beloved Héloise ; hence the significance of Rousseau's title, " The New Héloise." Burr's reference to the trees and walks of Montmorency and " the house of Eloise " have, however, a meaning. While writing his romance Rousseau had become greatly enamored of Madame d'Epinay's sister-in-law, Madame d'Houdetot, a matron of thirty years, not at all pretty. But Rousseau, who was applying his sensitive mind to the analysis of love, fell deeply in love with the first object he encountered, namely Madame d'Houdetot. He says of her : " I saw my Julie in Madame d'Houdetot, and soon I saw no longer anything but Madame d'Houdetot, clothed with all the perfections which I had just endowed the idol of my heart." Rousseau speaks in his " Confessions " of a meeting one night with Madame d'Houdetot out under the magnificent trees of Montmorency, in which there was given what he calls " *ce baiser funeste,*" that fatal kiss.

Montmorency or rather Bury in the *vallè de* Montmorency, May 7, 1810. Rose at 6. Cold, chilly, raining. At 9 set off for town. Mons. Froissart *en voit.*[1] with M'lle W. I, from choice, having something to say to Mr. S., in chaise with him. Arrived ½ p. 10. After *embrass.* of *mon aim. amie* M'e Pelough[2], off to Paschaud's. The *diablesse*[3] has gone to the country, too! Pure vengeance. Four times have I walked there (½ league) to-day and at 9 this evening she had not arrived. In the A. M. went to make peace with Mrs. Robertson. She is too good to harbor malice and received me very kindly. Staid two hours, reading over papers of business and talking of matrimony, on which head we have grave quarrels, for I am dead against it. "What!" says she, with temper and astonishment, "would you advise me to," &c. "*Madame, soyez indep.,*"[4] &c. Took soup there, and parted friends. On my return, called on Captain Lawson. He was all in the bustle of packing up and going off in ½ hour. At 8, however, this evening, he called to say that he should not go till 6 in the morning of to-morrow, and I am now *actuellement*[5] writing to my Juno and Minerva. *Excusez, Madame*[6]. Called also on Swediaur.

Paris, June 8, 1810. Rose 6. At 10 to *Roi West'l*[7] pursuant to appointment of Comte Fursten-

---

1 For *en voiture*. In the carriage.
2 For After *l'embrassement* of *mon aimée* amie, Madame Pelough. (Should be *mon amie bien aimée*.) After the embrace of my beloved friend, Madame Pelough.
3 The she-devil.
4 For "*Madame, soyez indépendante*." "Madame, be independent."
5 At this very time.
6 Excuse [me], Madame.
7 For *Roi de Westphalie*. King of Westphalia, Jerome Bonaparte.

stein. Waited an hour; not received. To Chabaud's, whom saw ½ hour. To Madame Robertson's, one hour. To Duc d'Alberg's ; out. Home. At 4 to Madame Paschaud's ; met Josephine with a note to me. *Y* dined. To the opera at 7. *En entrant le paterre Mon'sr on vous demande!*[1] Was placed well. *" Les Pretendus"*[2] and *" Persèe et Andromede "*[3] The scenery in the latter a perfect enchantment.

9. Rose 7. To Comte de Slubrendorf's at 11. To *ma pet. monstre*[4] to buy *les pretendus*[2] for you. To the Lyon. An American had called but would not leave his name. To Madame Paschaud's ; out. To Madame Loigerot's ½ hour. To Paschaud's again ; she came in ; ½ hour. To Vanderlyn's. *Y:* Madame de Castro and Madame Velè or Vellia ; *charmante*[5]. Dined with Vanderlyn. *Sor.* at ½ p. 6 to the Hotel du Ville[6] to see the preparations[7]; 18 francs for a place in the window for to-morrow! *Caused*[8], &c. To the *Ambigu Theatre*[9]. The *" Musico-Manie*[10]*"* et *" Les Highlanders."* On entering, a gentleman bowed, called my name, and said he had seen me in Philadelphia in '96· Between the pieces went to

---

1 For *en entrant dans le parterre on me dit*, " *Monsieur, on vous demande.*" On entering the pit some one said to me, " Sir, some one is asking for you."
2 For " *Les Prétendus.*" " The Engaged Couple.
3 " Perseus (*Persée*) and Andromeda."
4 For *ma petite monstre.* My little feminine monster.
5 Charming (woman).
6 For l'Hôtel de Ville. The City Hall. This building has played a great part in the different French revolutions, being the ordinary rallying-point of the democratic party as opposed to the royal palaces, the Louvre and the Tuileries. The present edifice was rebuilt after 1871, having been burned by the Communists in that year.
7 The preparations making for the parade on the morrow.
8 Probably means chatted, etc. This hybrid verb, which we have met before, is made from the French verb *causer*, to chat.
9 Probably for L'Ambigu-Comique. Literally, the Ambiguous-Comic. This was an old theatre founded in 1767, where one may still hear dramas, melodramas, and patriotic pieces.
10 *La Musicomanie* means the passion for music.

the *Jardin Turc*[1]. *Y* Ardefredi, now Madame Robin. Home at ½ p. 10.

18. *Couche* 12. Rose 7. To Fonzi's at 9. Home at 10. Engaged to dine with F. At 11 came in Borgo with the note and the outline of *projet*[2], translated to my satisfaction. He took them home to copy and was to send them to me at 3, which he did not. At 1 to Paschaud's; *y* two hours. Took circuit home by Pont Neuf or Neuve[3]. At 4 to Borgo's away in *la* Rue de Champs Eliseès[4]; out. To Fonzi's at 5. *Y:* A young handsome Neapolitan Baron and Vanderlyn; also a Spaniard. Much amused with the Baron. To Madame P.'s; out. Again at ½ p. 10 and staid an hour *t. a tet*[5].

19. Rose 6. At 9 to Dr. Swediaur's, calling on Madame P. on the way, but not see her. Went with the Dr. in his *cabriole* to pass the day with Mr. La Harpe. *Y:* Madame Bergère or some such name and her two daughters; M'lle ———, *artiste*[6] and M'lle ———, *botaniste*[7]; Mr. ———, brother of Madame La Harpe. Walked through his park and gardens. Eat fruit. Strolled an hour alone in the village. Walked an hour with L. H. *Din.* 4. At ½ p. 7 to the village of Schioux to see the dancing, &c., with

---

1 The Turkish Garden. Probably a restaurant for theater-goers.
2 Project, plan.
3 The former is correct. It means new bridge. This is one of the great bridges over the Seine.
4 For Rue des Champs-Elysées. Literally, the street of the Elysian Fields. It is ordinarily called simply Champs-Elysées. This magnificent street, with a sort of park on both sides, is now probably the finest street of Paris, extending more than a mile from the Place de la Concorde, formerly Place de la Révolution, to Napoleon's Arch of Triumph at the Star (l'Étoile).
5 For *tête-à-tête*. Literally, head to head.
6 Artist.
7 Botanist.

which was much amused. Home at ½ p. 9, calling on Madame P. on the way, who was out, to which circumstance you may ascribe these two pages. Nothing from Borgo.

Paris, July 2 or 3, 1810. To Fonzi's at 9; *y* two hours. He gave me ticket for the *Athenee*[1], this being the anniversary. Came home to dress and found note from Madame Paschaud with another ticket and inviting me to accompany her. So ran to Fonzi and apologized. Thence away to Madame Paschaud. She thought it too late and the weather too hot. We pouted and pouted. *Riz et lait* for *din*[2].

6 or 7. A very busy day. At 10 called on Borgo ; out. An hour with Fonzi ; ½ with Madame P. To Vanderlyn's ; took him out to *courir*[3] To the Hotel des Invalids[4] to pay my respects to the Duc de Montobello who lies there in state. Lamps innumerable ; hung with black ; inscriptions, devices. But what I was most desirous of seeing was the process of getting a soul out of purgatory. There was only one priest at work. Thence to the panorama of *le bat. de Wagram*[5]. Very beautiful, but not equal to that of Gibraltar which I saw in London. Thence to the Abbàye St. Martin to see the *depot des arts et*

---

1 For *Athénée*. Athenæum. The society of Paris known under the name of Musée took that of *Lycée* in 1794, and finally that of *Athénée des Arts* (Athenæum of the Arts) in 1803.
2 Rice and milk for dinner.
3 Literally to run; here to gad abroad, to ramble.
4 For L'Hôtel des Invalides. Literally house of the invalids. This is a military hospital or soldiers' home which was founded by Louis XIV. There is a well known war museum in connection with it. Here in the Church of St. Louis, beneath the conspicuous gilded dome, lie today the ashes of Napoleon the Great, and above the door of the crypt in which the sarcophagus is placed are seen these words taken from the Emperor's will : " *Je désire que mes cendres reposent sur les bords de la Seine, au milieu de ce peuple français que j'ai tant aimé.*" " I desire that my ashes repose on the banks of the Seine, in the midst of this French people that I have loved so much."
5 For *la bataille de Wagram*. The battle of Wagram, a battle won by the French under Napoleon over the Austrians in July, 1809.

metiers[1]. Thence home for ½ hour to smoke segar and repose   Then to ———, a sort of *gourman restaurateur*[2], where dined ; 4 francs 10 sous each. There we parted for an hour, Vanderlyn to see Flor entine and I to M'lle Prevost.   Found Vanderlyn at Fonzi's and thence we went to Tivoli[3]. *Les danses ; les* puppet ; *les ombres Chinois ; les* tight rope *sauts ; les grimaces ; les feu d'artifice*[4].   Home at 11 and at 12 am about to *couche*.

8.   Rose at 6.   At 10 to the club, to read gazettes and hear the news, which, I find, is of some consequence to me, if, indeed, anything be of any consequence.   To Borgo's ; out.   To *Le Conseil* to *Guerre*[5] to see the trial of Victor Hughes[6].   *Y* two hours.   To Vanderlyn's ; out.   Home at 4.   Dressed, and out to dine with Swediaur.   The first time since the fracture of the *machine electrique*[7].   On the way

---

1 The Abbey (or, as it is better called, *le prieuré*, the priory) of St. Martin. Here was established in 1794 an independent museum called *Le Conservatoire des Arts et Métiers*, the Conservatory of the Arts and Trades. Burr speaks of the collection as a depot (should be *dépôt*), a deposit or depository.
2 *Gourman* stands for *gourmand*, but should follow the noun. The phrase means gluttonous eating-house keeper. To judge by the price paid by Burr for this dinner, 4 francs 10 sous, it would seem that the word *gourmand* should refer to him.
3 The ancient Tivoli Garden is no more, having been buried long ago beneath five-story buildings and straight streets. A neighboring street, however, consecrates its memory. There were two Tivolis. The first, known under the name of Jardin Boutain, was, under the Directory, the rendezvous of the younger reactionists called *Clichiens*. The second Tivoli, occupying the same site, became a celebrated concert-garden where all sorts of amusements could be had. It became especially well known under the Restoration.
4 The dances ; the puppets, the Chinese shadows ; the tight-rope leapings ; the grimaces ; the fire-works. (The grimaces made a great impression on Burr, for he writes the word in the Journal in capital letters.)
5 For *le conseil de guerre*. The war council.
6 For Victor Hugues, a famous French soldier (1761–1826), who fought the English with great success in the West Indies and was notorious for his cruelties, becoming known as the " Robespierre of the West Indies." His corsairs were among the chief causes of the rupture between the United States and France in 1798. Under Bonaparte, Hugues was governor of Cayenne. In January, 1809, he surrendered the colony to the English, was accused of incapacity and treason, and was tried by court martial in Paris. The verdict, not rendered till 1814, was an acquittal.
7 For *machine électrique*. The electrical machine. These two words are by no means badly written in the MS., and yet in Davis's reprint of the Journal the word " limb " is substituted for *machine électrique* ! The reference here is to the electrical apparatus which Burr had broken, as mentioned in his Journal under date of April 27th.

called at Paschaud's. *Y* M. Chabaud, who, to my great regret, will leave town on Monday. At Swediaur's met again *le* Dr. Dirette, or some name near that. He says he will make me to be heard. Home at ½ p. 8. Madame P. promised to meet me here. She had been here but gone.

10¹. Rose 6. At 9 to Fonzi's. He gave me tickets for the *Athénée*², whose grand exhibition was this day. Home at ½ p. 11; found note from Madame P. offering ticket and asking me to accompany. Most certainly. Dressed as fast as I could and off to Fonzi's to apologize; thence to Paschaud's. It was ½ p. 12. Found her and Lou. dressed and looking rather sad. She thought it too late and too hot to go and coldly counselled me to go, which I declined. Parted rather *boudisly*³. Home and so lost the *Athénée* and disappointed *Madame et sa U* ⁴

*Hiatus valde deflendus*⁵ *!*

19. Called at Duke d'Alberg's. He had returned, but reported not at home. Left word that I would call at 11 to-morrow.

20. Called on the Duke at 11. The porter said again that he was out; that he had reported my name and message but received no answer. Not much like the look of this. Considered myself as denied and the last hope of communication cut off. On Monday, 9th, called on Mr. Roux to ask whether

---

1 It will be observed that the entry under this date is substantially the same as that under July 2–3. The Journal was often carelessly written.
2 The word is here spelled correctly.
3 Burr here makes an English adverb from the French adjective *boudeuse*, sulky.
4 For Madame and her maid (Jungfru?).
5 Latin. Exceedingly lamentable gap. (The reader will notice that the Journal skips from the 10th to the 19th.)

he would give me rendezvous to peruse with me a *memoire*[1] which I had been writing. He asked me to breakfast on Wednesday for the purpose. On Wednesday went, and we passed several hours together. He made some civil remarks, and proposed that I should write to the Minister to ask audience, which I declined.

21. Called on Duke d'Alberg at 10, and was received as usual. He apologized for my several disappointments. Had heard nothing of my note to Maret[2]. Looked at my memorial, &c. Went off to Argaud to get it copied. To Madame P.

22. All day at work with Argaud, getting my thing nicely copied. Called on Madame P. On Roux; out. On Madame Robinson[3]; out. Vanderlyn gone to the country. Dined *chez nous* for the first time in a month; for, perceiving that Madame meant to make no charge, I would not be a charge.

23. Up at 5. At 8 to Argaud's. The thing was done. Sent messenger with a note to the Duc to advise him, and that I would call at 10. At 10 called. We went over the thing. He approved. Wrote note to Maret and I took the packet and left it. *Voila fini.*[4] *S. M.*[5] will probably read it this day. To Madame Paschaud's, where met ———, an Italian musician; M'e———, and ———, a young *Genevois*[6]. Much talk. The former is to *ciserone*[7] me

1 For *mémoire.* Memorial.
2 Hugo Bernard Maret, Duc de Bassano (1763-1839), was a French statesman and diplomat.
3 Robertson ?
4 For *Le voilà fini.* There, it is finished.
5 For *Sa Majesté.* His Majesty.
6 For *Génevois.*
7 For *cicerone.* To guide. The word has been introduced into English.

to see strange things. Evening walked with Madame P. to Luxembourg[1]; thence to Vanderlyn's, who had not returned.

Tuesday, 25th it must be. Rose 6. M'lle Catherine came in and took breakfast with me. (No, that was yesterday.) *Sor.* at 10 (but just before Vanderlyn came in) to Terrien La Riviere's, where ½ hour. To Mr. N.'s ½ hour. Home, and at 4 to Vanderlyn's to dinner. Home. To Fonzi's. Home. Paid *commiss'e*[2] for three trips, 2 francs 5 sous.

25. (I have looked at the almanac; it is 25 July.) *Couche* 12. Rose 7. Settled with Jeanette for 1 mo. and paid her 18 francs. Omitted: On my return home on Saturday last about 2 P. M. found note from ———— saying that *une personne*[3] to whom I was unknown wished much to see me, and gave me rendezvous *au Thuleries*[4] on Monday. Doubting a little, hating mystery, and desiring to know at least the sex of the *personne*, wrote to have further *renseignments*[5], which got, and on Monday went to the place and actually met *une tres aimable personne. Au soir la meme* made me visit *chez moi*[6] and on Tuesday returned it *chez elle*[7].

25 continued. At 11 came in Vanderlyn. Went

---

1 This may mean the Luxembourg Garden, one of the most beautiful pleasure resorts of Paris, or else the Palace. The Luxembourg Palace has had a varied history. It was constructed from 1615 to 1620 for Marie de Médicis, widow of Henry IV. Various princes and princesses dwelt there up to the Revolution. The Convention made a prison of it, and it became in 1795 the Directorial Palace, then in 1799 the Palace of the Consulate up to the time when Napoleon went to live in the Tuileries, in February, 1800. Afterwards it was occupied by the Senate, by the Chamber of Peers and again by the Senate, under the second Empire. Since then it has been used by the Prefecture of the Seine, and again by the Senate.
2 For *commissionnaire.* Porter.
3 A person.
4 For *aux Tuileries.* At the Tuileries. Burr has a hard time with this word.
5 For *renseignements.* Information.
6 Met a very amiable person. In the evening the same made me a visit at my home, etc.
7 At her home.

together to Fonzi's. Thence to Abel, *m'd de Bas*[1], where we parted. Came home and thence to the reading room where I am *abonnèd*[2] for 6 francs per month. To Vanderlyn's to dine. Strolled with him through the Luxembourg[3]. Parted. To Madame Paschaud's. Home at 8. Did nothing till 11. Spent 5 livres[4] in nothings. If it had been nothings for you or Gam[5], it would have been something.

26. The saint, my neighbor, waked me punctually at 6, as I had requested. To the bath, which, at the cheapest rate, costs 40 sous. Having some very long *courses*[6] in view, took cabriolet. To M. le Montey, near the invalids[7]. There wrote note to the *Min. de la pol. general*[8], asking audience. M. le Montey took charge of the note. To the *Min. d'Exterieur*[9] to see Roux; not there. To M. Roux's; out. To Pelasges prison[10] where saw J. Swan; Mr. Lane, of New York, and Mr. Browne, of ———— Lane has been there three years. My cabriolet man set me down at the Pont Neuf. Paid him 5 livres for three hours he had been in my employ, and he was

---

1 For *marchand de bas*. Stocking merchant.
2 A hybrid verb from the French verb *abonner*, to subscribe. Here it means, where I have a subscriber's ticket.
3 The Luxembourg Garden.
4 A livre is equivalent to a franc.
5 For Gampy.
6 Jaunts.
7 For Les Invalides, the soldiers' home heretofore described.
8 For *Ministre de la police générale*. Minister of the general police.
9 Probably for *Ministère de l'Extérieur*. The Ministry of Foreign Affairs of France had until 1790 the title *la Ministère des Affaires Etrangères*, the Ministry of Foreign Affairs. In that year a change was made to the more convenient title, *la Ministère des Relations Extérieures*, the Ministry of External Relations. In 1794 this latter title was abolished, but in 1814 the department got back its ancient name which it had held down to 1790.
10 This was the prison known as Sainte-Pélagie. It was founded about 1665 as a convent. In 1792 it was converted into a prison for both sexes. From 1797 to 1834 it was more especially devoted to prisoners for debt, and, under the first Napoleon, to political prisoners. Here Bonaparte incarcerated such persons as displeased him, as not being in sympathy with his projects. It is said that at one period the Emperor threw into this prison, within the space of a few days, 500 persons whom he regarded as dangerous.

content. To Madame Paschaud's. To Fonzi's, where met Vanderlyn. I shall never get done with Fonzi. The morning was warm and it is now raining. *Din. chez moi. Bro. mjlk*[1]. Mem.: To tell you of the Pantheon[2]; Notre Dame; l'Abbaye St. Martin, where is the *depot des Arts et des Inventions Mechan.*[3]; Tivoli Jardin[4]; l'Hermitage[5]; College de ———[6].

27. Rose 7. Am trying to get rid of the use of sugar and coffee gradually. *Sor.* ½ p. 9 to Roux, whom found; but no news. Cold civility. To Duc d'Alberg. He has left town for three weeks. Forgot: On Thursday called on M'r Le Montey, the Prefet, to ask him to introduce me to the new Minister of Police[7]. He had offered to introduce to the former (Fauchet)[8], but got it through another channel. He declined, but offered to present a note if I would write one, asking audience, which is the *mode*[9]. Wrote note and left it with Le Montey to present. Shall never

---

1 For *brod och mjolk*. Bread and milk.
2 The Pantheon (*Le Panthéon*) is another building with a varied history. It was constructed between 1764 and 1790 as a church and dedicated to Ste. Geneviève, patron saint of Paris. In 1791 the Constituent Assembly converted it into a temple called Pantheon, which was destined for the burial of great men, as is indicated by the inscription upon its façade: "*Aux grands hommes la patrie reconnaissante*," "The grateful fatherland to the great men." It was given back to worship in 1806, transformed anew into a temple at the revolution of 1830, and again into a church in 1851, and since 1885 has been devoted to its early purpose of containing the tombs of great men. Victor Hugo's remains lie here.
3 For *Dépôt des Arts et des Inventions Méchaniques*. Depository or Museum of Arts and Mechanical Inventions. This was mentioned a few pages back as the Conservatory of Arts and Trades.
4 See page 448, note 3.
5 For *l'Ermitage*. In English it is known as the Hermitage. It was the name of Rousseau's cottage near Montmorency. See page 442, note 12.
6 Probably the reference is to the institution now known as *le Collège de France*. This was founded about 1530 by Francis I. and soon became known as *le Collège des Trois Langues*, College of the Three Languages (Greek, Latin, Hebrew). Under Louis XIII. and for some years thereafter it had the name of *le Collège Royal*. In the time of the Revolution its name was changed to *le Collège National*, which Napoleon again altered (in the year XIII., about 1806) to *le Collège Impérial*. This was its name at the time of Burr's visit. Later, under the Restoration, it was changed back to *le Collège Royal*, and finally to *le Collège de France*, which name it bears to-day.
7 Anne Jean Marie René Savary, Duc de Rovigo. See note further on.
8 Joseph Fouché, Duc d'Otrante.
9 Fashion.

hear   more   of   it.   From   d'Alberg's   to   Fonzi's.
Thence home to repose, smoke segar.   At 1 *sor.* to
the reading-room.   To Madame Pas.   Met her going
out.   Gave me letter from Chabaud, in reply to one I
wrote him a week ago.   He has gone home; (Nis-
mes).   Ten days ago wrote also to Lüning.   To Dr.
Swediaur's, who asked me to dine, but was engaged
with Vanderlyn.   To Mrs. Robertson's, who also
asked me to dine.   To Naner; out.   Left note which
I had written in case of not finding him.   To Vanderlyn's to dine.   After dinner together to Rue Hyacinthe[1]
to see M'lle; out.   To St. Martin's to get my razor.
To le *coiffeur's*[2].   To Fonzi's; out.   Home with
Vanderlyn.   Made ourselves a dish of coffee and at
10 he went off.   Now, Madame, shall tell you a
secret.   Despairing of any success in my project, a few
days ago asked passport to go to the United States,
which was refused.   Asked one to go to Rouen, to see
M'e Langworthy, which was granted, to *"circuler pour
un an!"*[3] which was more than I asked or wanted.
Was told that I could not have a passport to go out
of the empire.   *Me voila prisonier d'etat et presque sans
sous!*[4]   My different walks to-day amount to fourteen
miles, and all for nothing.   This evening received a
note from Swan, enclosing will for my advice.

    28.   This being the saint's day (one of them, for
there is a saint for every name) of my friend Madame

---

[1] Hyacinth street.
[2] A *coiffeur* is a hairdresser.
[3] To circulate for a year.
[4] For *Me voilà prisonnier d'état et presque sans un sou.* Here I am a state's prisoner and
almost without a cent.

Paschaud, went to dine with her. There were both families. The young *Genevois*, the mus.[1] Mr. ———, and two vacant places; guests bidden, but came not. We arranged a party for Versailles, which, however, I thought mere talk. Home at 9. At ½ p. 10 a special messenger from Vanderlyn proposing to visit St. Germain's *mardi le 9*[2], to which agreed.

29. Rose 6. Another proposition to go to Versailles. Went to P.'s; made a bad apology. Abandoned her party and went with Vanderlyn to St. Germain's[3]. Visited the Marli works[4]. Walked also to a village, formerly a strong town as defence against the Normans, one league below St. Germain's. The rain detained us all night.

30. We staid to dine, and then took *pot de chambre*[5] back. This vile name is given to a one-horse chair, with two rows of seats, holding four or six passengers inside and one or two outside. We were *nine* in that in which I returned. You pay about 40 sous for that distance (six leagues), but there is no fixed price for anything in Paris. You are not always safe in offering half the asked price. Those on board paid different prices, from 20 up to 50 sous. The forest and the *terras*[6] are the objects of curiosity at St. Ger-

---

1 For musician.
2 Tuesday the 9th.
3 Saint-Germain-en-Laye is meant. This a town about seven miles north of Versailles and ten miles west-northwest of Paris. There was there a magnificent chateau founded by Charles V.
4 About five miles north of Versailles is a hamlet called Marly-La-Machine. Here was established in 1676 the celebrated hydraulic machine known as the Marly machine which, for many years, furnished Versailles with water. Rennequin Sualem, a simple mechanic, was the originator of it. His primitive apparatus was defective and was replaced by a more pretentious one in 1804. This, which was built by the engineer Brunet, was also defective. In 1859 Dufrayer constructed there a masterpiece of hydraulic pumping which is still in use.
5 Chamber-pot.
6 For *La Terrasse*. The Terrace. This is a celebrated promenade more than a mile and a half in length on the edge of the magnificent forest of 8,000 acres and high above the Seine. It commands a superb view of the sinuous banks of the river and of the animated plain which its waters bathe.

main's. On alighting at the Thullieres[1], posted over to *ma belle ami*[2], about one mile. Gods, how cold, chilling! Not having said that I would be out all night, there was much inquiry and alarm. Finally it was discovered that I had been assassinated, and the maid had got all the particulars. *La Sainte*[3] was at work to get my soul out of purgatory, which she feared would be a long and hard job. But what devil can have got into Madame P.'s head? Called at Fonzi's on my way from P.'s. His warmth and kindness recovered me a little from the shock of P.'s *froideur*[4].

31. Insomnia, but got up at ½ p. 6. Did noth ing till 10, and then, did nothing till 12. To Stone's; out, and said to be at the manufactory; went thither and out again. Home. Then to Deschams[5]; fortun- ately *out*. To Prevost, more luck; out and all locked up. Ran great risks on my way home, but got home safe. Bought ½ doz. wine, a little white Burgundy which pleases me much; 15 sous the bottle. Bought *casa*[6], 20 sous. Home at 3. Two eggs for *din*. I have been trying, for some time past, to get rid, *grad- ually*, of the enormous quantity of sugar which I use (5 francs per pound!); finding I made no progress, have given it up altogether, and this morning took tea, *sans sucre*[7]. Doing unpleasant things *gradually* is very great folly; a protracted torment.

---

1 Burr has tried hard this time to improve the spelling of this name, with what success the reader can judge.
2 For *ma belle amie*. My beautiful lady friend.
3 The woman saint. This name Burr gives to one of the maids on account of her seeming piety.
4 Coldness.
5 For Deschamps, the name of one of Burr's many female acquaintances.
6 For German *Kase*, cheese ?
7 Without sugar.

Paris, August 2, 1810. At 11 a cruising; Virg. and *l'allemag.*[1] ; out. *Tant mieux.*[2]. To Fonzi's. To the *changeurs*[3] ; changed 3 guineas; they give 26:10, but cheat you out of 5 or 6 sous in the weight. To Deschamp's; 8 livres. Staid an hour. To Swediaur's, where met Madame P., being the first time I have seen her since my miraculous reception on Monday. We were very civil but no more. She went off with her friend and I to Crede's. Thence to Vanderlyn's to dine. He was with his model, who is spoiled for that business, being *enseignte*[4]. After dinner to Quai Pelletier[5] to get razors set; paid 3 livres for strop and parts. Thence to Rue Darè *au marois*[6] to find Howseal, a German interpreter, whom found and left for translation my letter to Cousin Jean Gotleib[7] Then home, tired. Note : Left with Crede to put in post-office my letters to Menard, to Lüning, to Menzzer, and a note to Swan.

From 2 to 10. On Friday the 3d wrote Mr. E. Gris.[8] About same time to Lüning, duplicate enclosed to Menzzer ; wrote also to our cousin John Gotlieb, and to Mr.——— (I'll think of his name presently), of Hamburg. On Saturday, 4th, passed the day at the Pelasgie[9] prison, aiding Mr. Swan to make his

---

1 Probably for Virginie and *l'Allemagne* or *l'Allemande.* Virginia and Germany, or the German girl, two more of his chance acquaintances.
2 So much the better.
3 To the money-changer's.
4 For *enceinte.* Pregnant.
5 This quay has now been absorbed by the Quai de Gèvres.
6 *Le Marais* has long been the name of one of the quarters of Eastern Paris. It was built in the reign of Louis XIII. The numerous kitchen-gardens (*maraichers*) there in those days gave it the name which it still bears. *Marais* means marsh, or kitchen-garden ground. *Au marais* means in the Marais quarter.
7 For Gottlieb.
8 For Mr. Edward Griswold.
9 The prison called Saint-Pélagic. See page 452, note 10.

will. On Sunday to Versailles, with Fonzi, Vanderlyn, and Hernandez. Called five leagues. Hired a coach for 14 livres to take us there and back. This and dinner made our expenses 6 francs 10 sous each. *Y* Madame Fonzi. The gardens at Versailles are in a style of magnificence surpassing anything I have seen. Returned the same evening. Went, forgot what evening, to see Mr. Pierre's *Theatre Mechanique et Picturesque*[1] and was much amused. He exhibits, like a scene in a theatre, a town, castle, or remarkable place, painted in the manner of panorama ; but you see carriages of all sorts, horses, men, women, children, dogs, cattle, all in motion like real life. Boats rowing and sailing. Sportsmen shoot ducks, and their dogs jump out of the boat, swim to the killed duck, and bring him on board. How Gampy would laugh and stare ! Another evening to the cosmorama, which is pictures (seen through camera obscura) of various antiquities. Balbec, the Coliseum of Rome, and one other, were pretty well executed. The rest execrable. On Monday, the 6th, called on Mr. Stone at his manufactory. He asked me to dine that day, which declined ; for Wednesday, to which, after some remonstrance, agreed. *Y:* Miss Williams and *le bon* Marron[2], *pres't du consistoire*[3], who was extremely civil. He engaged me to go with him the next day to hear the tryal[4] of ———, which excites much interest. Cards ; lost 30 sous. Home at 11. Found note

---

1 Mechanical and Picturesque Theatre.
2 The good Marron.
3 President of the Protestant clergy of Paris. (*Président.*)
4 So in the MS.

from Vanderlyn, who had been waiting for me an hour
and gone off.   On Thursday, the 9th August, with
M. Marron to the court.   Heard two lawyers.   Was
well pleased, much gratified, but cannot detail.
Breakfast this morning, 9th, at 7.   To Vanderlyn's.
Thence to Crede's ; thence to Marron's, a tour of
about two leagues.   At the court met General Waltershoff.   Note this day from Mrs. Robertson to dine,
which declined.   Another note in the evening to dine
on Saturday or Monday.   Engaged for Monday.
Dined Thursday *chez moi;* Friday with Vanderlyn ;
Saturday 11, *chez moi.*   But the most important event
of this month is the Hegira[1] of Madame Paschaud,
who has actually gone to join her husband at Geneva.
We had been *boudeing*[2], as you know, ever since my
return from St. Germain.   On Tuesday last, the 7th,
received message to dine with her that day, as she
should leave town next morning.   Dined there, but
was grave, silent, appetiteless, and without affectation.
Some engagement, forget what, called me away early ;
but at 10 returned.   She was out.   Went at 6 next
morning.   She had gone to the bath.   Followed *y*
and waited till she came out.   Walked a few minutes
in the garden, and had explanations, which were on
both sides declared satisfactory, and we kissed and
made friends ; but we are not such friends as we were
two months ago.   Went with her to the diligence

---

1   This unusual English word may need an explanation.   The Hegira, or Hejira, is the era
which forms the starting point of the Mohammedan calendar, July 15, 622, commemorative of
the flight of Mohammed from Mecca to Medina.   Burr uses it as synonymous with flight.
2   A hybrid present participle from the French verb *bouder,* to sulk.

office and saw her off. *Adieu, ma belle amie. Vraiment, son absence, m'attriste¹.*

Friday morning, 10th August, called on M. Marron to get the address of Valkenaer; out. To Baron d'Alberg's; not returned. It was yesterday, Friday, I dined with Vanderlyn. He came home with me and sat till 10.

11. Rose 6. At 10 to Marron's to get the address of Valkenaer to whom had letter from Strick, but supposed him (V.) to be at Amsterdam. V. is a *brave, franc, intelligent batave².* Sat an hour, and we were apparently equally amused. To Stone's manufactory to get Humboldt's work, of which he promised me the loan; out. Vanderlyn breakfasted with me this morning. (On Thursday Ternen came in and sat ½ hour.) From Valkenaer's to Mons. Le Montey's to see what been done about my note to the Duke, Minister of Police. It had been delivered, but no answer. Thence on my way to Madame Robertson's a *renc.³* Went into a *traiteur's⁴*; breakfast, though 2 P. M. *Muse,* &c.; 10 francs!! (How many good resolutions have been made since 3 to-day.) To Madame Robertson's; out. To Mr. Roux. He advises me to write to the Duc de Cadore about the refusal of the passport, which I shall do. Home at 3. Having bought coffee by the way, took coffee for *din.* Find coffee good after *muse.* At 6 to Crede's; out. Wrote him note on my return home. Home at 7.

---

1 Good-by, my handsome friend. Truly, her absence makes me sad.
2 A worthy, frank, intelligent Batavian, *i. e.,* citizen of the Batavian Republic. See page 462, note 3.
3 For *rencontre.*
4 Eating-house keeper's.

Tea and *bro.*, *w'tt-soc* & *mjlk*[1]. Letter from Swan enclosing his will for further amendments. Mem. of Notre Dame, Pantheon, the horse and gig in the China shop. *Bon soir a minerve*[2]. Dampier's "Voyage" or "Travels"; pray read it. I like much his manner.

12. At 9 to Fonzi's where dined and staid till 8. Then away to Crede's; no one at home, but met young Crede in the street coming home. At Fonzi's was a *garcon*[3] who imitated dogs, cats, &c., and played very prettily on a little flute flageolet about six inches long. He says the beautiful women of France are on the Rhone from Lyons down, particularly at Avignon, Valence, and Vien, and the Cote Roti[4], famous also for the wine bearing that name. Home at 9. *Tro. man. Rhe. rad*[5]; and coffee, *w'tt soc.*[6]

13. Rose 7 in bad order. At 11 to Abel's; 12 to Fonzi's; he not being ready, to————, with whom left my mem. for perusal. Anecdotes of L. and N. To *3 pet. Aug.*[7] to see Madame Pel. and to settle accounts; could not settle, but paid *30* francs for one month's room rent. To Fonzi's again and there till 4; not yet done. Thence home and dressed for dinner To Madame Robertson's. *Y* Sidney and Madame Menetza[8]. Md. Lewins est'd *bon et d'esprit*[9].

---

1 For *bröd, sockervatten, och mjölk.* Bread, sugar-water, and milk.
2 Good evening to Minerva. He means his daughter Theodosia.
3 For *garçon.* Boy.
4 For Côte-Rôtie, the name of a well-known vineyard on the banks of the Rhone, producing a wine of the same name.
5 For *Trop mangé* or *J'avais trop mangé. Radix Rhei.* Had eaten too much. Took rhubarb.
6 For *sockervatten.* Swedish for sugar-water.
7 For 3 Rue Petit-Augustin. Number 3 Little Augustine street.
8 For Menutzi.
9 Probably for esteemed *bon et d'esprit.* Esteemed good and intelligent.

Home at 10. Note : It is an hour's walk from my quarters to Madame Robertson's, being about one league.

15. To Valkenaer's to breakfast. *Y* a very interesting *Hollandois* [1] just arrived from Amsterdam. His name did not learn. Also a sensible *brave hom.* [2], also *Holland's* [1], formerly minister of the Bat'e rep. [3] to ————. The latter came to meet me and to talk, but was obliged to disappoint them, having made an engagement. The breakfast was Holland, that is, American, tea, bread, butter, slices of ham. Off at 11 and to St. Pelasgie [4]. *Y* an hour in correcting Swan's will. To Vanderlyn's ; out. To ———— to meet Mr. Lane, who has got out of prison, and expressed a great desire to see me. He did not come. At 4 to Fonzi's. Took a stroll through the Thuleries [5] to see what was doing, this being the Emperor's *jour de fête* [6] or saint's day. The morning was ushered in by cannon. Many people in the gardens ; few fashionables. Home at 6. Two eggs and *bro.* for *din.* At 7 came in Vanderlyn, and we went again to the Thull's [5] to see the illuminations. Rather faint. The musicians in the orchestra played several pieces. The Emperor appeared, as was said, in the balcony, but that not being lighted, we could not distinguish him ; but there were *vive l'empereurs* [7]. Home at 11. Called this morning on d'Alberg ; not yet returned.

1 For *Hollandais.* Hollander.
2 For *brave homme.* Worthy fellow.
3 The Batavian Republic. This was the name which the Netherlands assumed when a republic from 1795 to 1806.
4 The Sainte-Pélagie prison, heretofore mentioned.
5 For Tuileries.
6 Literally feast-day.
7 *Vive l' Empereur* means Long live the Emperor.

16. At 11 to the Louvre to meet Vanderlyn and to gaze. At ½ p. 12 to *le bureau du secretariat de la police general*[1] to meet there Mons. Le Montey, who was to introduce me to Mr. Saugnier, *le secretaire*[2]. Met him, and was introduced, and urged my demand for passport to go to the United States. He advised me to write to the Minister, and offered to hand him the letter, which I will do, but have little hopes. This morning received a letter from Mr. G.[3] in reply to one I wrote about ten days ago about money, which I had good reason to believe he would lend me, and which I begin to want. He cannot! This, Madame, is rather grave. Winter approaches, no prospect of leave to quit the empire, and still less of any means of living in it. So must economize most rigidly my few remaining louis. Met Mr. Lane at Paschaud's to-day. Thence to Fonzi's. Home at 3. Eggs and *bro.* At 8 came in Vanderlyn and sat an hour. Am reading Robin's "Travels in Florida, Louisiana, and the Mississippi." We have had about a fortnight of raw, chilling, uncomfortable weather; raining almost daily. I should be glad of a good fire, but see none.

17. Called again at d'Alberg's; not returned. To Fonzi's. To Terrien de Riviere; out. To Crede's; out. To Vanderlyn's to dine. *Y* model, with whom ½ hour. After dinner, home. Finished reading Robin's "Travels," being three volumes octavo.

---

1 The office of the secretaryship (*secrétariat*) of the general police.
2 For *le secrétaire.* The secretary.
3 Mr. Edward Griswold.

18. Dine at Fonzi's, being the *fete de Mad'e*[1]. *Y:* Dr. Swediaur, Vanderlyn, Hernandez, Mr. ————, *musicien*[2]; Madame Montalambert, *veuve du General*[3]; Madame ————, *souer de* Madame Castro ; Madame and M'lle Fabre. *Ayez un peu de menagement pour les beautes passeés. Ah, Madame D. encore enseingte? Je vous croyois accouchie il y a longtems. Mais ecst bien sur que je ne puis pas enseingte plus que 9 mois*[4]? Then a critical discussion on the possible time of gestation and how the date might be ascertained. Home at 10.

19. To Fonzi's at 12 and till 2. Home till 4 doing nothing. Then to Crede's ; out, but his son at home. To Vanderlyn's ; out. Home at ½ p. 6, having walked about two and a half leagues. *La S'te*[5] brought me a *bouillon*[6], before I went out ; very acceptable. On my return at 7 tea, *bro.*, egg for dinner and supper. *La J'te*[7] sat an hour telling her misfortunes. *La viell'de*[8] prays for me, so that my soul is in a good way. She is *devote*[9], goes daily to mass, and fills up the interval with cards. Vanderlyn had called twice

---

1 Mad'e for Madame. Madame's birthday (literally, feast).
2 Musician.
3 Widow of the General (*général*). Marc René, Marquis de Montalembert (1714–1800), was a celebrated French general and engineer. He was an acknowledged authority on fortifications, being a voluminous writer along this line. His chief work was " Perpendicular Fortifications," in eleven volumes, published from 1776 on, and re-edited in 1793 under the title, " The Defensive Art Superior to the Offensive." The great Carnot thought so well of Montalembert that he called him into his council. In 1770 he married a talented, beautiful lady of the name of Josephine de Comarieu, whose drawing-room became one of the most popular of all Paris. In 1792 he took her to London, where he left her and, returning to Paris, obtained a divorce and married the sister of Codet de Vaux, the celebrated chemist. After the death of Montalembert his former wife returned to Paris, where she lived until 1832. She was a novelist of some repute.
4 For " *Ayez un peu de ménagement pour les beautés passeés.*" "*Ah*, Madame D., *vous etes encore enceinte? Je vous eroyais accouchée il y a longtemps.*" " *Mais est-ce bien sûr que je ne suis pas enceinte plus que neuf mois?*" " Have a little consideration for past beauties." " Ah, Madame D., you are still pregnant ? I thought you had been confined long ago." " But is it quite certain that I am not pregnant more than nine months ?"
5 For La Sainte. The Saint. The name given by Burr to the maid who was so pious.
6 Broth.
7 For *La Jeannette.* Jeannette. This was the name of the maid whom Burr called the saint.
8 For *La vieillarde.* The old woman. (The feminine form of the noun *vieillard* is exceedingly rare.)
9 For *dévote.* Devout.

during my absence to-day. Forgot to say that I had yesterday a letter from Lüning *pere*[1], very amiable, and to-day another from our cousin, John Gotleib Burr, giving the history of his family, which will give me some trouble to translate, and then to reply in German. You did not know before I told you, and I have not told you yet, huzzy, that you are a Dutchman! But alas! in my affairs no advance; no passport; no money. " *Erotika Biblion,*"[2] *par* Mirabeau; duod., one volume, Paris: 1801. A very whimsical book, which I borrowed of Madame F., and read last week. Settle with Jeannet; 8 francs 10 sous.

20. Called on Duc d'Alberg; he returned yesterday but had walked out. To Fonzi's, where from 1 to 4. Home and thence to Vanderlyn's to dine. After dinner home at 8. Coffee, *w't. socer mjlk*[3].

21. At ½ p. 9 to Duc d'Alberg's, where ½ hour. Thence on to Roux's; out. To Madame Robertson's, where an hour; fruit, wine, sug. water[4]. Engaged me to dine to-morrow. To Fonzi's at 2. Home to change and dress and thence to meet Vanderlyn and two M'lls. Viol. *pas y* an hour[5]. Cooked three eggs which with *bro* for *din*. On way from Madame R.'s called at the *bureaux*[6], where found Roux. No answer from Minister about passport. Evening, a bottle beer, 7 sous. *La* Jeanette an *heur*[7]; *muse*, &c.,

---

1 Father.
2 A Greek title meaning " Erotic Book " or " Book of Sensual Passions " It was a collection of examples of deviations from true love among different nations. Mirabeau wrote it when, as a young man, he was imprisoned in a dungeon of the Vincennes prison, about 1780.
3 For *sockervatten och mjolk*. Sugar-water and milk.
4 Sugar-water.
5 Possibly for Violette *pas y ;* an hour. Violette not there; staid an hour. But probably for Violette. *J'y passai une heure*. Violette. Passed an hour there.
6 Offices.
7 For *heure*. Hour.

pour l'amour de dieu[1]. But after dinner walked to Crede's, which is a league; not come to town. So home. A very mild, serene, clear day, the only one this month.

22. Got *la* Jeanette to buy my coal and milk; got of both just double the quantity for the same price; of coal, indeed, nearly three-fold. At 9 to Staley's to get newspapers; got three of July, but nothing of interest. Thence to Vanderlyn's; out. Met his *bonne*[2] in the street. Home. Letter of business for *la* Jeanette. At 3 to Fonzi's. At ½ p. 5 to Madame Robertson's to dine. *Y.* Sidney, Madame Menutzi, Madame Lewins. *Le soir*[3], as always, came in Adamson. Staid till ½ p. 9; home at ½ p. 10. *Renc.*[4] but got safe home; only 7 *sous pour bout. de bierrè*[5]. Read an hour in the "*Journal del Adjutant-General Ramel l'un des Deportes a la Guina avec Pichegru et* 14 others." *Un volume octavo, Londres*[6].

23. To Fonzi's at 9, *mais rien fait*.[7] With Madame Pelough to Paschaud's to get letter. It is from Menard only to say that he had no letters for me. Changed 5 guineas at 26 francs 8 sous. To

---

1 *Muse*, etc., for the love of God.
2 Nursery-maid.
3 In the evening.
4 For *rencontre*. Rencounter.
5 For *sept sous pour une bouteille de bière.* Seven sous for a bottle of beer.
6 For "*Journal de l'Adjutant-Général Ramel, l'un des Déportés à la Guiane avec Pichegru et 14 autres,*" etc. "Journal of Adjutant-General Ramel, one of those Deported to Guiana with Pichegru and Fourteen Others." One volume octavo, London. Charles Pichegru (1761-1804) was a distinguished French general. In 1795 he conquered Holland and organized the Batavian Republic. Then he resumed command of the Army of the Rhine, of which he had been made chief in 1793, but entering into negotiations with the Bourbons and falling under suspicion on account of his activity and the reverses sustained by his army, he was deprived of his command in 1796. During the following year he was a member of the Council of Five Hundred, and was chosen its president; but his plottings with the Royalist party and the *émigrés* were discovered. He was therefore arrested, September 4, 1797, and transported to Cayenne, from which he escaped the following year to England. Later he was found in Paris, arrested, imprisoned, and in 1804 he was found strangled in his cell.
7 But nothing done.

Viol.'s[1], where an hour; *gr.*, *blo.*, *roug. chev.*[2] To Fonzi's; one piece is now, I think, complete[3]. Dined by invitation with Madame Pelough. After dinner came in Vanderlyn. After smoking segar, walked with him to Crede's to make money. *Merite*[4].

24. Wrote this morning to Duke Bassano, again demanding passport. *Sor.* at 2. To Roux to press the same demand on Duke de Cadore. R. is always civil. He had "*received no answer*" from the Duke (this is the diplomatic style of negation); but promised to state my further reasons and demand. Thence to Saugnier's, *le sec. de la police gen'le*[5]; out; left, enclosed to him, my letter, which is in English, to Bassano. To Vanderlyn's to dine; leaving an hour and ½ before dinner. Read out the first part of Burke's "Sublime and Beautiful." After dinner called on Crede; not in town. To the Luxembourg garden where I had rendezvous with Vanderlyn, but he came not; so home. At Vanderlyn's had the misfortune to break a spring of my *rat.*[6]

25. Rose this morning at 6 and with very pious resolutions to write a number of letters, &c. You shall see how faithfully executed. At 7 to Fonzi's about that spring. Home to breakfast. At 11 recollected a rendezvous foolishly made to Viol. You know how religious I am in the performance of all sorts of engagements, so went. Found M'lle in a

1 Probably for Violette.
2 For *grande*, *blonde*, *les cheveux rouges*. Tall, blonde, red hair.
3 Probably a reference to false-teeth.
4 For *Il a du mérite*. It (*i. e.*, the scheme) has merit.
5 For *le Secrétaire de la Police Générale*. Secretary of the General Police.
6 For *râtelier*. Set of false teeth. They were made with springs in olden times.

state of expectation and disposed to be amiable. *Y* an hour; 6 francs; never better pleased with red, which is my abhorrence in *theory*. Thence home. Changed 6 guineas at 26 franc 10 sous. To make a *cud.*[1] to Fonzi. Gave him 6 napoleons. Took a breakfast there of meat, bread, wine at 1 o'clock. On my way home the devil put in my way Flora, whom I had often before met and promised to call on; went to *sa cham. Jol. bon. vol.; y 2 h.*[2]; *7 francs.* Home at 3 and at 4 made myself coffee. At 6 came in Vanderlyn. Walked with him to show him Flora as he was in want of *muse; 3 francs; y 2 h.*[3] Home at 9 and rather disposed to go early to bed, having been kept awake till 2 this morning by the songs, &c. (a party below) and being obliged to be up at 6 to-morrow, and the labor of the day requires repose. So God bless and reform thee!

26. Went to bed last night full of penitence and contrition and promising you any number of times that I would never do so again. Full of apprehension, too, of some physical consequences. Rose at 6 and to my great surprise in perfectly good order. It manifests, at least, the good state of my health. Got breakfast at 7, and went at 8 to the rendezvous agreed on with Hernandez and Vanderlyn, about ½ league. They had just gone off to St. Germain[4], whither I was to have gone with them if they would have staid till

---

1 Possibly for *cadeau.* Present.
2 For went to *sa chambre. Elle est jolie, bonne, voluptueuse; y deux heures.* She is pretty good, voluptuous; staid there two hours.
3 There two hours.
4 Meaning St. Germain-en-Laye, a tranquil town outside of Paris. See page 455, note 3.

12. Nevertheless, was glad they were gone, for the jaunt would have cost me 8 livres. Home, and after changing and refreshing for an hour, for it is very warm, to Duc d'Alberg's. Very lucky I went, for he had been seeking me, and had lost my address. Offered to take me to the Duc Rovigo[1], to whom I have been trying these eight weeks to get access. The Duc wrote a letter demanding audience for us, which letter I took and left at Rovigo's. I suspect that His Majesty begins to think of me and my projects. From d'Alberg's to Madame Robertson's, where an hour. Took a second breakfast of ham, fruit, wine. Thence to Saugnier's. He refused to see me, but sent word by the servant that he had no answer to my letter. Home at 2. The Duc d'Alberg having requested another copy of my memoir, went out at 5 to get Argaud to make me another copy. He had moved to Rue Fer de Moulin, Faubourg Mareil[2], about four or five miles off. So came home, but after taking my *bro.* and *mjlk*[3], to Argaud's ; gave him my *brouillard*[4] with some additional notes, which I have

---

1 Anne Jean Marie René Savary, Duc de Rovigo (1774–1833), was a French general and politician who attached himself unreservedly to the fortunes of Napoleon. He fought in many battles. From the battle of Marengo on, he was Napoleon's aide-de-camp and confidential man. In 1800 he was named Colonel and Commandant of the Select Gendarmerie, which was commissioned to watch over the safety of the First Consul. In 1803 he became Brigadier-General and two years later rose to be Grand Officer of the Legion of Honour. In 1808, after serving as ambassador at St. Petersburg, the title of Duke of Rovigo was given to him by the Emperor. In 1810 he was called to succeed Fouché as Minister of Police. Of his nomination to that office he himself wrote : " I inspired fear in everybody. From the moment of my nomination people packed up. There was talk of nothing but exiles and imprisonments and things still worse. In fine, I believe that news of the plague having arrived on some point of the coast could not have occasioned greater fright than did that of my nomination to the Ministry of Police." On Napoleon's return from Elba, the Duke was made a peer and put at the head of all the gendarmerie of the Empire. He wanted to accompany Napoleon to St. Helena, but was not allowed to go. Seldom has a crowned head had a slave more willing than de Rovigo.
2 Iron-mill street. (*Rue Moulin-à-fer*) in the Marais suburb. How the name Marais came to be given has already been explained. See page 457, note 6.
3 For *bröd* and *mjölk*. It is remarkable how Burr sticks to these Swedish words.
4 Rough draft.

made to-day, and he promised to bring me a copy on Tuesday morning. Came home through the Jardin des Plantes[1] and the Boulevard, so that I have walked nearly twenty miles to-day, and am not the least fatigued. I grudged Gamp a coach on account of yesterday's extravagance. Jeanette brought me wine, bread, and melon to refresh and heated water for drink. Now I have to write a long letter of business for Jeanette.

30. Rose at 6 and at 7 to Fonzi's, where an hour. Home. Breakfast. Had lent my memorial to M. Pelough, and he had gone out. Dressed for the intended visit to Rovigo. There being a defect in the work of Fonzi[2], and being without my memorial, resolved to postpone the visit till to-morrow. *Din. bro. mjolk.* On my way home called at the Lyon and then on Scherer, who had a letter for me. It is from Bollman. The only one from America since October last.

31. Rose at 6. To Fonzi's at 10 and till 12. Then dressed, and to the Duc Rovigo's, armed with his note to d'Alberg. The *huissier*[3] told me that there were a great number of persons waiting audience ; that it would be very late before I could be received, and recommended me to come to-morrow at 1. *Din. bro. mik.*

---

1 Le Jardin des Plantes or Muséum d'Histoire Naturelle was founded in 1635 by Guy de . abrosse, a celebrated botanist, and was, as its name implies, intended for plants. It was entrusted to Buffon about a century later, who completely transformed it and organized natural history collections. Bernardin de St. Pierre transferred to it in 1793 the animals of the royal menageries of Versailles and other animals. In modern times it has become a very celebrated museum of natural history.
2 Fonzi was Burr's dentist.
3 Usher.

Paris, Sept. 1, 1810. Rose at 5, having slept enough, though it was 12 when I *couched*[1]. At 1 to Duke Rovigo's. I was the first, and placed in the antechamber. The *huissier* told me that the audience would not begin till 2. "Why, then, sir, did you bid me come at 1 ?" "That you might be ready at 2." There came in to the number of forty-seven ; a majority women. Two English women sat next to me. At ½ p. 2 the doors were thrown open, and a *huissier* cried out, "*Mesdames et messieurs, entrez*"[2]. I was quite surprised, expecting we were to be called in one by one, as I had seen practiced by Fauchet[3] and Champigny. We all went in. The Duc, in full dress, was at the farther end of the room, and we stood, forming a sort of horseshoe, of which the two ends approached him. He began on his right, and so on, hearing and answering, generally, in about one minute. Some of the women kept him three or four minutes, and some talking on after he had given his answer, till he turned his back and addressed the next. His first question was, "*Qui etes vous?*"[4] One very ill-looking fellow he asked, "*Etes vous le* Colonel Burr?"[5] By which I learned that he had that person in his mind. I shifted my place so as to be last; but some three or four others, with the like design, got after me. At length my turn came. I announced myself, and told him I had been refused a passport, at which I was the more

---

1 A hybrid verb from the French verb *coucher*, to go to bed or put to bed.
2 " Ladies and gentlemen, enter."
3 For Fouché.
4 For "*Qui êtes-vous ?* " " Who are you ? "
5 " Are you Colonel Burr ?

surprised, as he probably knew the nature of the business which had brought me to France. "*J'en ai entendu paler mais je ne connois pas les detailes.*" "*Je serais charmé, Monsieur, d'un occasion de vous les faire connoitre. J'ai n'ai pas eu le bonheur d'avoir été ecouté par un soldat et un autre nest pas capable de juger de mon affaire. Le genie militaire de votre Excellence scaurait apprecier mes veus et je serais desolé de quitté la france sans avoir été entendu et compris.*"[1] Then he asked me to walk aside that he might hear it. I told him I had it in writing. "*Ah, donnez le moi. Je le lirai avec empressement.*"[2] So I drew it from my side pocket and gave it to him, and was going to renew the question of passport. "*Ah, nous conferons de ca aprez j'aurai lu votre memoire. Je vous ecrirai pour vous donner rendez-vous particulier en peu de jours;*"[3] and turned off to another. So that after all my pains to get an audience, it has amounted to just nothing. It was unlucky, however, that, through ignorance, I should have stumbled on his public day. On any other he gives private audiences to all who are permitted to come in. I like much his appearance and manner. A handsome man, about 42, very prompt and decided, but sufficiently courteous; the appearance of intelligence and good breeding; all which is better than I had been taught to expect. Got off at 4. To Paschaud's,

---

1 "I have heard it mentioned (*parler*), but I do not know (*connais*) the details." "I should be charmed, sir, to have an opportunity to make you acquainted with them. I have not had the good fortune to have been heard by a soldier and no other is capable of judging of my affair. The military genius of your Excellency can (*saurait*) appreciate my desires (*vœus*) and I should be very sorry (*désolé*) to leave (*quitter*) France without having been heard and understood."

2 "Ah, give it to me. (*Donnez-le-moi.*) I shall read it with eagerness."

3 "Ah, we shall consult together about that after (*conférerons de cela après*) I shall have read your memorial (*mémoire*) I shall write (*écrirai*) you in order to give you a private interview in a few days."

where had agreed to meet Vanderlyn at 3. He had been and gone, leaving a note for me to dine with him. Home ; changed my dress, and to Fonzi's ; thence to Vanderlyn's, distant one league, where had a model, not exquisite. After dinner we walked by pon nuf to Pal. Roy.¹ ; parted and I came home, having agreed that he should call on me at 11 to-morrow, to arrange about going together to St. Germain's, where is a *fête* and *foire*². Crede came to town Thursday ; called on me twice, but missing me, left a note saying that he would be at home all the evening. Called and saw him in the evening. Walked together to the Luxembourg gardens, where I staid till he went to make a neg'n³ for me. He was successful, and returned. After walking an hour, home at 10. His zeal is great and unabated.

2. Rose at 6. At 9 to d'Alberg's ; gone to the bath. To Valkenaer's, where took a second breakfast and staid an hour. Home at 11. Came in Vander lyn. Walked together by the Thulleries⁴ to Port Royal⁵ to get a passage for *me* to St. Germain, Vanderlyn having resolved not to go. Found a carriage with four ; I made the fifth. He wanted but one of his complement. After sitting in the carriage thirty-five minutes, two of the passengers got out of patience, *sacre'd* and *diable'd*⁶, and went to seek some other pas-

---

1 For Pont Neuf to Palais Royal.
2 Festival and fair.
3 Possibly for negotiation ; but financial or amorous ?
4 For Tuileries.
5 The Boulevard de Port Royal.
6 These two hybrid verbs are made by Burr, the one from the French verb *sacrer*, to curse, and the other from the French noun *diable*, devil. Hence, they cursed and swore.

sage. Then came up three who wished to go to Versailles. The coachman asked if any of us within would go to Versailles; two said no, the third yes. So we two Noes were turned out, and he changed his destination to Versailles. After waiting ½ hour longer, without being able to get a passage, gave up the jaunt and came home. Just now, 3 P. M., *la* Jeanette brought me a bowl of soup. Every day some such attention and good office; and now, at 5, I am going to stroll an hour and fear greatly some accident. I ask your prayers for my safety. Evening. Felicitate me on my safe return. I did, indeed, spend 6 livres, viz., 5 livres 10 sous for a pound of sugar, and 10 sous for fruit. Note: This is the only sugar bought in a month, and it will last me a month, for I use none at breakfast. Have been reading " *Tableau de l'Amour Conjugal*¹," *par* Vernette, two volumes, Paris : 1810. Seeing it announced in several *affiches*², I wondered what could be said on such a subject to fill two volumes. Looking at the table of contents, found the heads of chapters inviting, and bought it. A most stupid book. I met in every chapter disappointment and nothing else.

3. Rose at 6. At 9 to Fonzi's, who was abed. To d'Alberg's, who had walked out. On my return bought *Boccace nouvelles librement traduits par*³ Mira beau (who makes everything amusing), eight volumes

---

1 " Picture of Conjugal Love."
2 Placards.
3 Boccacio's novels freely translated (*traduites*) by Mirabeau. This was the famous "*Decamerone.*" Mirabeau's translation was made during the time of his imprisonment and was published in 1802. The "*Decamerone*" consisted of one hundred stories published by Boccacio in 1353, ranging from the pathetic to the licentious.

duod. Also, Boccace's something, French and Italian ', one volume; Rochefoucauld's "Maxims"², one volume; for the whole paid 12 livres. Then to Fonzi's again. To d'Alberg's; always frank and kind. He engaged me to meet him to-night at ½ p. 8 at Duc Rovigo's, than which, you know, nothing could be more agreeable to me   Thence to Madame Robertson's, where an hour, and took soup. She urged me to dine, which I declined on account of my evening engagement. Went with her in her carriage to see the M'lles Evans; and thence I called on Swediaur, where ½ hour, and then home. Took two eggs for *din.* To Beret's, *coiffeur*³, to engage him to call this evening; but saw only his wife, *qui est fort gentill.*⁴ Home. Made my *toilette* without Beret. Vanderlyn came in and we walked by way of Pal. Roy.⁵ (a route he always prefers *a cause des filles*⁶). A thundershower, that is, much lightning, a little thunder, and about ten drops of rain. At the Duc's was a great assemblage; perhaps one hundred gentlemen, and twenty or thirty ladies. Met there the Duc d'Alberg, who presented me in form to Duc Rovigo. Staid an hour to see the show, with which I was amused, because it furnished something to amuse you. The Duc told me he had read my *memo.*⁷, and said some

---

1 Boccacio wrote many works and it is impossible to conjecture to which reference is here made.
2 The French title of this work is " *Réflexions ou Sentences et Maximes Morales du Duc de la Rochefoucauld.*" It was written during the age of Richelieu and had a wide and salutary influence.
3 Hair-dresser.
4 Who is very pretty. (*Gentille.*)
5 For Palais Royal.
6 Because of the girls.
7 For *mémoire.* Memorial.

civil things. Off at ½ p. 9 and home. *Bon soir, chere T.*[1] Mem : Took coffee before going out this evening, contrary to all habit, and much afraid of insom., to guard against which have drank a ½ bottle of wine.

4. The coffee did keep me awake till about 3 ; nevertheless rose at 6. *Sor.* 9 to Terrien de Riviere's villa, Rue du Temple, about 1½ miles ; out. Then by the *quais*[2] to Baron d'Alberg's, Rue Concorde, about two miles. *Y* an hour. Then to Fonzi's where engaged myself to dine. Home at 2. Read about sixty pages in the " *Fiametta* " *de Boccace*[3], which found dull, the French being antique and difficult to understand. Finding myself drowsy, took a nap in my chair of an hour. To Fonzi's at ½ p. 5 to dine. *Y* the famous young ———, whose father I met there some time ago. Came in after dinner Mons. Isidore and wife and three *enf.*[4] He had been a year in England as *emigré*[5]. A very pleasant, well-informed man. Urged me much to come and pass a day with him at Passy, where he resides. This is the first Frenchman who has offered me the slightest hospitality since the 7 mo. I have been in France. Home at 9. *Seul* ½ hour with Mr. and Madame Pelough. *Couche* at 12.

5. Lay till 9 to sleep off a headache. In bad order. Took a bowl of tea, but ate not. At 1 to

---

1 For *Bon soir, chère* Theodosia. Good evening, dear Theodosia.
2 Quays, wharfs.
3 Boccacio's "*L'Amorosa Fiammetta*," an allegory as tedious as it is long, of the amours of Boccacio and Princess Marie.
4 For *enfants.* Children.
5 Emigrant.

Rovigo's; gone to St. Cloud's[1]. To Dr. Swediaur's ½ hour; then walked along the *quais* an hour, looking at the books which are there exposed[2]. They are second-hand books and odd volumes, but so amazingly cheap that it is tempting to buy, but bought none. Saw an edition of Boccace for 6, 10[3], which is 2 livres less than I paid for mine, and which I thought so very cheap; 1 livre a volume, there being eight volumes, what cheaper could be desired? To Fonzi's; engaged. Home and at 4 made breakfast, the head ache having passed off. Did not go out again. At 8 came in Vanderlyn and sat two hours. To-morrow shall go again to Rovigo's, when it is hoped I may have something to tell you.

6. *Couche* 12. Rose 6. One sound nap. *Sor.* at 9 to a bookstore in St. Honoré[4], where bought for you and Gamp to the amount of 16, 10[5]—just 3 dollars. I mean to buy you about fifty plays of those written since '88· You will see from them much of the change of manners. On my way home changed three guineas. Then to Fonzi's; engaged. Home and dressed for the Duc Rovigo's; went there at 1. Was told by the *huissier* that he was in council of state, which might last till 4, but advised me to come at 3. Paschaud's bookstore being just by, went there to pass the two hours. At 3 returned to the Duc's and, after staying

---

1 St. Cloud is a small town on the Seine about six miles southwest of Paris. Napoleon was very fond of this retreat, probably because there was effected the *coup d'état* of November 10, 1799, which placed him at the head of the government.
2 Many travelers in Paris are greatly tempted as Burr was by the remarkable bargains in old books which are to be had at numerous book-stalls along the Seine.
3 Meaning 6 livres or francs and 10 sous.
4 Meaning Rue St. Honoré.
5 Meaning 16 livres 10 sous.

an hour in the antechamber, was told that the council might still sit a great while, and that I had better come to-morrow at 1. So off to Fonzi's; still engaged. Home. Coffe.[1] and *bro.* for *din.* At 7 to Fonzi's, a visit. He is not only a *dentiste*, but a man of education, of talents, and considerable acquirements; *franc et enjoué*[2]. I met there, also, a very amiable Spaniard, *c. d. prete*[3]; has passed many years at Constantinople, attached, I believe, to the Spanish embassy. He has great love for personal independence and ease, that he has refused a brilliant place at court, and prefers to learn Fonzi's art. Vanderlyn was there also. Staid till 9, then home, and have read an essay on lotteries, *par* Bardini. A title full of pretension, but the pamphlet has very little either of fact or reasoning. Read also one of your plays, " *La Famille Americaine,*"[4] *par le Citoyen* Bouilly[5]. Very pretty. Yesterday, no, it was Tuesday, the weather changed, and it is now so cold that I should be glad of a fire; but to that there are great objections; for what would become of the fifty plays, and of something, I won't tell what, which I meditate to buy for Gampillo[6], that will make his little heart kick?

7. *Couche* ½ p. 12. Rose ½ p. 6. How divinely I sleep. "Divinely?" Do the gods sleep?[7]

---

1 Probably meant for *café.* Coffee.
2 Candid and merry.
3 For *ci-devant prêtre.* Formerly priest.
4 "The American Family."
5 By Citizen Bouilly. The appellations citizen (*citoyen*) for men and citizeness (*citoyenne*) for women were universally employed under the Republic for Monsieur and Madame. Under the Consulate these titles disappeared from public acts and official language.
6 Little Gamp or Gampy, Burr's favorite nickname for his grandson.
7 The reader will note Burr's play on the word " divinely," which is derived from the Latin *divinus,* belonging to a god.

At 9 to Valkenaer's, where an hour, and took a second breakfast, tea, *bro.*, but., and smo. beef shard[1]. To d'Alberg's an hour. Home and dressed for Duc de Rovigo's, where at ½ p. 12. The *huissier* told me that *S. E.*[2] did not *receive* to-day. " *Néanmoins faites passer mon nom.*"[3] Several others also came in. Was seated with my back to the door of entrance. But the story is too long to write. I will tell it you. The conclusion is, that after waiting three hours, I got sight of his Excellency by force, and demanded my passport. " *J'en ai parlai a S. M. avant hier et il a con senti, mais il faut que j'en parle au Min. de Rel. Ext'r et je vous enformerai,*"[4] and turned his back and made his escape. The assurance that H. M. has consented is something, though I am very sorry to say, not much. Words cost nothing here, and there is often an immensity of time and space between the promise of a courtier and the performance. At 4 to Fonzi's and thence to Vanderlyn's, where dined at ½ p. 6. We walked together as far as *le passage faydeau*[5] and thence I came home. Found a note from Madame R'n, requesting me to dine to-morrow, as being " *probably the last time.*" Replied yes. On my way from the Minister's, went round by Rue Cadran to Stone's manufactory, and he not being there, to Rue Bondi ;

---

1 For tea, *bröd*, butter, and smoked beef cut in thin slices. (Shard for shared.)
2 For *Son Excellence.* His Excellency.
3 " Nevertheless, take in my name."
4 For " *J'en ai parlé à Sa Majesté avant-hier et il a consenti, mais il faut que j'en parle au Ministre des Relations Extérieures et je vous en informerai.*" " I spoke to His Majesty about it day before yesterday and he consented, but I must speak about it to the Minister of Foreign Affairs and shall let you know."
5 There is in Paris a short street named Rue Feydeau leading from Rue Richelieu to Rue Montmartre. Burr may mean this, or there may have been an arcade (*passage*) of the same name.

out. Left a note which I had written in case of not finding him. The note was rather dry, and may probably terminate our acquaintance.

8. *Couche* 12. Rose 6. At 9 to Fonzi's. At 10 to Duc d'Alberg's, to whom related my interview of yesterday. He advises me to go to his evening party on Monday, and there again press the subject, and he will meet me there. Back to Fonzi's and there till 2. Then at 4 to Fonzi's again and at ½ p. 4 walked off to Madame Robertson's to dine. *Y:* Evans *l'ainee*[1] and Madame Menutzi. Staid till 9 and then home. Wrote a note to Crede, who, I fear, is not pleased that I did not pass Sunday last with him as I had engaged. See the "*Journal de l'Empire*"[2] of this day. The contrast between France and England. Wrote note to Crede which sent by the *messagerie*[3] to beg him to advise me of his advent.

9. At 8 came in Mr. Howseal, whom I detained at breakfast, and had a great breakfast below; coffee, sugar, *bro.*, butter, eggs, fruit. He staid nearly two hours, and amused me with his adventures. He has only thirteen children, but expects five or six more. At 10 to Fonzi's, where found Vanderlyn, but F. was engaged. Home and read in "*Les abus Dans les Ceremonies et Dans les Moeurs,*" *devellopes par* Mr. L., *auteur du* "*Compère Matthieu.*"[4] *Octavo; 175 pages.*

---

1 For *l'aînée.* The elder Miss Evans.
2 The "Journal of the Empire."
3 Coach or coach-office.
4 "Abuses in Ceremonies (*Cérémonies*) and Customs," Developed or Expanded (*développés*) by Mr. L., author of "*Le Compère Matthieu*" (Godfather Matthew). This was a satirical romance published in 1765 by Abbé Henri Joseph Dulaurens. At its appearance it enjoyed such success that it was attributed to Voltaire.

Imp. a Blois. *2ᵐᵉ an. de la Rep. fr.*[1] There is wit in the preface and dedication and some learning in the body of the work, but the subject has lost its interest except as mere matter of curiosity. At 2 to Fonzi's again and there two hours, and got fitted so as to be at ease. For two days past have had much plague and pain with my jaws. Dined with the family to-day, and have not stirred out. Vanderlyn came in at 8 and sat an hour. Had a note from Mrs. Robertson this evening, asking me to draw a power atty. and to dine with her to-morrow ; replied, assenting to both. No reply from Stone. What the devil did he mean by offering me, near six weeks ago, the loan of Humboldt's works, and neither to send it nor answer my notes ? This is English.

10. At 10 to d'Alberg's. He had heard nothing concerning me, but persisted that I should go this evening to Duc Rovigo's. Home, and drew and copied a power atty. for Mrs. Robertson. Then at 2 to Fonzi's. Then *au Musée*[2] to meet Vanderlyn and to examine the pictures exposed for public inspection. Every two years there is an exhibition and competition for prizes. Every ten years a great exhibition and great prizes. This is both the biennial and decennial exhibition. As I buy the list and explanation of all such things, will give you my remarks when we shall read that over together. At 4, home to dress for dinner and for the evening. As I was obliged to wear

---

1 For *Imprimé à Blois dans la deuxième année de la République Française.* Printed at Blois in the second year of the French Republic. (The French Republic was founded Sept. 22, 1792. Then began the year I., called by the French *L'an I.* Hence the year II. was at some time in the years 1793–1794.)
2 To the Museum.

chapeau bras[1] for the evening, and could not come home from Mrs. Robertson's, was necessitated to take a hack, 32 sous. At dinner, Nancy Evans, Madame, and myself. Mrs. Robertson will certainly marry that young Adamson very soon. Neither she nor Mr. Evans can get passport. You see I am not the single victim. Left Madame Robertson's at ½ p. 7, and to Duc Rovigo. There was an immense crowd; perhaps one hundred carriages at the door. Was presented to *la* Duchesse Rovigo, who is a *belle Creole*[2]. Met there Duc d'Alberg *et ux.* and was again much amused with the spectacle. The gentlemen all stand. Now and then one advances and says some commonplace to one of the ladies. Then retires to the male side. They seem to *ennui*[3] themselves quite as much as in England or America on like occasions. I was almost the only person who was laced and *gallonèd*[4]. Home at ½ p. 9. Observe how very reasonable and sage I have been for ten days. I never spend a livre that I do not calculate what pretty thing it might have bought for you and Gampillo ; hence my economy.

11. Rose at 5. Scarcely light enough to see. There must be something in the air or stars, for the family, who are never stirring till 9, were up at 7. Took my breakfast at 7. At ½ p. 9 to Valkenaer, where took a second breakfast. Last evening I had a note from him, saying that he had something to tell

---

1 See Glossary.
2 A beautiful Creole. (*Créole*)
3 See Glossary.
4 A hybrid perfect participle from the French verb ga*lo*nner, to adorn with gold or silver lace.

me. It was about the Spanish Cap.[1], but how to get at him I have not yet discovered. To Fonzi's an hour. To Abel's, where paid my account, 59 livres, and exchanged three *pr. de bas de cot.* for *tant de filozel* and ordered a pattern for *culottes en soye noir tricote en maille fixe*[2]—a piece of extravagance which you will find venial. *Din.* with Swan at the Pelasgie[3], where met my friend McRae, whom I did not recollect, he is so pale and thin. (He married two years ago a young wife.) Not a cent for *muse* since last Saturday week[4]. Staid but a few minutes. He had heard nothing from V———. Engaged to call on him again this week to hear something "important" he had to communicate.

12. Rose 6. At 8 a special messenger from Crede, begging me to call immediately, that he had something very important to communicate. What the devil can it be? Good or bad? Or, perhaps, something which I shall consider of no importance at all? Posted off about a league, and found him waiting. The arrival of G.[5] is what he had to tell me, and perhaps it may be important. We shall know to-morrow. Thence about a league more to d'Alberg's; out. To Fonzi's an hour, and did nothing. Then home to receive Howseal, who was to call with some of his children. He came at 4, and brought M'lle, who is very pretty and *gentil*[6], and three boys, Edward,

---

1 Is this for Captain?
2 For three *paires de bas de coton* for *tant de filoselle*, etc. Three pairs of cotton stockings for as many of floss silk, and ordered a pattern for breeches of black silk (*soie noire*) knit (*tricotée*) in fixed stitch.
3 The Sainte-Pélagie prison.
4 This sentence is crossed out by Burr in the MS.
5 For Mr. Griswold.
6 For *gentille*. Pretty, genteel.

————, and ————. We had a little repast of peaches, grapes, bread, butter, cheese, and wine, which cost about 3 livres, and nosegay for M'lle. Staid till 5. Before their arrival, I being hungry, took my *fillibonka*[1] and ate again with them. Madame P. asked me to dine, as she does almost every day, but I had dined.

13. Rose 6. At 9 to Mr. G.'s; not up. To Baron d'Alberg's; not up. Now it seems the air and stars have taken a drowsy turn. Waited at d'Alberg's till he got up, and passed ½ hour. He says that the Duc Rovigo told him that Mons. *le* C. B.[2] might have his passport whenever he would call for it. This was great news; very great, if true in the event. To Mr. G.'s, who received me very courteously. Began with my business—the most awkward of all sorts of business, *l'argent!*[3] Spoke of his losses, &c., which I knew to be very true. He has been infamously swindled by men who hold unmerited estimation in the world. Agreed to take breakfast with him to-morrow at 10, which I shall not forget. To Fonzi's, who was very much occupied. To Saugnier's, *sec. de la police generale*[4], to demand my *passeport*. He would not see me. These fellows are often more difficult than their masters. Sent in a note to him, and received verbally in reply that he had no instructions from the Duke about my pasport[5], but would see him on the subject to-day. Thence to the *prefecture*[6], where the *passe-*

---

1 Davis substitutes the word share.
2 Colonel Burr.
3 Money.
4 For *Secrétaire de la Police Générale.* Secretary of the General Police.
5 So in the MS. Burr may mean it for the French form, *passeport*, which he sometimes uses.
6 For *préfecture.* The office of the *préfet* or prefect.

ports are finally had and *paid for.* The *chefι du bureau*[1] made me the same reply as Saugnier. Thence on to Pelasgie[2], where dined with Swan. The important concern is about merino sheep. No doubt there is a great deal of money to be made by it, but it it out of my line. Home at 7. To Pelasgie[2] from my quarters is more than three miles. Vanderlyn came in and sat two hours. Had *coffee blanc*[3]. I am making an experiment of coffee not burnt, having somewhere read that the burning made the oil acid, which was the cause of the nervous effect. I have drank two large cups. You will know to-morrow how I sleep. Vanderlyn found it detestable, and I confess it was somewhat mawkish.

14. *Couche* 12. Rose 6, having slept perfectly well, the white coffee notwithstanding. Have taken a large dose this evening, and something stronger than that of yesterday. Found it more intolerable to the taste. Wrote a letter to Duke Rovigo, *q. v.*, to remind him that he had assured me of his Majesty's assent to my passport; that I had applied, and the answers I had received. Sent it by a *commissionaire ;* 15 sous. To Mr. G.'s[4], where took a second breakfast. He let me have 2,000 francs, about 333 dollars, for which I gave a receipt, containing a request for you to pay it, in case I should not pay it within a year. This will enable me to get to America if I should ever get *passeport.* Passed two hours with G. You know

---

1 The Chief of the Bureau or Department Chief.
2 For Sainte-Pélagie.
3 For *café blanc.* Literally, white coffee.
4 Griswold.

that I have always thought he had one of the most acute, logical heads of our country. To Fonzi's where till 4, doing very little, for we were constantly interrupted. Home for an hour and then to Vanderlyn's, where dined. Walked with him to Fonzi's where ½ hour. On coming home, met on the Boulevard what he thought a model. He went to take information, and I sagely home, where, having taken my *caffee blanc*, I have now at ½ p. 11 the honor to bid you good-night.

15. *Couche* 12. Rose 6. The white coffee maintains its reputation, and I became more reconciled to its flavor. In a little while I shall like it. The disadvantage is, that it takes double the quantity. Don't imagine that I use it perfectly raw. Not so, Madame. The roasting took me two hours, so afraid was I that it would be spoiled. I succeeded to dry it in an iron machine made for the purpose of " burning coffee," till the whole was nearly a cream color, more nearly approaching very pale cinnamon, or something between both. At 10 to d'Alberg's. He advises that I go again to the Duke's this day, being his day of public audience. Went on to Madame Robinson's[1], where an hour. Wine and water, bread, butter, and ham. Gamp was hungry. She urged me so much to come back and dine, that I consented. Thence to Saugnier's, secretary of the police. He would not see me, but sent me word by the *huissier* that he had no instructions about my *passeport*. Then to Fonzi's an hour,

---

[1] For Robertson.

but did nothing. Home, and dressed for the audience of the Minister, and went. Had a few words with him. He said that H. M.[1] had not yet given his signature, but that he would procure it in the course of the next week. Perhaps so. Home ; changed my dress, and to Fonzi's another hour and did nothing. Then to Madame R.'s, where dined. *Υ:* Sidney and Madame Menutzi, *la mere* Evans[2] and James, and Mr. Adamson came in to tea. Off at 8, and directly home without accident, though I had some narrow escapes. While I was in Saugnier's *antichambre*[3] there passed a *marchand de nouveates et varieties*[4], with whom I had, some weeks ago, been bargaining for an old painting which I had thought of buying. He saluted me very respectfully by the title of baron ; said he had my works which he had read with great pleasure, &c. ; to all which I bowed. Who the devil can he take me for? Have been taking my *caf. blanc*[5], and reading two hours in some books I have been buying for you, of which shall say more anon.

16. Rose 7. Very chilly. A fire would be comfortable. At 10 to Valkenaer's, where took a second breakfast and staid two hours. He is amusing and instructive. To Mr. G.'s ; out. To Fonzi's, and there till ½ p. 3. We finished the work[6], and I believe it is at length perfect. Home. *Bro.* and *cas.*

---

1 His Majesty.
2 Mother Evans or Mrs. Evans.
3 Antechamber.
4 For *marchand de nouveautés et variétés.* Merchant of novelties and miscellanies.
5 For *café blanc.*
6 Set of false-teeth, probably.

for *din.*[1]   A packet from Mrs. Robinson and request
to dinner on Tuesday ; agreed. Wrote note to Crede,
and went out to leave it in case he should be out. To
Crede's ; you know, I don't believe you know,
though I have told you three times, hussy; why, then,
again, it is a league. Home at ½ p. 6. At 7 came
in Vanderlyn and sat an hour. Have taken *caf. blanc*
but *san. socer*[2].

17. Slept sound till 7. What can have produced
this lethargy ? Not the white coffee, surely. At ½
p. 9 to d'Alberg's ; told him of my interview of
Saturday. Says there must be something more than
ordinary. Thence to Roux's ; out, as was said. To
the *marchand des varietés* to look again at that picture,
and finally bought it, thinking it would please you ;
48 francs ! What extravagance ! But that is by no
means the worst article of this day's work. Thence to
Michaux's, the botanist, who was many years in the
United States, and has written a valuable little book of
his travels. He is now publishing his account of our
trees, which will be extremely interesting. It demon-
strates that we (not the whole continent but the United
States alone) have three times the number of useful
trees that Europe can boast; but I will bring so much
of his work as is published. I called on him yesterday, but he was out, and out again to-day. Thence to
Vanderlyn's, which is near (that is, about a mile), and
at 1 back again to Michaux's, whom I found. My

1 *Bro.* for Swedish *bröd*, bread ; *cas.* for German *Käse*, cheese, and *din.* for French *dîner*.
Including English, four languages are drawn upon to form this little sentence of five words!
2 *San.* is for French *sans*, without. *Socer* may be for Swedish *socker* or French *sucre*, sugar.

business was to ascertain the identity of a plant and a tree, both vaunted here in medicine, and Mr. M. gave me the most perfect satisfaction. Thence home, but alas ! on my way a p. of *dem.*¹, and so 8 francs. How many curses have I heaped on poor Gam., and yet he is rather to be pitied ; only see how for the last fifteen days he has been so good and considering his habits, and considering, &c., &c. And so we will try to forget it till next time. Got home at ½ p. 2. Smoked my segar. Ate bread and cheese and drank *vin* and water. Then dressed for dinner. At ½ p. 4 to Dr. Swediaur's, calling on the Lyon on the way to see my taylor², a great rascal, but if I change I shall get a greater. The porter at the Lyon told me that a gentleman had called there to see me, and she had given him my address. "And, pray, where did you direct him ?" "Why, to No. 9 Rue du Croissant³." Now, as I am at No. 7, she might as well have sent him to the Boulevard Parnasse⁴, and so I have not seen the gentleman. It was, as agreed, a *tête-à-tête* with Swediaur. The story of William Vance, charged with forgery, to whom Armstrong gave a passport under a feigned name to favor his escape. Of Upson, whom he wished to charge with despatches for England, but required a receipt for a sum of money not paid. Of ———— ; I don't know, but a great many others. Home at ½ p. 7. Drank too much wine. Have taken my *caf. blanc* still stronger. Found, on

1   This may stand for a pair of *demoiselles*, girls, or *demireps*, women of questionable character.
2   So in the MS.
3   Street of the Crescent.
4   For Boulevard du Montparnasse.

my arrival here, a letter from Scherer and Fringestin, enclosing one from Gahn, open. An apology from S. and F., which was unnecessary, for it is known that all foreign letters go to the police for examination. If you should have written me by the same occasion, the letter has not been delivered. Perhaps you had a few words of cipher ; if so, I shall never see it. But, ah, perhaps that gentleman whom I have not seen had letters for me ! Curse the porteress. Some weeks ago, the 24 sous and 12 sous pieces were, by an im-perial decree, put down to 20 and 10 sous. I paid my quota of the tax, having just then received about twenty of those pieces. There was a publication by authority on the occasion. Then, after an interval of about fifteen or twenty days, the louis, the old crowns and half crowns were reduced. To this, also, I con-tributed, having had the same luck as before. On Friday or Saturday last, the 6-liard[1] pieces (1½ sous) were put at 1 sou, or reduced to nothing, as they ought to have been, I don't know which ; of them I had for the first time about forty in my possession ; but as this bore hard on the very poor, the 6-liards were, by a proclamation in the evening, restored to their nominal value, which is a pity. The sooner the old money is out of the way the better, for it makes a deal of intricacy and confusion in dealings, whereas the new is all in decimals like ours ; is also well struck, and very handsome, so that I should very cheerfully pay my quota.

---

1 The liard was a small coin worth a quarter of a sou. The 6-liard piece was, therefore, worth, as stated, 1½ sous.

18. *Couche* 1. Rose 7 something the worse for the dinner of yesterday. At 10 came in Mr. G. and sat till 12. He has a most profound, analytic head. At 1 to Fonzi's. Thence to Bourgoin, the *jouallier*[1], to order a pair of springs. To the taylor's[2] at the Lyon. Home. Dressed for dinner and off to Madame Robertson's. Was, by appointment, to be there at ½ p. 4 to talk of business. *Y* to dine, M'lle J. Evans and Madame Menutzi, and, after dinner, Mr. Adamson. Staid till 9. Home just before 10. Not permitted to walk through the Thulleries[3] at that hour.

19. At 10 to Valkenaer's, where took a second breakfast. To Roux's, from whom got the usual answer. To Saugnier's to inquire for a small parcel of books which I supposed I had left there, but found it afterward at Paschaud's. Home. *Fillibonke,* and at 4 set out on a very long walk to Howseal's, Rue Doré. He had removed to Isle St. Louis[4], about as much farther. Went on, and there found him and his eight *enf.*[5] Home at 7. Tired, and must go to sleep, but will have a supper first. Eggs and white coffee.

20. To Mr. G.'s, where an hour. To Fonzi's, where met Vanderlyn, who told me that Peale will leave town to-morrow for l'Orient[6] to sail thence for Philadelphia. Home to write, but could send you

1 For *joaillier.* Jeweler.
2 So in the MS.
3 For Tuileries.
4 This island is one of two islands in the Seine situated in the very heart of Paris; the other, connected with this by a bridge, is l'Isle de la Cité, Isle of the City. It is upon this that the celebrated cathedral of Notre Dame is situated.
5 For *enfants.* Children.
6 A seaport of France.

nothing, not knowing any single person in Philadelphia to whom I could intrust a parcel to you. Yes, J. Barclay now occurs to me, but it is too late, for my letters are gone. One to you, to Bollman, and to Gahn. Vanderlyn called at 8 this evening and we went together to hand the letters. Thence home safe.

21. After writing you last evening, I made draught of a letter for Mrs. Robertson to her lawyer, and did not go to bed till 1. Rose 7 and at 9 to Fonzi's, where two hours. Thence home. At 2 set out to go to St. Pelasgie¹, but found it too late, and so stopped at Vanderlyn's, where, as was agreed last evening, we took an early dinner that we might go to the opera to see the *" Bayarderes "*². It was said that the Emperor would be there. On the way from Vanderlyn's called on Crede, whom found, and agreed to breakfast with him to-morrow. Thence to the opera. The decorations and the ballet are magnificent. The * * * * *ennuyes*³ everybody, yet in every theatre they have a parcel of rascals hired to applaud everything, from twenty to fifty of them, who are placed in the middle of the *paterre*⁴, and are a great nuisance. Home at ½ p. 10, and found a note from Madame Robertson, and another from Swan. Just 12. Must *couche;* have answered both notes. Have not taken my *caf. blanc* this evening, having no coal;

---

1 Burr has mentioned the Sainte-Pélagie prison several times, but never before with the word St. prefixed.
2 For *Bayadères.* A name for dancing girls in the East Indies.
3 The * * * * annoys everybody. Burr's verb is a hybrid from the French verb *ennuyer*, to annoy, bore. The undecipherable word probably means *claque,* meaning paid clappers at the theatres.
4 For *parterre.*

so consoled myself with milk punch. My uncle Stephen lived on milk punch, and at the age of 86 mounted by the stirrup a very gay young horse, and galloped off with me twelve miles without stopping, and was, I thought, less fatigued than I. On my way from Vanderlyn's called on Crede and agreed to break fast with him to-morrow morning.

22. Rose 6. The *caf. blanc* maintains its repu tation. Was at Crede's just before 9, and there took breakfast. We went together to St. Pelagie', where he left me, and I passed an hour with Swan, talking principally of sheep. On coming home, found the card of Captain Skiddy, with message that he would call again between 3 and 4. Doubtless some American captain with a letter from you. Intended to have gone to the Duc de Rovigo's, but was tired, and it is a most unpleasant ceremony, and I shall get only the usual answer. At 4 comes in Captain Skiddy. He is from New York; in the employ of Jamel, and his business is to present for payment an order which I drew on Mr. Alston² about fourteen months ago, in Sweden, in favor of Captain Barry, for 80 pounds sterling. Captain Barry sends me word that he had written frequently to Mr. Alston, who has never answered him! Very pleasant! To Madame Robertson's to dine at ½ p. 5. *Y:* Jane E. and Madame Men.³ After dinner Madame reproached me in terms which did not please me with machinations against her

---

1 Burr has finally almost attained to the correct spelling of this name. It should be Sainte-Pélagie, or Ste-Pélagie.
2 Burr's son-in-law.
3 For Madame Menutzi.

intended match, which is not true. Her expressions were so unkind that I left the room without replying and came off and think I shall not go there again. Home at 8 and did not go out again.

23. Rose 6. At ½ p. 8, as was agreed, Crede came in to take me to breakfast with his friend Mancel. A very pleasant young man, who has a very handsome establishment for a *garçon*[1] of 25. He meditates to remove to United States, and his younger brother is now there exploring. We had tea, cutlets, and dessert of fruit. Staid till 1. A very important discovery has been made here, viz., to make vinegar, of excellent quality, from the sap of any trees. The process gives you all the moisture in vinegar, and all the wood in carbon. I shall get the details if I can find money to pay for it, that is to say, about 100 dollars. Walked with Crede to buy a sample of this vinegar; but the store was shut, being Sunday. We went then to see Mons. Cagniard[2], and his new invention of raising water and performing any mechanical operation. His apparatus is a screw of Archimedes turned the reverse, air, water, and quicksilver. Cagniard was abroad; but we saw a model, and worked it, and got the report of a committee of the Institute[3] on the subject. If the thing performs what is said, I will apply it to give water to Charleston. Walked with Crede about half way down St. Denis and then came

---

1 Bachelor.
2 Cagniard de La Tour (1777–1859) was a celebrated French physicist and engineer who performed many notable experiments in physics and became an inventor of considerable repute.
3 Meaning the Institute of France. This great institution is divided into five academies, one of which, the Academy of Sciences, interests itself in all things relating to the mathematical and physical sciences.

home. *Bro.* and *mjlk.* At 4 to Fonzi's ; he was out, but met Vanderlyn to whom gave a commission. Home at ½ p. 6. *Caf. blanc bien fort.*[1] Vanderlyn came in at 8 and sat an hour. A note from Madame R. Very amiable ; must make up. So wrote a very amiable answer, *q. v.* Poor good soul, she is grievously tormented by her lovers and will probably finish by marrying one of them. A note also from Swan. Still sheep!

24. Very early sent off my note to Madame Robertson by the *commissionaire*[2], which costs 15 sous. At 10 went out to call on Skiddy; met him in the street with Howseal. To Duc d'Alberg's ; *y* an hour; took breakfast *a la fourchette*[3], &c. Madame is handsome and lovely. They go to Rovigo's to-night, and will ask about my passport. I declined going. On to Madame R.'s. She always keeps me about ½ hour while she makes her *toilette.* She appeared *abbattu*[4]. We did not talk of our quarrel. Coming from Madame's called on Baron Claybrooke, who has returned to town after three months' absence. Home leisurely. Found that Crede had just called. We had agreed that he should call between 2 and 3, and I was home five minutes before 3. He left word he would call again ; and, as I wished much to see him, I staid at home till ½ p. 5 ; but he came not. So wrote him a note, and went and left it at his lodgings, about one league. Home at ½ p. 7. At 4 *bro.* and *cas.* and

1 *Caf.* for *café.* Very strong white coffee.
2 For *commissionnaire.* Porter.
3 A meat breakfast.
4 For *abattue.* Depressed.

this evening white coffee. Answered Swan's note this P. M. Rumors of changes intended by the Emperor in Spain, in Poland, and in Naples. They are but rumors. Read a *memoire*[1] on the state of Europe before the discovery of America.

22. To Duc d'Alberg's at 10. *Y* breakfast and prateings[2] with *la Duc'se.*[3] He promises to talk with Rovigo of my affairs on Monday evening. To Madame Robertson's ; still dismal. She will finish by marrying Adamson against her own will and judgment. No, all this was on Monday the 24th. I have already written you Saturday but can't find it. But in writing Saturday I forgot to mention (being engaged by the *brouille*[4] with Madame R.) the incident of *la boit'se*[5]. I do not find that Montaigne *a raison*[6] on that subject.

23. Went with Crede to breakfast with his friend Mancel. This I have also written you.

24. See above. We may as well do the thing in gross for I am now writing Thursday evening, 27th September, 1810. This morning on my return from Madame R.'s called on the Baron de Claybrooke. (This I have also written, but can't find.) Home at 2 to wait for Crede, who had promised to call between 2 and 3. He had called just before 2 and gone. He will as well have called[7] at 8 as at any other hour. He left word he would call again. Waited till 5. He

1 For *mémoire*. Memorial.
2 So in the MS.
3 For *la Duchesse*.
4 Quarrel, disagreement.
5 For *la boiteuse*. The lame girl.
6 Is right. Does he refer to the great French essayist Montaigne (1552–1592)?
7 So in the MS.

came not and to his lodgings, which you know, is a league; nobody at home. Left under the door a note which I had written.

25. At 10 called on Mr. G., where a few min utes. We searched the code and talked of Bentham, and of vinegar, &c. Thence to d'Alberg's to hear his report. The Minister of Police said that he had made a report to the Emperor of my demand of passport, and had *received no answer.* Did not know when one might be given; so that I am just where I was four months ago, only with less money, and the fine season gone. Home. At 1 *sor.* and met young Crede. His father left town yesterday, and uncertain when he will be back. Dined at home with the family. To-day a *mauv. recont.*[1]; not good; 6 francs; *bah!*

26. To Valkenaer's, where breakfast a second time, for my first breakfast is generally made at 7. Valkenaer always amuses me. To Mancel's, where ½ hour. He engages me to dine on Friday. The first invitation of any sort from a Frenchman since being in France, now near eight months. On my return home last evening found a note from Vanderlyn, saying that Mr. Warden, by whom I proposed to write to America, would leave town to-morrow morning. Wrote to you, to Gahn, and to Bollman, and to Greenwood the *dentiste* and at 7 this morning sent a special messenger with the letters to Vanderlyn. At 5 to Vanderlyn's to dine. After dinner we walked by the way of the Thuilleries[2] to Fonzi's, where an hour

---

1 For *une mauvaise rencontre.* A bad rencounter.
2 So in the MS. Burr has great difficulty with this word.

and thence home, where we took *caf. blanc.* Took
bath before dinner; 40 sous.

27. Now I have got up with you and will try
to keep even[1]. Yesterday called on Sisto, the Spanish
mait de languas[2], to engage him to give me a few lessons in his language. This morning at 9 he came and
staid an hour. I would do nothing but read aloud
after him, to catch the pronunciation, and translate.
Have laid out a louis in grammars, dictionaries, and
some other books, for which expense I console myself
that they will be useful to you and Gampillo. Wrote
you another letter, and one to Hosack, with a parcel
for each of you, and went to Vanderlyn's with them.
He went to Warden's, who, learning that the letters
and parcels were from me, would not take them.
Home and dined on *fillebonka.* After dinner to hunt
two or three pamphlets. Home at 6. *Caf. blanc.* A
long visit from Jul.[3] to talk about her business, and to
get me to write some more letters. Poor soul, she
repeats over her instructions 200 times, for fear I
should forget them. Have read this evening Molle-
ral's pamphlet on the wood vinegar; a very important
discovery; and Parmentier's on the management of
wine; very stupid and unsatisfactory. To-day bought
½ pound of *sirop de raisins*[4], for experiment. It is
something like very dirty molasses diluted exceedingly
with dirty water. The taste corresponds to the
appearance. I can make no sort of use of it. Cost

---

1 Referring to his Journal, which he had neglected.
2 For French *maitre des langues*, or Spanish *maestro des lenguas*. Language master.
3 For Julie, a woman previously mentioned.
4 Grape sugar.

12 sous, and 5 sous for the bottle. Grapes are now from 3 to 8 sous a pound, and I eat about two pounds a day.

28. At 10 to Mr. G.'s[1], where ½ hour talking of vinegar and other projects. Thence to Valkenaer's to get a pamphlet which I had borrowed from d'Alberg, and lent him. He had *lent it to a friend*, so I think it is in a fair way to be lost. Thence home to get another pamphlet about vinegar, which I had promised to G. Called again at G.'s, and thence to d'Alberg's, where ½ hour. Thence to Sisto's to say that I could not take a lesson till Monday. Home and at 3 to Rue St. Denis to buy a toy for Annabella. Got in trouble by the way and spent 6 francs. Home to dress for dinner. Vanderlyn came in and we walked together to Fonzi's and to Marcel's where met Crede and a young Frenchman, Bourdelet, a handsome, intelligent man of about 36. We were five at table. A plain, good dinner, intended to suit my taste. A pleasant, chearful[2] party. Off at ½ p. 8. Mancel and Bourdelet walked with us, and we took ice creams on the Boulevard. Then parted. Crede and I walked together ½ hour, and agreed to meet at 10 to-morrow morning. On my arrival home, found a note from Swan, containing at last some news from V., but not perfectly satisfactory; also a verbal message from Mrs. Robertson, left by her coachman, begging me to call on her to-morrow morning, and by no means to fail. What the devil can be now in the wind? It is quite

---

1 Griswold's.
2 So in the MS.

malapropos[1], for I am engaged to go with G. to-morrow morning in the country

29. At 10 to G.'s, where met Crede. Found G. ready for the country jaunt, but asked an hour's delay, that I might go and see what was Madame R.'s distress. Took *cabriole*[2] (the first time in a month) and drove to Madame R.'s. Found her unusually well, and expecting that I would dine with her, which was the only message by her servant. The rest was the invention of our deaf Jeanette; so drove back again to G.'s. Having last evening written to Swan that I would call upon him this evening, wrote from G.'s that I must postpone my visit to him till to-morrow morning. Went with G. in *cabriole* to see a place he had thought of buying. Passed two or three hours there, and got in town at ½ 5. Took dinner with him at the ———, a famous *restaurateur's* on the Boulevard. At 7 we parted. I to F. where met the beautiful Madame C. and her beautiful daughter about 4 years old. "*Ma petite, montrez ta piece de mariage*"[3]; and she showed it. There were three ladies and four gent. Engaged to pass some hours with F. to-morrow to finish our business. Just as I got home came in young Crede, to say that his father had engaged Mancel to take me out to pass the day at his house at St. Germain's[4], and to set off at 8. I had

1 For *mal à propos*. Ill-timed.
2 A one-horse vehicle. *Cabriolet* was a lighter vehicle of the same kind. From this word comes our word cab. Cabs, or cabriolets, as they were first called, were not known to the English till 1820.
3 For " *montre ta pièce de mariage.*" A *pièce de mariage*, literally marriage-piece, was ordinarily a medal of gold or silver given by the husband to the wife during the marriage ceremony. Here it may be called the engagement present. In spite of her slight age the child may have been already affianced.
4 Burr uses these names of places as if they were the names of persons. He should say, of course, at St. Germain.

much desired this party, and Crede had made it to gratify me ; but how unfortunate ! What is to be done with my engagements with F. and S?

30. In my great *embarras*[1] I resolved to disappoint Crede, though sorely against my will. At 9 called on Mancel to tell him so. He had already gone. Hence to Fonzi's, on whose account I gave up the other engagement. Found him engaged, and the *bijoutier*[2] not come. Home to get my permission for the Pelasgie[3] Thence to the *bijoutier's* to engage him to go to F.'s ; then to St. Pelagie, where passed a few minutes with Swan ; thence to Vanderlyn's to meet me at dinner at F.'s; then to F.'s. For these courses took *cabriole*, which cost me 3 francs. Note, Madame, it is the first time in a month that I have paid carriage-hire. F. and I did very little ; but we dined and smoked segars. Hernandez and Vanderlyn, and the *bijoutier* were our party. Vanderlyn came home with me at 8 and we took *caf. blanc* together. Found on my return home another letter from Gahn, dated 30th July, referring me to former letters which have not been received, but saying that he has forwarded me many letters, of which, however, I have not seen one.

---

1 Perplexity.
2 Jeweler.
3 Permission or permit to visit the Sainte-Pélagie prison.

CPSIA information can be obtained
at www.ICGtesting.com
Printed in the USA
BVOW03s0251261116

468717BV00008B/198/P